UNDERSTANDING SPORT

In the decade or more since publication of the first edition of *Understanding Sport*, both sport and wider global society have undergone profound change. In this fully updated, revised and expanded edition of their classic textbook, John Horne, Alan Tomlinson, Garry Whannel and Kath Woodward offer a critical and reflective introduction to the relationship between sport and contemporary society and explain how sport remains an important agent and symptom of socio-cultural change.

Fully integrating historical, sociological, political and cultural analysis, the book covers every key topic in the study of sport and society, including:

- debate, interpretation and theory
- sport and the media
- sport and the body
- sport and politics
- commercialisation
- globalisation.

Retaining the accessibility and scholarly rigour for which *Understanding Sport* has always been renowned, this new edition includes entirely new chapters on global transformations, sports mega-events and sites, and sporting bodies and governance, as well as a brief commentary on researching sport. With review and seminar questions included in every chapter, plus concise, helpful guides to further reading, *Understanding Sport* remains an essential textbook for all courses on sport and society, the sociology of sport, sport and social theory, or social issues in sport.

John Horne is Professor of Sport and Sociology in the School of Sport, Tourism and the Outdoors at the University of Central Lancashire, where he is Director of the International Research Institute for Sport Studies (IRiSS).

Alan Tomlinson is Professor of Leisure Studies and Director of Research and Development (Social Sciences) at the University of Brighton, and has authored and edited numerous volumes and more than 100 chapters/articles on sport, leisure and popular culture.

Garry Whannel is Head of the Centre for International Media Analysis, Research and Consultancy (CIMARC) at the University of Bedfordshire, is one of the world's leading experts on the cultural analysis of media sport, and has written extensively on media and culture for over thirty years.

Kath Woodward is Professor of Sociology and Head of Department at the Open University and works in the Centre for Research on Socio-Cultural Change (CRESC) on feminist materialist critiques, most recently in the field of sport, especially boxing. She has published extensively on identities and diversity and on issues in social science.

CULTURE, ECONOMY AND THE SOCIAL

A new series from CRESC – the ESRC Centre for Research on Socio-Cultural Change

EDITORS

Professor Tony Bennett, Sociology, Open University; Professor Penny Harvey, Anthropology, Manchester University; Professor Kevin Hetherington, Geography, Open University

EDITORIAL ADVISORY BOARD

The *Culture, Economy and the Social* series is committed to innovative contemporary, comparative and historical work on the relations between social, cultural and economic change. It publishes empirically-based research that is theoretically informed, that critically examines the ways in which social, cultural and economic change is framed and made visible, and that is attentive to perspectives that tend to be ignored or side-lined by grand theorising or epochal accounts of social change. The series addresses the diverse manifestations of contemporary capitalism, and considers the various ways in which the 'social', 'the cultural'and 'the economic' are apprehended as tangible sites of value and practice. It is explicitly comparative, publishing books that work across disciplinary perspectives, cross-culturally, or across different historical periods.

The series is actively engaged in the analysis of the different theoretical traditions that have contributed to the development of the `cultural turn' with a view to clarifying where these approaches converge and where they diverge on a particular issue. It is equally concerned to explore the new critical agendas emerging from current critiques of the cultural turn: those associated with the descriptive turn for example. Our commitment to interdisciplinarity thus aims at enriching theoretical and methodological discussion, building awareness of the common ground that has emerged in the past decade, and thinking through what is at stake in those approaches that resist integration to a common analytical model.

Series titles include:

The Media and Social Theory (2008)
Edited by David Hesmondhalgh and Jason Toynbee

Culture, Class, Distinction (2009)
Tony Bennett, Mike Savage,
Elizabeth Bortolaia Silva, Alan Warde,
Modesto Gayo-Cal and David Wright

Material Powers (2010)
Edited by Tony Bennett and Patrick Joyce

The Social after Gabriel Tarde: Debates and Assessments (2010)
Edited by Matei Candea

Cultural Analysis and Bourdieu's Legacy (2010)
Edited by Elizabeth Silva and Alan Ward

Milk, Modernity and the Making of the Human (2010)
Richie Nimmo

Creative Labour: Media Work in Three Cultural Industries (2010)
Edited by David Hesmondhalgh and Sarah Baker

Migrating Music (2011)
Edited by Jason Toynbee and Byron Dueck

Sport and the Transformation of Modern Europe: States, Media and Markets 1950–2010 (2011)
Edited by Alan Tomlinson, Christopher Young and Richard Holt

Inventive Methods: The Happening of the Social (2012)
Edited by Celia Lury and Nina Wakeford

Understanding Sport: A Socio-Cultural Analysis (2013)
John Horne, Alan Tomlinson, Garry Whannel and Kath Woodward

Rio de Janeiro: Urban Life through the Eyes of the City (forthcoming)
Beatriz Jaguaribe

Interdisciplinarity: Reconfigurations of the Social and Natural Sciences (forthcoming)
Edited by Andrew Barry and Georgina Born

Devising Consumption: Cultural Economies of Insurance, Credit and Spending (forthcoming)
Liz McFall

Diasporas and Diplomacy: Cosmopolitan Contact Zones at the BBC World Service (1932–2012) (forthcoming)
Edited by Marie Gillespie and Alban Webb

Unbecoming Things: Mutable Objects and the Politics of Waste (forthcoming)
Nicky Gregson and Mike Crang

Centre for Research on
Socio-Cultural Change

E·S·R·C
ECONOMIC
& SOCIAL
RESEARCH
COUNCIL

UNDERSTANDING SPORT

A socio-cultural analysis

SECOND EDITION

**JOHN HORNE, ALAN TOMLINSON,
GARRY WHANNEL AND KATH WOODWARD**

Routledge
Taylor & Francis Group

LONDON AND NEW YORK

First published 1999 by E & FN Spon, an imprint of Routledge

This edition published 2013
by Routledge
2 Park Square, Milton Park, Abingdon, Oxon OX14 4RN

Simultaneously published in the USA and Canada
by Routledge
711 Third Avenue, New York, NY 10017

Routledge is an imprint of the Taylor & Francis Group, an informa business

British Library Cataloguing in Publication Data
A catalogue record for this book is available from the British Library

Library of Congress Cataloging-in-Publication Data
Understanding sport : a socio-cultural analysis / John Horne... [et al.]. – 2nd ed.
p. cm.
Prev. ed. cataloged under Horne, John.
Includes bibliographical references and index.
1. Sports–Great Britain–Sociological aspects. 2. Sports–Great Britain–History.
I. Horne, John, 1955– II. Horne, John, 1955– Understanding sport.
GV706.5.H664 2012
306.4'830941–dc23
2012006470

ISBN: 978-0-415-59140-9 (hbk)
ISBN: 978-0-415-59141-6 (pbk)
ISBN: 978-0-203-80713-2 (ebk)

Typeset in Zapf Humanist and Eras
by Keystroke, Station Road, Codsall, Wolverhampton

CONTENTS

X

contents

ILLUSTRATIONS

FIGURES

TABLES

PREFACE

This book is a revised, second, edition of *Understanding Sport: An Introduction to the Sociological and Cultural Analysis of Sport*, first published by Routledge in 1999. The subtitle of this second edition – 'a socio-cultural analysis' – retains the interdisciplinary focus of the first edition, combining scholarship and research from history, politics, sociology, and cultural studies. The first edition's authorial team has been expanded, with the addition of the contributions of Kath Woodward on sporting bodies and governance. The new edition is also framed not just in terms of the study needs of students on the sport studies courses that have grown so successfully in the last third of a century; it is also revised in the light of a broadening interest in the cultural profile and social significance of sport in contemporary society, as manifest in the book's place in the 'Culture, Economy and the Social' series of CRESC (Centre for Research on Socio-Cultural Change).

In the late 1970s, only a very few colleges or universities offered degree programmes in sport-related subjects. Over the following three decades, more than a hundred institutions have moved into this field. The importance of the field was also recognised in its research profile. In 1996, the higher education funding bodies of Britain (in their Research Assessment Exercise) recognised sport-related subjects as a discrete and distinct area of research activity. In 2011, these bodies confirmed 'sport and exercise sciences, leisure and tourism' as a specialist sub-area within the 2014 Research Excellence Framework (REF). In this context, the teaching base established so strongly over recent decades has been matched by the recognition of the quality and importance of sport-related research. This growth in the academic study of sport, and the volume of research into specialist aspects of sport, culture and society, have produced a burgeoning literature, in books and specialist journals.

We commented in 1999 that there were good books – both readers (collections of seminal or original articles) and textbooks – on sport in the USA and in other societies and countries, and on sport in cross-cultural and political contexts; research monographs, including detailed and illuminating social historical studies, also enhanced our understanding of sport in modern society. But, we added, there was a surprising lack of books attempting to produce an integrated socio-cultural analysis of sport in modern Britain. The first edition of this book offered such an analysis, in accessible yet simultaneously rigorous and scholarly form, aimed explicitly at the needs of undergraduates. We invited students who may have studied sport studies at school or college to develop their understanding in greater depth, and to encounter and engage with original sources, and polemic and debate within the field. That invitation is repeated in relation to this new edition. The book takes a predominantly sociological perspective, but draws too upon a number of complementary approaches and frameworks. The authors' own backgrounds embrace critical social science and interdisciplinary humanities.

Although sport has been a subject for degree level study in its own right for more than thirty years, some still express surprise that the subject is considered appropriate for academic analysis. It is seen by some as too trivial, marginal or epiphenomenal to warrant serious attention. Others view sport as a hermetically sealed world of its own, apart from the rest of society. Indeed, for participants and spectators, this perceived apart-ness may well be precisely part of its appeal. Yet by any standards, sport is a set of cultural practices with significant historical and sociological resonances. To give some examples: sport in nineteenth-century public schools was seen as a vital form of moral character training that produced the leadership and teamwork skills required by the dominant class, both domestically and in governing the Empire; while the structure of amateur sport served the interests of elite groups, football, in its professional form, had by the 1920s become the major leisure interest of the male working class, and an important expression of community identity; during the 1930s the government was disturbed enough about the poor physical condition of its citizens to mount a National Fitness Campaign; in post-war Britain, National Sport Centres were established as part of a pursuit of elite-level success; and in a potential chemistry of elite success and popular passion, the London 2012 Olympics brought the global audience to that city's third staging of the world's highest-profile sporting event.

Sociologically, sport and fitness loom large in the media. Sport programmes, dedicated sport channels, sports pages and sport supplements in newspapers, specialist sport magazines, and sport-related websites have become increasingly prominent. Although only a small minority of the population are active participants, a great many more have some degree of interest in following sport. The images derived from sport play a significant role in constituting our notions of the body and how it should, ideally, look. In both representational forms and in lived practices, sport is one of the cultural spheres that most distinctively marks gender identities and differences. The activities of top sport stars are highly publicised, and debate rages about the extent to which they are role models who have a responsibility to set a good example. Many politicians are fond of sporting metaphors, and former UK Prime Minister John Major spearheaded a drive to regenerate sport in schools, couched in terms that echo the Victorian confidence in its capacity to train character and instil moral values. Alongside this, sport has consistently provided a forum for the expression of national identity.

Sport studies courses have a strong scientific element – physiology, psychology and biomechanics are quite rightly regarded as integral elements in the multi-disciplinary approach characteristic of such courses. But the historical formation of sporting practices and institutions, and their place in the wider social formation, are also of great importance to a full understanding of sport. All the scientific understanding of the sporting body and mind in the world is of little use to sports development unless the nature of the wider social and cultural environment is understood. This book is designed to offer a framework for those seeking a conceptually informed but empirically grounded understanding of the place of sport in the modern world.

This book will not offer any simple essentialist definition of sport. An historical and sociological understanding of sport and its place in processes of social change and cultural reproduction makes it clear that 'sport' has no such fixed meaning – it has had different meanings in different societies, and refers to different activities at different historical moments. Most people would not now regard cruelty to animals as a sport, but until the early nineteenth century, cruelty to animals was a central aspect of sport. Hunting and shooting are now seen as rather marginal sporting activities, yet in the eighteenth century they would have been at the heart of the meaning of the term, indeed, the very notion of the sporting man referred to the hunting man. The meaning of the term sport, therefore, involves a form of social construction, which can be analysed from a socio-cultural perspective.

Sociologists and social-cum-cultural historians have been demonstrating for some time now that sport's role in society is an important one, and is becoming still more important within social and cultural formations; that in some important respects the phenomenon of sport can be seen to lead or shape society. In 1997, Martin Jacques, academic and journalist, and former editor of *Marxism Today*, recognised that sport had become more than a mere pastime or hobby, that it might be seen as a symbol of a changing society, or even as a pervasive metaphor and rationale for mainstream sections of society such as business and the media; and that sport is critical in terms of contemporary conceptions of the body: 'It would be an exaggeration to say that society is being refashioned in the image of sport, but there is a kernel of truth in the proposition' ('Worshipping the body at altar of sport', *Observer*, 13 July 1997, pp. 18–19). Any such proposition must be subjected to informed evaluation and rigorous analytical scrutiny that fits well with the CRESC mission to stimulate 'theoretically directed, inter-disciplinary empirical research on socio-cultural change in the UK', also placing this in 'comparative and historical perspective'. This revised edition of *Understanding Sport* brings together relevant evidence, scholarship and theoretical debate in order to allow such evaluations to take place, and to indicate – to the beginning student, the more general social scientist, or the curious sports enthusiast – where one might look to find out still more about the social bases and cultural characteristics of the sport phenomenon.

The book is simple to use. The chapters are designed to be read, either in whole or in part, and reviewed in group discussions. They are designed, too, as foundations and introductions, which should stimulate interested and committed students to explore further sources. Some further reading is indicated after each chapter, and all references cited in each chapter are listed in the Bibliography.

The book has been produced collaboratively, although initial authorial responsibility was as follows: Chapters, 1, 2, 3 and 4, Tomlinson; Chapters 5, 8, 10 and 13, Horne; Chapters 6,

11 and 12, Whannel; Chapters 7 and 9, Woodward. Tomlinson drafted the Introduction and Conclusion (with Woodward). Horne and Tomlinson completed final editing work on the entire manuscript. We are grateful to our publisher, Routledge, for its patience in awaiting delivery of the manuscript, to the anonymous readers/reviewers for their perceptive comments in response to the proposal; comments that confirmed our plans for the reworking and reshaping of this revised edition. We hope too that the book will make a mark beyond specialist sport studies readership and constituencies, through its location in CRESC's book series.

Finally, we would be pleased to receive comments and responses on the book, individually and collectively, on matters of both accuracy and interpretation.

John Horne, University of Central Lancashire
Alan Tomlinson, University of Brighton
Garry Whannel, University of Bedfordshire
Kath Woodward, Open University
February 2012

ACKNOWLEDGEMENTS

The authors would like to thank their families, friends, colleagues and former students for contributing in so many different ways to this book and members of the editorial team at Routledge for their efficient professionalism in bringing the book to completion.

XVii

acknowledgements

CHAPTER ONE

INDUSTRIAL SOCIETY, SOCIAL CHANGE AND SPORTS CULTURE

INTRODUCTION

Modern sports have exhibited some core characteristics that make them specifically modern, and these can best be understood in contrast to earlier forms of sports. These earlier forms have been described and classified as *popular recreations* (Malcolmson, 1973), *mediaeval sports* (Guttmann, 1978), or *folk sports* (Dunning and Sheard, 1979). To clarify the differences between the older and modern forms of sports, it is necessary also to understand the changing nature of the society of which these sports forms are a part. Therefore, in the first two chapters of this book we review important elements of social change and their cultural implications; outline on a general level the primary features and characteristics of those sports forms, comparing the modern forms with older types of games; demonstrate the importance to the emergence of modern sports of athleticism in the British public schools, and its impact in spheres beyond the school, alongside the impact of reformers; provide case studies of major team sports and individual sports to illustrate the tensions at the heart of the amateur–professional dynamic in those sports, and the working through of these tensions into the late modern period; and review the principal features of and trends in the development of modern sports in contemporary Britain up to the end of the first decade of the twenty-first century (see Chapter 2).

SOCIAL CHANGE AND THE CULTURAL IMPLICATIONS OF CHANGE

Malcolmson (1973) has argued that traditional recreation was rooted in a society that was, in its core features, vastly different to the society produced by the processes of urbanisation and industrialisation. Popular recreations of a traditional kind were features of a society that was predominantly agrarian, strongly parochial, and had a deep sense of corporate identity. The changing society – the inchoate modern industrial society – was very different indeed. It was urban-centred, and generated uniquely congested cities; it was governed by contractual relations, in spheres of life such as work and the family, and increasingly in leisure; it was biased towards individualism, prioritising the unit of the self or the individual rather than the collective or the corporate; it was rooted in factory-labour discipline, rather than the social relations of the community or the inherited relations of the community; and it was based on free enterprise, with all the concomitant volatility that the release of the entrepreneurial spirit implies. Societies so different would obviously generate cultural, leisure and sports forms with very different characteristics. Culture does not change immediately in the wake of social change, however, and Griffin (2005) has identified the spatial dimensions of popular sports that persisted and developed at uneven historical rates. Malcolmson himself recognised an interregnum between popular recreation and the growth of the sports of the industrial society, and suggested that, for many people, this interregnum 'was filled by the public house' (Malcolmson, 1973: 170–171). Indeed, as the 'new world of urban industrial culture' (Holt, 1989: 148) was established in nineteenth-century cities, the role of the pub was far from diminished, and social drinking around sport was an important dimension of male leisure: 'the new generation of publicans seemed to have taken over the role of sporting enthusiasts with as much gusto as the ale-house and tavern-keepers of the past. This was a powerful source of continuity in popular culture' (ibid.: 148). Holt's work shows how 'half hidden continuities between generations' might be as significant as more dramatic transformations in understanding the growth of modern sport, and stresses the 'gradual shift in cultural attitudes towards popular recreation' as much as 'sudden changes or discontinuities brought about by the onset of industrialization' (ibid.: 3, 4). In studying the emergence of a specifically modern sports culture in Britain, and the main effects wrought by the hugely influential process of industrialisation, it is important to bear in mind these insights from Holt's authoritative and sensitive historical analysis.

James Walvin, in the context of his study of the demise of the folk form of football, identified four factors as the main influences upon the decline of the game (1975: 26–27). These were: (1) a growth in the policing powers of the state; (2) a tightening of labour discipline, based upon the longer controllable working hours that were possible in the new forms of industrial production in the factory; (3) the take-over of urban space inherent in the process of urbanisation; and (4) the rise of 'a new middle-class mentality', which was to effectively marginalise popular traditional sports and codify some into new forms for the privileged classes, and to encourage the development of forms of rational recreation (those forms of activity deemed to be worthy rather than worthless, and often of potential benefit for self-improvement) for the popular and working classes. It is clear that the new and emerging society did not spawn new sports in any inexorably natural way. These social changes involved sets of interests and forms of cultural brokership in which some activities were deemed as of more value than others. John Hargreaves (1982: 37–39) has provided an outline of the development of modern sports, which suggests that the key social changes represent 'organised interests'. He points to five aspects of social change that create the climate in which modern sports emerge. First, the way of life of the majority of people is subjected to attack; second, for many people, time and space is eliminated; third, patrician patronage is the basis of the reconstruction of some sports; fourth, forces of social class affect the way new sports forms are developed, with 'games' being produced for the leaders and 'drill' the physical diet recommended for the subordinate class. Finally, there is an expansion of commercial provision in the new society. For Hargreaves, the social changes in which the modern sports culture emerges are revealing of 'a bringing to bear of pressure on subordinate groups; pressure ranging from outright coercion and the use of material incentives to moral exhortation' (ibid.: 38).

There is an interpretive consensus concerning the major aspects of social change that demarcate the limits and possibilities for cultural expression in the sphere of sports. The preindustrial social order was based more on traditional relationships than on essentially contractual ones. Time becomes more quantified in the new industrial order. Space becomes more rationalised, and functionally defined in ways that are, in their precision, excluding as much as enabling. Social groups are, in industrialising society, defined anew in terms of their position with regard to the newly dominant industrial economy and its division of labour – defined, that is, as social classes. And leisure and sports are seen as important forms of cultural expression, though the basis and expression of their importance are far from shared by the different social classes. Alongside exploitative and monotonous work, for instance, many working people also had to endure a 'loss of leisure and amenities' (Thompson, 1968: 222).

Seminal social historical studies have drawn out some of the cultural implications of these social changes. In his majestic and imaginative study of the centrality of new modes of time-keeping, E. P. Thompson (1967) lists the ways in which the new industrial order fundamentally restructures the basis of everyday life. His analysis is premised upon the recognition that 'the transition to mature industrial society entailed a severe restructuring of working habits – new disciplines, new incentives, and a new human nature upon which these incentives could bite effectively', and he then asks 'how far is this related to changes in the inward notation of time?' (ibid.: 57). Thompson reviewed anthropological and cultural sources that indicate how time has been related to 'familiar processes in the cycle of work or of domestic chores' (ibid.: 58). For the Nuer, the cattle clock served the function of a daily timepiece; time was determined by 'the round of pastoral tasks'. Bourdieu's early anthropological work showed how Algerian peasants were nonchalantly indifferent to the passage of time, seeing the clock as 'the devil's mill'. In the Aran Islands, people's sense of time depended upon the direction of the wind. This kind of task-orientation, seen by Thompson as 'more humanly comprehensible than timed labour' and more conducive to the intermingling of 'social intercourse and labour', is less tolerated by those who are ruled by the clock: 'to men accustomed to labour timed by the clock, this attitude to labour appears to be wasteful and lacking in urgency' (ibid.: 60). As the industrial society attaches measurable value to labour and its output, the task becomes less important, and time's value in cash terms becomes dominant: 'Time is now currency: it is not passed but spent' (ibid.: 61).

Thompson lists seven ways in which the 'new labour habits were formed, and a new time-discipline was imposed . . . by the division of labour; the supervision of labour; fines; bells and clocks; money incentives; preachings and schoolings; the suppression of fairs and sports' (ibid.: 90). Modern sport, as it was shaped in the context of such cataclysmic changes in conceptions of time and work, must be understood as, if not a directly determined product of,

3

then certainly a cultural corollary of, these major processes and influences. This can be seen in the recognition, within social historical work (Brailsford, 1991), of the importance of shifting conceptions of time in the development of modern sports.

In the early 1880s, one contemporaneous critic of the Industrial Revolution recognised its essence as 'the substitution of competition for the mediaeval regulations which had previously controlled the production and distribution of wealth' (Toynbee, 1967: 1). Its 'facts', as Toynbee called them, were straightforward enough: the rapid growth of population; cataclysmic agricultural changes as the common-field system was destroyed, enclosure of commons and waste-lands was effected, and large farms became the main form of ownership; technological inventions affecting the nature of manufacture; advances in the means of communication with important consequences for the expansion of trade; a revolution in the distribution of wealth, constituting 'a great social revolution, a change in the balance of political power and in the relative position of classes' (ibid.: 5); and the substitution of a 'cash nexus' for the more traditional human tie. All of these six facets had implications for the context and meaning of recreational activity and sports practices.

The identification of such features at the core of the new industrial society has an impressive intellectual pedigree, deriving as it does from the classical sociological thinkers of the late nineteenth and early twentieth centuries: Marx, Weber and Durkheim. As Krishan Kumar observes, the 'sociological image of industrialism, in its details' (1978: 63) derives from the work of these founding fathers. Kumar sets out six 'elements of the contemporary sociological model of industrialism' (ibid.: 64): (1) urbanism as a way of life; (2) the demographic transition; (3) the decline of community; (4) a specialised division of labour; (5) centralisation, equalisation and democratisation; and (6) secularisation, rationalisation and bureaucratisation. These constitute not just social influences; they become primary social relations and, as Giddens notes, industrial capitalism's world-wide expansion 'brought about social changes more shattering in their consequences than any other period in the whole previous history of mankind' (1982: 17). It is important to grasp the scale of change in the vision – often of loss and anxiety, anger and despair – underlying the analytical and theoretical treatises of the classical sociologists. Kumar summarises the foci of the latter:

> In the dead prose of a multitude of textbooks on 'industrial sociology' lay buried and congealed the passionate accounts of Marx and Engels on the conditions of the proletariat; Weber's icy and characteristically ambivalent dissection of bureaucracy and bureaucratization; Durkheim's concerned vision of industrial man in the state of *anomie*, impossibly striving after infinitely receding goals.
>
> (1978: 63)

These theorists were seeking to make sense of a new social order, an emerging cultural universe, of which sport was a part. We will see in the classifications and case studies covered in Chapter 2, and in illustrative material presented in Chapter 3, how important these social changes and their cultural ramifications are for an understanding of the forces shaping modern

4

sport. Peter Bailey's (1978) study of the early industrial period argues that the growth of new forms of leisure and sports in the kind of cultural climate evoked by Thompson should be seen as a form of cultural struggle: the development of rational recreation – the use of sport and leisure activities in 'the creation of a healthy, moral and orderly workforce' (Holt, 1989: 136) should be seen as an element in the contest for control of industrial society's new culture (Bailey, 1978). Bailey's emphasis is an important one, for it warns against any simple reduction of the character of sport to a mere mirror image of the society. At the same time, though, there is no doubt that the features of the newly emergent and dominant sports forms were in many cases close to the core features of the new social order. There was a consonance between the core values of the societal form of industrialism and the sports forms that emerged within that societal form. It is hardly surprising, then, that any classification of the core features of those sports will comprise elements that are also characteristic of the society itself.

THE CHARACTERISTICS OF PRE-INDUSTRIAL AND MODERN SPORTS

Several typologies have been developed offering valuable classifications of the features of modern sports. Allen Guttmann presents a typology of this sort for each of four societal types: primitive society, classic civilisations (Greece and Rome, treated separately in Guttmann's analysis), mediaeval society, and modern society. This is worth presenting in full (Table 1.1).

Reservations might be expressed about the accuracy of some aspects of this classification. There is evidence, for instance, of the prominence of records and of the quantification of performance in the ancient Olympics in Greece (Young, 1984). Also, it has been pointed out (Tomlinson, 1992), that the classification could be seen as championing a relatively linear and evolutionary process, with the sports of a primitive society appearing to be almost completely the opposite of the sports of a modern society. But Guttmann himself has shown some awareness of these implications (1986) and believes that it is a harsh criticism to hold them against him (1992). The main achievement of the Guttmann classification is that it highlights, in an illuminating

Table 1.1 Guttmann's characteristics of sports in various ages

	Primitive	Greek	Roman	Mediaeval	Modern
Secularism	Y&N	Y&N	Y&N	Y&N	Yes
Equality	No	Y&N	Y&N	No	Yes
Specialisation	No	Yes	Y&N	No	Yes
Rationalisation	No	Yes	Yes	No	Yes
Bureaucracy	No	Y&N	Yes	No	Yes
Quantification	No	No	Y&N	No	Yes
Records	No	No	No	No	Yes

Source: Guttmann (1978: 54).

5

comparative framework, the specificity of the nature of sport in different and distinctive social contexts. The framework demonstrates how sports cultures and forms vary across time and space, showing that sport is socially constructed and not some sort of trans-historical and supra-social phenomenon. Guttmann defines sports as 'playful physical contests', that, in the modern age, have come to express an increasingly scientific view of the world. In his later work, Guttmann defined sports as 'autotelic physical contests' (2004: 2), implying that sport practices have their own ends and purposes, but his classification beds sports cultures of particular times within their wider social context. Gruneau has criticised Guttmann's work for what he calls its 'theoretical affirmation of voluntarism and the merits of liberal democracy' (1983: 43), and for its implication that sports, being inherently playful, are also therefore 'voluntary and free' (ibid.: 44); Tomlinson and Young (2010) subject the 'Weberian' basis of Guttmann's framework to close scrutiny. But despite such critical reservations, Guttmann's broad perspective is upheld in seminal work on the origins of British sport. All of the characteristics of the Guttmann model bar one – secularism – are stated or implied in Eric Dunning and Kenneth Sheard's path-breaking typology of what they call 'the structural properties of folk-games and modern sports'. This classification was developed in the context of Dunning and Sheard's brilliant study of the development of rugby football (1979), but it focuses invaluably upon the general characteristics of sports in the transformative period of industrialisation (Table 1.2).

Table 1.2 The structural properties of folk games and modern sports

Folk games	Modern sports
1 Diffuse, informal organisation implicit in the local social structure	1 Highly specific, formal organisation, institutionally differentiated at the local regional, national and international levels
2 Simple and unwritten customary rules, legitimated by tradition	2 Formal and elaborate written rules, worked out pragmatically and legitimated by rational-bureaucratic means
3 Fluctuating game pattern; tendency to change through long-term and, from the viewpoint of the participants, imperceptible 'drift'	3 Change institutionalised through rational-bureaucratic channels
4 Regional variation of rules, size and shape of balls, etc.	4 National and international standardisation of rules, size and shape of balls, etc.
5 No fixed limits on territory, duration or numbers of participants	5 Played on a spatially limited pitch with clearly defined boundaries, within fixed time limits and with a fixed number of participants, equalised between the contending sides
6 Strong influence of natural and social differences on the game pattern	6 Minimisation, principally by means of formal rules, of the influence of natural and social differences on the game pattern: norms of equality and 'fairness'

6

7 Low role differentiation (division of labour) among the players	7 High role differentiation (division of labour) among the players
8 Loose distinction between playing and 'spectating' roles	8 Strict distinction between playing and 'spectating' roles
9 Low structural differentiation; several 'game elements' rolled into one	9 High structural differentiation; specialisation around kicking, carrying and throwing, the use of sticks, etc.
10 Informal social control by the players themselves within the context of the ongoing game	10 Formal social control by officials who stand, as it were, 'outside' the game and who are appointed and certificated by central legislative bodies and empowered, when a breach of the rule occurs, to stop play and impose penalties graded according to the seriousness of the offence
11 High level of socially tolerated physical violence; emotional spontaneity; low restraint	11 Low level of socially tolerated physical violence; high emotional control; high restraint
12 Generation in a relatively open and spontaneous form of pleasurable 'battle excitement'	12 Generation in a more controlled and 'sublimated' form of pleasurable 'battle excitement'
13 Emphasis on physical force as opposed to skill	13 Emphasis on skill, as opposed to physical force
14 Strong communal pressure to participate; individual identity subordinate to group identity; test of identity in general	14 Individually chosen as a recreation; individual identity of greater importance relative to group identity; test of identity in relation to a specific skill or set of skills
15 Locally meaningful contests only; relative equality of playing skills among sides; no chances for national reputations or money payment	15 National and international superimposed on local contests; emergence of elite players and teams; chance to establish national and international reputations; tendency to 'monetisation' of sports

Source: Dunning and Sheard (1979: 33–34)

'Structural properties', as Dunning and Sheard call the core values of modern sports, do not spring from thin air: they are cultural constructions, socially shaped. Important economic and social developments in industrialising and urbanising Britain provided the setting in which modern sports emerged. Golby and Purdue (1984: 110) see the transformation of popular culture as strongly influenced by four factors in particular, from the 1840s onwards: (1) the rise of public transport in the form of the railway system; (2) a reduction in working people's working week, providing, by the middle of the century, the Saturday half-day for leisure; (3) an increase in real earnings, particularly in the last decades of the century, providing unprecedented levels of disposable income; and (4) an expansion of commercial provision in leisure, 'marked especially by the growth of the music hall, and of the popular press,

7

professional sport and seaside holidays'. But such influences alone do not in any simple fashion shape the contours of the emerging sports cultures: they are the necessary conditions for certain changes and developments. For the sociologist of sport, the important task is to identify those social influences and social relations that are the most important in the process whereby some 'structural properties' and values rather than others come to the fore. In the making of modern sport in Britain, it was athleticism – the cultivation of the values of amateur sport – and rational recreation – conceived as a transformative project for the improvement of the masses – that were the most telling (in the case of rational recreation, albeit in unanticipated ways) of such influences. In the rest of this chapter, the nature and impact of these influences are reviewed. In Chapter 2, in the context of selected case studies, their relationship to (and in many respects struggles with) other influences such as professionalism and commercialism are illustrated.

ATHLETICISM AND ITS CONTRIBUTION TO THE GROWTH OF MODERN SPORTS

Many of the core characteristics of modern sports were shaped in the British public schools of the nineteenth century. This is widely acknowledged and useful accounts and discussions abound (Hargreaves, 1986: 38–45; Holt, 1989: 74–86). But the definitive source for an understanding of the nature and impact of the public schools' approach to games, sport and physical activity remains the work of J.A. Mangan. In his seminal study of athleticism in the public schools of the nineteenth and early twentieth century, Mangan (1981) produced a substantial empirical study of the genesis and impact of what he labelled the 'ideology of athleticism'. Six case study schools were chosen for the study. Harrow was chosen as representative of the great public schools. Stonyhurst (1873) was the denominational type (though these spread across Catholic, Quaker and Protestant). Proprietary types, with shareholders, were represented by Marlborough (1843). Uppingham (1853) was the selected elevated grammar. The Woodard Anglican middle-class type of school was represented by Lancing (1948). And individually financed and owned private venture schools were represented by Edinburgh's Loretto (1862). In selecting these six types of school, Mangan was confident that his case study material would be extensive enough to permit generalisations about the significance of athleticism in the public schools generally. He could then assert with confidence that four educational goals were stressed by physical educators in the public schools. Physical education, it was believed, would cultivate desirable moral values: physical and moral courage; loyalty and cooperation; the capacity to act fairly and take defeat well; and the ability to command and obey (Mangan, 1981: 9). With such an agenda, the public school educators attributed to sports a capacity for character building. As Mangan shows so vividly, riotous and brutal forms of activity by the undisciplined public school youth – such as 'a brutal frog hunt in the school grounds' in the early 1840s at Marlborough, in which the frogs were beaten to death and the bodies piled high (ibid.: 18) – were replaced by formalised disciplined activity. From around 1870, Bamford notes, 'there was a subtle but organized drive by authority to

8

understanding sport

sublimate the boy's self to a team' (1967: 83); a drive so successful that the rhetoric of athleticism took such a hold that it could resonate across the British Empire (Mangan, 1986; Holt, 1989: 204–211; Mangan, 1992); and early in the twentieth century could be heard from the 'donkeys' (Clark, 1991) on the battlefields of the First World War (Mangan, 1981: 191–196). The discipline of the Victorian upbringing could become a template for conduct, notions of chivalry and decency and the rules of the game dictating an unthinking conformity in battle (Clark, 1991: 174); and when the 18th London Regiment lost 1200 men in a single hour at Loos, they had 'dribbled a football in front of them as they crossed No-Man's Land' (ibid.: 150). These may be extreme and tragic instances of the wider manifestation of athleticist values, but the particular achievement of the public schools in sport was the development of a vehicle for the transmission of moral values to newly educated generations of upper-class and upper middle-class males. In his 1904 book, *Let's Play the Game: The Anglo-Saxon Sporting Spirit*, Eustace Miles wrote that cricket could illustrate:

> such valuable ideas as co-operation, division of labour, specialisation, obedience to a single organiser (perhaps with a council to advise him), national character, geography and its influences, arts and artistic anatomy, physiology and hygiene, ethics and even – if the play can be learnt rightly – general educational methods.
>
> (cited in Dobbs, 1973: 28)

There is a clear manifesto in this list of ten 'valuable ideas' for the production of the disciplined individual with a set of socially acceptable moral values. It would be difficult to overestimate the importance of what Peter McIntosh has noted as the equation of physical education with moral education. McIntosh notes too that the recognition that physical education can contribute to moral education emerged in the late eighteenth century, arising from the ideas of French philosopher and educationalist Jean-Jacques Rousseau, concerning the body–mind relationship, and out of pioneering developments in gymnastics on the European mainland. But the public schools were to institutionalise such ideas into powerful sets of principles and a coherent working ideology. As McIntosh puts it:

> It was in the Public Schools during the second half of the [nineteenth] century that two basic new theories were developed. The first was that competitive sport, espe-cially team games, had an ethical basis, and the second was that training in moral behaviour on the playing field was transferable to the world beyond.
>
> (1979: 27)

Lest one might think that such theories have been long discredited, consider how much they have in common with the declarations of then Conservative Prime Minister John Major in his Introduction to the policy document, *Raising the Game* (DNH, 1995). Framed as 'ideas to rebuild the strength of every level of British sport', and claimed as 'the most important set of proposals ever published for the encouragement and promotion of sport' (ibid.: 1), the policy document was rooted in the founding principles of the morality of athleticism. *Raising the*

Game argued that sport should be cherished for its capacity to bond and bind people together across ages and national borders and, 'by a miraculous paradox', also to represent 'nationhood' and 'local pride'. In doing this, sport is claimed to do the following:

- through competition, teach lessons which last for life;
- be a means of learning how to be both a winner and a loser;
- thrive only if 'both parties play by the rules', and accept the outcome 'with good grace';
- teach how to live with others as part of a team;
- improve health;
- create friendships.

(ibid.: 2)

The vehicles for the inculcation of these values were 'our great traditional sports – cricket, hockey, swimming, athletics, football, netball, rugby, tennis and the like' (ibid.: 3) – an explicit acknowledgement of the moral values long attributed to the playing field and, above all, to team games. This kind of thinking continued to bolster sport policy and pedagogy in Britain, throughout the administrations of the 1997–2010 Labour government and the Conservative–Liberal Democrat Coalition government that took power in 2010. It also underpinned the winning of and run-up to the London 2012 Olympics, despite the fact that participation in traditional team games was in consistent decline, as we show in Chapter 4.

Compare the Major eulogy for sports with celebrations of the values of games from a century earlier. Mangan reported the beliefs of an early apologist for public school games who believed that these games could help produce:

> a manly straightforward character, a scorn of lying and meanness, habits of obedience and command, and fearless courage. Thus equipped, he goes out into the world, and bears a man's part in subduing the earth, ruling its wild folk, and building up the Empire.

(cited in Mangan, 1981: 9)

Well prepared by his grounding in the 'institutional wars on the playing field . . . The alliance between character-building and games promoted self-restraint and cooperation without wholly destroying a competitive sense of struggle' (Wilkinson, 1964: 30). In 1909, the captain of the Cambridge University cricket team of twenty-five years before could still write, in the *Empire Annual for Boys*, that to play the game was to exhibit a 'supreme standard of excellence'. From such a perspective, three main sporting values were worthy of cultivation: 'to aim high, to never lose heart, and to help your neighbour' (Kanitkar, 1994: 187). Cricket, rugby and football were the sports that featured most in this kind of rhetoric. Arthur Mee, too, famous in mid-century as the author of the *Children's Encyclopaedia*, stressed the importance of the playing field for the laying down of the 'laws of honour'. Belief in the importance of games and sport was deeply rooted in the schools, and practice matched rhetoric throughout the

10

twentieth century. In the mid-1960s, most (boarding) public schools still allocated three or more half-days per week to organised games (Kalton, 1966: 110); in 1963, sporting activities could still serve as a primary form of 'ritualistic symbolisation of the social values on which . . . the public school system rests' (Wakeford, 1969: 124); in the academic year 1993/4, 83 per cent of 11-year-old pupils in independent secondary schools had more than two hours of physical education per week, compared to 48 per cent in state schools, and weekend, lunch time and after-school sport was reported to have further decreased in the state sector (Secondary Heads Association, 1994: 8). The legacy of athleticism was still being widely preached in the pedagogy of the privileged close to a century and a half on from its inception (see Horne *et al.* 2011).

Belief in the appropriateness of sport and physical activity as a means of developing moral values was not exclusive to male educational establishments. At the end of the nineteenth century the institutional foundations were laid for several influential colleges of physical education for women. Although the existence of these colleges did not guarantee radical feminist outcomes – Hargreaves observes that the profession idealised the role of the woman within the family, and 'the colleges reproduced the structure and ideologies of the "perfect" Victorian home, thus reinforcing conventional sexual divisions in society' (1994: 78) – they nevertheless established a parallel character-building agenda to that of the public schools and their university counterparts. The pioneering Swedish educational gymnast Madame Österberg opened a college in 1895 in Hampstead, North London, and this moved to Dartford in Kent ten years later. Dartford College 'offered the first full-time specialist course in the theory and practice of physical education in England' (ibid.: 74) and was the exemplar for other innovative initiatives of the late Victorian and early Edwardian period. Anstey College (1907), Chelsea College (1898), Bedford College (1903) and Liverpool College (1904) followed the pioneering model of Osterberg's Dartford.

Dorette Wilkie was the 'Founder' of the Chelsea College, which became the Chelsea School in the University of Brighton in 1992. She initially founded a Gymnastic Teachers' Training Department in connection with a Day College for Women and associated with the Chelsea Polytechnic in London – this was launched in 1898, with six pioneer students and Dorette Wilkie as 'Headmistress' (Clarke and Webb, 2005). Wilkie, an 18-year-old Prussian immigrant to England in 1885, had suffered from a spine condition and came to England to seek a cure, entering the Training School of Adolf A. Stempel's gymnasium. Benefiting directly and dramatically from the curative effects of gymnastics, she made physical education her career, anglicising herself still further on naturalisation by dropping the title 'Fraulein' and adding an 'i' to the Prussian name Wilke. Establishing a Saturday afternoon games session for the deprived children of Battersea Park, south London, she saw sport and physical activity as a form of escape, declaring that 'the time for fairyland is half-past two till four pm, and the only condition of entrance is a desire to play and be happy' (Webb, 1979: 45). In a *fin-de-siècle* lecture, Miss Wilkie preached the philosophy of sports values and physical education, specifying three core aims in physical education training (ibid.: 57). First, the development of 'a body as hard as steel' would help 'to bear up against our many difficulties'. Second, the physical educator

11

should help students cultivate 'a mind as clear as crystal, to see and understand all that is good and noble and beautiful in the world, and also to distinguish the true from the false'. Third, Miss Wilkie recommended an emphasis on empathy, in nurturing 'a heart as warm as sunshine, so that we may feel and sympathise with the ways and troubles of our fellow creatures'. In 1903, Miss Wilkie confirmed her feminine if not feminist mission: 'it is no use setting a man to drill girls. He does not understand them as does a woman. His place is to drill an army; we do not want our women for the Army' (ibid.: 59). In terms of gender, such institutions were to pursue separatist missions until the last quarter of the twentieth century, with important implications for the nature of generations of girls' (and so of course boys') experience of sport and physical education in school.

In summary, public school sports and games were not conceived as some innocent pastime. They constituted a vehicle for powerful and prestigious social actors, for the transmission of preferred values and for the generation and perpetuation of a particular form of culture, stressing the moral responsibilities of an elite and the manly virtues (Maguire, 1986) that were seen as the basis of the execution of such responsibilities. And the conception of sports fostered in those schools closely matched the political agenda of sports-reared politicians, many of whom were the products of the schools themselves. A.J. Balfour – prominent Scottish landowner, Cambridge philosopher and golf zealot as well as Conservative prime minister – was a tireless spokesman for the provision of 'healthy means of recreation for all classes in the community', as he put it in 1899 (Balfour, 1912: 276). Balfour sang the praises of sport for performers and spectators alike in 'Tom Brown's Universe' (de S. Honey, 1977: 117).

Educators, industrialists, priests and soldiers – as well as politicians – emerged from these institutions with a belief in and a commitment to spread the gospel of athleticism. This was accomplished in their own universities as they became undergraduates, and in their professional lives in the institutions of the new industrial communities. The clerical sponsorship of weekend football, for instance, was 'promoted as a wholesale alternative to drink' at certain points during the nineteenth century, and many churches at the turn of the nineteenth and twentieth centuries 'were energetic pioneers of new popular pastimes' (Harris, 1993: 162). This contrasted with their equivalents in mid-Victorian Britain, 'when clerics were more often engaged in "rationalizing" or repressing the archaic pleasures of the poor' (ibid.).

As the nineteenth century progressed, the gospel of athleticism was made manifest in the institutional form of amateur sport. The process of ascendancy of this model of sports can also be linked to the desire to produce a modern healthy model of the physical. The cultural historian Bruce Haley has captured the importance of this health rationale, and its inter-connectedness with established sets of interests, in the rise of organised games: 'in playing the game, the moral faculty took over entirely from the cognitive. The healthy body was an instrument not for understanding the ineffable, but for ritualizing an obedience to the reasonable' (1978: 259).

Through the athleticist model of sport, the public schools framed the beliefs and practices of many of the privileged and the powerful. In this sense, as Hargreaves (1986: 38) states, the 'importance of the public schools in the development of sporting forms and in articulating them on the power network in this period can hardly be exaggerated'; the athleticist ideology actually permeated the country's political culture and had 'long-lasting effects on the character of sport in Britain' (ibid.: 45).

'TEACHING THE POOR HOW TO PLAY': RATIONAL RECREATION AND THE STRUGGLE OVER SPORT

As noted above, rational recreationists saw some forms of sport as a means of moral education, a source, as Holt (1989: 136) observes, for the cultivation of a 'play discipline' capable of 'teaching the poor how to play'. Golby and Purdue observe how, early in the nineteenth century, new industrial workers experienced a reduction in leisure time. But 'religious, humanitarian and educational bodies' became concerned, as the century progressed, that the labouring classes should be provided with 'as many accepting and improving activities as possible', contributing as 'members of a culturally harmonious society' (1984: 92).

Throughout the century, 'rationality implied both order and control' (Cunningham, 1980: 90). The spirit, intent and impact of the rational recreationists can be seen clearly in a wide range of cases and initiatives. For illustrative purposes, four such cases are outlined here: (1) developments in the culture of the London working class; (2) football in the urban industrial cities of the Midlands and the North of England; (3) physical drill for the working classes in schools; and (4) the provision of open space, in the form of parks, within cities.

First, Stedman-Jones (1983) has shown how in the last three decades of the nineteenth century a conservative (in the sense of forgoing political activism) working-class culture was established. At the beginning of the century, it could be said that, even though social distinctions might be clear, 'there was no great political, cultural or economic divide between the middle class and those beneath them . . . All classes shared in the passions for gambling, theatre, tea gardens, pugilism and animal sports ' (ibid.: 185). In the first half of the nineteenth century, however, political and religious/evangelical concerns and a move to the suburbs by the propertied classes fuelled a separation between the classes. The working class became more and more widely perceived as a problem, and three waves of anxiety consolidated this: in the 1840s/1850s around the political activism of the working classes and the European revolutions; between 1866 and 1872 around the Second Reform Bill and revolution in Paris; and in the late 1880s around high unemployment, urban overcrowding and ethnic immigration into London. At each point, the 'respectable and the well-to-do' were concerned that the working class would pose a threat to the social order, and numerous organisations were founded 'to hasten the work of christianizing and "civilizing" the city' (ibid.: 191). This was the basis for the rational recreational initiative aimed at the London working class. This constituted a project to 'create a physical and institutional environment', via legislation, which would undermine working-class habits, and promote the inculcation of 'a new moral code' through private philanthropy. Stedman-Jones (ibid.: 194–195, 202–203) catalogues the successes of such a

13

project. By the end of the century the following popular cultural practices had all but disappeared from the public life of London: gin palaces, cock fighting, bear baiting, ratting, rat-baiting, bird singing competitions, street gambling. In their place there emerged 'a growing number of parks, museums, exhibitions, public libraries and mechanics' institutes, which 'promoted a more improving or innocuous use of leisure time' (ibid.: 195). Without doubt, the institutional and everyday environment of the London working class was altered by these interventions, but the new working-class culture was itself distinctive:

> it was clearly distinguished from the culture of the middle class and had remained largely impervious to middle-class attempts to dictate its character or direction. Its dominant cultural institutions were not the school, the evening class, the library, the friendly society, the church or the chapel, but the pub, the sporting paper, the race-course and the music hall.
>
> (ibid.: 207)

Second, rational recreationists were important figures in the formation and early development of many football clubs which were to feature in the formation of the professional game. Public school and Oxbridge-educated enthusiasts for the game, middle-class missionaries seeking to reform the populations of the new cities, may well at times have provided an important basis for the growth of the game. Aston Villa, Bolton Wanderers, Wolverhampton Wanderers and Everton (from the north-west of England and the West Midlands, the cradle of the professional game) were all associated originally with religious organisations (Cunningham, 1980: 127). Other clubs, in Preston and Sheffield, for instance, were initiated by local employers or industrialists. Between 1870 and 1885, in Birmingham, around one in four football clubs and around one in five cricket clubs were connected to religious organisations (Holt, 1989: 138). But the initiative in some cases came from the ordinary people themselves, and the development of spectatorship was hardly the stuff of which the rational recreationists' dreams were made. In the last year of the century, one commentator could observe that 'football in the North is more than a game. It excites more emotion than art, politics and the drama, and it awakes local patriotism to the highest pitch' (Mason, 1996: 50). Aston Villa may have been founded by young male members of a Wesleyan Chapel in 1874, but its pitch was provided by a local butcher and a local publican provided the dressing room. Cunningham points out that any working men wanting to play football would not have been worried about the motives of their providers and were 'prepared to accept for as long as necessary, the fact of middle-class sponsorship, but not its ideology' (1980: 128). Rational recreationists in the middle class might have promoted football as one of several means geared towards the bringing together of classes, the goal of class conciliation, but working men made the sport their own and the development of the professional game with its boisterous and visible public culture both on the field and off defied the worthy objectives of the moral improvers of the time.

Third, in schools, the working classes were denied any potential benefits of organised games' moral worth until after 1908, when trainee teachers began to be trained in physical education,

14
understanding sport

giving some substance to the 1902 Education Act, which had recommended a wider programme of physical education for elementary schoolchildren (Holt, 1989: 139) – not unconnected to the concern felt by the state at the poor levels of health and fitness of conscripts during the Boer War campaigns. The 1870 Education Act had permitted, though not required, the instruction of schoolchildren in drill: 'Military drill fleshed out with some general exercise was considered to be all that the ranks required' (ibid.: 139). Reformers like Chadwick, Hargreaves (1986: 50) points out, promoted drill, not sports, for the working class, and physical space in state schools was minimal. Consequently, some priests or schoolmasters – or 'dedicated improvers of the young' as Holt calls them – devoted their own time to organising extra-curricular initiatives, sometimes prompting developments on a more formal level, such as the formation of Schools' Football Associations. Here, the interventions of the rational recreationists can be seen to have at least loosened the stranglehold on working-class children's schooling of a restricted form of physical activity.

Fourth, if middle-class reformers saw disorderly public sports as undesirable, they argued the need for and benefits of appropriately designed and constructed open spaces in urban areas, which it was believed would both contribute to the reduction of crime, drunkenness and immorality, and check the spread of infectious diseases (Golby and Purdue, 1984: 102). Britain's legacy of municipal parks stems from such concerns, along with the desire of local notables and dignitaries to inscribe themselves in the history of their locality by gifting land to the town for the public good (Cunningham, 1980: 94–95). A public meeting in Manchester in 1844 recommended the provision of parks in the town, as they would 'contribute to the health, rational enjoyment, kindly intercourse and good morals of all classes of our industrious nation' (Golby and Purdue, 1984: 102). Although initially many such spaces were educational – providing a guide to nature, and a source for healthy exercise, walking (Cunningham, 1980: 95) – the space secured by them provided a vital long-term resource for the playing of sports. Rightly – as a stroll through any town or city in the country will show over a hundred years on, with the town's parks laid out in mosaics of bowling greens, football pitches and tennis courts – the establishment of municipal parks can be seen as the most important and long-lasting achievement of the rational recreationists.

Overall, then, the rational recreationist project – in Hargreaves' summary, 'the attempt to spread bourgeois mores concerning the use of free time', in promoting activities 'that would be "improving", educational, respectable and more refined than the boisterous and dissolute pursuits of popular culture' (1986: 22) – was far from successful in its primary goal of cultural transformation, for those at whom it was aimed could use facilities for their own purposes, could appropriate them for their own ends and imbue them with their own meanings. Nevertheless, reformers created spaces, facilities and resources for new ways of playing, even if the meanings of that play for the poor and the popular classes could not be dictated and controlled by the reformers.

15

CONCLUSION

Modern sports in Britain emerged as the male-dominated cultural products of a rapidly industrialising society undergoing unprecedented levels of change. But that is not to say that the sports simply reflected the characteristics of the society. Rather, they were – and are – a product of the social relationships within that changing society. Tensions between the gospels of athleticism and rational recreation, and the emerging forms of professional and commercial sport, would shape the future of sport in Britain. It is to selected cases of that future that we turn in Chapter 2.

ESSAY QUESTIONS

1   Discuss the main changes, accompanying the Industrial Revolution, that reshaped the social basis of popular recreation.
2   How successful was the character-building project of athleticism/organised games in the nineteenth- and early twentieth-century public schools?
3   Apply *either* the Guttmann or the Dunning/Sheard classification of the features of modern sport to the analysis of one sport that you know well.

EXERCISES

1   Make a list of the municipal sports facilities in your home town, from parks to playing fields to swimming pools. Find out how old they are, who founded and funded them and how they might have connections with the rational recreation initiatives of the nineteenth century. Compare your findings with those of classmates, making urban/rural and any other comparisons.
2   Drawing upon your personal history of involvement in sport, consider how and when you might have embodied the values of athleticism in your own sporting practice. Has sport, for example, been good for the character?
3   How important are social conceptions of time and space for the formation of modern sports?

FURTHER READING

A. Guttmann, *From Ritual to Record: The Nature of Modern Sports* (New York, Columbia University Press, 1978), provides a provocative discussion of the comparative characteristics of sports in different types of society and at different points in history.

J.A. Mangan, *Athleticism in the Victorian and Edwardian Public School: The Emergence and Consolidation of an Educational Ideology* (Cambridge, Cambridge University Press, 1981), is a seminal study in the field, illustrating the nature of the formative influences upon modern British team games.

CHAPTER TWO

CASE STUDIES IN THE GROWTH OF MODERN SPORTS

INTRODUCTION

Case studies can illustrate clearly how particular sports have manifested the features pointed to by Guttmann, and Dunning and Sheard, in their taxonomies discussed in Chapter 1; how such features have been more or less characteristic of the amateur and professional forms of those sports; and how they must be located in their social and social-historical context. As John Bale has put it: 'Sport, bound by rules, precision, quantifying, record-seeking and under bureaucratic control, increasingly came to mirror society at large' (1989: 42), and in this process the 'transition from folk game to sport typically followed five stages': (i) the folk game stage; (ii) the formation of clubs; (iii) the establishment of a rule-making national bureaucracy; (iv) the diffusion and adoption of the sport in other countries; and (v) the formation of an international bureaucracy. In this chapter we offer two case studies cast in terms of this type of stage analysis, recognising its general applicability, but adding a more sociological and British-based emphasis, rather than Bale's international and geographical dimension, in the consideration of later phases. Athletics is the first case study, in recognition of its 'key role in the development of amateurism' (Whannel, 1983: 43); cricket, the second. They provide focused empirical cases of the process of the commodification of sport, the intensifying production of sport and sport-related goods for the market, for sale and for profit.

ATHLETICS

Whannel has summarised the pre-modern form of athletics in Britain, which had existed for centuries:

> The rural festivities of the sixteenth and seventeenth centuries featured running races. A tradition of rural athletic meetings in the eighteenth century became particularly strong in the north of England and Scotland with events like the Highland Games and the Border Games. Pedestrianism and the running of head-to-head matches for gambling were well-established before the nineteenth century. In the nineteenth

century it is known that there were both open professional athletic events, with prizes, and open meetings that were mainly middle-class affairs, with low-value prizes.

(Whannel, 1983: 43–44)

The amateur form of athletics superseded these established practices, in the context of class disputes and tensions, as upper-class, middle-class and working-class enthusiasts struggled to gain control of the emerging institutional base of the sport. If the traditional forms can be seen as the first phase in any periodisation of the historical development of the sport, then the succeeding phases were: (1) the formation of clubs and the struggle to lead the sport, rooted in class-specific tensions over the amateurism issue; (2) the dominance of the amateur ethos, during which time women's athletics also developed; (3) a period of athlete power in which the premises of athleticism were questioned, disputed and opposed, and which also coincided with the high point of 'shamateurism'; and (4) the impact of commercialism and of open professionalism, in intensifying forms as media interests and sponsors effected a commodification of the athletic event and its champions and stars, with the production of the athletic event and the construction of the athletic celebrity (and associated goods and products) in increasingly uncompromising market terms.

Whannel argues persuasively that 'the rigid distinctions erected between the amateur and the professional were in the end rooted in class domination' (ibid.: 53), and the consensus among specialist historians of the later nineteenth century confirms this emphasis upon class: 'many historians of different ideological persuasions have identified the last quarter of the nineteenth century as the period in which the tentacles of class became all-embracing, in which all other social and cultural attributes became reducible to class categories' (Harris, 1994: 6). Sport, resonant of the new and rooted in the social relationships of the time, could hardly be immune from this. Definition of amateur status was commonly based upon forms of privilege and power rooted in class position and relations. The AAC (Amateur Athletic Club, formed in 1866, later to become the three As, when 'club' was changed to 'association') formulated an influential definition of the amateur (Bailey, 1978: 131) which affected a range of sports. The Club was formed to enable 'gentlemen amateurs' to practise and compete among themselves 'without being compelled to mix with professional runners'. The AAC offered an elitist and excluding definition of 'amateur':

Any person who has never competed in an open competition, or for public money, or for admission money, or with professionals for a prize, public money or admission money, and who has never, at any period of his life, taught or assisted in the pursuit of athletic exercises as a means of livelihood, or is a mechanic, artisan or labourer.

(ibid.: 131)

So, just in case any non-elitist athlete might qualify for membership, the AAC came clean in its last clause, and expressed the class basis of its constitution.

The Amateur Rowing Association and the Bicycling Union also barred such workers from membership, on the rationale that workers who worked physically so much would enjoy an unfair advantage in competition with the more sedentary professional, and were really in need of more mental exercises away from work. In golf, too, similar emphases were articulated concerning the material gains that might accrue from playing or providing services for sport (Cousins, 1975: 39), though the English Amateur Athletic Club's definition did not explicitly exclude on the basis of social class or type of work. But generally, professionals were defined as an unacceptable other, on the basis of criteria of exclusion – if you were characterised by X, then you could not be included in category Y. The organisation and administration of athletics were shaped by such excluding principles.

The modern form of athletics was modelled on the Amateur Athletic Club's first championship, held in the mid-1860s. Clubs were formed within the networks of the public schools, the universities, the professions and business (Crump, 1989). The notion of the club was critical, providing 'an element of collective endeavour' (ibid.: 44) which fuelled the team spirit characteristic of organised games, and marked the new sport off from the competitive individualism of pedestrianism, the established form of running races. The Amateur Athletic Association (AAA), formed in 1880, was the initiative of three former Oxford University athletes, and successfully united amateur athletics in England, at least until the British Olympic Association was established to organise the 1908 Olympic Games in London (Tomlinson, 2012: 3), and the Women's Athletic Association was established in 1922. The AAA campaigned against professionalism and illegal payments to athletes, defending the purity of the amateur ideal, which was bolstered in the 1890s by the formation of the Olympic movement by the French aristocrat Baron Pierre de Coubertin. We have seen that the Amateur Athletic Club's 1866/1867 definition of amateur ruled that no mechanic, artisan or labourer could be accepted as an amateur, reasoning that manual labour would give such people an unfair advantage in athletic competition. This definition was loosened in 1868 but still stated that 'An amateur is a gentleman who has never competed' (Crump, 1989: 51). The AAA revoked this 'gentleman' clause, but fought a long-term offensive against professionalism. Professional athletics continued to flourish, nevertheless, especially in regions such as the north of England, and in the Scottish Highlands. The AAA excluded professionals from other sports, such as cricket and football, in 1883 and 1899 respectively, and funded the prosecution, for fraud, of those breaching the ban, some offenders even receiving prison sentences. In 1899, the AAA authorised payment of travel expenses to athletes, and it appeared that the leadership and shape of the sport were by then well established, in class-based and amateur form; so much so that in the 1920s the gentleman amateur dominated British athletics, and the national team was made up in most part of members of the Achilles Club, which had been established by and for Oxbridge graduates.

Women's athletics developed separately from men's. The first women's athletics club to be formed in England was the London Olympiads Athletic Club, formed by women returning from the Women's Olympiads in Monte Carlo in 1921 and Paris in 1922 (Hargreaves, 1994: 130). Most of these women were from the Regent Street Polytechnic and, with others who ran and played netball for England, they provided the basis for the formation of the Women's Athletic Association (WAA). Women's athletics, Hargreaves argues (ibid.: 131), was less exclusively middle class than many other female sports as it was considered to be unladylike. Indeed, the administrators of the WAA commissioned a medical report in 1925 which argued that 'even if one does not see any ill results at the time from too strenuous devotion to athletics, the final result may be very deleterious to the girls' health and natural functions' (ibid.: 133). The report claimed that child-bearing could be adversely affected by participation in athletics, and the WAA accepted the report without question. Although some women may have challenged class dominance in developing women's athletics, prejudices about the female body continued to inhibit the sport's development. Fragmentation in the organisation of British athletics was such that when the Scottish Amateur Athletic Association complained to the International Amateur Athletic Federation about the power and nature of the AAA, the British Amateur Athletics Board (BAAB) was set up in 1932. In 1981, the Minister of Sport, Neil MacFarlane, was shocked to find that nineteen organisations could claim to control some aspect or other of British athletics (Crump, 1989: 49). This organisational complexity continued to characterise the British sporting scene, as commercial, political, and voluntary interests struggled to defend and/or control their stakes in the development of sport – a theme that we consider, in relation to state strategies, in Chapter 8.

The final phase in the growth of athletics saw it break free from the stranglehold of the amateur ideal and open the door more widely to the forces of commercialism, and to open professionalism. In this, a form of athlete power was important, when the International Athletes Club was formed in 1958, developing out of the dissatisfaction felt by non-university athletes during and after the 1956 Olympics in Melbourne, Australia, and disputes concerning the payment of pocket money to athletes. A confusing period of 'shamateurism' – with underhand payment to so-called amateurs, in association with manufacturers such as Adidas – was followed by the introduction of the trust fund in 1982. This fund enabled athletes to keep all appearance, sponsorship and advertising income for the purposes of subsistence, training and retirement, while retaining the status of amateur. The BAAB retained the right to authorise arrangements for any trust funds.

Reports and committees in the 1960s and the 1980s were to warn that unless British athletics united, increasing sponsorship income could be misdirected. These reports were shown to be timely when the boom years of athletics in the 1980s, with Sebastian Coe, Steve Ovett, and Daley Thompson prominent in a new generation of athletic superstars, were followed by the bust years of the 1990s. Ignominiously, the national federation plunged into financial crisis with little explanation as to what had happened to the huge income flowing into the sport during its prosperous years. Emblematic of such mismanagement was the famous race between Zola Budd and American Mary Decker-Slaney in 1985 (Crump, 1989: 56; Channel 4, 1986).

Decker-Slaney had raced against Budd in the final of the 3000 metres at the 1984 Los Angeles Olympics, blaming Budd for a collision and a fall which she claimed lost her the race. The rematch, at Crystal Palace in July 1985, attracted £200,000 sponsorship from a US television company. Budd, a South African running at the Olympics by claiming British citizenship, was paid £90,000; Decker-Slaney received £54,000. It was widely perceived that Decker-Slaney was the superior athlete, with a personal best 8 seconds faster than Budd's. Budd herself commented at a pre-race press conference that 'I certainly don't think I can win', but that 'anything can happen in a race'. The stadium was far from full, as the meeting had been stretched into a second day in order to accommodate Saturday coast-to-coast coverage of the race in the USA. Many spectators at the first day were therefore disgruntled at the changed schedule and the unpredictability of the line-up in other races, as Sebastian Coe, Steve Cram and the Brazilian Cruz were announced as running in separate races, or not at all. Meanwhile, behind the scenes, the sponsor of the event, Peugeot Talbot, entertained its 900 key customers in its hospitality suite, the company's director Tod Evans welcoming these clients as family and friends. Peugeot was also taking advantage of a new regulation which permitted sponsors to advertise during programme breaks of programmes that they were themselves sponsoring. Cavalcades of Peugeot's new model were filmed on the track, and a special advertisement had been made for broadcasting over the two days of the meeting. Peugeot's John Russell could draw analogies between his own company's values and those of athletics, the latter described as clean, lively, full of integrity and dynamic. Professional commentators were less fulsome in their praise. Steve Goldstein, print journalist from Philadelphia, commented that 'this is one of the biggest showbiz extravaganzas that's ever taken place in sport', comparing it to soap opera and the television audience expectations for a mix of drama and celebrity. Sports journalist Colin Hart (of the *Sun*) described the contest as 'an event not a race, no contest, a mismatch . . . they're selling advertising, it's money'. Alan Pascoe, of Alan Pascoe Associates, the man responsible for guaranteeing British athletics a sponsorship income of £3 million over five years, labelled the event as 'one of the big personality races of the century'. Created for television, this 'head-to-head that had to happen' was a complete mismatch, heralding an era of event management in the sport, in which entertainment and celebrity would become as important as competitive realities. New alliances between the sport, sponsors and television – brokered in important ways by marketing figures such as Pascoe – established a financial bonanza for British athletics. But as Decker-Slaney strolled to her victory at Crystal Palace, British athletics proceeded down the road to its eventual insolvency. Individual athletes such as Daley Thompson, Linford Christie and Sally Gunnell would benefit greatly, but athletics itself failed to disseminate its newfound riches, with entrepreneurial opportunists doing little for the wider development of the sport (Downes and Mackay, 1996). In this process, too, the *esprit de corps* of the amateur ideal and national pride has given way to a more individualistic ideal: 'the athlete's effort and dedication are directed at least as much to self-realisation and to the peer group of athletes as to the national team and the wider public' (Crump, 1989: 59).

Such self-realisation has been driven as much by financial motive as by performance aspiration. Downes and Mackay (1996) see the Budd versus Decker-Slaney event as pivotal in the transformation of athletics, a process which they label as a 'loss of innocence' based upon the perceived market value of individuals, and the ascendancy of appearance over competition: 'The sport's values soon began to warp'. (ibid.: 18).

Such warping or distortions would include not just made-for-TV fiascos such as Budd versus Decker-Slaney, but also a range of examples corrupting the values of fair competition. British athletics promoter Andy Norman, for instance, ensured that top stars were not present and offered payment to a runner not to win in the 'carefully orchestrated event' that was Alan Pascoe's last race, in front of a capacity crowd at Crystal Palace in 1979 (ibid.: 91). In 1995, Kenyan Moses Kiptanui, running in Sweden, deliberately avoided breaking his own world record in the 3000 metres steeplechase World Championships final, so that he could reap all the benefits on offer at the meeting in Zurich later in the week – where, as the first man to run under 8 minutes, the Kenyan's bonuses and fees amounted to around £130,000 (ibid.: 114–115). Corrupt officials would contribute to fixed outcomes. International Amateur Athletics Federation president Italian Primo Nebiolo built an extra lane and bent the rules to get the host nation into the final at the Rome World Cup in 1981; and was implicated, in the cover-up at least, when long-jump measurements were fixed in the computer at the 1987 World Championships in Rome, thus guaranteeing an Italian competitor a medal (ibid.: 133–135). Nebiolo is also reported to have rigged the voting in the poll for World Athlete of the Year in 1995, so robbing English hurdler Sally Gunnell of a second successive such honour (ibid.: 140); and to have covered up a positive drug test on an Italian hammer-thrower at the 1984 Los Angeles Olympics (ibid.: 135).

The systematic use of drugs has also distorted the record books, especially up to the point at which Canadian Ben Johnson set his steroid-aided all-time 100 metres record at the Seoul Olympics: 'in the doping control clampdown that followed the Johnson scandal, there was not one world-record set in a women's Olympic event for five years' (ibid.: 158). Not just state-centred regimes such as East Germany and Bulgaria were prominent in the administration of performance-enhancing substances. A sudden emergence to prominence of Italian distance runners in the mid-1980s has been attributed to doping by steroids, and blood transfusions (ibid.: 223). In Britain, top performers such as Linford Christie and Sally Gunnell have achieved great performances in the post-clampdown period – though they have not always been available when drug-testing teams have sought to administer random tests at the athletes' home base. In 1999, in Germany, Christie failed a drugs test, and was suspended from athletics for two years for using the performance-enhancing substance nandrolone.

Athletics – in its basic form, the glorious epitome of sporting competition – has emerged as a celebration not merely of individual athletic talent, but as a sport increasingly vulnerable to exploitation by individual performers, administrators, and political and market forces. The riches that poured into British athletics in the boom years of the 1980s and the early 1990s – redistributed at times 'in a brown paper bag' and 'a stack of used notes' (Downes and Mackay, 1996: 108) by Andy Norman – did little to secure the longer-term prosperity of the sport. The case of the Chafford Hundred Athletics Club is a revealing one, related by Downes and Mackay (ibid.: 104–111). This club was created in 1991, and became, overnight, the richest athletics club in Britain, though entering and competing in no team competitions: 'Chafford Hundred AC was established purely as a marketing ploy, a one-stop shop for sponsors wanting to become involved in one of Britain's most successful sports' (ibid.: 104). Top British athletes – including Christie, Gunnell and John Regis – could wear the vest of this fictional club on the international Grand Prix circuit, plastered with whatever logo the elite group agreed to display from the favoured sponsor. Income into the sport would thus flow into the individual accounts of a few stars, bypassing the development programmes of the grass roots of the sport. The Chafford Hundred Club – named after an Essex housing development close to Andy Norman's home, and managed by Fatima Whitbread, former javelin world champion and Norman's fiancée, twenty years later a participant in Independent Television's *I'm a Celebrity, Get Me Out of Here* – diverted potential income away from the sport's federation and real conventional clubs, and was 'just the latest manifestation of the greed and money motive that threatens to corrupt athletics forever' (ibid.: 104). In the light of marketing initiatives such as this, and the collapse of the financial infrastructure of British athletics, it is no surprise that Peter Radford, former Olympic sprinter and erstwhile head of the British Athletics Federation, argued that sport is too important to be left to the sports organisations and other agencies, and that a heightened degree of state involvement and direction was necessary if sport was to fulfil its true potential (BBC Radio 4, 1998). Two years earlier the British contestants at the Atlanta Summer Olympics had returned with just one gold medal, won by rowers Matthew Pinsent and Steve Redgrave in the coxless pairs; twelve years after this nadir of British sporting performance, the newly rebranded 'Team GB' returned from Beijing with 19 gold medals, but only one in athletics, for the women's 400 metre victory by Christine Ohuruogu. The Olympics is not of course the only measure of competitive athletic quality, and distance runner and marathon champion Paula Radcliffe was still world-record holder on the eve of London 2012, and had won seven World Marathon Majors between 2000 and 2009 (Tomlinson, 2011: 79). On one level – fun-runs, charity runs, half-marathons, park runs – Britain had never had more active running enthusiasts than in the first decade of the new century. But organised athletics had a decreasing profile in the wider sporting culture and the sport media, and despite the profile of double Olympic champion Dame Kelly Holmes at Athens in 2004, or gold medallist heptathlete Denise Lewis at the Sydney 2000 Games, athletics was no longer among the leading or dominant sports within British sport culture.

CRICKET

Cricket's development has been traced by Brookes (1978: 7) across five phases. These are: (1) the pre-1660 folk game; (2) a period of aristocratic patronage of the game; (3) the prominence of the professional XIs in the mid-nineteenth century; (4) the rise and dominance of amateurism as the basis for the game; and (5) the commercial and business years, which Brookes takes up to the mid-1970s, on the brink of the years of the widespread influence of the Australian magnate Kerry Packer's World Series Cricket initiative. A sixth phase can be added: one of intensifying spectacularisation and commodification of the cricket product, especially in its televised form and shortened form of 20-over encounters, Twenty/20, indeed its de-Westernisation with the growth of the Indian Premier League. Williams comments: 'Throughout the twentieth century cricket has been inseparably intertwined with the class system and its history does much to make clear the changing nuances of social relationships within Britain' (1989: 116). The same can be seen to be true of the longer-term history of the game. In this case study – particularly as more modern phases in the history of the game will feature in some of the specific themes covered in later chapters, but also because 'by 1840 it had more or less crystallized into the form into which it is still being played today' (Sandiford, 1994: 1) – it is the earlier phases of the game that are concentrated upon.

The first two phases in the game's development must be understood in the context of the social class dynamics of a changing society, and the inherent game form would evolve in tandem with the sorts of social changes discussed at the beginning of the chapter. Brookes summarises the three main sorts of folk games prominent in the society of the early seventeenth century (1978: Chapter 2). First, a collective team game involved players on the move (using hands, feet or an instrument such as a stick to control the ball) seeking to score by hitting the ball towards a goal. Second, direct competition between individuals involved a stationary player hitting the ball away from the body with an implement, and using the strokes to direct the body towards a hole or across a course. Third, a team game involved co-operation, with one side pitching its individuals against the collective opponents: in this form, a stationary player struck a ball or piece of wood away from his or her person, and registered scores by running between two or more fixed points. Football exemplified the first type, golf the second, while cricket in its folk form was the third sort of game, along with stoolball, tip-cat, trap-ball and cat and dog.

The folk version of cricket was a relatively unorganised game, fluid in form and therefore difficult to police, and played by the popular classes and the peasantry in typically unstructured and varied ways. Cricket's second phase is really a story of appropriation of the popular recreational form by the aristocracy. Brookes identifies 'four main reasons why the aristocracy patronized and played the game' (ibid.: 38). The first reason was, by mixing with a wide range of people through the game, to impose or at least reassert local authority over the people living on the landowner's estates. A second reason was social, with cricket providing the opportunity to reaffirm or establish friendship networks. The way that Brookes describes it, the cricket match was a gossip shop and a plotting cabal as well as a game. Third, the aristocracy could sustain a public declaration of personal rivalries safely, without the risks of duelling. Finally, it was a cultural form and ritual ideally suited to the lifestyle of a powerful and privileged leisure class, providing 'a source of entertainment, exercise and excitement for a group of people who possessed almost infinite amounts of time and money to devote to the cause of leisure' (ibid.: 40). The implications of the aristocracy's involvement in the game were profound. Matches became organised in more elaborate ways, it was recognised that rules needed to be standardised, and the rivalries between individual aristocrats bred the game's first professionals, and the consequent improvement in playing levels (ibid.: 45). In this phase of the game, two forms of organisation predominated: country house cricket and London-based matches among the aristocracy; and local village contests involving the gentry, shopkeepers and craftsmen as well as the aristocracy. Sir Horatio Mann, Member of Parliament for Sandwich for thirty-three years and extensive landowner in Kent, was the quintessential aristocratic patron of the game. His 1814 obituary in *The Gentlemen's Magazine* emphasised the importance of leisure in a life 'rather dedicated to pleasure than to business . . . he was much attached to gymnastic exercise, especially cricket' (ibid.: 46). By the plate depicting this man of leisure in post-hunt repose, Brookes reports on his reputation as 'agreeable, gay and affable', noting too that 'he once staged a match in which both teams played on horseback' (ibid.: plate opposite p. 114). In those forms of cricket involving groups from across the community it was 'the bond of communal sympathy which motivated both players and spectators' (ibid.: 53). The famous Hambledon Club represented this form of the game. In the 1770s, crowds of 20,000 would watch the team, costs for players could be covered, and 'bonds of birth and residence' (ibid.: 60) provided the framework for the club's prosperity. The Marylebone Cricket Club (MCC), formed in 1787, was to surpass the influence of the Hambledon Club and help usher cricket into the emerging industrial society. In the nineteenth century, cricket was remoulded under the influence of the middle classes and the working classes. From the turn of the century and up to the middle of the nineteenth century, cricket was remade, from 'an aristocratic diversion . . . on the way to becoming a sport, an occupation and a career' (ibid.: 83).

League, club and county cricket had established a sound foundation and organisation in England by the last quarter of the nineteenth century, but:

> [The] vast bulk of first-class cricket during 1845–70 had been provided by the great All England and United professional touring teams, led by William Clarke, George Parr, the Lilywhites and John Wisden, who popularized cricket by taking it virtually to every nook and cranny of the kingdom.
>
> (Sandiford, 1994: 58)

Clarke had formed the first all-England XI in 1846 and, helped by the new transport infrastructure of railways and communications infrastructure of popular media, established a successful initiative which was continued by his successors and which 'demonstrated that there was an almost insatiable demand for cricket of high quality and generally showed how that demand could be met' (ibid.: 59). The impact of the professional XIs was undeniable, but they were in effect a travelling circus and, as Brookes succinctly puts it, they 'lacked all but the vaguest geographical identity about which supporters could rally' (1978: 116), and the XIs' strength meant that the matches were inherently uncompetitive. In the 1860s and the 1870s public school, university, North vs. South, Gentlemen vs. Players and inter-county games (Sandiford, 1994: 59) captured centre stage in the unfolding drama of cricket's contribution to Victorian culture. The county game became the essence of English elite cricketing culture, W.G. Grace its personification.

County cricket grew in 'haphazard fashion', as Sandiford puts it, but by 1873 nine counties were playing in the first-class competition: Derbyshire, Gloucestershire, Kent, Lancashire, Middlesex, Nottinghamshire, Surrey, Sussex and Yorkshire. Five further counties – Denbighshire, Essex, Hampshire, Leicestershire and Warwickshire – joined in 1895, and Worcestershire joined in the last year of the century. 'The sporting press . . . played the leading role in determining the champion county' (ibid.: 60) by logging performances, and also catapulted W.G. Grace into the centre of the celebrity culture of the time.

Grace, with his 'modern scientific batsmanship . . . did much to modernize cricket during the 1870s' (ibid.: 130, 131). Grace dominated the sporting press, doing 'most to transform Victorian cricket into a full-scale spectator entertainment' (ibid.: 131). He was also renowned for his gamesmanship, and for his manipulation (despite his avowedly amateur status) of every commercial opportunity – Midwinter (1981: 156) estimates that Grace pocketed an income equivalent to a million pounds in 1980s values. Early women's cricketing initiatives were frowned upon by Grace, who (drawing somewhat dubiously perhaps upon his professional medical background) pronounced women as 'not constitutionally adapted to the sport' (Sandiford, 1994: 46). Just as his middle-class status placed Grace in a bridging position between upper-class and lower-class adherents to cricket (Midwinter, 1981: 9), so it allowed him to bend the codes of amateurism in what were really ungentlemanly and rather professional practices – 'his attempts practically to instruct umpires in their duties bordered on the unfair and the autocratic' (ibid.: 157). But whatever these failings – or perhaps aided by them – his achievements in first-class cricket, mostly for his county, Gloucestershire, were legion and fabled: 54,896 runs and 2,876 wickets. In one eight-day spell in August of 1876, his feats led one journalist of *The Saturday Review* to conclude that he was 'wholly indifferent to atmospheric influences' (ibid.: 61). Throughout all this, he sustained his medical career.

Cricket was seen as contributing to health by strengthening physique, but was also seen as valuable for producing mental alertness and spiritual adequacy (Sandiford, 1994: 171). It shared the core values of the ideology of athleticism. Grace's career and impact show both the centrality of that ideology in the formative phase of development of one of England's major sports, and the rhetoric and hypocrisy at its core. These latter were to persist right through the first three-quarters of the twentieth century, until what became known as the 'Packer Revolution' effectively challenged the old order, when the cream of English cricketing talent ignored appeals to traditional loyalties and joined Australians, South Africans, Indians, Pakistanis, West Indians and New Zealanders in the Australian media magnate Kerry Packer's World Series Cricket initiative. It was only in 1953 that the England cricketing side was first captained by a professional, the Yorkshire player Len Hutton, and some traditional inequalities persisted still later, such as separate entrances for amateurs and professionals, and different ways of listing their names. It was not until 1963 that the MCC abolished the distinction between (amateur) gentlemen and (professional) players.

Asked in June 1993 what the legacy of Packer's late 1970s initiative was for cricket in general and cricketers in particular, the English wicketkeeper-batsman and Packer recruit Alan Knott was in no doubt about its benefits:

> It was the best thing that ever happened to cricket. It gave the player a different position in terms of respect as well as being financially better off. The game has gone forward regarding TV coverage; fitness is far more important; and it showed the appeal of one-day cricket. Over here the administrators are trying to kill one-day cricket which is ridiculous. I can see one-day cricket becoming the major world game; if you travel the world, people don't go to Test Matches but they flock to one-day cricket.
>
> (Luckes, 1994: 151)

Interviewed in January 1993, another WSC recruit, former England fast bowler John Snow, commented how the world's top players from the West Indies, Australia and England were:

> frustrated by the workings and attitudes of those running the game and were quite happy to go to Packer in order to change the game. It was like coming up against a brick wall all the time . . . the dead wood needed to be cut out . . . Something had to shake the game up, Packer went in, in a commercial way, and why not – if someone comes with a lot of money, you don't tell him to bugger off: you see what he can do for you and you for him.
>
> (ibid.: 155)

Ironically, the great amateur W.G. Grace's actions – if not his expressed principles – concurred with such a philosophy.

> In his person he symbolized the game's progress from the loosely organized structure of his youth to the formalism of test matches and the county championship, its links with empire and Commonwealth, and its technical advances, which set the pattern for the twentieth century. His public image and performances were widely reported in the expanding journalism of his day; his presence attracted supporters in huge numbers and sometimes doubled the entrance-charge to grounds.
>
> (Howat, 2004)

Without doubt, though, and after a century's stability in English cricket, the Packer intervention heralded a new phase in which it became clear that 'social standing and a sense of heritage' were 'ill-equipped to resist a concerted and determined assault by an entrepreneur backed by the crucial factor of commercial funding' (Luckes, 1994: 1). Sponsorship of tournaments and individual players, and new television deals with broadcasters such as Sky Sports, heralded the new age of the cricketing product, with rule changes designed to produce exciting

understanding sport

spectacles, sometimes played under floodlights by sides clad in colourful costumes rather than the traditional all-white kit. The scene was thus set for the further exploitation of the commercial potential of the packaged product, embodied in the new century in the dramatic emergence of the Indian Premier League (IPL) and the 20-20 format. Individual players such as Andrew Flintoff could pick up lucrative end-of-career earnings even for under-par performances, bought by the Chennai Super Kings for $1.55 million in 2009. The Indian subcontinent has come to generate 70 per cent of world cricketing revenue, and the IPL sold its broadcasting rights for US$1 billion, its team franchises for $700 million (Szymanski, 2010). In 2005, the International Cricket Council (ICC) left London to relocate in Dubai. The ICC had been founded at Lord's Cricket Ground in London in 1909 as the International Cricket Conference, renamed the International Cricket Conference in 1965, then the International Cricket Council in 1989. Its founding members were England, South Africa, and Australia. In 2012, the ICC president Shara Pawar, former president of the Board of Control for Cricket in India, presiding over the world game in the tax-attractive haven of the United Arab Emirates, symbolised the story of cricket's growth from its British imperial roots to its commercial expansion in the Indian sub-continent. Although England's men's test team reached World Number 1 position after defeating India in 2011, and could recall glorious Ashes triumphs over Australia in recent years, the traditional base of English top-class cricket was dwindling, with negligible crowds watching county sides shorn of their star players who were obligated to the schedules of the international calendar. Despite its top position in world Test Match rankings, England's men had still not, after 10 attempts since 1975, become World Cup winners, unlike the England women's cricketers who took the world title in 1973, 1993, and 2009 (see Malcolm et al., 2010, for an illuminating overview).

MODERN SPORT: THE NATURE OF CONTEMPORARY SPORTS CULTURE AND THE SOCIAL INFLUENCES UPON IT

We have seen how a sport can be analysed in terms of shifts and continuities in the social context in which it has emerged, prospered or declined, determined by essentially material social and economic factors in interplay with the human cultural response to those determining factors. The pull between the past traditional practice and the novelty or the necessities of the present has often been a tense dynamic, a feature far from exclusive to sports. The whole period of the last third of the nineteenth century and the decade and a half up to the Great War has been characterised as a volatile one. Changes and collapses, as Harris has put it, were widespread across social institutions and cultures, with 'many countervailing pressures of locality and custom', and 'in the last resort patterns of employment, settlement, taste, consumption and value were all subordinate to the pursuit of "comparative advantage"' (1993: 5).

Britain's free trade policy allowed home producers no protection against American wheat and this led to the 'consequent collapse of archaic rural communities, an explosion of migration

29

to great cities, a rapid rise in living standards for those in secure employment, and an invisible revolution in the structure of class power' (ibid.: 5). These processes constituted the infra-structural base of the society in which the parameters of modern sport were set. Harris goes on to depict the material and the mental pressures and contradictions of this society in the making, which she sees as exhibiting 'a certain latent instability' characteristic of the industrial world. In this society, 'change was a norm of life in a way that had not been true in past ages' (ibid. 5). New forms of sport could both reflect that change and offer sources of cultural identity that might calm the seas of such tempestuous changes.

The making of modern sports has, too, been a predominantly masculinist narrative, with women marginalised or disenfranchised at most stages of the narrative. We have reconstructed the developmental histories of what became the dominant male forms, recognising in that context the experiences of women. Women's involvement in cricket was marginalised early on, and Sandiford notes that cricket was seen as too much a 'manly sport' even for the tennis-and hockey-playing women students at the Universities of Cambridge and Oxford in the late nineteenth century (1994: 44). It was not until 1926 that the British Women's Cricket Association was founded, by hockey and lacrosse players from Malvern College (Hargreaves, 1994: 123). It thrived rapidly, in the institutionalised context of schools, colleges, universities and clubs, away from the more public face of cricket, which remained 'a traditional bastion of male chauvinism' (ibid.: 123). Evidence of *some* cricketing initiatives among women in working-class areas, or of informal cricketing games between young boys and girls, remains evidence of a marginalised and widely scorned activity. Even in 1993, when the English women's cricketing team became World Champions – at precisely the time when the English men's team was plummeting towards new lows of performance in international competition – press coverage of this tremendous achievement was tinged with a patriarchal hue. The persistence of such situations is explored in more ethnographic detail in Chapter 4.

The major English sports have developed as male-dominated activities, and most female involvement in those traditional sports forms has been in middle-class sports such as golf and tennis. A balanced social history must recognise the dominance of the male form and the persistence of the male-dominated sports culture that was established in key formative phases in the growth of sport. This established a sporting culture of a predominantly patriarchal character, at all of its levels from the school to the stadium.

Sport's place and meaning in everyday life are negotiable and are culturally created, not simply socially imposed. The working through of social and cultural change is a complex and uneven process. In this sense, any socio-historical periodisation of phases in the growth of sports is vulnerable to the criticism that it simplifies social and cultural realities. But without any such periodisation, the history of sport risks becoming what has been called a Book of Genesis version of history (Tomlinson, 1984) or an internal inventory of the features of a particular sport (Hall, 1986). Both of those methodological warnings are reminders that the deeper meanings of a sport cannot be found outside of an understanding of the relationship of a sport to its society. This is not to say that a sport is merely the reflection of a society; rather, that sport has social meanings and, despite senses in which it can be seen as relatively autonomous (Gruneau, 1983; Hargreaves, 1986), is in itself a social product.

Social historians, sociologists and cultural researchers are united on this final point, and the analysis of the tensions between the social determinants of sport and its cultural location and context forms the recurrent focus of researchers in the field. In this chapter we have focused upon just two case studies to exemplify and explore selected themes. A wider sample of case studies would identify comparable interpretive themes (and in the first edition of this book we also included association football and golf, see Horne et al., 1999). In Mason's (1989) very valuable collection, the contributors were asked to concentrate on the themes of competition, physical activity and spectacle in examining ten sports, and to 'give some idea' of each sport's 'origins, the power structure within it, the relationship between the participatory mass and the spectacularly eminent' (ibid.: 9). Though looking specifically at British sports, contributors were also encouraged to consider gender, Gaelic and global aspects of the case studies. Extracting major concerns from the case studies as a whole confirms the centrality of a number of themes to the sociological and cultural analysis of modern sport, and to the understanding of sport culture in the second decade of the twenty-first century:

- A decline in live attendance levels in the later twentieth century; this has been a continuing trend, as forms of media sport have drawn increasing numbers.
- An intensification of commercialism in sport, in close connection with professionalisation, a process commodifying still more the sport product and experience.
- An increasingly sophisticated technological base to sport, affecting sport as a mode of production.
- A rise in individualism in sport (in squash and running, for instance), constituting a new mode of consumption articulated around fashion and narcissism, trends that have escalated in recent decades.
- The explosion of media sport – television-made events impacting upon established sports phenomena such as national leagues and, more globally, the football World Cup and the Olympic Games.
- The competition to sport of emerging alternative modes and forms of leisure consumption, particularly in the new media.
- Moral and political debates about the significance of sport and popular culture, which persist in the defence of sport as a worthwhile human and cultural endeavour.
- The contestation of space, and the aspiration to and desire to acquire or provide space for new types of cultural expression, more and more manifest in the construction of spectacular sporting sites.
- Americanisation and its impact upon more localised and traditional sports cultures, amplified in recent years by the search for new global markets.
- The gendered nature of sports – sport as an element within more general forms of male domination, but simultaneously a focus for women's challenge to established forms of male dominance. This remains a core dynamic of sport cultures.

31

- The reluctance to excel – in traditional British sports, a wariness about producing top-quality players in the professionalised and increasingly globalised sports arena. Since the late 1980s, British sport has overcome this in focusing upon top competitive performance and preparation.
- The invisibility or marginalisation of race within sports cultures. Sport has in recent decades been a focus for anti-racist developments, and continues to be a sphere in which important questions concerning race and ethnicity can be raised.

CONCLUSION

We conclude this chapter with reflections on the core changes in the longer story of British sport. At the level of high-profile and top-level competitive sport the last third of the twentieth century saw some radical changes. Whannel has argued that this amounted to 'a period of transformation which constitutes a remaking of British sport' (1986: 129). The key influences in this remaking were television and sponsorship, between them producing a 'cultural transformation' when 'the traditional amateur, benevolent paternalism of sport's organisation came under pressure from entrepreneurial interests as the contradiction between sport's financially deprived organisations and its commercial potential widened' (ibid.: 130). The characteristics and contours of this transformation have been signalled in the case studies in this chapter, and are examined in more detail in later chapters. Two points are worthy of note, though, at the end of this review. First, Whannel's emphasis on the process of transformation reminds us of the essential features of the traditional organisations of sport: undemocratic, elitist in class and gender terms, yet dedicated often in a voluntarist way to service and resource distribution. Second, a thrusting entrepreneurialism brought more money into sport and released its meritocratic and democratic potential. But this was to focus resources more exclusively at the elite performance level. Thus were the fears of the nineteenth-century paternalist defendants of amateurism borne out. And thus is shown the importance of the understanding of the past, for the crises and contradictions in early twenty-first-century British sport have deep roots in a complex social and cultural history.

ESSAY QUESTIONS

1   'The amateur and professional dynamic in the formative phase of modern sports was an expression of class power and class rivalry.' Discuss.
2   Taking one sport of your choice, consider the ways in which its post-Second World War history has been shaped by new economic forces.
3   Discuss the emergence of the sports 'star' during the second half of the nineteenth century.

EXERCISES

1   Talk to three of your colleagues/peers from different sports specialisms and ask them to summarise their views on the *social* values of sport. Do these vary from sport to sport? Are there echoes of old debates in the responses?
2   Interview a sports administrator of the sport in which you are most involved and consider whether he or she represents the trend towards entrepreneurial rather than patrician forms of provision of and involvement in sport.
3   Consult some of the main sources on sports participation (for example, up until recent years, the General Household Survey and the annual Social Trends and, from 2006, Sport England's Active People Survey, in which different sources are summarised) and consider why, in terms of participation, an activity of such minority significance has such a high profile.

FURTHER READING

R. Holt, *Sport and the British: A Modern History* (Oxford: Oxford University Press, 1989) is an elegant, scholarly and accessible account of the influences upon and the context of the growth of sports in modern industrial Britain.
T. Mason (ed.), *Sport in Britain: A Social History* (Cambridge: Cambridge University Press, 1989) provides lucid and informed accounts of the social history of Britain's most prominent sports.

CHAPTER THREE

DEBATES, INTERPRETATIONS, THEORIES

INTRODUCTION: THE HISTORY AND SOCIOLOGY OF SPORT IN CREATIVE TENSION?

In this chapter, we consider debates within and between different theoretical frameworks and traditions that have been utilised in the analysis of the social and cultural roots and contexts of modern sport. In the previous chapter, several case studies established some major common and recurrent themes in the social history of sports in England, and to a lesser extent, Britain. Those themes will vary in importance within particular parts of Britain, and specific studies of sport need to recognise the distinctive trajectories of sport culture in the different cultures and countries of the United Kingdom and the British Isles (Jarvie and Walker, 1994; Bairner, 2005; Johnes, 2005). Generally, though, we have sought in the previous chapters to blend the historical with the sociological, led by a simultaneous concern with both the past and the present, and the relationships between them. Too often a sociological approach has nodded in tokenistic fashion in the direction of the historical, given some space to the portrayal of an historical backcloth, and then proceeded to offer sociological analysis *detached* from that historical basis. A critical analysis concerned with history as process and society as product must avoid this.

The chapter is, as in any exercise of academic analytical judgement, selective. The task of critical sociology and cultural studies involves demanding theoretical questions. It is on this level of theory that sometimes the sociological and social historical agendas have differed. It is this issue that is the concern of the first section of the chapter. A particular case – the political suppression of folk football in the mid-nineteenth century – is then considered as a common reference point for the evaluation of a range of theoretical perspectives that have been brought to bear upon the social history of sports in modern England and Britain.

Three of the most distinguished and prominent social historians of British sport have raised important issues concerning the respective character and merits of the social historical and the sociological approaches. Robert Malcolmson's contribution to the inaugural edition of what, reversing contemporary trends in political and economic history, was *The British Journal of Sports History* but soon became *The International Journal of the History of Sport*, raised broad thematic and conceptual issues central to the analysis of sports in society. Tony Mason, in his book on *Sport in Britain* (Mason, 1988), reviewed a couple of prominent sociological theories under the label of 'Theory'. And Richard Holt, after, rather than in, his magisterial study *Sport and the British: A Modern History* proffered an Appendix comprising 'some observations on social history and the sociology of sport' (1989: 357–367).

Malcolmson – specialist scholar of popular recreations in the preindustrial period – prefaced his contribution to the inaugural issue of *The British Journal of Sports History* with a reaffirmation of what he described as a 'contextual approach to the history of sports' (1984: 60). By this, he referred to the recognition that there are 'conditioning influences of the wider society . . . upon the practice and character of sporting activities' (ibid.). Such influences, for Malcolmson, include the distribution of property in a society and the structure of power and ideologies characteristic of that society. From this perspective of social influences, it can be seen that sports are in many respects '"determined" forms of conduct' (ibid.). Malcolmson exemplified his approach to the social history of sports in early modern England by concentrating upon three themes: first, the links between popular sports and forms of work; second, how sports patronised by the privileged social groups were connected to a concern for 'social discipline, popular quiescence, and theatrical display'; and finally, the embeddedness of sporting activities in processes of social and cultural conflict. Malcolmson laid out and prioritised here a clear set of working assumptions and themes for enquiry. They sound very much in common with those of many sociologists, a point which will be returned to in the concluding section of the chapter.

Mason, recognising that 'serious thinkers' no longer 'ignore sport' and that 'the sociology of sport has become a vigorous sub-discipline' (1988: 69), offered some discussion of 'two sociological theories of sport and its place in society' (ibid.: 77). The first of these was the seminal work by Thorsten Veblen on the place of conspicuous consumption in the leisure cultures of the privileged social groups in late nineteenth-century USA, *The Theory of the Leisure Class* (1899). No critical evaluation was offered of this famous text. Mason then took as representative of a critical neo-Marxist approach the work of Bero Rigauer, summarising his forceful critique of sport, in which it is trenchantly argued that sport is structurally analogous with work. Mason acknowledges the strength of Rigauer's argument but, citing intra-class disputes in British sport over the respective merits of amateurism and professionalism, comments that Rigauer 'has little patience with such niceties' of historical reality (1988: 73). Sympathetic as Mason is to some of the forceful and persuasive ideas of Rigauer, he remains critical of what he sees to be a theoretical inflexibility: 'It is the rigidity of Rigauer's theory, however, which eventually undermines it. In the end there seem too many empirical objections' (ibid.: 75) and 'Rigauer sees society as domination by one set of values which are largely unquestioned. But such a view does not seem to fit the complexities of the actual world' (ibid.: 77). The empirical realities of historical actuality, then, disturb the coherence, for Mason, of any 'comprehensive critical theory of contemporary sport' (ibid.: 73). Mason has also referred somewhat condescendingly, in his work on football in Latin America, to the conceptualisation and theorisation of contemporary social trends. In his postscript to the study, he discusses the possibility that variety in styles of play in world football has given way to a standardised approach to the game:

> Caution is the watchword; the game is not to lose. Perhaps this is an aspect of that globalization or homogenization of the sporting world about which sociologists excitedly chatter . . . if the homogenization theory is true, something which made football vital and attractive will have been lost.
>
> (Mason, 1995: 157)

Here, in an implied critique of social science theorising, the sociologist is reduced to a figure of fun, a naïve gossip. But it is a bogus critique, and ultimately disingenuous – for Mason then proceeds to contextualise his own specialist analysis and interpretation within the framework of the theoretical issue about which he is initially so sceptical. Despite his expressed reservations concerning sociological theorising, Mason seems to find (some of) them interesting enough to use.

Richard Holt's appendix to *Sport and the British* begins with a succinct presentation of the source of dispute between the historian and the sociologist, and of some awareness of the respective need the one has for the other. This is worth quoting in full:

> Sociologists frequently complain that historians lack a conceptual framework for their research, while historians tend to feel social theorists require them to compress the diversity of the past into artificially rigid categories and dispense with empirical verification of their theories. In truth both disciplines need each other, and distinguished authorities in both areas have recently emphasized the interdependence of sociology and history in the identification and pursuit of common problems in social science.
>
> (1989: 357)

Yet immediately following on from this statement, Holt writes that the 'apparatus of theory' can weigh down history in a crude fashion, and that enjoyment of a subject can be spoiled by the use of 'specialist language' that does nothing to enhance the understanding of the subject. Railing, then, against theory, Holt lists what he calls 'some highly abstract formulations' up against which 'few stay the course and the gap between the new theorists of sport and the ordinary historian can seem unbridgeable' (ibid.: 357). He then goes on to cite an excerpt of social theory, 'an excruciating sentence' (ibid.: 358), to describe it as 'pretentious and incomprehensible' and then to offer his own interpretation (presumably a comprehension) of the incomprehensible! There is a tension running throughout Holt's discussion in this appendix, between his recognition of the value of social theory and his irritation at the obscurantisms and neologisms characteristic of the forms of expression of such theory. For both the historian and the sociologist, he believes, 'the crux of the matter . . . is the perception of sport and the varying cultural meanings that are attached to games – sometimes to the same game – by

understanding sport

different social groups or by different forces within the state that command our attention' (ibid.: 360). At the same time, if the sociologist gets too theoretical about this, he or she is seen as reducing, erroneously, varied realities to a 'single essence' (ibid.: 362):

> What may seem conceptually confused and unacceptable to the theorist may be appropriate and right to the historian drawing on different theories to illuminate different aspects of what is in reality not a single phenomenon but a set of loosely related activities shifting their forms and meanings over time. Eclecticism is justified provided it is reasoned and critical.
>
> (ibid.: 362)

Variety, reality, these are what the historian often asserts to be trampled underfoot by the standardising and homogenising sociological theorist. Not all historians are so dismissive, and Martin Polley is more sympathetic to the potential of historical sociology (Polley, 2008). Not just sociologists, though, are adjudged by Holt to be guilty of missing the critical historical point. In an essay on the Scottish footballer Denis Law, 'Cultural analysis' is dismissed as 'impenetrable jargon', 'left too much to the Left Bank' and 'at its worst [it] airily dismisses the need for evidence, experience and even clarity of expression' (Holt, 1994: 58). The charge is obscurantism, then, plus finding the facts to fit the theory. John Hargreaves' seminal *Sport, Power and Culture* (1986) comes in for particular criticism here, the 'theoretical neatness of this account' leading 'to problems when dealing with the complex historical reality' (Holt, 1989: 363). What Hargreaves stands accused of here is a selective use of evidence in the construction of a sophisticated and all-embracing theoretical analysis.

The problem of any historically insensitive sociology is that the theory will predetermine the empirical task and that a rigid and prior interpretation will shape the analysis, and this can lead to distortions and misrepresentations of historical realities and complexities. But history without adequate conceptualisation or theorisation can be little more than a form of antiquarianism – an important retrieval of the past, but decontextualised, an academic and anodyne version of the heritage industry. Some sociologists should certainly do more careful and more rigorous historical work, sensitive to the methodological demands and possibilities of detailed historical scholarship. But at the same time, it would be unwise for social historians of sport to ignore the central theoretical debates of the social sciences, for this could consign important scholarship to the margins of academic debate. It could also constitute a lost opportunity, in that the historically sensitive study of the place, role and nature of sport in modern societies has the potential to enhance the analysis and understanding of the wider society and culture. For example, the study of sport spectacle and the ceremonial and ritual around a global phenomenon such as the Olympic Games (Tomlinson, 1996) can illuminate our understanding not just of sport itself, but also of international relations, and media-based and cultural dimensions of globalisation itself. Such a study of sport can contribute to the generation of a fuller theoretical understanding. An adequate socio-cultural approach to the understanding of sport needs, therefore, to be receptive to the potential contribution of a variety of theoretical frameworks.

37

In the next section of this chapter, a descriptive case study of football during a key transitional phase in its history is provided, and this is followed by illustrations of how the case study might be interpreted from some such theoretical perspectives.

FOOTBALL IN TRANSITION: THE FOLK FORM IN DERBY

This case study is derived from the work of Anthony Delves (1981). We offer a purely descriptive account of the culture of the Derby game in the early nineteenth century, the social context in which it thrived and then was increasingly less prominent in the local culture, and the sporting developments that took place as football's prominence decreased. We are aware, of course, that the case study is dependent upon the historical scholarship of Delves, and that his decisions as to the importance of a source were informed by some conceptual preoccupations. We will make his theoretical tendencies explicit at the beginning of the following section. In this section, we present as objectively as it is possible to do – without having buried ourselves in Delves' primary sources – the empirical realities of the story of football in Derby in the mid-nineteenth century.

The popular recreational form of football bore very little resemblance to more modern forms of football. The game of football in its pre-modern form – street football, as Delves chooses to call it – was 'highly popular, rowdy and controversial' (1981: 89). There was little demarcation between players and supporters. Not much kicking took place either, and, as another name for the activity – 'hugball' – indicates, the primary mode of possession was manual. Numbers were flexible and uncontrolled, hundreds and sometimes more than a thousand on each side. The game was characterised by hours of 'rough horseplay and brawling, leaving a trail of physical injuries, petty vandalism, assaults and much heavy drinking' (ibid.: 90). The all-male playing cast, reflecting the 'masculine republic' (Harrison, 1971: 46) of the pub and the drinking place, was complemented by women spectators. Women were not in merely passive roles, but at critical moments could be instrumental in defence of the game and defiance of those who sought its suppression. In the mid-1840s, at one point a woman was reported in the local press to have smuggled the ball into the market-place to enable play to begin.

This form of football attracted holidaymakers from far afield, and as such operated not just as a contest, but also as a popular participatory festival. Attempts at suppression of the game had not succeeded in 1731, 1746 and 1797, and active opposition was rekindled and fuelled from the 1830s onwards. By 1845, representation, claimed to emanate from many working-class as well as middle-class quarters, was made to the Mayor of Derby, in which the game was alleged to cause:

> the assembling of a lawless rabble, suspending business to the loss of the industrious, creating terror and alarm to the timid and the peaceable, committing violence on the persons and damage to the properties of the defenceless and poor, and producing

in those who play moral degradation and in many extreme poverty, injury to health, fractured limbs and (not infrequently) loss of life; rendering their homes desolate, their wives widows and their children fatherless.

(*Derby Mercury*, 29 January 1845, cited in Delves, 1981: 90)

Accurate or representative or not, this appeal had an immediate impact: the Mayor pronounced the game illegal. Players were threatened with prosecution, and offered alternative outlets. Cash prizes were offered for organised competitive athletic sports and cash inducements also offered to players to play outside the town. Some defied this and tried to play in the town centre, leading those in authority to cancel the alternative sports. This left people without either football or the planned alternatives. A vigorously contested game then took place (on Ash Wednesday), following which a few players were made an example of, being prosecuted and fined. The following year, 1846, saw those opposed to football increase the pressure against the game. Magistrates issued warnings against playing the game, and some negotiation took place. When some footballers handed over a ball to the Mayor in a public meeting, he promised to negotiate with local employers for time off for workers, and to subsidise a free railway excursion instead of football.

This negotiation came to nothing though, with employers asked *not* to release workers for the holiday, no alternative sports arranged and several hundred local citizens recruited as special constables. The Mayor and magistrates also arranged for a troop of cavalry to be brought in for the holiday. On Shrove Tuesday 1846, the streets were full of spectators and roving groups of youths. A ball appeared at the customary hour in the town-centre market-place and the crowds started to play, in the event taunting and physically provoking the special constabulary. Hit by a missile, seeing the riot as 'dangerous and appalling' and concerned at the highly charged atmosphere, the Mayor read the Riot Act and called in the troops. The footballers were chased and the crowds broken up, regrouping to play the game beyond the borough boundary. Local moral outrage condemned the game. In the *Derby and Chesterfield Reporter* of 8 May, it was alleged to be 'of so low and degrading a nature that it should be swept away from our land as bull-baiting, cockfighting and other brutal sports had been of late years' (ibid.: 95). Legal charges were taken against fifteen of the football organisers, for obstruction or for playing the game or for enticing other players to play it. Five of these were prosecuted and bound over to keep the peace. In succeeding years, the calendar of the traditional game continued to stimulate elaborate public order alarms, with special constables dispersing crowds, troops on the alert and, in 1848 – that most cataclysmic of revolutionary years – another alternative sports arranged and subsidised from the public purse, for the Thursday following Ash Wednesday. Preparations to counter any revival of street football were still being made towards the middle of the following decade.

Football was popular for the way in which it symbolised a two-day holiday for mill and factory workers whose annual holidays totalled only eight days. The game provided a catalyst for the reunion, too, of family and friends. It could also serve as a vehicle for other forms of organisation, so that for insecure framework-knitters in 1845 the holiday, the large crowds and the

39

game could provide a possibility of social protest, as they planned and projected trade union organisation.

INTERPRETATIONS ILLUSTRATED

How, then, do we go beyond the mere telling of the story or the detailed portrayal of the event? The facts of the matter are undeniable. Though the representation of any historical fact outside the pure context of the historical source can always be claimed as an interpretation or as a selective telling, the facts of this particular matter are surely undisputed. Ideally, we would know more about the main players in the story. Who were the five ringleaders, prosecuted successfully but not sentenced with severity? Who were those who most actively campaigned against street football, in the cause of 'rational recreation' and in opposition to traditional popular cultures perceived as dangerous, threatening and unrespectable? And what is the overall picture that emerges of the society and culture of the time, and the place of popular recreations in that society and culture?

Nevertheless, with the picture provided by Delves we are in a position to outline major theoretical approaches to historical analysis, to consider concepts such as hegemony and power in the making and remaking of sport, and to articulate the methodological principles and theoretical preoccupations that we believe most usefully inform critical work on both the social history and sociology/cultural analysis of sport. The two influential interpretations selected for consideration are:

1 developmental/figurational sociology (exemplified in the work of Elias and Dunning);
2 critical materialism (as in the work of Bailey, Hargreaves, and Clarke and Critcher).

Other approaches – in liberal history, feminist theory and postmodernist theory – could be used in the same way. But this chapter is not an attempt at any comprehensive review of the social history, sociology and social theory of sport. Jarvie and Maguire (1994) have provided such an overview, concentrating upon social thought and social theory and their application to the analysis of sport and leisure; and Giulianotti (2004) has compiled a collection of overviews of critical and social theorists' work that might be drawn upon in theoretical debate. The selection of approaches covered here is more modest in intent, designed to transmit, to the newcomer to the field, some of the spirit and liveliness of the debates that characterise humanities and social science-based approaches to understanding sport.

Developmental/figurational sociology

The impact of the work of Eric Dunning and others following him in the advancement of developmental, figurational sociology and its application to the history and sociology of sport

understanding sport

and leisure has been immense. This work has been a running collaboration and debate with Norbert Elias, revolving around the nature and application of his contribution to social theory and cultural analysis. Prior to summarising the theoretical and conceptual features of Dunning's approach, it is useful to consider some of the main thrusts in the work of Elias himself. For this purpose, we consider here two of his works – *The History of Manners: The Civilising Process*, first published in German in 1939, and in English in 1978, and *What is Sociology?*

The History of Manners (Elias, 1978b) is a dazzling combination of empirical research and theory, depicting the developing inhibitions in social conduct that characterised the period in Western Europe of the emergence of the bourgeoisie and the modern nation-state. From eating habits to sleeping patterns, from breaking wind to urinating, Elias shows how behaviour became more rigidly conditioned throughout the sixteenth, seventeenth and eighteenth centuries. It is argued that these social influences are internalised to the extent that adults act *as if* they are restraining themselves in purely personal terms, that is, the bourgeois personality presents a social code *as if* it is a matter of individual initiative. But, Elias argues, drives are modelled in terms of a particular moment of social structure and personality structure:

> The pattern of affect control, of what must and must not be restrained, regulated and transformed, is certainly not the same in this stage as in the preceding one of the court aristocracy. In keeping with its different interdependencies, bourgeois society applies stronger restrictions to certain impulses.

> (ibid.: 152)

The overriding theme of Elias' study is the proposition that affect control (what amounts to the increasing tendency of the modern individual to de-primitivise all aspects of human behaviour) is a central feature of the historical development of Western societies. Elias' method can make the most impressive interpretive connections on the basis of this emphasis. Thus, the discussion of the fork can become a prelude to the description of the modern individual's notion of the body:

> What was lacking in this *courtois* world, or at least had not been developed to the same degree, was the invisible wall of affects which seems now to rise between one body and another, repelling and separating, the wall which is often perceptible today at the mere approach of something that has been in contact with the mouth or hands of someone else, and which manifests itself as embarrassment at the mere sight of many bodily functions of others, and often at their mere mention, or as a feeling of shame when one's functions are exposed to the gaze of others, and by no means only then.

> (ibid.: 4)

The construction of such a wall included the intensification of provision of facilities and objects for a more privatised existence. Individuals were to have their own plates, their own beds, and

41

articles such as the handkerchief became *de rigueur*. The toilet claimed its own room, so enclosing the individual in the most privatised of settings for the most natural of acts. For Elias, the 'pattern of affect control, of what must and must not be restrained, regulated and transformed' (ibid.:152) pervades the whole of social life.

Interested in a sociology of processes rather than of states (ibid.: 228–235), the exploration of 'the figuration, a structure of mutually oriented and dependent people' (ibid.: 261), and the impact of forms of affect control within the long-term civilising process, the Elias of this majestic study offers an attractive framework for sociological analysis of historical (or developmental) processes. It is cross-cultural and comparative in scope; it stresses the processual dimensions of social reality, striving for a balance between historical and structural levels of analysis; it is innovative in the analysis of empirical phenomena; and it treats culture and social consciousness (sentiments, feelings, attitudes) as objects worthy of rigorous sociological attention.

In *What is Sociology?* (1978a) Elias reiterates some of these principles, and in his joint work with Eric Dunning (Elias and Dunning, 1986), these central points are reaffirmed. There has been considerable, and lively, critique and counter-critique on figurational sociology and its application to sport and leisure (for instance, Horne and Jary, 1987; Dunning, in Rojek, 1989; Horne and Jary, 1994), but undeniably the contribution of the figurational approach to understanding sport has been formidable. How, then, would the sociologist working within this framework make sense of the story of street football in Derby in the middle of the nineteenth century?

The key point in Elias' figurational sociology for the investigation of the developmental history of sport is the contention that affect controls intensify within sport as the civilising process advances. The uninhibited physicality, therefore, of street football, its inherently uncontrolled and anarchic form, becomes subject – to paraphrase the words of Elias – to forms of restraint, regulation and transformation. The popular recreational form is out of tune with the refrains of the marching band of the emergent classes which are at the centre of the civilising process. The key features of the traditional form of street football – its disorderliness, violence and open-endedness – are anathema to these newly powerful social groups and the alliances of interest that bind together some of those groups, and sectional interests within and between those groups of 'mutually oriented and dependent people'.

Street football or the folk antecedent of modern forms of football involved, for the figurational sociologist, 'wild and, according to modern notions, savage brawls. Their violence probably constituted one of the sources of enjoyment' (Dunning and Sheard, 1979: 25). Such folk games 'were rough and wild, closer to "real" fighting than modern sports' (ibid.: 30). It is, effectively, the lack of affect controls that becomes, logically, the major analytical emphasis for the figurational sociologist: 'folk games retained a distinct family likeness determined . . . above all, by the fact that, correlative with the stages in a "civilising process" through which pre-industrial Britain passed, they were rough and wild' (ibid.: 32). Dunning and Sheard recognise the importance of changes in time in the industrialising context, and of the decline in the availability of open space in which to engage in activities like street football. But the 'more deeply-rooted "social forces"' to which they point transcend, for instance, social class differences:

> Englishmen during the early stages of industrialization underwent a 'civilizing' change . . . this period (1780–1850) formed a watershed, a stage of rapid transition in which there occurred a 'civilizing spurt', an advance in people's 'threshold of repugnance' with regard to engaging in and witnessing violent acts.
>
> (ibid.: 40)

The street football of Derby, from this perspective, became an unacceptable form of public spectacle. Its suppression was accelerated by new and more effective forms of social control, and by the lack or withdrawal of local patronage (the Mayor explicitly opposed the game in Derby; his counterpart in 1866 in Kingston 'refused to comply with the old custom of kicking off at the start of the Shrovetide match' (ibid.: 43)). But, despite the range of elements recognised as important by Dunning and Sheard in the decline of folk football, the central influence, they argue, is 'the demand for greater orderliness and more "civilized" behaviour characteristic of an advanced industrial society' (ibid.: 44). The key conceptual emphasis in figurational sociology is upon 'different degrees and types of regulation' (Elias and Dunning, 1986: 190) in the evolution of modern sport forms from their folk-game predecessors.

Critical materialism

In this section we consider the major interpretive emphases of two prominent social historical works on the nineteenth century, and of two studies by sociologists to whom the analysis of the process of history is paramount. The work of E.P. Thompson – and of the radical analysis and cultural Marxism of other prominent figures in the English New Left of the 1950s and 1960s, such as Stuart Hall and Raymond Williams – has been important to this approach. Thompson's stress on the lived experience and everyday culture(s) of the popular classes, on the creative dimensions of cultural life, and his concern with the fundamental transformations wrought by industrial capitalist society (and the concomitant cultural struggles and class conflict) have inspired generations of critical materialist scholars. Malcolmson's groundbreaking work on popular recreations was undertaken under the supervision of Thompson, who suggested 'early lines of enquiry, frequently offered advice on source materials, on several occasions suggested further, and fruitful, approaches to the subject' (Malcolmson, 1973: ix). Thompson's works on the emerging class dynamics of early industrialism, and on the features of the new industrial order, feature in significant ways in the work of Bailey, Hargreaves, and Clarke and Critcher. Indeed, for the latter co-authors, his classic work *The Making of the English Working Class* 'marks the emergence of cultural history':

> Everyday life became more than the cold indices of the standard of living; class consciousness was understood to take forms other than political or trade union

organization; and perhaps most importantly, ideas about class conflict were extended beyond the issues of economic and political power to encompass struggles over the cultural legitimacy of images, definitions, meanings and ideologies embedded in social behaviour.

(Clarke and Critcher, 1985: 49)

This is not to say that Thompson's work is all-embracing, and Clarke and Critcher list four reservations about Thompson's pioneering approach and the historical work inspired by it (ibid.: 49–50). First, its concentration on working-class leisure is at the expense of the leisure histories of other classes and strata. Second, the historical research focuses selectively upon '*institutional* forms of leisure practice', marginalising our understanding of the unorganised or the informal. Third, its history is primarily that of '*male* leisure'. And fourth, the approach has not generated historical material of high quality on the more recent periods of British history, such as the post-Second World War period of the twentieth century. Nevertheless, they reassert, the work of the cultural historians has been of great value. How, then, would scholars working within or out of this framework account for Delves' Derby case study? Peter Bailey's study clearly states its primary themes in its title, *Leisure and Class in Victorian England: Rational Recreation and Contest for Control, 1830–1885*. His core case study is of the Lancashire industrial town of Bolton. Impromptu holidays (at the time of political elections) and lively street entertainment were features of a 'public and gregarious . . . working-class leisure' in the 1830s, based around the social setting of the pub, or the public space of the street. The basis of this leisure culture and its sports corollaries was undermined by, as Bailey puts it, paraphrasing the classic work of the historians Barbara and John Hammond, 'the curtailment of time and space, and the hostility of the superior classes' (1978: 11). Factory employers and middle-class evangelists combined in the first third of the nineteenth century 'to police the amusements of the poor', their 'principal targets' being 'animal cruelty, Sabbath breaking and intemperance' (Bailey, 1978: 17, 18). In Bolton, in 1844, for instance, local authorities responded to the urgings of such constituencies, the local clergy lobbying the magistracy to prohibit Sunday performances at the Star Museum and Concert Hall, the town's leading singing saloon. This was not an all-embracing opposition. Some elements – licensed victuallers, for instance – objected to the constraints, clearly putting business concerns before moral outrage. But there was no doubt that the new officers of the police were having a widespread effect on the nature of popular recreational practice. Peel had reformed the Metropolitan Police in London in 1829 and parallel forces were established around the country. These officious and at times zealous bobbies enforced the law against blood sports and 'were also effective in curtailing other wild sports, such as the Shrove Tuesday game in Derby' (ibid.: 21). The police force in Bolton was far from universally popular in Bolton and its locality, in its early days even among the middle classes. But the forces soon began to operate more effectively in the name of respectability: they 'invaded the daily occasions for recreation as well as the popular festivals of the fair and the race meeting' (ibid.: 21). The middle classes had less and less time for the theory that the street games and public recreations of 'a hard-driven working people' acted as a safety valve for their frustrations and discontents (ibid.: 22). And certainly, the profile of

44

an activity like the Derby street football was a symbol to the local middle classes of a lack of public order. Bailey captures vividly this clash of cultures. The hostility of the reform associations and local authorities was only the most forceful expression of a general middle class impatience with the intractable crudities and excess of so much of popular recreation:

> [The] respectable citizens of Bolton who demanded police action against street games were not just concerned to criticize the efficiency of a distasteful new service, but were genuinely affronted by what they saw and heard of. In an age of progress and rationality it was frankly incomprehensible that people should amuse themselves by eating scalding porridge with their fingers or stripping the wicks from a pound of candles with their teeth, all for the sake of a wager and the applause of an audience of like-minded boobies. These folk pleasures were popular contests at the yearly Halshaw Wakes held near Bolton, but similar feats took place all year round – eight pounds of treacle consumed in twenty minutes by a butcher's assistant (the commonest of participants) provides a ready example. Such displays were generally attended by a great deal of drinking and gambling. The gentry and respectable middle classes recoiled from such uncouth congenialities and, like the clergy, no longer appeared as patrons of the local fairs and feasts.
>
> (1978: 21–22)

In this metaphor of recoiling, Bailey evokes the tensions between the social classes of the time, and demonstrates the cultural incompatibilities that were manifest in disputes over the acceptability of recreational activities and folk pastimes. Documenting the 'language of resistance' of many working people to the marginalisation and undermining of their culture, he indicates the political basis of sports and popular culture in the class dynamics of this formative period. Street football in Derby could be, from such a perspective, a major symbol of the social tensions and cultural struggles at a time when the social order and the new modern society were in the making; and at a time, it is well worth recalling, when popular revolutions were sweeping away old hierarchies across Europe, and collectivist political agitation in England (the fight for trade unionism, the Chartist Movement) rendered the privileged classes paranoid at the prospect of a popular uprising. It is in such a climate that the reformist interventionists framing new forms of leisure and sport developed their initiatives. The 'voices of improvement', as Bailey puts it, of the rational recreation movement had more in mind than merely the calming of the crowd. Reform of popular recreations would be 'a constructive contribution to the general drive for social amelioration or "improvement" . . . improved recreations were an important instrument for educating the working classes in the social values of middle-class orthodoxy' (ibid.: 35). Policies developed for the regulation of amusements, albeit in sympathy with the need and conditions of the urban masses, constituted, in Bailey's terms, the implementation of a 'rationale of social control' (ibid.).

Hugh Cunningham's careful scholarship has reminded us that despite the reformist interventions, the practitioners of many popular recreations were resilient. Street football in Derby was not wiped out overnight, and the immediate impact of official action was not always translated into long-term importance. Cunningham describes how a reformist curate, the Reverend Grimshaw, arrived in the West Yorkshire village of Haworth in 1742. Praying strategically in opposition to local folk games, and serendipitously helped by adverse weather, he succeeded in ending local horse racing and other activities. But soon after Grimshaw's time, regular Sunday football with neighbouring parishes was back on the agenda. Cunningham's insight holds for the case of street football in Derby – the resilience in the face of hostility and the resistance to reformist campaigners were widely characteristic of working people's responses. Cunningham recognises the main hope of the interventionists as, through the management of acceptable forms of leisure, the achievement of 'a reconciliation of classes, a recreation of community and a reassertion of paternalism' (1980: 123). For four reasons, he points out, this was an over-optimistic 'hope'. First, many of the events that were claimed as testimony to class conciliation, and where this principle was preached, were in fact one-offs: they were a-typical, exceptions to a rule of cultural separatism. Second, while claims were made for class conciliation in leisure, the intensification of labour discipline and the consolidation of new forms of labour relations had the opposite effect, and 'work is of primary importance in determining class relationships' (ibid.: 125). Third, when social classes 'did meet in leisure they often interpreted the meaning of the meeting in different ways' (ibid.: 125). And fourth, aspirations to achieve a mingling of the classes in leisure did not include a mingling of the sexes. Male liberal rational recreationists left their wives at home. Cunningham shows how alliances formed in opposition to activities like street football were not inexorably to succeed, and indeed, quoting Delves, he points out that some liberal recreationists were opposed not so much to the practice of popular recreation, but to the form it took and the way in which it was organised: for them, a more entrepreneurial approach could have economic spin-offs as well as moral credibility (ibid.: 78). And on a wider point, reviewing the inter-class dynamics of the early stages of football in England, he makes the astute observation that in certain circumstances 'the working class, for lack of any alternative, was prepared to accept for as long as necessary, the fact of middle-class sponsorship, but not its ideology' (ibid.: 128). 'Give me the resources and facilities, and stuff your sermons' might have been the motto of such a response.

In a conclusion which is really a conceptual and methodological appendix rather than a summative review of his study, Cunningham acknowledges his debts to the work of E.P. Thompson, Raymond Williams and the Italian Marxist theorist Antonio Gramsci. Such sources are important too to the work of Hargreaves, and Clarke and Critcher.

John Hargreaves' social and historical analysis of popular sports in Britain stresses the interconnectedness of three elements which form the title of his book: *Sport, Power and Culture*. The examples of street football that he cites are the Derby game (for which the source is Malcolmson) and (quoting Storch, 1976) the banning of football in Leicester in 1847. For Hargreaves, the Derby story is primarily one of suppression, with agencies of repression – the police, the troops – brought in as, in Storch's phrase, 'domestic missionaries of the bourgeoisie'.

These initiatives, perceived by working-class communities as outright attacks on their traditional freedoms and on their right to assemble, were examples of blatant ruling-class oppression of an exploited working class. The story of street football in Derby and the attempt to construct more acceptable alternatives is evidence, from a perspective such as that of Hargreaves, of how sport was seen as either playing a part or having the potential to play a part 'in the pattern of working-class accommodation to the new social order' (Hargreaves, 1986: 26).

Clarke and Critcher identify violence and brutality as 'major features of popular culture' in the early 1800s, when 'life, on or off the streets, was often nasty, brutish and short' (1985: 53). Yet still, at the turn of the eighteenth and nineteenth centuries, prominent popular cultural forms were, as they note, endorsed by powerful groupings, by the aristocracy and the gentry. Economic, political, religious and cultural cum consumerist forces were, Clarke and Critcher emphasise, to change that. From such a perspective, the concerted strategy to outlaw street football in Derby was part of a wider trend across the industrialising, modernising society:

> [L]ooking overall at the trends evident by the 1840s, the clearest impression is of the wholesale changes in the rhythms and sites of work and leisure enforced by the industrial revolution. It was during this period that what we have come to see as a discrete area of human activity called 'leisure' became recognisable. But, contrary to the account offered by sociological orthodoxy, it did not develop in any simple linear fashion, as an aspect of industrialised progress. It was enforced from above as a form of social control, by magistrates, clergymen, policemen, mill owners, poor law commissioners. Its rationale was in the end, despite religious and moral camouflage, that of the economic system. It concerned, most simply, the taming of a workforce.
>
> (Clarke and Critcher, 1985: 58–59)

This is not to say that the suppression of street football is a mere reflection of the economic order, rather that the cultural resonance of such an activity was inimical to the expressed values and priorities of that order – regular and anarchic folk forms were not the sort of non-work recreational activities of which factory owners and local authorities would approve, in a climate in which older patterns of life were being reorganised 'under new moral and social auspices' (Hall, 1986: 24). Avoiding any crude economic explanations Clarke and Critcher (1985: 227) propose that the concept that 'provides a model for analysing culture as creation from below and appropriation from above' is hegemony, for it addresses the dynamics of contested power and recognises the importance of negotiation as a form of contestation within power relations. And certainly the notion of hegemony helps account for how sports cultures in particular circumstances can contribute to the manufacture of consent.

We have called the framework of the writers covered in this sub-section a critical materialist one. By materialism we mean the *historical materialism* of the great multi-disciplinary social scientific thinker Karl Marx, through which the mode of production of a society and the labour process can be seen as having a primary role in the development of human history (Bhaskar,

1993: 372) and upon the nature of social relations. By critical, we mean (following Marx's *Theses on Feuerbach*) the recognition that analysis and theory might also have the capacity to affect, if not effect, change, in both comprehension and practice. Other perspectives (such as Hughson *et al.*, 2005) complement such a critical materialist approach, and suggest too that such work on sport contributes to the analysis of the overall social and cultural order, and not just the sporting sphere alone.

CONCLUSION

Other theoretical frameworks could be instanced. For example, John Hughson *et al.* (2005) provide an alternative reading of cultural theorists of sport that owes more to the work of Richard Hoggart in founding cultural studies. Liberal historians have disputed the analyses of critical materialists, seeing in the concept of hegemony 'a brilliant attempt to span the chasm between the evidence and an unsatisfactory theory' (Golby and Purdue, 1984: 13). They argue that nineteenth-century popular culture may well have expressed 'the aspirations and desires of most men as most men are' (ibid.). From such a perspective, the demise of street football could be seen as a kind of popular progressivism, the more orderly conception of sport representing an emerging consensus. Feminist scholarship would point to the absence of women from the street football ritual as an indication of its deep-rooted patriarchal nature, and to its endemic violence and physical roughness as an elemental form of masculinity.

The beginning sociologist or cultural analyst of sport might wonder how it is that scholars and writers sharing so much in common – after all, aren't they all sociologists or social historians? – can spend so much time at loggerheads. But one of the main sources of excitement in the social sciences is the challenge of interpretation, and debates over the respective merits or validity of different concepts and theories are central to this challenge. To recognise this is to debate the nature of history and its legacies, to assess the impact of relations between dominant and subordinate groups in a particular society, and to illuminate the place of a cultural form such as sport in history and society. Jarvie and Maguire have also stressed the commonality of different approaches, pointing to three core 'common hallmarks of good sociology': (1) the examination of the nature of 'structured processes understood to be concretely situated in time and space'; (2) the recognition of unintended as well as intended outcomes of social processes; and (3) an awareness of the interrelationships between individual lives and the structural context of those lives (1994: 256).

Some of the most influential sociologists of the modern age have been at pains to emphasise such common preoccupations. Mills (1970) argued for the development of a sociological imagination in which self and structure, individual and history, were understood together. For Giddens (1982), the sociological imagination is at once critical, anthropological (or comparative) and historical. Though there may be theoretical disputes over the balance between and emphases of competing conceptualisations, the broader sociological agenda should be acknowledged and the crafts of social history absorbed. But if the nature of historical

48

scholarship is not recognised, then sociologists run the risk of theorising in a vacuum. In interpreting the growth of modern sports, and seeing the respective possibilities, merits and deficiencies in theoretical and conceptual approaches to that growth, sociology needs history, and history can benefit from a partnership with sociology.

ESSAY QUESTIONS

1   With reference to one sport other than football, discuss the contribution that figurational sociology can make to an understanding of the sport's growth.
2   'Contestation is a central dynamic of sports cultures.' Evaluate this claim with reference to critical materialist accounts of sport.

EXERCISES

1   Review one journal article on the history of sports, summarising its argument, listing the types of sources upon which it is based, and evaluating its theoretical stance (300 words).
2   Interview, for 20–30 minutes, one person aged 70 years or more who has had an active life in sports, asking him or her to comment upon how the meaning of sport has changed. Make notes of the main points of the interview, and speculate upon how you might theorise the account, and the changes in meaning documented in it.
3   List the different kinds of documentary and oral sources upon which the social historian and the sociologist draw. Write down any differences in how they use those sources, and draw out any interpretive or theoretical implications.

FURTHER READING

R. Holt, *Sport and the British: A Modern History* (Oxford: Oxford University Press, 1989) includes, in the appendix, a provocative discussion of the difference between historical and sociological styles and approaches.

G. Jarvie and J. Maguire, *Sport and Leisure in Social Thought* (London: Routledge, 1994) provides an overview of leading social theories and schools of thought, and their relevance for the analysis of sport and leisure.

CHAPTER FOUR

SOCIAL STRATIFICATION AND SOCIAL DIVISION IN SPORT

INTRODUCTION

Sport is often seen as the domain of fair play in which opportunity is said to be open to all. From such a perspective, the legacies of the values of athleticism as established in the nineteenth century – playing to the rules, honouring one's opponent, for instance – blend with the meritocratic rhetoric of modern sport. Yet throughout modern history, sport participation and its meanings have been differentiated and diverse, rooted in social inequalities and divisions. Sport has been developed and sustained in a modern society characterised by deeply embedded forms of social stratification; it is hardly surprising, therefore, that sports forms and practices are themselves indices of such differences. In this chapter we consider the primary sources of stratification in sport – social class, gender and ethnicity – in illustrative detail, and signal other sources of division in examining how social inequalities and divisions have been variously and recurrently manifest in sporting forms and practices.

The term 'stratification' derives from the technical geological word for the different layers of the earth's crust. Figuratively, in sociology, it has come to refer to the way in which a society comprises layered groupings, separate yet interconnected within a totality – the organic power of the metaphor has persisted. By the second half of the nineteenth century the term was beginning to be applied specifically to society. As the German Baring-Gould could put it in 1879: 'The stratification of the German classes, and of the aristocracy, is most peculiar' (OED, 1979: 3084). It has become a central concept in the analysis of societies:

> In all complex societies, the total stock of valued resources is distributed unequally, with the most privileged individuals or families enjoying a disproportionate amount of property, power or prestige . . . most scholars . . . identify a set of 'social classes' or 'strata' that reflect the major cleavages in the population. The task of stratification research is to specify the shape and contours of these social groupings, to describe the processes by which individuals are allocated into different social outcomes, and to uncover the institutional mechanisms by which social inequalities are generated and maintained.
>
> (Grusky, 1993: 610)

A classic formulation of stratification in American society points out that it is in societies in which success, equality and classlessness are claimed as central social values that many people are blinded to 'the contours, and the pervasiveness of social stratification' (Hodges, 1964: x):

[O]urs is in fact a multi-layered society, a hierarchical society in which whole classes of people are quite commonly accorded low, middling or high social esteem, power and material wealth . . . Complex societies are everywhere and always *stratified* societies: this is inescapable fact. It is a fact as true of today's United States – and of contemporary Japan or the Soviet Union or Thailand or Paraguay – as it was of medieval Europe, classical Greece, or ancient Mesopotamia.

(Hodges, 1964: x–xii)

Although sport has in some cases offered opportunities for dramatic and spectacular individual social mobility – sports stars earning money and accruing status undreamt of in the social and cultural milieux of their origins – sports have, at most levels of commitment and performance, exhibited the differentiations and divisions of the wider, stratified social context. This is not to say that sport is always no more than a mere reflection of the society: sporting practices and cultures can break the mould of inherited inequalities, or challenge an existing order of division and inequality. In such ways, a particular sporting form can exhibit a complex mix of the residual, dominant and the emergent (Williams, 1977a; 1977b) within a society and a culture. But for the most part, sport cultures have contributed to the reproduction of existing patterns of social stratification and division, and status inequalities. Sugden and Tomlinson (2000: 309) comment:

[I]n the context of British society, involvement in a polo match in the grounds of Windsor Castle, participation in Henley's boating regatta or a trip to the grouse moors of Scotland can be taken as clear signals of high social status. Similarly, playing golf at Royal St Andrews, attending Twickenham for a rugby international, having a season ticket for a Premier Division football club, turning out in the park for the local pub's football team, and keeping and racing pigeons, all convey messages about the social location of the participants.

These sites of sport are, then, places in which social class values are generated and perpetuated. Bourdieu connects the rationalisation of games into modern sports forms with a class-based philosophy of amateurism: 'the modern definition of sport . . . is an integral part of a "moral ideal", i.e. an ethos which is that of the dominant fractions of the dominant class.' (1978: 825). To play tennis or golf, to ride or to sail, was, as Bourdieu argues, to bestow upon the participant *'gains in distinction'* (ibid.: 828). Sports in which lower middle-class or working-class adolescents participate develop 'in the form of spectacles produced for the people . . . more clearly as a mass commodity' (ibid.: 828). For Bourdieu, then, sport acts as a kind of badge of social exclusivity and cultural distinctiveness for the dominant classes, for the social elite, and as both a means of control or containment of the working or popular classes and a potential source of escape and mobility for talented working-class sports performers. Sports, therefore, are not self-contained spheres of practice:

> [C]lass habitus defines the meaning conferred on sporting activity, the profits expected from it; and not the least of these profits is the social value accruing from the pursuit of certain sports by virtue of the distinctive rarity they derive from their class distribution.
>
> (ibid.: 835)

From this perspective, then, sports participation is not a matter of personal choice, of individual preference. It depends upon the financial resources available to the potential participant, the social status of those prominent in that activity, and the cultural meaning of a sport and the individual's relationship to those meanings. The notion of the habitus is central to the Bourdieuian framework: 'different conditions of existence produce different habitus – systems of generative schemes applicable, by simple transfer, to the most varied areas of practice' (1986: 170). The habitus embodies both that which is structured and that which is structuring: 'As a system of practice-generating schemes', it 'expresses systematically the necessity and freedom inherent in its class position and the difference constituting that position' (ibid.: 172).

The concept of habitus reminds us of the boundedness of sports cultures, and the ways in which sport acts a source of capital. Sport is one sphere of practice, often institutionalised, which creates a form of capital through which distinction can be bestowed, and cultures challenged or reproduced. But the momentum of Bourdieu's analysis is towards the shaping of status by the dispositions of habitus. The cultural significance and social power of the habitus are manifest in particular sport contexts and settings, characterised as they might be by social class, gender, race/ethnicity, or potent combinations of these.

SOCIAL CLASS

Social class has been a central concept in the social sciences, 'one of the best established approaches for analysing data on social structure' (Wesolowski and Slomczynski, 1993: 82). This has been accomplished by looking at how social classes differ according to the share of unequally distributed goods, their varied opinions and attitudes, their group actions and political beliefs and behaviours, and the extent to which they are socially mobile (that is, able to move between classes).

The rigidity of class boundaries may have decreased in some ways, and sociological debates have raged on the 'mounting evidence that societies like Britain are more open than they had believed' (Saunders, 1997: 282), but in contemporary sports cultures class categories – in terms of socio-economic classifications, in which the combined influence of economic, status and cultural factors have persisting influence and impact – continue to influence participation and activity. The figures in Table 4.1 also suggest that, taking the case of golf in the late 1980s and early 1990s, the largest fall-off in participation was among the best and least well-off social groups: such trends are clearly connected to economic cycles of boom and recession. But the broad parameters of the sporting milieu remain unaltered. More generally, 82 per cent of people in professional occupations 'had taken part in at least one physical activity in the previous four weeks in 1993–94 compared with only 48 per cent of those in the unskilled manual groups' (CSO, 1996: 224). These differences in levels of participation persisted over the following decade and a half. Nick Rowe, Head of Strategy Research and Planning at Sport England, acknowledged in 2004 that 'participation rates have remained stubbornly static and inequities in participation between different social groups have continued largely unchanged over the last 30 years or so with perhaps the exception of more women taking part in fitness related activities' (Rowe, 2004: 2–3). Social class differences have continued to characterise what Rowe calls the 'stubbornly static' participation rates of active sport participants

Class cultures in which the meanings of sport are rooted do not disappear overnight. Even in the traumatic context of the mid-1980s coal dispute in northern England, it was traditional cultural, leisure and sporting strategies that continued to 'shape family life, social relationships and leisure' (Waddington et al., 1991: 104). And 'Sports and social clubs, pubs and churches seemed to provide most of what local adults wanted' (ibid.: 103). Further qualitative, ethnographic work in sociological community studies, anthropology and cultural studies illuminate the deep-rootedness of such cultures. The social and economic conditions that formed the basis of the place of rugby league in the community life of an early post-Second World War northern English mining village (Denis et al., 1995) may have undergone dramatic change. But the values of working-class community that were at the heart of that culture were still important influences upon the game where it survived in the mid-1990s:

> the working class maleness that forms part of the values of the Sudthorpe social networks of the imaginary community of 'the game' is in tension with the expressions of masculinity in Australian league, and the discourses around the Super league.
>
> (Spracklen, 1995: 116)

In their participant observation studies of working-class male youth groups in the early 1970s, in the West Midlands and north-east England respectively, Paul Willis (1977) and Paul Corrigan

Table 4.1 Participation in golf, by socio-economic group, 1987, 1990 and 1993 (%)

Year	Professional	Employers and managers	Intermediate and junior non-manual	Skilled manual, own account non-professional	Semi-skilled manual and personal service	Unskilled manual	Total
1987	11	12	8	5	5	4	7
1990	13	10	4	5	2	1	5
1993	9	10	5	6	2	2	5

(1979) demonstrated the cultural resistances of working-class males to formal institutional structures and official cultures of school and sport. The studies gave prominence to the views and voices of their respondents.

Willis' study of twelve secondary-aged male working-class pupils in an English West Midlands school in the early 1970s identified the intensely hostile attitudes of 'lads' to an official culture of the school. Lads who may have begun secondary school with what teachers saw as a positive outlook to educational life are drawn into what Willis calls a process of *differentiation* from formal school life, a process whose 'dynamic is opposition to the institution which is taken up and reverberated and given a form of reference to the larger themes and issues of the class culture' (Willis, 1977: 62–63). To the institutional leader, as Willis puts it, the teacher, this is an individual pathology, a personal failure. The following report on the pupil Spanksy captures both the process and the institutional response:

> [Spansky] in the first three years was a most co-operative and active member of school. He took part in the school council, school play and school choir in this period and represented the school at cricket, football and cross-country events.
>
> Unfortunately, this good start did not last and his whole manner and attitude changed. He did not try to develop his ability in either practical or academic skills . . . his early pleasant and cheerful manner deteriorated and he became a most unco-operative member of the school . . . hindered by negative attitudes.
>
> (ibid.: 62)

For a working-class pupil such as Spansksy, the street culture, the commercial dance and the prospect of the excitement of the evening against the mundanity of the daytime offer more meaningful cultural values than the dubious promise of schooling. And sport becomes widely associated with the formal, official school culture.

Corrigan's ethnography of the school and leisure lives of 14- to 15-year-old boys in Sunderland, north-east England, makes still more explicit this incompatibility between the expressed class culture of the boys and the sports culture of the school. Corrigan notes that sociologists had recorded previously the reluctance of such kids to play school sport or represent the school at sport, but adds a fresh layer of interpretation, exploring what he calls the *mode* of sport offered by the school and the alternative mode of playing preferred by the kids away from the school:

> School sports are not simply an attempt to allow the boys a chance to enjoy themselves, they are meant to instil a certain attitude to sports as their prime reason for being on the timetable. Playing football for the school represents a certain form of 'playing football' which by no means represents the 'normal' way of playing football for the boys in this study . . .
>
> *Question* Do you like football?

Bert Yes, a lot. I used to play for the school team only you had to turn out every Saturday, and you had to buy a bag so I dropped out.

Question Where do you play football around here?

Bert Used to play outside the metalwork shop. But the coppers came and said 'Next time we catch you here you're gonna get summoned'. He took the ball away in his panda. [Author's note: 'panda' is the vernacular for the police car.]

(1979: 101)

Corrigan shows that there are numerous ways of playing the game – modes of involvement and commitment – for the boys in his study and that 'for most of them the activity of playing football was not that of the structured game' (ibid.: 102). There is a complex relationship between class cultures, or habitus, and formal sports institutions. The work of Willis and Corrigan shows how class is an objective feature of social relations, a dynamic framing the lived realities of their subjects. Hargreaves (1986) also reminds us of the class dynamics that frame different opportunities and experiences for class fractions.

Urry (1989: 87–88) summarised major trends in social class in Britain on the eve of the century's final decade, listing six points:

1   The traditional working-class has shrunk, as manufacturing industry and manual work have employed fewer people.
2   Social inequalities between the 'have-nots' and the 'have-lots' have increased.
3   Limited chances for upward social mobility have been evident, mainly for white men.
4   Middle-class groupings have become differentiated in more complex ways.
5   Occupations are not wholly patterned by the capital/labour relationship.
6   The 'institutionalisation' and 'internationalisation' of capital have become more advanced.

To take Urry's points one by one. First, traditional and often collective working-class sports may persist in some regions, but the community and urban base for such sports has been to a large extent eroded. Second, sports participation data do corroborate the existence of inequalities, with 'issues of access and exclusion' (Tomlinson, 1986) still at the heart of Britain's sports cultures. Third, it is clear that some sports professionals' careers provide dramatic evidence of income and status-based forms of social mobility, and some sports audiences are also testimony to the shifting boundaries of life-chances and cultural opportunity. Fourth, and relatedly, *nouveau* elements within the class structure (and particularly the newer middle classes, or relatively unskilled income earners who see themselves as middle class rather than working class) have more opportunity to play sports such as golf, tennis or squash than in earlier generations. Fifth, on the level of sports workers and occupations, the expansion of public sector sports provision, the fragile but persisting profile of clubs and voluntary sports bodies and institutions, and the growth in the private-sector sports industry have all contributed to a growth of far from easily classifiable forms of work and occupation in sport. Finally, sport has become more and more internationalised as multinational capital and international media and marketing have fundamentally reshaped traditional sporting institutions and practices and sought to import sporting cultural products (such as American football, basketball and sumo). Rather than indicating the 'end of class', these trends and exemplars of trends have pointed to a complex repositioning of some traditional social class groupings and sub-groupings, and the continuing importance of sport as a barometer of social change and continuity. But as Tomlinson (2007: 4698) puts it: 'Class habitus and cultural capital remain major determinants of everyday practices and cultural institutions.'

GENDER AND SPORT PARTICIPATION

Gendered differences in sport participation have been, and remain, marked, despite well-intentioned interventions, by bodies such as the Sports Council (London, UK), its successor Sport England, and UK Sport, to raise girls' and women's participation. For increased participation is no simple index of a move towards gender equality. Researchers have pointed to the vulnerability of women in settings such as the aerobics class:

> [T]he body is exposed to the gaze of others . . . The great fear of aerobics is to be caught under the gaze of others . . . most participants are most comfortable at the back of the class, anonymous, where they can see and not be seen, follow the movements of others and not be seen.
>
> (Flintoff *et al.*, 1995: 98, 99)

Sport and the physicality embodied in sport render it a major source for the reaffirmation of traditional gender relations, in some cases in public spheres where initially and potentially women's sport constitutes a progressive intervention in, and sometimes a challenge to, dominant male assumptions concerning the place of sport and women's relationship to traditional forms of sport. Striking examples of this are available from feminist ethnographers: the research of Prendergast on women's stoolball in the south of England; and Middleton's work on the gender dynamics and struggles surrounding the use of a (cricketing) sports facility in a Yorkshire village.

Prendergast studied the stoolball case during 1977, when she was living in a rural parish in the Kent/Sussex Weald. She was astonished that 'the playing of stoolball was surrounded by a whole mythology of meaning and explanation, in the minds of men particularly, that simply did not occur in the equivalent male game, cricket' (1978: 15). Her study illustrates the way in which sporting practices can be determined by and implicated in wider issues of sexuality and gender identity. Modern changes in work patterns and labour opportunities meant that village households have become much more dependent upon the women of the locality continuing to live, and to work, in or within the vicinity of the village. The stoolball team in the village was also a catalyst for wider aspects of village life, and connected in important ways with women's involvement in community issues, child-rearing and work in the fields. Prendergast argues that this strong combination of interests was threatening to the males in

the village, and to their sense of masculine identity. Women's stoolball practices were characterised by banter, joking, gossip, physical exuberance and display, and some male reactions – of young men on cycles and motorbikes, old men with their lifelong assumptions – were to disrupt the women's activities by riding through the practice area itself, or to label the women as promiscuous, as feminine failures:

> The remark of an older man, a shepherd, perhaps serves to illustrate the particular combination of explicit sexual meanings of the game, as read into it by men, with its corollary, the suggestion that men could easily control this display if they so wished:

> 'I'd be in two minds as to send me old dog down there and get 'em all up for the tup' . . . He was saying in effect, that the women were like the ewes that were, on the word of the farmer, brought up from the marshes and mated with the rams, in order to lamb in the Spring.

> (Prendergast, 1978: 19)

The stoolball game, Prendergast argues, is seen by the village males – young and old, around the village and in the pub – 'as a manifestation of the strength of women when they act as a group, rather than their "ideal" state of division and isolation in the home' (ibid.: 22). In this context, the abusive joking of the males is a means of attempting to reposition and reassert control over women's behaviour. Women with a firm economic base and financial independence, and a public and confident sports culture, are doubly threatening to the males of the village, whose main response is to abuse, harass and vilify the women.

Middleton's study identifies a village sports institution – the cricket club – as a revealing instance of how social boundaries are established and reaffirmed. She is concerned with the economic and the political boundaries that constrain women (Imray and Middleton, 1983), but also with the ways in which the boundaries between public and private operate in practices like sport, in the rhythms of everyday village life. Her fieldwork was carried out between 1979 and 1982 in a village in the English county of Yorkshire, and she questioned the assumption that men and women experience 'the village' in the same way: 'social movement in all its aspects – travel, employment, mobility, social contact and, most tellingly, use of village space – is consistently curtailed for women' (Middleton, 1986: 121). The institutions of the village to which women were seen to have access – the village hall, the shops, the school, for instance – were those in which they were expected to fulfil a public dimension of their domestic, household roles as parent, wife/partner, family carer or household manager. Their access to certain resources was limited. As Mary put it, with reference to the family car: 'I can't have it just when I want it – not for too flippant a reason' (ibid.: 125). Mary's last daytime use of the family car had been to take a son to hospital; shopping was seen, by her partner, as in the 'flippant' category. As Middleton (ibid.: 125–127) observes, for women:

> [R]ole-sets become frozen while their husbands' are extended . . . Women have only limited entry to places of leisure; they may be tolerated in these but with restrictions.

57

They are in fact kept on the fringes of community space . . . much public space is off-limits to women.

Women alone, 'manless' as Middleton puts it, using public leisure spaces such as the river and its surroundings, or the pub, were seen as 'asking for it', or offering themselves as 'fair game'. The overall picture painted by Middleton is of a village life in which public space is dominated by men, and 'the two sexes have distinct lives and inhabit different domains' (ibid.: 132). When women sought to make inroads into public sporting space in the village, they were seen as a threat to established male activity and territory.

Imray and Middleton describe in detail the way in which the men of the village discriminate against women, using their labour to support their own sporting institutions and practices, and generating ritualistic forms of affirmation of their own superiority and dominance over women. The village cricket team – comprising males of both working-class and middle-class backgrounds, from the ages of 14–60 – were the prima donnas of village life, expecting widespread support for their own activities, but giving no support to other village activity. They dominated the bar space of the sports and social club and forbade other forms of activity on what they saw as exclusively their playing pitch. The space around the clubhouse, the seating arrangements and the playing area were seen as spaces for men: 'But in the private sphere, women are hard at work producing leisure for men', washing whites, providing teas, activities vital to the 'production of a cricket match' (Imray and Middleton, 1983: 23). Women prepare drinks for players, but can go no further than the edge of the cricket pitch, where a man takes over the carrying duty and takes them to the square at the centre of the pitch. The men's changing room was off a corridor which linked the bar to the kitchen. Women working in catering who needed to go from the kitchen to the bar had to go outside and round the building. Once a year, on a weekday evening, men played women. The club fielded a young inexperienced male side. The women wore badminton skirts, tan tights, men's long sweaters and plimsolls. On the club veranda, segregated spectators comprised male cricketers on one side, women on the other. Veteran players yelled obscene comments at women during the play. The young men played with the cricket bat weaker-hand-round. The ritual end was a victory for the women by one run. In this apparently harmless and playful annual event is inscribed a deep-rooted male-dominated power and status structure:

> Once a year, then, members of the private sphere are allowed onto the 'square' where they are encouraged to flaunt their femininity and where inexperienced cricketers are defined as 'women', being beaten by them . . . a calendrical rite of status reversal . . . (which has) . . . the long-term effect of emphasising the strength and permanence of the usual order.
>
> (ibid.: 24)

Going beyond the role of uninvolved, detached observer/researcher, Middleton became secretary of the sports and social club, and attempted to organise the space for women to play seriously in team hockey. The cricket club offered initial support for use of the outfield of the cricket pitch for winter-season hockey, but, seeing the seriousness of the proposal, did not sustain the support: 'if women are allowed on the cricket pitch, this village will fall apart' (ibid.: 25) was the masculinist view that prevailed.

Communal space for stoolball in the locality; and space for organised sport in a voluntary sector club – two distinct contexts across time and space. But the interpretive messages have much in common, and the cases illustrate the importance of several themes in understanding the gendered basis of sports practices and institutions. First, the social space in which sports occur is to a great extent characterised by gender inequalities. Second, time itself is less flexible and malleable for women than for men. Third, sports as institutions are widely – both formally and informally – controlled by men, at the levels of organisation, and supported and serviced by women. Fourth, sports continue to be seen as affirming of stereotypes of masculinity and femininity, and as spheres in which gender prejudice can be confirmed, even to the point of abuse.

Sexuality and the dimensions of power and status associated with sexual identity are important persisting influences upon the making and remaking of sports cultures (Scraton and Watson, 2000; Scraton and Flintoff, 2002). Women's initial experiences of sport, in school-based physical education, have also been shown to be a source of girls' resistance to involvement in sport, for the culture of femininity so important to schoolgirls did not fit with what they perceive as on offer from PE:

(a) the development of muscle;
(b) sweat;
(c) communal shower/changing facilities;
(d) 'childish', asexual PE kit;
(e) low status activities.

(Scraton, 1987)

Forms of out-of-school involvement in sports clubs have also been male-dominated at the level of administration and management (White *et al.*, n.d.), and in terms of an organisational sexuality that can render girls and young women vulnerable to a range of forms of harassment and abuse (Tomlinson and Yorganci, 1997). In a number of key sites of social life – the family, the school, the community, the club, the local authority facility – forms of prejudice, discrimination, harassment, and sometimes abuse, have curtailed the scope and level of women's involvement in sport.

More generalised accounts of women's sport and leisure activities and experiences (Deem, 1986; Wimbush and Talbot, 1988; Green *et al.*, 1990) confirm the widespread persistence of such gendered inequalities. Quantitative signs (in participation figures) that women's participation in sport has increased in the final quarter of the twentieth century, as recognised by central policy makers such as Nick Rowe cited above, must be contextualised within an understanding of the nature of the particular activities or sports. Some 'new sports' as Bourdieu called them (1986) – windsurfing, surfing, fitness activities – have offered new possibilities to those women with the available resources in time and money. But aerobics, however potentially empowering, appears to have confirmed rather than challenged traditional and established models of femininity (Hargreaves, 1994: 160–162; Flintoff *et al.*, 1995; Tomlinson, 1997). Where other inroads have been made into traditional male territory – as in sports presentation within the broadcasting media – parallel paradoxes are evident. Although the Channel 5 presenter Gail McKenna's career profile from aspirant nun to tabloid Page 3 girl, through pantomime and soap opera *Brookside*, was hardly typical of the emergent women's presence in sports broadcasting, it is clear that in large part the women's contribution is seen, even by the presenters themselves, as complementary to rather than challenging of traditional modes of presentation by men (Thompson, 1997). The explosion of sport coverage on channels such as Sky Sports News has done little to shift what comes close to a sexist stereotype of the glamorous and sexualised female (Sugden and Tomlinson, 2010).

There have been important critiques of the gender order in sports, fuelled by feminist scholarship and activism. Hall (1996: 101) has acknowledged, in this context, a 'notion of sport as a site of cultural struggle', a sense of the 'history of women in sport' as 'a history of cultural resistance'. Apparent increases in the number of women participating in sport can veil the basis and nature of women's participation, which is often reaffirming of the established structures and stereotypically treats 'women as unitary subjects' (Hargreaves, 1994: 241). Citing a Sports Council pamphlet on 'Sport for all Women', Hargreaves points to the consequences of this:

> One million more women have been attracted to sport in the last five years BUT the benefits of increased participation are not being shared by all women. Particularly under-represented are: black and ethnic women, girls and young women, house-wives, single mothers, unemployed women, those on low incomes, and women with disabilities.
>
> (ibid.: 241)

The newly active women participants are, then, affluent, middle-class, able-bodied, white and adult. Gender inequalities are compounded by other dimensions of stratification and sources of social and cultural division. The mode of participation in sport – its location and frequency – continues to set women's sport cultures apart from those of men. The sociological evidence indicates clearly that in the sphere of sports, a hegemonic masculinity – 'defined as the con-figuration of gender practice which embodies the currently accepted answer to the problem of the legitimacy of patriarchy, which guarantees (or is taken to guarantee) the dominant position of men and the subordination of women' (Connell, 1995: 77) – continues to prevail. Such gendered values as masculinity are not innate, as Connell (1983) also notes: sport is not a vehicle for the articulation of an inherited manliness. Rather, a sphere such as sport provides a regular and routinised forum for the promotion and expression of a learned and generated masculinity, as is considered in more detail in Chapter 5 (on socialisation) and Chapter 7 (on sport and bodies). As Salisbury and Jackson (1996: 208) note: 'School sport . . . locks many boys into an aggressively virile culture through the masculinising of their bodies.'

Despite the values that may be claimed for sport as a form of egalitarian or meritocratic physical practice; or the social and health benefits that some sports undeniably generate; or the innocently framed pleasure, fun and enjoyment that accrue to participants from many sports – despite the importance of these meanings of sport, it would be an incomplete sociological and cultural reading of the meaning of contemporary sport that failed to recognise the large degree to which it acts as a source of and an expression for stratified status based upon gender. Such gendered status is fiercely and cunningly defended within the institutional structures of sport, though sport spaces and places offer the potential to challenge and contest conceptions of gendered physicality (Scraton and Watson, 2000), within the context of what Whitson (2002) calls the gendered subjectivities that are embodied in individual sportsmen and women.

RACE, ETHNIC IDENTITY AND SPORT

Ethnicity and black identity have been identified as important areas of research into the social and cultural role of sport in modern Britain. It has been established that black people are disproportionately under-represented in participation patterns across sport, but over-represented in certain elite levels of sports such as athletics and football. Sport policy makers and providers have at times seen the problem of participation as a general one, 'with no clearly articulated understanding of the issues relating to ethnic minorities and sport . . . initiatives seem largely to have been aimed at the general community in the vague hope that minority groups would join in' (Kew, 1979: 29). Alongside such ethnocentric provider philosophy, limited examples of black people's high profile in sport (as documented in Cashmore, 1990: 84) and the negative effects of stereotyping black people as 'naturally' good at certain sports, and so restricting opportunities in other spheres of life (Cashmore, 1982), have provided the basis for a complex picture and pattern of participation. Fleming (1995) reminds us of the essential heterogeneity of South Asian cultures and of the varying place of sport in the wider ethnic culture. Participation rates vary across ethnic groups and between genders within ethnic groups. As Verma and his collaborators reported (1991: 335), males in all ethnic groups participated in sport more than did females.

This gender pattern pervaded the findings:

> The difference in participation levels between the most active group of males – Chinese – and least active – Pakistani – was much smaller than the difference between the most active females – Chinese – and the least active – Bangladeshi. The differences between Chinese, White British and Caribbean males and females were quite small whereas those between Indian, African, Pakistani and Bangladeshi males and females were significantly greater.
>
> (Verma et al., 1991: 335)

Some black sports stars such as footballers achieve their goals against a backdrop of racial harassment and abuse (Fleming and Tomlinson, 1996), which has persisted, if more muted, despite the well-intentioned development of anti-racist initiatives (Garland and Rowe, 1996; Horne, 1996). It is well established that ethnically based forms of sport have often flourished as a means of asserting a distinctive identity, in response to discrimination. For instance, 'Bermudian blacks responded to segregation by forming their own clubs, mainly for sports and recreation', and also for arts, charity work and fashion (Manning, 1973: 29). Similarly, some responses within the black British community have prioritised a cultural autonomy in sport. The Muhammed Ali Sports Development Association, in the 1970s, stressed 'the importance of having black leaders in institutions and of designing projects specifically for black youngsters' (Kew, 1979: 30). Twenty years later, the all-black Accra Football Club in Brixton represented the pride of black identity and was seen by one of its organisers as 'a valuable social institution which can help prepare young black men for the difficulties they are likely to encounter in a racist society' (Fleming and Tomlinson, 1996: 93). One response to racism has been, therefore, to turn inwards. Carrington's study of the Caribbean Cricket Club illustrates the rationale for and nature of such a response (1997; see also Carrington, 2002 and 2010).

The Caribbean Cricket Club was formed in Leeds in 1947, by West Indian Second World War veterans who had settled in the city. Both a social and sporting club, it offered a black community space for the following half century and a means of achieving at a high level in the local sports culture. Carrington (1997) emphasises the importance of the Caribbean Club and its ground and clubhouse (dating from the 1980s), The Oval, on the edge of the Chapeltown area, as a 'discursively constructed black social space':

> [In] the discussions and interviews . . . the club is mentioned as a 'black space', by which is often meant a place where black people can 'be themselves', free from the surveillance imposed by the 'white gaze'. . . In this sense the club's significance goes beyond merely being a cricket club and assumes a heightened *social* role as a *black* institution within a wider white environment. This can operate on a number of related levels, from being a space removed, albeit not entirely, from the overt practices of white racism; as a social and cultural resource for black people; and an arena that allows for black expressive behaviour.

Carrington's interviewees recall the importance to them of the club, as a focal and survival point. One 17-year-old who played for other sides where he was one of only two blacks described how he could face racial abuse there, whereas no opposing side would abuse a Caribbean side that was predominantly black. As the club expanded in achievement and, concomitantly, profile, more teams were established and its junior teams comprised a wider ethnic mix of white, Asian and Chinese players. Its gender complexion remained exclusively male, with women's inputs being support-based and marginal, and talk of the development of a women's team never leading to action. The achievement of the Caribbean Cricket Club has been, nevertheless, to prosper and diversify, by adopting a strategy of the affirmation of cultural identity and therefore difference. This has shown the capacity of sport to both confirm yet challenge the sources of social division and stratification, to challenge racist stereotyping and prejudice by positive action and achievement. Sport provides a forum in which communal identity can be expressed and – in the case, for instance, of the northern English rugby league – some stereotypes challenged: 'at the symbolic level at least, the increased participation of . . . Asian players in the "hard white working class culture" of rugby league would make the stereotyped claims about Asian passiveness and fragility all the more difficult to sustain' (Long et al., 1996: 13). Nevertheless, as Burdsey's research (2007) has demonstrated, a passion among Asian males for amateur football does not translate into representation in the professional ranks of the game; and anti-racist initiatives have done relatively little to attract Asians onto the terraces.

CONCLUSION

This chapter has concentrated upon primary aspects of stratification and sources of social division, and some of their interrelationships. Others include age (Long and Wimbush, 1979; Woods, 1994; Abrams, 1995) and disability (Collins with Kay, 2003; and Thomas and Smith, 2009: 108). Sport at all its levels can therefore be seen to express social divisions on the basis of a range of sources of stratification. The social class, gender or ethnic category into which an individual is born will affect the status outcomes of any single individual's life. As Dahrendorf emphasises in his neo-Weberian approach, 'life chances are a function of two elements, *options* and *ligatures*' (1979: 30). In this formulation, options refer to possibilities of choice and ligatures are allegiances, bonds or linkages. The social habitus (Elias, 1993: 32) can also be conceived in this fashion, with the tribe or the community placing the individual in the particular context, and the development of individual strands, at the level of instincts and feelings, indicating options for the future. All social groups experience, in different ways, the process through which a stratified social order is constructed, maintained and amended. Sporting possibilities and prospects are not immune from these central dynamics of a society and its cultures. Patterns of stratification are not laws of nature: they can be contested. But it would be sociologically naïve to ignore their prevalence across time and space, and the persisting influence of forms of habitus and their capacity to effect social closure in sports cultures. Where a dominant sports culture is challenged by an emergent one, negotiated concessions can be made which modify but preserve the basis of privilege and dominance. In such ways can hegemony be sustained. When such a basis is marginalised, the previously dominant culture will often find ways of surviving in a residual form. Sport can encapsulate the contested and shifting dynamics of stratified societies, and can make some contribution towards challenging or reshaping those dynamics, but as a form of contemporary conspicuous consumption, sport has continued to be a major site for the explicit demonstration of difference framed by hierarchy, and of publicly expressed forms of social division.

Three primary dimensions of social stratification have been conceptualised by Turner (1988: 65–67): first, status as a legal-political phenomenon – a sense of entitlement based upon a principle of citizenship within a nation-state; second, the cultural dimension of lifestyle; and third, economically derived class position, referring to the individual's possession and effective control of economic resources. Turner argues that in a postmodern society – 'one in which, among other things, cultural styles become mixed, inter-woven and flexible, precluding any clear maintenance of hierarchical distinctions' (ibid.: 75) – social differentiation and social evaluation are not eroded, but are expressed in the possibility of 'more fluid cultural styles and the decline of conventional hierarchies' (ibid.: 76): 'The conventional hierarchies within the cultural system appear to be more fragmented and diversified than in any previous period' (ibid.: 77), producing 'an explosion of cultural signs and a cacophony of lifestyles' (ibid.: 78). In the sports cultures of Britain in the late 1990s and into the twenty-first century, some trends in sports participation seemed to bear this out. Relatively new, and individualistic, sports such as windsurfing, snowboarding and skateboarding appeared, on the surface, to be class-less and gender-less in comparison with more traditional sports. But research revealed that committed windsurfers were very much middle-class professionals, youths or young adults, able-bodied in their conspicuous consumption, and that – despite inroads by highly independent and competitively successful women – the windsurfing culture, for instance, was deeply masculinist (Wheaton and Tomlinson, 1998; Wheaton, 2004; Tomlinson et al., 2005). Also, it was clear by the end of the new century's first decade that fewer people are looking to commit to traditional team sports and clubs: 'New social practices', as Ravenscroft puts it, underlie contemporary forms of participation: 'It seems to be increasingly accepted that people are becoming more reluctant to join clubs and societies' (2004: 129).

The data generated by Sport England's Active People Survey (APS) from 2006 onwards (Sport England, 2006) has confirmed the stratified patterns of sport participation discussed in this chapter. Ethnic minorities play less, volunteer and organise less, and have fewer sporting role models than their white counterparts (Sporting Equals, 2007). In the APS5, covering 2010–2011, age was shown to be a major factor correlated to regular activity: 26.1 per cent of 16–34-year-olds participated in, on average, three sessions a week of exercise over the previous four weeks. The figure for 35–54-year-olds was 16.2 per cent, and for those aged 55 and over – arguably, those who stood to gain most from regular physical and sporting activity – a mere 7.7 per cent (1,126,800 people). Occupational status – and concomitant economic means – affected participation too: higher and lower managerial occupations, and intermediate occupations, managed to sustain and even increase their sporting commitments and participation. Men (20.5 per cent of the sample/population) participated more than did women (12.4 per cent) whose participation level was reported as declining compared to results from the survey in previous years (2007/8). People with a limiting disability/illness were, though, participating a little more in sports than in previous years. While some sports were reported to have slightly increased participation numbers – running/jogging, boxing, table tennis and mountaineering – 19 saw a decrease in participation rates between 2007/8 and the 12 months to October 2011: swimming, football, golf, badminton, tennis, equestrian, bowls, rugby union, basketball, snowsport, hockey, weightlifting, sailing, rugby league, gymnastics, rowing, volleyball, rounders, and judo (Sport England, 2012).

General statistics tell one story, and the APS narrative is one of sporting activity in decline. But why? It is hardly a surprise that sporting participation decreases at a time of global economic crisis and national recession, and extended qualitative research into the range of sports cultures in contemporary Britain would be likely to show that into the twenty-first century the classic sources of social stratification remain primary determinants of who was involved in what sports culture, and where and why they were involved in that particular way. The meanings of sports are not independent of the social setting, but are an indicator of the forces by which societies are stratified, often reproduced and sometimes changed.

ESSAY QUESTIONS

1   Discuss the ways in which sport participation statistics reflect the stratified nature of contemporary British society.
2   With reference to qualitative studies of sport culture, consider the ways whereby gender inequalities are reproduced through sport.
3   How can sport contribute to challenging prejudice and cultural stereotyping? Discuss with particular reference to issues of women's empowerment through sport, and black identity in sport.

EXERCISES

1   Consult data on sports participation for men and women in the Active People Survey, and earlier publications such as *Social Trends* and the *General Household Survey*, and list the possible causes of the different rates of participation recorded.
2   Interview one person under 25, and one person over 55, whom you know to be active in sport, and list their activity patterns at succeeding stages of their life-cycles. What influences have affected these patterns?
3   Make some notes on your own involvement in sport. Who do you play with? Where do you play? What do you have in common with those with whom you play? How, if at all, does sport contribute to your own male/female, black/white identity?

FURTHER READING

Journal of Sport and Social Issues, vol. 22, no. 2, August 1998, contains articles on ethnicity and gender, framed in terms of themes of social division, power, domination, resistance and empowerment.

M. Polley, *Moving the Goalposts: A History of Sport and Society Since 1945* (London: Routledge, 1998), covers the relationship of sport to gender, social class and ethnicity, in Chapters 4, 5 and 6 respectively.

CHAPTER FIVE

THE SOCIAL CONSTRUCTION OF IDENTITY AND CULTURAL REPRODUCTION

INTRODUCTION

The first four chapters have discussed the broad social and historical context within which sport has developed and the structural influences on current participation patterns. Structural analysis can sometimes be accused of 'reification' – ignoring the processes involved, the people or agents who attach meanings to, and have specific motivations for, their actions. Structural models – for example, Marxists using concepts like 'social reproduction' – suggest that the concept of socialisation is an overly functionalist and even out-dated notion. Yet as is clear from the work of Bourdieu (introduced in Chapter 4) who uses the concept of 'habitus' rather than 'socialisation' but refers to essentially the same phenomenon, structural social scientists recognise the need to be able to explain how and why people become involved, or not, in sport.

This chapter focuses on ways in which sporting affiliations and practices are developed through the life course, by an examination of some of the ways in which socialisation can be seen to take place in sport. Pivotal moments in socialisation processes have particular resonance in sport, for example, through education and through informal sporting practices, some of which can be seen to constitute resistance, such as the growth of subcultures and alternative sports.

This chapter also turns the spotlight on the processes by which people acquire an interest in (or a dislike for) sport. It looks at the development of human beings who do not have 'natures' or instincts for particular types of behaviour – some timeless or fixed set of behavioural characteristics (e.g. aggression, tenderness, nurturance, competitiveness) – but are people who acquire these characteristics through interaction with their social circumstances. The notion of socialisation focuses attention on the socio-cultural influences that shape human beings, their patterns of life and biographies. An individual's personal identity is still viewed as a cultural and structural product – the result of the influence of family, friends, educational, neighbourhood, legal and religious institutions and the mass media. In this chapter, our approach asks, from the point of view of those involved, what is going on in their participation in and involvement with sport?

Finally, this chapter considers the notion of identity and sport. Identity simply refers to a sense of who we are and how we are connected to the social order. It involves a psychological process of association between oneself and with something else, often someone else. In the past twenty years this concept has become more influential in sociological and cultural studies as it serves to link external, social, and internal, psychological, factors and processes and the complex interplay between them in the shaping of contemporary lifestyles (Watson, 2008: 140).

WHAT IS SOCIALISATION?

Socialisation is often defined as the process by which individuals learn to conform to social norms and learn how to behave in ways appropriate to their culture. From this approach the individual *internalises* these social norms and becomes committed to them and thus internalises the 'social rules' of behaviour. This happens because individuals want to gain acceptance and status from other people. An individual becomes socialised as they learn to act in a way that is in keeping with the expectations of others. In short, socialisation is the transmission of culture. Another approach talks about socialisation as a process of social learning and development that involves social *interaction* and *identity formation*. (Coakley and Pike, 2009: Chapter 4). Irrespective of approach, the major agencies within society that are involved in the socialisation of individuals are the family, the school and the mass media. These institutions can all influence an individual's socialisation in interacting and sometimes contradictory ways. We will look at the influence of these on sport experience shortly.

Clearly the process of socialisation begins early in life. A distinction has been drawn between primary socialisation and secondary socialisation to distinguish what happens to young children and what happens as people grow up and move through the life course. Primary socialisation is the first socialisation an individual undergoes in childhood and through which he or she becomes a member of society. Secondary socialisation refers to socialisation after childhood, and in interactionist theoretical approaches involves the consideration of careers in adult life.

Human infants spend much time undergoing primary socialisation in a family setting. During primary socialisation a child gains his or her conception of self or personal identity, and learns the rules and norms of society to which the child belongs. The sociological conception of socialisation therefore stresses the capacity of human beings to adapt to their environment through processes of learning. Ideas, attitudes and body movements associated with a given sport, for example, from the physical attributes, skills and techniques of coordination, agility, speed, power and stamina, through to the psychological aspects of play, sport and athleticism, all have to be socially acquired. Both the psychological disposition to play particular games and the mentality for competitive sport have to be learned.

As we have seen, French sociologist Pierre Bourdieu (1984), using the concept of habitus, has suggested that primary socialisation, via various social experiences prior to involvement in formal sport, can be seen as crucial for sports participation. Habitus refers to a set of acquired

patterns of thought, behaviour and taste. Continuing involvement in sport through adolescence and later adult life is, he believes, connected to the internalisation of specific manners, deportment and demeanours in childhood (Jarvie and Maguire, 1994: 183ff). The acquisition of particular tastes and dispositions for different sport and leisure activities in the family home is connected to differences in social class and gender habituses.

Ken Roberts and David Brodie (1992) carried out a study of involvement in sport in six inner city areas: Belfast, Camden, Cardiff, Chester, Glasgow, and Liverpool. They surveyed approximately 7000 users at sport centres and conducted panel discussions with participants and non-participants over a two-year period. They provide a useful comment that helps to illustrate the concepts of habitus and the importance of early socialisation in the acquisition of an interest in sport. They note that nearly everybody at some stage of their life is involved in physically active leisure when they are young. The question is often asked: why do some (the majority) drop out shortly afterwards while others persist? Research has often been carried out into the movement from youth to adulthood to try to find an answer. In fact, the answer lies in individuals' experiences in sport during childhood and youth. Roberts and Brodie argue that 'provided young people had been given secure foundations in sport, the chances were that they would continue into adulthood whatever happened in other life domains' (ibid.: 41). It was not the amount of sport played in childhood and adolescence that provided a 'secure foundation', however, but the number of different sports that respondents to their survey had become involved in. In short, early sport socialisation is a major determinant of people's participation in sport. If acquired early on in life, the propensity to be involved in some form of physical activity, although not always the same sport, is more likely to continue throughout the life course.

This propensity is not only related to social class, as the previous chapter outlined, but also gender. Iris Young (1980: 146–147) provides a useful illustration of gender differences in bodily experience:

> Women often approach a physical engagement with things with timidity, uncertainty, and hesitancy . . . Women tend not to put their whole bodies into engagement in a physical task with the same ease and naturalness as men . . . the whole body is not put into fluid and directed motion, but rather, the motion is concentrated in one body part . . . The woman's motion tends not to reach, extend, lean, stretch, and follow through in the direction of her intention . . . We often experience our bodies as fragile encumbrances, rather than the media for the enactment of our aims.

That this gendered experience of the body is a result of socialisation and not part of natural difference can be illustrated by reference to anthropological research. We will look at this below.

Both the existence of culture and the process of socialisation are distinctive features of human society. The large variations in social life that anthropologists have shown suggest that 'human nature' is highly variable. In language, dress, values and beliefs and in patterns of acceptable and unacceptable behaviour, human beings have been shown to exhibit great plasticity. Even in the area of such apparently 'natural' behaviour as sex roles, the division of the human group into males and females, it is clear that cultural definitions of behaviour are vital.

Socialisation is therefore above all a learning process. Human beings are not born to be competitive or co-operative, aggressive or passive, naturally 'good' or 'bad', but behave as they do because of culture. Whatever biology predisposes human beings to be and to do, it is only through socialisation that they become part of their social group and culture. The norms and values that constitute the 'rules' of a social group are therefore culturally specific, that is, different cultures educate and socialise their children differently. A fascinating example of this in sport is the case of the taketak game played by the Tangu tribe of New Guinea (Leonard, 1984: 76):

> The dominant social value among the Tangu is equivalence. The idea of defeating opponents through competition disturbs them, since they believe it fosters ill-will and contempt among the participants. Hence although taketak is a team sport – a game resembling bowling in which teams take turns to bowl a dried fruit at a number of coconut stakes – the aim of the game is not to knock over as many stakes as possible, but for both teams to remove the same number of stakes. Winning is completely irrelevant.

Compare this with Britain and the USA where 'win–loss' tables are vital ingredients of the most popular team sports. Increasingly draws are resolved through 'sudden-death' playoffs or penalty kicks. The axiom, attributed to Vince Lombardi, that 'winning isn't everything, it's the only thing', increasingly reigns supreme. Although there are similarities between the USA and the UK, it is hard to imagine the sports press in the States getting as worked up over a drawn cricket match as British journalists still can.

Socialisation into sport thus involves someone's abilities, characteristics and resources. It also involves the influence of significant others and the availability of opportunities that are attractive to individuals. From this emerges a commitment to participate or be involved in or with sport. Studies of involvement in sport suggest that processes involved include growing association with a sport of physical activity, exhibiting knowledge and how to think about a sport as well as being accepted by others engaged in the practice (Donnelly and Young, 1988; Wheaton, 2004).

Not only are there cultural differences in the meaning of sport and recreation between different societies, there are important differences in the meaning of sport within single societies. It is important to account for the fact that although everyone undergoes socialisation, not everyone undergoes the same socialisation experiences. Indeed, this is what makes people 'individual', according to one theoretical model. As we saw in Chapter 4, there are certain social forces and relationships – most notably social class, gender and ethnicity – that have a reality *sui generis* (literally, in their own right) that affects socialisation. Hence according to social class, gender and ethnic group, people will have different 'ways of seeing' the same event, situation or object. It is useful to examine gender socialisation as an illustration of these ideas.

GENDER SOCIALISATION

In 1935, the anthropologist Margaret Mead published *Sex and Temperament in Three Primitive Societies*. Based on fieldwork conducted in New Guinea, it revealed considerable variability in the behaviour patterns of men and women in three tribes living within a hundred miles of one another. Among the Arapesh tribe, both men and women exhibited characteristics associated in the West with femininity – non-aggressivity, gentleness and passivity. In the Mundugamor (formerly headhunters), both sexes were assertive and very aggressive – traits typically associated with masculinity in the West. Finally, among the Tchambuli tribe, a 'role reversal' was apparent – males appeared to take on feminine qualities and females those of masculinity in the West: 'the men act according to our stereotype for women – are catty, wear curls and go shopping, while the women are energetic, managerial, unadorned partners' (Mead, 1977: ix). Each society had its own 'natural' behaviour patterns, which were in fact products of culture.

Undoubtedly the family continues to play an important role in the gender socialisation process. Research has shown that male and female babies are dressed in different colours, given different toys to play with and treated differently (Bellotti, 1975). Boys are not expected to cry, girls are praised for their appearance. Institutions outside the family contribute to this process through, for example, the different language used to describe the behaviour of boys and girls (Stanworth, 1980). If a child is quiet or withdrawn, a girl will be described as 'shy', while a boy is a 'strong silent type'; if a child shows emotion freely, girls are 'oversensitive' while boys are 'wet', 'cry-babies' or 'softies'; a girl who takes the initiative can be 'bossy' while a boy is seen as a 'born leader', and so on.

The writer and broadcaster Garrison Keillor offers another illustration of these processes:

> Girls had it better from the beginning, don't kid yourself. They were allowed to play in the house, where the books were and the adults, and boys were sent outdoors like livestock. Boys were noisy and rough, and girls were nice, so they got to stay and we had to go. Boys ran around in the yard with toy guns going kksshh-kksshh, fighting wars for made-up reasons and arguing about who was dead, while girls stayed inside and played with dolls, creating complex family groups and learning to solve problems through negotiation and role-playing. Which gender is better equipped, on the whole, to live an adult life, would you guess?

> (1994: 12)

An important influence on the behaviour of boys and girls are their adult carers – usually biological or social parents. Studies have shown the importance of adult/parental interaction with a child on their development. Adults and parents act differently when they know the sex of a child – they are more likely to prevent a boy from crying; encourage girls to smile; allow boys to crawl more and go further than baby girls; boys are treated 'rougher' especially by their fathers, while girls are very soon taught about 'appearance'. Girls are protected more, and given less encouragement, generally, than boys. The implications of these different responses in terms of male and female physicality and emotional displays can be seen at an early age. By the time they are 3 or 4 years old, girls and boys start drawing conclusions about who they are and what the world is like – the formation of 'self'. Experience of parents and family life in general help to shape some of our most important conceptions of self (Coakley, 1994: 233).

The school is another major agency of socialisation (Byrne, 1983). It has both a formal curriculum and an informal 'hidden' curriculum that helps to reproduce the gender order. While overt differentiation on the basis of gender is only rarely practised today, boys and girls are encouraged to take different subjects through more subtle methods, through clashes on the timetable, for example. Even if there appears to be an open choice, it takes considerable determination for a boy or girl to opt for a subject that is not considered suitable for their gender. Boys and girls are expected to behave in different ways (Stanworth, 1980).

In physical education and sport, a form of 'aversive socialisation' occurs for girls and young women – sport is tied up with, and more complementary to, emerging male sexuality and gender identity than female sexuality and identity. For young women, it is as if a choice has to be made between female identity and sports involvement (Scraton, 1987; 1992). This is not the case for most young boys, although of course not all boys play and enjoy sports to the same extent, and some girls excel in them (Connell, 1983; 1987; 1995). For girls, however, as they grow up, the stakes of staying in sport are far greater. Participation in sport and organised physical activity is associated positively with masculinity and sexual identity and boys respond to this accordingly. The opposite still remains largely true for girls. Not only do girls risk being considered unfeminine if they remain involved in demanding sports and physical activity into adolescence, but they also risk their sexuality being questioned.

The mass media enhance these differences and play an important role in reinforcing socially acceptable norms and values. On television it has been suggested that women are under-represented in action drama series, and when they do appear they are featured in a narrow range of roles – 'the virgin, the madonna or the whore'. Women are more often shown in domestic settings than in paid work and usually shown as incompetent in anything other than domestic roles. Women, far more often than men, are the helpless victims of violence, and are usually rescued by men. It is with some justification that Gaye Tuchman (1978) suggests television performs the 'symbolic annihilation of women'!

The reinforcement of sex-role socialisation through television portrayals of women (and men) is important because of its potential impact upon young children. Research has shown that heavy television viewing is associated with extreme stereotyping of sex roles among boys and girls (Gunter, 1986). Sex role stereotyping occurs in other media beside television, notably in reading material directed at young children and adolescents. Studies have shown the male dominance of many preschool and early school reading books. Girls or female characters are often shown as passive and housebound, while boys and male characters are more often seen outdoors and involved in exciting adventures. Comics aimed at young children also play a part in the socialisation process. Many of them are linked specifically to a particular product or television programme (see Dixon, 1977a; 1977b; 1990).

In comics for older age groups, the differences between male and female interests has often been accentuated even further (Dunne, 1982). Most boys' comics still feature action-packed adventures, where soldiers or football players lead active and dangerous lives (Tomlinson, 1995). Comics for girls have undergone a change. While they were full of romantic love stories in the 1970s, it was suggested that in the 1980s the almost exclusive concentration on romance and dependency on boys was replaced by a new focus. The practices and rituals of femininity portrayed in the magazines for adolescent girls were presented as being on behalf of the development of a more independent self, not with the singular aim of attracting a 'fella' (McRobbie, 1991: 183; see also Philips, 1995; Whannel, 1995). In the 1990s it appeared that both emphases could be found in teenage magazines. Regular articles featuring sport and physical activity involving girls are still not as commonplace as those featuring boys and young men.

In their classic study *The Femininity Game*, Boslooper and Hayes (1973) argued that the predominant idea in the USA in the 1960s and early 1970s was that 'feminine' women were not supposed to take any form of strenuous physical activity. Despite the changes that have been taking place throughout the Western world since then, it is not difficult still to find examples of the sort Boslooper and Hayes cited. The mass media provide stereotypes of what type of body image is beautiful and sexually attractive for males and females. The 'ideal' male shape is mesomorphic (muscular) and the 'ideal' female is ectomorphic (lean).

Phrases such as 'unfeminine' and 'butch' are flung at strong and competitive women, whereas these attributes serve to mark out the 'real men' from the boys in the school playground and elsewhere. Physical education in school tends to reinforce these cultural stereotypes of body image ideals (Scraton, 1992). The mass media often present female athletes in terms of their sexuality, physical attractiveness, etc. while this is rarely, if ever, done for male athletes. Female athletes still face either trivialisation or exclusion from the mass media (Sabo and Jansen, 1992; see also Hargreaves, 1994, on the 'sexualisation' of female athletes). Boslooper and Hayes's (1973: 45) comment with regard to the USA in the 1970s is still applicable to the UK today: 'American society cuts the penis off the male who enters dance . . . and places it on the woman who participates in competitive athletics.'

The physical body holds social meaning. It is not a natural thing, purely physical, but a part of culture. Physical sex differences become cultural – they are used, modified, reinforced and accentuated as part of cultural beliefs about the real and the ideal attributes of men and women. Culture projects certain images and influences ideas about gender difference.

Recognising the central importance of socialisation to the construction of culture enables the sports sociologist to pierce through these cultural preconceptions. Gender is a cultural construct and therefore subject to change and variability. Yet it is important to realise that although the mass media do reproduce gender stereotypes, readers and viewers are not simply passive recipients of media messages. It is a mistake to think that people simply absorb media messages uncritically and reproduce what they are told. Not all the girls who read *Jackie* in the 1970s and 1980s, or its equivalent in the 1990s, passively absorbed the idea that their one aim in life was to 'catch a man' (Fraser, 1987). While the television programme, newspaper, comic or magazine may have a preferred reading, some people may read them in different, more critical, ways. Media messages are part of the process of socialisation, but so too is the active involvement of people.

While much research into socialisation has focused upon primary socialisation – in which it is held that the basic values and knowledge essential for living in a social community are acquired by infants and young children – it is now widely recognised that socialisation is a lifelong process. Throughout the life course and especially in the socialisation of children, there are strong prescriptions against acting in ways appropriate to the other sex. Recognition of the importance of secondary socialisation agencies and experiences, socialisation after childhood and processes of social development in adult life, is largely the product of an alternative approach to socialisation.

SPORT AND CHARACTER BUILDING

Undoubtedly one of the foremost expressions of the relationship between sport and social-isation is the idea of an association between a healthy body and a healthy mind. This goes back at least to the English public schools of the mid-nineteenth century (see Chapter 1). Since then, there has been a widely held belief in the advanced capitalist countries – such as Britain, the USA and Canada – about the effectiveness of sport in dealing with various perceived 'social problems', such as the prevention of crime and delinquency among adolescent boys and young adult males. '*Mens sana in corpore sano*' – the notion that sport was character building – was conveyed through the English public school system and 'athleticism' became a key attribute of 'the proper Christian Gentleman' during the last century. The belief that sport produces disciplined, responsible and self-reliant men has been sustained throughout the twentieth century by being incorporated into the basic principles of physical education in both state and public schooling and on occasion being re-emphasised by leading industrialists, police chiefs, members of the armed forces, politicians of all political persuasions and other members of the 'establishment'. Prince Philip, the Duke of Edinburgh, a forthright advocate of the character building qualities of sport and former President of the Central Council for Physical Recreation (CCPR), set up his award scheme in the mid-1950s following his expe-riences as a pupil under the physical fitness and training regime established by Kurt Hahn at the exclusive public school Gordonstoun, in Scotland.

A number of official inquiries set up at the end of the 1950s to look into the 'problem of youth' in Britain voiced concerns about the state of sport and physical activity in Britain. The

Wolfenden Report on Sport and the Community (1960) included a concern for how potentially troublesome groups of youth spent their leisure. Their findings, or rather assertions, about the preventive properties of sport and other constructive forms of recreation did much to shape subsequent policy. The Wolfenden Report (1960: 2) noted that: 'It is widely held that a considerable proportion of delinquency among young people stems from a lack of desire for suitable physical activity.' A little further on, it continued:

> [Although we] are not suggesting it [i.e. criminal behaviour] . . . would disappear if there were more tennis courts and running tracks . . . at the same time it is a reasonable assumption that if more young people have opportunities for playing games, fewer of them would develop criminal habits.

Speaking in the 1980s, when there had been several successive years of inner city disturbances involving young people, the chairman of the CCPR pronounced:

> We want people, young people particularly, off the street corners, getting them away from frightening old ladies and breaking windows, and getting them into sports areas where they can participate at their own level, have fun, enjoy themselves and really feel that they are part of something that is totally enjoyable and that is being a Briton and enjoying life in Britain.
>
> (Peter Lawson, speaking on BBC Radio 4 programme,
> *Children and Sport*, March 1986)

In their study of sport in a divided Ireland, Sugden and Bairner (1993: 1) suggest that the British Government, from the 1960s onwards, sought to exert a greater degree of influence over sport in Northern Ireland than anywhere else in the British Isles out of the recognition that sport can play an influential part in an individual's political socialisation. The justification for the inclusion of physical education and games in the school curriculum has largely been based upon their supposed 'efficacy as agents of socialisation' (Stevenson, 1975: 287). An emphasis upon the instrumental rationale for sport provision pervades the growth of state intervention in sport in Britain (see Chapter 8). Iain Sproat, as Conservative Minister at the Department of National Heritage responsible for sport in the mid-1990s, clearly believed that team sport might solve many of the country's problems. 'If we had more organised team games in schools', he told a meeting of sports writers in 1994, 'we'd have fewer little thugs like those who murdered James Bulger' (quoted in the *Guardian*, 1 March 1994, p. 2).

How accurate is it to believe that there is a strong relationship between involvement in sport and PE and the development of good character? While this connection is still widely held to exist, the relationship between physical activity and mental health, and the impact of exercise on psychological well-being, is not so straightforwardly a positive one. The remarkable thing is that while the validity of these beliefs has been taken for granted and routinely espoused by those associated with organised competitive sports, it was not until the 1950s that people actually began to use research to subject the belief to a systematic examination (Lee, 1986). A textbook on psychology in sport concludes that psychological-based research suggests that physical activity can only promote mental health if 'exercise is kept within certain limits and when the reasons why people exercise are intrinsically healthy to begin with' (Kremer and Scully, 1994: 15).

David Robins (1990) reviewed the research literature into this question from a sociological and criminological viewpoint. He found some research in the USA pointed to a positive relationship between sports participation and less delinquency. But another author in a major review of fifty studies on socialisation and sport carried out in North America could only conclude that 'to date there is no valid evidence that participation in sport causes any verifiable socialisation effects' (Stevenson, 1975). A piece of work carried out for the Scottish Sports Council concluded that it was not possible to say definitely 'that the correlation of high level of sports participation/low frequency of delinquency holds good in the UK' (Coalter, 1987: 2).

Robins (1990: 2) concluded that:

> It is an open question whether participation in sports or the provision of sports facilities have any effect on levels of delinquent behaviour at all, or whether perceived associations can be accounted for in other ways.

He continued:

> A research project which sought to examine and control for all possible aspects of the relationship between participation in sports programmes and delinquency is theoretically possible, but it would necessarily be extremely complex and expensive, requiring a large sample and longitudinal design.

Possibly the best that can be said with certainty from British-based research is that sports participation does not make things much worse. There is research in the USA, however, that provides reason to doubt even this rather weak conclusion. A study by Hughes and Coakley (1991) suggests that sport programmes can create a tendency for over-conformity and what they call 'positive deviance' which can be as socially dysfunctional as other forms of antisocial behaviour that sport programmes are usually set up to try and deter. 'Positive deviance' is one way of explaining cheating, the pursuit of gaining an unfair advantage, through, for example, the use of performance-enhancing drugs and other substances. Sports participants become so involved in the desire to achieve and win through competition (the 'sport ethic') that they are prepared to break the spirit of play in order to succeed.

understanding sport

SOCIALISATION, IDENTITIES AND SPORT: AN OVERVIEW OF RESEARCH TRADITIONS

It is an axiomatic assumption of both academic and political discourses on sport that it has effects on identities, both collective and individual. This assumption underpins the three main approaches relating sport, socialisation and the construction of identities that have developed in the sociology of sport. The dominant view until the late 1970s – *socialisation-as-internalisation* – assumed that people were relatively *passive* recipients of information and social influences. An alternative approach (*socialisation-as-interaction*) was based upon a different model of the human actor. People were conceived of as more *active and interactive*, interdependent with others. Following the so-called 'cultural turn' in the 1990s, the notion of socialisation has been challenged and replaced by a focus on identity, formed through the process of *identification* via language, discourse and power. The focus on identity questions the coherence and stability of subject formation and pluralises the sources of social power. In the following section these discourses on the relationship between sport and socialisation will each be critically explored as historically rooted and thus contestable.

All social scientists recognise the need to be able to explain how and why people become involved in society, as the following quotations demonstrate:

> Socialization is a complex developmental learning process that teaches the knowledge, values, and norms essential to participation in social life.
>
> (McPherson *et al.*, 1989: 37)

> Socialization is a theory concerning how individuals grow and learn into becoming full members of society. Clearly any such theory presupposes a firm grasp of what society is like and it supposes that individuals are brought into that reality whatever their level of activity.
>
> (Jenks, 1998: 274)

The notion of *socialisation* focuses attention on the *socio-cultural*, and therefore *temporal* and *spatial*, influences that shape human beings, their patterns of life and biographies. Next we identify the main perspectives in the shift among social scientists of sport from an 'over-socialised' conception of human beings to more dynamic models of socialisation into and through sport. At the outset three features of these research perspectives are particularly worth commenting on. First is that, while they draw upon translations of European theorists, they are primarily Anglo-American. This might be seen as a shortcoming or a consequence of the global dominance of Anglo-American social science. Second, they do not all take into account the social, cultural and economic transformations that sport has undergone in the past thirty or forty years with equal emphasis. We argue that the meanings and context of sport are centrally important in asking questions about sport's effects. Third, we consider that the three approaches exhibit different ways in which difficult questions about the relationship between agency and structure have been *avoided* in social theory. We suggest that the attempt to comprehend this relationship by Pierre Bourdieu offers a fourth, and possibly more fruitful, approach to understanding sport and socialisation (see Figure 5.1).

Socialisation as internalisation

Key concepts	social role, system
Key theory	functionalist
Key feature	socially deterministic
Image of actor	individual receives Society's messages; a 'scripted actor'; passivity; over-socialised conception of 'man'
Sport interest	technical-instrumental outcomes; behavioural

Socialisation as interaction

Key concept	self-identity
Key theory	interactionist
Key feature	anti-deterministic
Image of actor	individual interprets and responds to Society's messages; individual as 'active' or creative; a 'role-taker'
Sport interest	practical experiences/redistribution; incorporation/resistance

Social construction of identities

Key concepts	subject, discourse
Key theory	post-structuralist
Key feature	anti-essentialist, socially indeterminate
Image of actor	instituted through difference; performative; contradictory, changing and multiple identifications; importance of social and historical context
Sport interest	experiences/recognition; spectacle/performance

Social construction of habitus

Key concepts	habitus, field, cultural capital
Key theory	practice
Key feature	dualism
Image of actor	habitus sets parameters *and* enables individuals to be creative; resources drawn upon can limit potential; importance of social and historical context
Sport interest	sport as relatively autonomous field; sport as space of body practices/sport as spectacle

Figure 5.1 Four approaches to socialisation and the social construction of identity

understanding sport

SOCIALISATION THROUGH SPORT: AN OVERVIEW OF THE FUNCTIONALIST APPROACH

Who plays sport and what happens to them? What processes are involved in becoming and staying involved in sport? What happens to people by being involved in sport? The following extract from Coakley's overview of the field indicates the sort of issues traditionally investigated:

> Early research on socialization and sport was typically grounded in widespread concerns about who participated in sports, how they became involved, why they participated, and how they were changed by participation. Those who asked these questions were often associated with organised sports programs, and they usually had vested interests in recruiting new participants into their programs and promoting programs by linking participation in them to positive developmental outcomes . . . Researchers were also interested in discovering whether . . . participation in sports builds character and shapes people in positive ways.
>
> (Coakley, 1993: 169)

This, the dominant view until the late 1970s, which Coakley calls *socialisation-as-internalisation*, was based on a model of the human actor as a *tabula rasa* or blank slate, upon which society writes 'its' messages. The assumption was that people were relatively *passive* recipients of information and social influences. Human beings were passive learners, 'socialised into, out of, and through sport' (ibid.: 191).

Between 1950 and 1980 many studies tested hypotheses based upon a variety of popular beliefs held about the social developmental consequences of sport participation, such as:

- the development of positive character traits;
- producing better academic attainment in young people;
- promoting conformity and reducing delinquency rates;
- establishing strong achievement orientations and moral development.

The focus of most of the research was normally on children and young people, rather than adults, which reflected the assumption that adults were no longer in a formative stage of development and that adult lives were so complex that the effects of sports participation were minimal compared to the socialisation effects of other experiences.

Research into the issue of socialisation through sport dropped off during the 1970s and Stevenson suggested that this was for two main reasons. First, there was a long record of inconsistent findings, and most studies found little or no significant socialisation effects of sports participation. Second, research priorities shifted to focus on how to promote sports involvement, especially among young people with the potential to become top-class athletes (Stevenson, 1985; see also McCormack and Chalip, 1988).

INTERACTIONIST APPROACHES TO SOCIALISATION

An alternative approach to socialisation and sport (*interaction-as-interaction*) was based upon a different model of the human actor. People were conceived of as more *active and interactive*, interdependent with others. Socialisation occurs through interaction between active and creative agents. *Interactionist* studies of sport socialisation looked at the social construction of *identity*, the *dynamics* of participation decisions and the social *meanings* underlying sport participation. Sport participation was not conceived of as a 'once and for all' type of experience to be explained through traditional quantitative survey methods. Instead this approach viewed initial participation and continued participation in sport as just as 'problematic' (i.e. in need of explanation and investigation) as 'non-participation' and 'dropping out'.

Interactionist approaches to socialisation in sport involve four central assumptions:

1   Becoming involved in sport involves a *process of identity construction and confirmation*. Identity formation related to sports participation occurs over time and depends upon a number of processes, including the acquisition of knowledge about a sport, being associated with a sport group, learning the values and perspectives of the sport group, and earning the acceptance of those in the group so that one's identity as a participant is affirmed and reaffirmed over time. Donnelly and Young (1988) provide a good example of these processes in their study of climbing and rugby football sub-cultures.

2   The process of becoming involved in sport among elite athletes is initiated through a process of recruitment in which first-time participation experiences are supported, coerced or subverted by people who are important in the athletes' lives. Involvement in sport is never established in any final sense (Stevenson, 1990).

3   Decisions about participation in sport by young people were often linked to considerations of the implications of these decisions for the opportunities it gave them for further extending control over their lives, for becoming adults, and for developing and displaying personal competence. Gender and socio-economic status were directly related to the control young people had or perceived they had over their lives. The problematic nature of the decision to participate or not to participate in sport schemes, for example, and whether to maintain participation thereafter, was considered by White and Coakley (1986; and Coakley and White, 1992) in their study of sport participation patterns among 60 adolescents in south-east England.

4   Interactionist approaches to socialisation emphasise the extent to which individuals and groups *create and negotiate* their involvement in sport. Socialisation is not the primary focus of research: instead it is the struggle associated with the determination of what sport will mean in the lives of particular groups or categories of people. The focus is upon the *dialectic of control* and *power relations*. This approach suggests that the connections between patterns of individual involvement and participation in sport and leisure and wider relations of cultural reproduction, subordination and oppression are more clearly linked through the notion of sport and leisure sub-cultures (see Donnelly, 1985).

As Jeff Bishop and Paul Hoggett (1986: 43–44) suggest:

> Sub-cultures can . . . be seen to occupy an intermediate position between the individual or club engaged in a leisure activity and the wider social order. Sub-cultures are often very active elements, deliberately negotiating and restructuring this intermediate position . . . leisure sub-cultures are an aspect of society's internal social organisation which is actually thriving and constitutes a crucial vehicle through which dominant values are transmitted, resisted or negotiated and new sets of values, which may take as their point of origin a different mode of production and social organisation, emerge. In particular, collective leisure offers opportunities rare – if not unique – in our society to reassert values related not to passive consumerism but to production for one's own use and enjoyment.

Interactionist approaches to socialisation suggest that sport participants encounter a wide variety of experiences. The meaning of sport participation – and the values thereby encountered – make sense only in the context of the experiences and social relationships of those involved. Hence for some participants, sport builds character, for others, it does not. There is no single response to sport participation – sport is not a carrier of one single message or set of messages; nor are participants recipients in a deterministic fashion of a single message. Hence, 'Sport has as great a capacity for producing bullies and thugs as it has good citizens and saints' (Professor John Evans, quoted in the *Guardian*, 1 March 1994, cited in Horne et al., 1999: 154).

Interactionist approaches to socialisation focused on: the process of identity development through sport participation; the ways in which sport is connected to the production and reproduction of knowledge, meaning, social practices and power relations at personal, cultural and structural levels; and used interpretive methods of social analysis to carry out research – collecting data (usually 'talk') through in-depth interviews and/or detailed observations, case studies and ethnographies (Coakley and Donnelly, 1999). For this tradition of analysis, sports participation is a social process that has emergent qualities that reflect the interests of those involved and the context in which it occurs.

THE SOCIAL CONSTRUCTION OF IDENTITY THROUGH SPORT

The focus on the construction of identity that has emerged in sociology in the past twenty-five years also views identity as an ongoing project. However, previously, the self was either considered as 'a fully centred, unified individual, endowed with the capacities of reason, consciousness and action' or someone 'formed in relation to "significant others"' though interaction between self and society. Now the subject, rather than 'having a unified and stable identity, is becoming fragmented; composed not of a single, but of several, sometimes contradictory or unresolved identities'. This is what Stuart Hall called 'the post-modern subject' in which identity becomes more of a '"moveable feast": formed and transformed continuously in relation to the ways we are represented or addressed in the cultural systems which surround us' (Hall, 1992: 275–276). Identities are constructed through language, discourse and cultural texts, but questions remain about how, from what, by whom, and for what purposes?

That identities can be constituted through involvement in sport and leisure is the basic assumption of this third approach to socialisation which is often referred to as post-structuralist. For post-structuralists, socialisation cannot produce monocultural citizens or subjects. Gender, ethnicity, sexuality as well as class differences shape identities. At the same time the identity categories used in previous research are considered to be unacceptable abstractions. Post-structuralists replace a notion of class primacy with a conception of social power related to identity, language and culture. Discourse, governance and the formation of subjectivities through governmentality reveal the influence of Michel Foucault (see Chapter 9 for more information on governance and this related concept).

Attention focuses on identity and the plural repertoires of identities, created through difference. Personal identities and collective or group identities – shaped through imaginative involvement with imagined communities – are marked by fluidity and not fixity. Globalisation stimulates the further destabilising of identities, while also creating the conditions for conflicts between traditional, fundamentalist identities and novel (what Hall calls postmodern) multiple identities. The emphasis on treating socialisation as an active process moves attention away from the constraints imposed by social contexts on to an interest in the control people try to exercise on the circumstances under which they live. Social change creates new possibilities and expectations of people but also new uncertainties and potential insecurities.

The emphasis on choice and negotiation in the establishment of identity is in marked contrast to the first two approaches, but also creates the basis for several criticisms of the approach. First, the focus on discourses, culture and identity draws attention away from class and material social inequalities that continue to shape people's lives. Second, the concept of agency is confused with identity, rather than being seen as a modality of social life. This means that material and structural conditions (including social class) that influence the formation of identity are not seen as central to agency. Third, post-structuralists argue that it is no longer relevant to seek the truth, or a single explanation for an issue. Critics suggest that knowledge is not simply a weapon in power games, but the search for truth, understanding and explanations of life circumstances is a central task for social scientists. This may seem a long way from explaining why, for example, the authors of this book have supported, and therefore identified with, Burnley, Chelsea, Fulham and Sheffield Wednesday football clubs during their lifetimes. But it does remind us that identification can outlast changes in social circumstances.

SPORT, GLOBALISATION AND HABITUS

The previous outline has remarked upon a shift in approach to the relationship between sport and the formation of human beings as members of society. The shift broadly follows that also to be found in studies of mass media audiences – from what sport does to people to what people do with sport. In addition, like the study of media audiences, there has been a third development emphasising the greater involvement (agency) of people in constructing their involvement. The three previous approaches can be characterised as focusing on internalisation, interaction and identification.

While there are obviously several alternative theoretical approaches in sociology of sport, and it is not our intention to argue specifically for one or other of these here, we do consider that the ideas of some other social theorists remain underdeveloped in terms of understanding sport as practice and sport as spectacle in the contemporary hyper-commodified world of disorganised, global capitalism. Here we briefly mention Pierre Bourdieu's contribution, and in particular his conception of the 'habitus' as an organising principle of social structure.

According to Richard Giulianotti, Bourdieu, who died in January 2002, wrote about sport to examine 'behind-the-scenes factors of socialisation and social differentiation that instil different sporting tastes' (Giulianotti, 2005: 152). Habitus, which Bourdieu also referred to as structurising structure, comprises an individual's preferences, dispositions, inclinations and perspectives. The concept enables Bourdieu (to claim) to bridge the gap between structuralist and social interactionist theories. As an internalised system of unconsciously held patterns of behaviour, the habitus generates behaviour, taste, perceptions, and convictions. For Bourdieu, the habitus of different social classes is revealed through sport and other cultural pursuits (Bourdieu, 1984). His ideas underpin subsequent research into sport and cultural activity in other parts of the world including Australia and the United Kingdom (Bennett *et al.*, 1999; Bennett *et al.*, 2009). One specific example of the use of this idea in sport research can be found in David Howe's study of Pontypridd RFC, a professional rugby club in Wales (Howe, 1999, 2001). Howe argues that the habitus of the (male) players was transformed as the club's relationship to commercial enterprise altered. Pressure to perform for the team heightened and this meant, for example, that an injury might be treated differently depending on the hold a player had on their position in the team.

Bourdieu held a view of society that rejected the objectified notion of social classes opposing each other in their struggle for dominance. Instead for him, the social world is conceptualised as a multi-dimensional social space rooted in various patterns of differentiation and distribution. Social space is structured according to the specific distribution of different forms of capital, which can be of material as well as of symbolic quality. Cultural capital, which depends to a great degree on upbringing and schooling, and social capital, which is based on the usage of institutionalised social networks, can be transferred into economic capital, which is also convertible to other forms of symbolic capital. Thus, the specific value of a form of capital is determined by its assessment in relation to alternative variants within a social field. These are largely autonomous realms in which and between which struggle and contestation over resources take place. The acquisition of capital, and the position of an individual within a field, are directly linked with the habitus, or the individual's embodied social history. This is particularly of relevance when thinking about choice and action in a contemporary context where common-sense ideas about life and society, the social order and even the global system have fallen prey to the rhetoric of neoliberalist globalisation.

Bourdieu (1978; 1990) suggested it was useful to think about the practice and consumption of sport as a form of supply that meets a specific social demand. Such an assessment necessitated, first of all, conceiving of the production of sport as an autonomous field with its own logic and distinctive history, and, second, to think about the social conditions that enable members of society to acquire these sports products. Transformations of the supply side depend on the relation between the kinds of sports, new entries and technologically altered products; on the demand side, sport preferences are embedded into the habitus and thus subjugated to broader transformations of society. While Loïc Wacquant (1995; 2007) has used such ideas in his research into boxing, Bourdieu's influence has been greatest in the French sociology of sport where studies of combat sport, gymnastics and team sports all have been carried out using his concepts (see Defrance, 1995).

Globalisation impacts on both the supply of, and demand for, sport. The contestation of sport games has come to be challenged, if not dominated, by certain sports, such as association football, in social fields which are no longer exclusively based on their locally distinguishable past. The recognition that the global has to be local somewhere has improved research in sport since the 1990s as it promotes detailed empirical case studies of sport in specific social and cultural contexts. Like Bourdieu, however, we would not want such studies to be read in a particularised manner, but rather in terms of the general analytical and structural features that they draw attention to. The aim is to explore the dialectics of particularism and universalism further in order to investigate 'the particularities of different *collective histories*' (Bourdieu, 2000). As one of us wrote a few years ago:

> Sport cultures and practices have continued to be shaped by human agents drawing on their various reserves of different types of capital, in the construction of class and gender-influenced habituses that have characterised the field of sporting practices.
>
> (Tomlinson, 2004: 171)

CONCLUSION

The basic message of this chapter (and the book as a whole) is that sport matters differently at different times and in different places for different groups of people. The overall social significance of sport is conjunctural. Similarly, different interests underpin different conceptions of socialisation and sport (Habermas, 1972). A focus on outcomes is related to a technical-instrumental approach to sport, a focus on experiences tends to be interested in practical engagements in sport, including but not necessarily implying the socially redistributive potential of sport, while concern for the social construction of identities in and through sport has implicit emancipatory interests based on a politics of recognition. Socialisation into sport and its relationship to sport should therefore be understood as an historically rooted, contradictory

84

and political process, with different meanings according to time, place, and social location. Socialisation may have given way to discussions of identity in sociology, but the attempt is still made to relate sport to formations of persons, selves and cultures.

The impact of sport on people's lives is increasingly studied through the voices of sports participants, subcultures of sport and alternative sports and physical activities (for example, see Young *et al.*, 1994; Fleming, 1995; Wheaton, 2004). There has been a shift in research orientation from seeing sport as a *cause* of specific socialisation outcomes, to seeing sport more as a *site* for socialisation and identity formation (and reformation) experiences (Coakley and Pike, 2009: 119). Sport – understood as either spectacle or practice – has become more of an integral part of the economies of signs and space of late capitalist modernity in the past twenty years, but it has not always been so. But sport does not straightforwardly cause changes in character, attitudes or outcomes. Rather it provides a social site or space for social processes through which certain socialisation outcomes may occur. Hence attention to specific social and cultural contexts is essential for the clarification of claims made about sports' effects on individuals, communities or societies (Horne, 2006).

ESSAY QUESTIONS

1 'Sport has as great a capacity for producing bullies and thugs as it has good citizens and saints' (Professor John Evans, quoted in the *Guardian*, 1 March 1994). Discuss.
2 British identity is in decline in England and Scotland, as a result of devolution. What might be the consequences for sport?

EXERCISES

1 Debate the proposition that: 'The culture of masculinity can be, and should be, addressed as a sport policy issue.'
2 The Nobel Prize-winning novelist and philosopher Albert Camus famously noted that all he learned about life, he learned on the football field (he played in goal). Have you learned any lessons in this way, and in what ways has competitive sport prepared you for life? Compare with a partner.

FURTHER READING

J. Coakley and E. Pike, *Sports in Society* (Maidenhead: McGraw-Hill, 2009), Chapters 4 and 5 synthesise vast amounts of evidence, from British work as well as US research on socialisation and young people and sport.

P. Donnelly and J. Coakley (eds) *Inside Sports* (London: Routledge, 1999) remains an excellent collection of accounts, discussions and interpretations of identity, experience and interactions within sports cultures.

CHAPTER SIX

SPORT AND REPRESENTATION

INTRODUCTION

We commence this chapter with an example that encapsulates many of the issues for any analysis of sport representation – stardom and celebrity, national identity, race, class, gender, risk and the body. In 2010, Nike distributed a 3-minute advertisement called *Write the Future*. According to the web video analytic company, Visible Measures, it proved to be one of the most successful viral ads ever, achieving a new record of 7.8 million views in its first week. The advertisement features very fast cutting, and although the initial impact is compelling, it requires repeated watching to work out what is going on. A great deal is compacted into three minutes. It encapsulates key elements of live sport – the stars and the action, the immediacy and uncertainty, the drama and mythology, success and failure, blame and redemption, dream and nightmare.

It offers an image of the globalised game, consumed live around the world via television, pulling the audience into its vortextual moment (Whannel, 2010). The globalised world it portrays, however, is not simply one of unity; it shows the working of global and local upon each other, though as a smooth and naturalised process. It does not centre upon the team but upon the exceptional and heroic individual, the person capable of producing the transcendent moment of magic – precisely the brand image around which Nike advertising has been constructed since the huge success of its association with Michael Jordan, and the Air Jordan campaign (see You Tube at http://www.youtube.com/watch?v=ISggaxXUS8k; [accessed 14 January 2012]).

The advertisement is constructed around a set of mini-narratives. Didier Drogba almost scores, to the huge excitement of Ivory Coast fans; but the ball is intercepted at the last moment by Italian defender Cannivaro, who is then rewarded with a guest appearance on an Italian entertainment TV show. Wayne Rooney's long pass is intercepted by the Frenchman Ribery. Rooney's vivid and fearful fantasy of the consequence is portrayed (opprobrium, followed by obscurity). Galvanised, he wins the ball back and becomes the nation's hero. Ronaldhino's step-over becomes an iconic trick, reproduced by fans, by people around the world and in an exercise video. Ronaldo's talents on the pitch lead to a film of his life and the construction of a giant statue. He powers through but is fouled. Fans pray as he runs up to take the free kick. Before we know the outcome, the advert ends with its concluding banner 'Write the Future' (the above description derives from an unpublished paper by Steven Conway and Garry Whannel).

MEDIA SPORT ANALYSIS

Our understanding of sport is shaped by representations – by how it is photographed, filmed, written about and talked about. Detailed and systematic analysis of media sport coverage began to develop during the 1970s with the work of Buscombe and Peters in England, and Birrell and Loy and the contributors to the *Journal of Communication* in the USA. *Football on Television* (Buscombe, 1975) drew on film theory, as did similar French analysis (Daney, 1978; *Télécine*, 1978), and concentrated on close textual analysis along with consideration of political and ideological signification (see also Peters, 1976; Nowell-Smith, 1978). The influence of Buscombe can also be detected in North America during the 1970s, alongside more traditional forms of content analysis (see *Journal of Communication*, summer 1977, special issue on media sport; and Real, 1975).

These early analyses, heavily influenced by film theory, were supplemented by work that sought to understand the television medium with its twin impulses to be realistic and to entertain (see Birrell and Loy, 1979; Bown, 1981; Clarke and Clarke, 1982; Whannel, 1982). Alongside studies of British television sport (Bamett, 1990; Whannel, 1992), there are a range of North American studies (Rader, 1984; Cantelon and Gruneau, 1988; Chandler, 1988; Wenner, 1989; Gruneau, 1989; Real, 1989) and the rapid growth of cultural studies in Australia during the 1980s has spawned several studies of media sport (see Goldlust, 1987; Lawrence and Rowe, 1987; Rowe and Lawrence, 1989); and Blain, Boyle and O'Donnell (1993) look at the European media in a cross-cultural perspective.

Such analyses are broadly constructionist – they contend that television and the other media do not simply reflect the world, but rather construct versions, or accounts, of it. Buscombe's football monograph analyses in detail the way that camera positions, cutting patterns, modes of editing, commentary, title sequences and presentation material all serve to construct a particular image of football. Similarly, Peters analyses the ways that television's visual and verbal conventions serve to relay a particular picture of the 1976 Olympic Games. Birrell and Loy (1979) analyse the ways in which television re-arranges time and space in order to produce sport in televisual form. Buscombe (1975) and Peters (1976) both argued that while television sport claimed to be merely presenting reality, it was in fact constructing a version of it, viewed from the position of an imaginary 'ideal' spectator.

The combination of direct and indirect address in television sport, the use of visual devices like slow motion, and action replay, and the use of graphics, cannot simply be seen as a variant of the realist conventions of narrative fiction. To dissect the complex combination of title montages, presentation, contributors, clips, action replays and actuality, it is more useful to think in terms of conflicting tensions between attempts to achieve transparency and a desire to build in entertainment values in representing sport.

NARRATIVES, STARS AND SPECTACLE

The contributors to the *Journal of Communication* special issue on sport analysed the ways in which commentaries function to produce drama (see Bryant *et al.*, 1977). Such analyses served to highlight the focus of television coverage around action and spectacle, star individuals and drama. Whannel (1982) examined the coverage of athletes Coe and Ovett, and argued that television narrativises events, turning them into stories with narrative structures that correspond in some ways to the conventions of literary narrative. Such narratives are used as part of the process whereby readers are addressed and positioned, aiding the gaining and retaining of audiences.

Television has, since the 1950s, undergone a process of spectacularisation, dramatisation and personalisation. The percentage of close shots in sport coverage has increased dramatically. In the 1966 World Cup Final, close-ups amounted to around 13 per cent of all shots. In an analysis of four major matches between 1988 and 1992 close-ups provided between 20 and 30 per cent of the total. The average shot length in 1966 was 20 seconds, while in the 1990 World Cup semi-final between England and West Germany, it was 10 seconds, and in the 1990 FA Cup Final replay (BBC), it was around 6 seconds. Television does far more than simply relay an event. It selects, frames, juxtaposes, personalises, dramatises and narrates. In the process, space and time are re-composed in order to enhance the entertainment value.

In the television age, sport has been turned into mass spectacle, a process that arguably began at the start of the 1960s (Crawford, 1992) and is epitomised in major sport events like the Olympic Games (McPhail and Jackson, 1989; Brennan, 1995), the World Cup (Nowell-Smith, 1978; Wren-Lewis and Clarke, 1983; Geraghty *et al*, 1986), and the Superbowl (Real, 1989). The English football cup final has been analysed as a site on which representations of tradition, ritual and royalty are joined to the tension and drama of 'the people's game' (see also Colley and Davies, 1982). Van de Berg and Trujillo (1989) examine the centrality of winning in American sporting ideology and the ways in which the Dallas Cowboys were represented as a symbol of success. Young (1986) examines media coverage of the Heysel Stadium disaster, charting the various ways in which blame was attributed. Gruneau's (1989) case study of television ski-ing describes the need of producers to make the event look more dramatic and 'make the course look faster'. Tomlinson's analysis of Olympic ceremonies explores the ways in which television's global spectacles are framed (Tomlinson, 1996; 1999)

Morris and Nydahl argued that, in the 1980s, television producers designed sport spectacles laced with visual surprises that present a range of dramatic experiences that the live event could not, thus inventing an original form of drama. In particular, slow motion replay offered entirely new events outside of real time and space. Slow motion replay not only altered our perception of the action it reviews, but it also established our expectations (Morris and Nydahl, 1985). The power of television is such that, as Barnett (1990) suggested, stadia are increasingly prepared to adopt the role of a surrogate TV producer, introducing huge TV screens with close-ups, slomo and advertising.

IDEOLOGY, DISCOURSE AND THE BODY: COMPETITIVE INDIVIDUALISM

A major impetus behind much of this analysis was to trace the presence and operation of ideology within representation. Ideology is one of the more complex terms in sociological and political debate. Work in the semiologic approach developed by Roland Barthes conceptualises ideology as an all-pervasive way of seeing that is taken for granted and naturalised. It is a partial view of the world, systematically favouring the interests of dominant groups at the expense of subordinate groups.

The study of individual media texts revealed that the terms of which they are made up do not acquire their meanings in isolation. Language is a system, or set of systems, within which terms already have meanings with connotations, according to how they are used and have been used in other contexts or 'discourses'. Take words like freedom, fair play, commitment, flair – they are all shaped by the contexts in which we are accustomed to hearing them used. They exist within particular discourses – organised sets of utterances. It is possible, for example, to regard the emergence of fitness chic in the late 1970s as a discourse that linked up a whole set of terms (work, pain, fit, individual) and gave them specific meanings.

Sport inevitably involves forms of body transformation, whether conscious, deliberate and strategically planned, as in elite sport, or as the coincidental by-product of active physical activity, pursued for other reasons. Jean-Marie Brohm regards sport as a form of Taylorisation of the body, an attempt to produce maximum productivity through a sado-masochistic training regime which instils an ability to withstand pain, to train and compete beyond the pain threshold. This concept of sport training is a typical aspect of sport films such as *North Dallas Forty* and *Rocky*. The rise of Thatcherism in the 1980s was accompanied by the growing prominence of a new competitive individualism in which sport became work, fitness classes became work-outs and the new common sense was constituted by phrases like 'no pain, no gain', 'feel that burn', and 'if it ain't hurting, it ain't working'. Going on through the pain signified commitment. This self-focused culture of competitive individualism is, arguably, more striking than ever, with new technologies of body transformation prominent in every high street.

Placing the body in jeopardy, in a position of danger and risk, also appears to be a part of the production of sporting spectacle. Certain events signify danger – skiing, boxing, motor racing, mountaineering, American football – and thrills and spills are a major point of appeal. For the television audience, motor racing, skiing and ice-skating all carry promise that something will go wrong. Risk and the threat of an accident contribute to the spectacle – it is part of what binds an audience to these events – and it underlines the heroic nature of those who compete – they place their bodies, and hence their lives, in jeopardy. The growing popularity of extreme sports in general and the ultra endurance events, such as the Iron Man triathlon are examples. The 'celebrated body' is for some the end product. The celebrated body is that body seen at the moment of victory, breasting the tape, receiving the trophy, waving to the crowd, in an image to be recycled a hundred times. The celebrated body achieves recognition and admiration, it acquires immortality, in the words of the song 'Fame', 'I want to live forever . . .'. It is in this sense that we can speak of a discourse of competitive individualism.

GENDER

Of all cultural practices, sport is, arguably, the one that most prominently serves to demarcate the genders. Boys grow into a world in which sport is a significant component of masculinity. Being sporting provides an ease of entry into masculinity, while to dislike sport prompts unease and doubts about whether one is a 'real man'. By contrast, interest in sport is aberrant within the confines of conventional femininity. Sport and femininity are set up as conflicting systems so that reassurance has constantly to be offered that despite an involvement in sport a girl is also feminine. Such difference is not, of course, produced by representation alone; lived sporting practices themselves have always had masculinity structured in dominance. As such, they are means by which patriarchy has been able to reproduce its power and authority in society.

Of the small proportion of media content that is devoted to women, much of it goes to those supposedly aestheticised sports – such as gymnastics and skating – in which supposedly feminine qualities are to the fore. As the number of women who are active in sport has increased, so the quality of elite performances has risen and the gap between women's and men's performances has shrunk, leading some to predict a continuing process of gap narrowing. However, as Paul Willis (1982) argues, the implication here that women's performances are only valid by comparisons with men's, itself only serves to reproduce women's subordination.

Dunne (1982) found that while magazines aimed at pre-pubescent girls feature positive images of sport, by the teen years, in magazines, sport is something that boys do and girls have little interest in. Leath and Lumpkin (1992) found that as the magazine *Women's Sport and Fitness* switched emphasis towards fitness, it featured more non-athletes and fewer athletes on the cover. Females were more likely to be posed rather than performing, aggressive sports were covered less than traditional female-appropriate sports, and female athletes were liable to be described in terms devaluing their sporting achievements. The portrayals of sport and fitness in magazines represented a reworking of femininity that tried to reconcile active women with femininity (see Bolla, 1990; and Horne and Bentley, 1989). Shifflett and Revelle (1994) conducted a content analysis of *NCAA News* and found that 73 per cent of space in *NCAA*

91

News was devoted to male athletes and only 27 per cent to female, and more than three times as much space was devoted to photos of male athletes. In 2011, a controversy developed after the BBC announced a shortlist for the award of Sport Personality of the Year that contained no women. This issue has consistently caused the BBC embarrassment. The award, which is not for the sports*person* of the year but the sports *personality* of the year, was previously described as the *television* sports personality of the year. Since the BBC ceased to be the dominant broadcaster for television sport, it now has to confront the problem that major stars may emerge in events or sports that it does not televise. Similarly public pressure has developed to recognise stars in sports such as yachting that do not attract television audiences. All of this is underpinned by the inherent male dominance of the cultures of both sport and sport journalism.

Such gender constructions are structured by power relations: by the subordination of women within patriarchy (see Duncan and Hasbrook, 1988). Higgs and Weiller (1994) found that although women were given greater coverage in individual sports, that coverage was divided into shorter and more heavily edited segments. In addition, commentators relied on gender marking, biased and ambivalent reporting, and a focus on personalities as opposed to athletic abilities when covering women's sports.

Williams, Lawrence and Rowe (1987) argued that despite any gains that women have made in the struggle to obtain equality in Olympic competition, their participation was limited and their image, as defined by the media, is structured according to prevailing gender stereotypes (see also Yeates, 1992).

Feminist scholarship does not just document the construction of gender difference and the underlying power relations, but also challenges such image production. Halbert and Latimer (1994) have argued that although women have made great strides in sport, their achievements will continue to be meaningless as long as sports broadcasters undermine, trivialise and minimise women's performances through biased commentaries. MacNeil (1988) has argued that leisure is a site of contestation in which women's participation presents new ideas of physicality, but residual patriarchal notions that sport is for men are difficult to alter. She describes the commodification of the feminine style through aerobic classes, sports clothes and videos, and argues that patriarchy is reproduced in a newly negotiated form that attracts women to buy a range of narcissistic commodities. She concludes that this exploits women by creating 'needs' that are in reality only 'wants' – female sexuality and glamour help to sell physical activity to women – and that advertising is a major impetus in the acceptance of the aerobic ritual and its style as 'feminine'. Media representations of active women, in activities such as aerobics and body-building, are aligned with dominant hegemonic relations. They reproduce male dominance by continuing to associate women more with appearance than performance, objects for the gaze rather than acting subjects.

If the discourses of sport have historically served to mark both gender difference and male domination, their contestation has helped open up space for the transformation of images of women in the last twenty years, The rise of feminism and the women's movement has prompted legislative and social change. The fitness chic era has produced a whole new range of imagery in which being physically active and sporting is no longer portrayed as unfeminine. However, as Jennifer Hargreaves (1994) argues, this has also led to a heightened sexualisation of the female body, whereby sporting imagery merely offers another form of objectification of the female body for the male gaze. The stress on work and pain in the discourse of fitness chic in the context of the political ideology of Thatcherism also appears to provide a link between the reformulation of femininity and more traditionally masculine ideologies of work, during the period in which women's employment, both full- and part-time, was growing.

So masculine imagery has been at the heart of sporting discourse. Representations of sport celebrate supposedly male virtues – strength, toughness, determination, grit, aggression, commitment and single-mindedness (Messner et al., 1993). There are close links between the cultures of sport and dominant constructions of masculinity (Miller, 1989). It is a world of toughness, competence and heroism which celebrates traditional 'masculine' qualities (Sabo and Jansen, 1992).

However, just as there is no single monolithic femininity, nor is there a single simple homogenous masculinity. There are a range of images of masculinities available within images of sport, although these are typically delimited by the parameters of 'masculinity'. The world of American football is viewed, critically, in the film *North Dallas Forty*, as a tough brutal world in which there is no room for doubt or uncertainty (Whannel, 1993). The terrace sub-cultures of English soccer celebrate a tough, aggressive self-asserting localism (Williams and Taylor, 1994). The rise of men's style magazines in the late 1980s marks a distinct commodification of masculine appearance, in which sport iconography plays a significant role.

Yet while male vanities are nurtured in media representations of sport, these still characteristically offer a vision in which emotions are only readily expressed in specific contexts like sporting victory, and in which relationships, feelings, and desires are frequently rendered marginal. Neale (1982) analyses *Chariots of Fire* in terms of male gazes at each other, implying a sexuality the film cannot acknowledge. Scorsese's *Raging Bull*, an antidote to the rather more glorified version of violence in boxing in *Rocky*, is seen by Cook (1982) as portraying a masculinity in crisis – only able to express emotion through violence.

The rise of feminist scholarship, the growth of an interest in the study of masculinity, and a growing body of work on sexualities have brought the body centre stage as an object of study. Work-outs, weight training and bodybuilding have foregrounded a new masculine muscularity (see Chapter 7 on bodies, and also Klein, 1990). Gymnasia have become the site of cultural contestation, as the rituals of gay, straight and female users struggle to establish sub-cultural space (Miller and Penz, 1991). Sporting imagery also constitutes one of the few cultural spheres in which women (and men, gay and straight) can legitimately gaze at male bodies, often semi-naked. For much of the history of media sport, this sexual dimension has been repressed and unacknowledged. However, one trend in the past twenty years is very striking. It is not just women's sporting bodies that are now sexualised but also male bodies. This is not a trend limited to sport – advertising and cinema have prominently featured images of semi-naked male flesh, offered up for the admiring gaze, and this trend is increasingly striking in sport coverage.

Sport stars are often dubbed role models, although what precisely this means is rarely clearly specified (Hrycaiko, 1978). They certainly do function as stars and top-level sport has developed an elaborate and marketable star system. Hill (1994) discusses the problems associated with understanding heroes, stars and what they represent (see also Nocker and Klein, 1980). While pundits constantly assert that sport stars can be moral exemplars or bad influences, the relation between these images, morality and the youth market is undoubtedly more complex (Whannel, 1995b; also Whannel, 2002). Adherence to heroic figures is socially constructed. It rests also on popular memory, and popular tradition, and thus is historically constructed (see Holt et al., 1996).

CLASS

Class is striking both by its presence and by its absence in representation. Sports themselves are heavily and distinctly class stratified. The distinctive class cultures of Wimbledon tennis, Royal Ascot, rugby league, squash or greyhound racing are very clearly marked. Yet in the media, particularly on television, such differences tend to be downplayed and masked. Television rarely alludes specifically to class difference, and in its sport coverage tends to minimise the difference between the rooted cultural contexts of sports and work to produce more of a unity than is apparent in lived social experience. Indeed, as Critcher (1979) argued, writing before the development of satellite broadcasting, television itself exerted a transformative effect on a sport like football, helping to weaken its traditional working-class roots and foster the movement of the game away from shared collective communality towards a modernised commercialised form of individual consumption.

Television's own selection of sports has tended systematically to favour those that neatly fit, or can be made to fit, its own needs. Highly popular sports like badminton, speedway, and greyhound racing have occupied a low place in the hierarchy of television. Of course, this is a complex issue. Darts and snooker became major television sports, and during the same period showjumping declined significantly. However, even in the case of darts, television does little to further accentuate the visible working-class locale, and in the case of snooker, television and the promoters seem to have gone to considerable lengths to diminish the traces of the working-class smoke-filled snooker hall image.

RACE

We live, many would argue, in a society in which racism is endemic, deep-rooted and pervasive, as the recent outcome of the Stephen Lawrence murder trial and the background

94

story to the murder have indicated. Images of black people in the media have typically fallen into two categories: victims and perpetrators. Black people are portrayed in terms of social problems. In this context, at first sight, sport might appear to offer something very positive. Here, uniquely, we see black people as active and successful, achieving goals and receiving popular acclaim. In athletics, football and cricket, black sportspeople have achieved a prominence much greater than their proportion within the population might suggest. Media sport offers a fund of images of black people achieving success and therefore offers role models to young black people. However, the picture is not quite so positive, for two reasons. First, the portrayals of black athletes still serve to reproduce stereotypes that underpin racism and, second, such images offer false hope – like the entertainment industry, sporting success can only provide an escape from poverty for a very small minority. While purporting to condemn any form of racism in sport, the popular media know that the theme of racism guarantees a good headline and an effective storyline.

The principal stereotype that is reproduced through sporting imagery, according to Cashmore (1982), is the myth of natural superiority – the concept that black people by virtue of racial/genetic characteristics are especially well equipped to succeed at sports, particularly those requiring speed. The assumption can be detected in the constant references to silky skills, natural rhythms and natural ability to be heard in commentaries. There is little evidence to support the notion of natural ability, especially given the lack of validity of the concept of fundamental differences between racial groups. It has two consequences. First, some teachers, coaches and football managers believe that because blacks are well equipped for sport, they are less well equipped for other tasks. Second, black people themselves may tend to accept the stereotype and underachieve in other areas as a result. In the age of celebrity and reality television, the attempt to seek fame through sport or show business can prove a beguiling temptation, and especially to those who may come to feel that, through racial discrimination, they will encounter barriers in pursuing other avenues.

In the USA, stereotypes held by coaches and others about the ability of black athletes have been detected in the process of stacking, whereby black American footballers are found in disproportionate numbers in some positions, where speed and strength are essential, and not found in positions, like quarter-back, where mental abilities are seen as central. Similarly, Maguire (1988) demonstrated the degree to which black soccer players are found in highest proportion in peripheral, as opposed to central, positions. The process of becoming popular, too, is subject to significant limits. Boxer Frank Bruno became a popular hero by being modest, unassuming, genial and almost Uncle Tom-ish, whereas the more street-wise flash and sassy Lloyd Honeyghan never won the hearts of the white public. This phenomenon has been manipulated very successfully by Chris Eubank and his manager Barry Hearn. Together, they have carefully forefronted Eubank's arrogance in order to attain fame and hence marketability using that classic boxing promotion strategy of creating the man they love to hate. Eubank's rather arcane posturing and provocative stylistic pastiche of the clothes of an English country gentleman seem calculated to tease the racist underbelly of the white working class. The contrast between Bruno and Eubank marks vividly the limitations upon this road to black success. (See Gilroy, 1990, on Bruno, for comparison and also Fleming, 1991, 1994; and Jarvie 1991.) More recently, boxers such as Prince Naseem have used similar arrogant performativity in careful calculation of its impact in attracting attention. The demarcation between respectable and provocative is still very striking in the way it is applied to black sports stars, as a study of media coverage of Lewis Hamilton will reveal.

Sabo *et al*. (1996), in a study of American televising of international sport, found that producers appeared to make efforts to provide fair treatment of athletes, but that the treatment of race and ethnicity varied across productions. There was little evidence of negative representations of black athletes, but representations of Asian athletes drew on cultural stereotypes, and representation of Latino-Hispanic athletes were mixed, with some stereotyping.

Wonsek (1992) found that the majority of black college athletes were exploited by their institutions. She argued that, within a historical and contemporary racist culture, some black athletes are elevated to super-stardom while other black athletes do not receive an adequate education. The image of black success in athletics tends to support the stereotypical view that black students' abilities lie with sport rather than academic work. She concluded that the media perpetuates the image of the young black male as athlete only, with advertisements playing a significant role in this process.

Wenner (1995) identified a good guy/bad guy frame of reference that served to mark differences between sport stars like Michael Jordan and Mike Tyson. Crawford (1991) examined the limited range of stereotypes of black athleticism in American movies. Majors (1990) argued that the cool pose adopted by black athletes provided a means of countering social oppression and racism and of expressing creativity, but the emphasis on athletics and cool pose among black males was often self-defeating, and came at the expense of educational advancement. Perversely, the very success of black athletes, generating a fund of 'positive' images, at the same time reproduces a negative stereotype, because of the lack of positive images of black achievement in other areas. There is a complex relationship between images of black people as sport stars and the social and historical determinants which have shaped images of black people. Analysis of such images needs to place them in this context and examine the relation of black and white in representation and in social relations. The image of stars such as Michael Jordan and Mike Tyson is not merely an issue of sport (see Carrington, 2010).

When Tiger Woods emerged, he was a marketer's dream – young, black, cool, good-looking and the dominant figure in his sport. He was not merely one of the best ever, he appeared almost unbeatable. He made the perfect billboard for Nike, with the Nike swoosh constantly visible on his clothing. His advertising value peaked in 2005 when after a long putt, the ball remained balanced on the edge of the hole for an eternity, the Nike swoosh perfectly positioned, before dropping in. Then came calamity – an incident in which Woods crashed his car and his wife smashed the rear window with a golf club. While the precise details remained unclear, the incident was the prelude to a series of revelations, rumours and allegations about Woods' private life and affairs with other women. The marriage broke up, Woods' form on the golf course declined dramatically and his value to sponsors and advertisers was greatly

diminished. From being an advertiser's dream, the image of Tiger Woods now became linked to a very old racist stereotype – white fears of black male sexuality.

NATIONAL IDENTITIES

National identities are complex – analysts have spoken of the production of imaginary coherences (Poulantzas, 1973), imagined communities (Anderson, 1983) and of the invention of tradition (Hobsbawm and Ranger, 1983). Media coverage of sport arguably plays a significant part in the construction of national identities. Our sense of our own national identities and our characteristic stereotypical images of other nations can be traced in the ways in which the media represent sport. Nowell-Smith (1978) has discussed the ways in which World Cup football coverage establishes a difference between the North European and Latin styles of play. The British media typically contrast us with grim, humourless East Europeans, happy-go-lucky Africans and over-resourced Americans, suggesting that only the Brits have the balance right (Whannel, 1983).

Blain, Boyle and O'Donnell (1993) analysed over 3000 press reports from ten countries, taking as their key examples the 1990 World Cup, Wimbledon 1991, and the Barcelona Olympics of 1992. To illustrate the narrative frame through which the European media interpret the relation of the 'small' sporting nations like Cameroon and Costa Rica to Europe, they string together quotes from eight sources to demonstrate a hyper-narrative in which the 'insolent, impudent upstarts' are 'put in their place', 'taught a lesson' and given 'a harsh lesson in realism' by the European powers. At stake here, of course, is not just national identities but the construction of a 'European' identity (see also O'Donnell, 1994).

In this process of construction, audiences are characteristically positioned as patriotic partisan subjects. National belonging-ness is inscribed in the discursive practices that seek to mobilise national identities as part of the way in which our attention is engaged with a narrative hermeneutic. We want to know who will win and 'we' hope that it will be our 'own' competitor (see Whannel, 1992).

National identities clearly and visibly have considerable prominence in the process of cultural mapping, yet the internationalist impulse is also a factor in the contested process of representation. Controversy developed during the Euro 1996 football tournament when the *Daily Mirror* ran a front page proclaiming, 'Achtung, Surrender: for you Fritz ze Euro 96 is over'. The bellicose tone misread the popular mood, and the following day the paper ran a conciliatory shot of the editor presenting German captain Klinsmann with a hamper, with the rather weak 'Peas in Our Time' headline as an attempted apology.

Clearly national identities are constructed upon difference; upon oppositions between 'our' qualities and 'theirs'. British and English images of self in the tabloid press often stress the Bulldog spirit, the willingness to take bruises in the cause of Queen and Country, the love of pageantry and tradition, the honour of playing for the country and the commitment to fair play.

Such representations serve to produce and reproduce 'common-sense' assumptions about 'our' national character.

Nations are, in Benedict Anderson's phrase, imagined communities (Anderson, 1983). They are the product not simply of wars or of linguistic communities, but also of symbolic practices – mapping, flag design, emblem construction, and so on. Such is also the case with Europe. In such symbolic practices, national media systems are part of the constant marking and remarking of difference. As Blain et al. (1993) suggest, 'Television and the press need a variety of Europes.' French, German, British and Italian media will construct Europe differently. There is no single simple or essential Europe – it is an area that has had shifting geographic divisions. The historical legacies – wars between England and France, Napoleon, the rise of Germany, the World Wars – have a continuing resonance. The threat from outside – from the USSR, from the USA, from the Third World – have all featured in the construction of a commonality of interest within 'fortress Europe'. Yet, in England, the notion of Europe as 'other' is still remarkably strong, reinforced by a legacy of war imagery. Even the liberal Observer drew on this and commented at the commencement of Euro 96, 'Will it be V.E. Day on 30 June?' (Observer, 2 May 1996).

From a British perspective, of course, the Channel always intervenes as a factor in our imaginary landscape, producing a difference between island and mainland. British teams win and 'get into Europe'. It is deeply inscribed in our sporting language that we are not in Europe, that we have to win our way into Europe, that we go there, that it is a foreign place, alien. We go there on a trip, as football supporters, like an invading army. You can get knocked out of Europe, and then you have to try and get back in next year. Far from being trivial or irrelevant, this perspective, constructed in sport, has close relations to the Eurosceptic sensibility that conceptualises Europe as 'somewhere else'.

The concept of national identity is made more complex by the particular nature of the British state. The United Kingdom is a product of the process of establishing English dominance. The very name of the British state is a source of confusions: British/English/Great Britain/Great Britain and Northern Ireland/ United Kingdom/British Isles – few seem to understand clearly the distinction between these terms. While the British are not unique in having this blurred and confused identity, the particular role of the British in the development of world sport reproduced these confusions on the world stage. The Celtic nations, Wales, Scotland and Northern Ireland, are not yet fully independent states, but do, in many sports, have their own representative teams (see Whannel, 1995a).

England has dreamed for many years of producing a male Wimbledon champion, no British tennis player having won the title since Fred Perry in 1936. The best prospect for many years, Tim Henman, attracted a huge following, and an almost hysterical press coverage, which dubbed the sloped ground at Wimbledon where events can be followed on a giant screen, 'Henman Hill'. However, Henman failed to get to the final, let alone win, and he was replaced as 'the great British hope' by Andy Murray. However, Murray's representation has taken a different course. As a Scot, he has made it clear that he does not want to be regarded as British (and certainly not English), implicitly resisting the role of 'first Brit since Perry to win'. While Tim Henman's slightly bashful and distinctly non-macho style sowed doubts over his competitiveness under pressure, it may have added to his appeal for some. By contrast, Murray's rather dour and humourless public persona has not succeeded in building a big public following south of the border, where he has not been adopted as 'ours', nor does he wish to be. If Murray does succeed in winning a Grand Slam or Wimbledon title, it may well be accompanied by a Scottish referendum vote for independence. Representations of sport do not merely reflect our complex ideas of national identity, but play an active role in the constant reconstruction and negotiation of national identities.

STARS IN POSTMODERN CULTURE

There have been some significant and far-reaching transformations in the forms through which sport has been represented in the media over the past decade. Television's increasing use of montage sequences, with music, overlaid graphics, visual colorisation and dubbed music produces a juxtaposition of surface appearances in which appearance subsumes substance. The tabloid press has undergone three dramatic revolutions in the past twenty-five years. First, from the start of the 1970s, the new Murdoch-owned *Sun* set the pace in pushing a brasher variant of tabloid style in which larger headlines, more pictures, shorter stories and greater sensationalism were central elements. Second, from the mid-1980s, the defeat of the old print unions and subsequent introduction of new technology had a transformative effect of even greater visibility. The introduction of colour, electronic data handling and computerised page layout meant that sports pages developed a collage style in which the old divisions of content type were less rigid. As stories shortened and photos grew in size, the combination of picture and headline increasingly carried the weight of the meaning, with body text often reduced to caption length. Third, all newspapers now have linked websites and their financial futures are closely linked to the success of those sites – whether in generating advertising, encouraging subscriptions or in developing other forms of revenue.

This revolution is also highly visible in the magazine market, especially in that sector targeting the youth market – such magazines are all collaged layouts. However, this collaging of media form is not simply part of the postmodern glissage whereby surface appearances continually float before us in a never-ending process of arbitrary re-juxtaposition. Beneath these forms lie real relations which help to determine in a very direct way the production of images.

The increasingly close links between top sports stars, sports agents, advertisers, sponsors and image producers is a case in point. Take an example from basketball. Michael Jordan became a major basketball star in the USA because of his remarkable talents. His position enabled him to secure lucrative clothing contracts, such as that with Nike. Nike designed a whole range of clothing which traded on his name – Air Jordan – and his image. They produced ads which reified and fetishised the sight of his body soaring into the air to score. This brand name and image then proceeded to catch the imagination of a worldwide youth market, many of whom probably never saw basketball itself, or knew that much about Jordan beyond the image. It was one of the most compelling demonstrations of the power of a well-constructed image in recent years (see Andrews, 2001).

Following this well-trod path, the career of Shaquille O'Neill was stage-managed according to the same blueprint. On his autumn 1993 visit to London, the capital was saturated with enigmatic ads showing 'Shaq' leaping to a basketball hoop suspended from the Post Office Tower. More than ever, sport stardom can increasingly become disconnected from the sport itself. Jordan and Shaq seem almost to float above the sport, as if basketball itself was rather superfluous. Carefully chosen performers from other countries can link star image to pro-motional strategy – the presence of Chinese basketball player Yao Ming in the NBA has produced huge new television audiences and shirt sales in China. In many cases, far more people are aware of and know the star than follow the sport. This was probably the case with Michael Jordan. Female sport stars whose image can be readily sexualised are particularly likely to be caught up in this phenomenon. The fame of Anna Kournikova far outstrips those of her fellow competitors, as her image has been reproduced in secondary circulation to a far greater extent, not least in men's magazines.

Such star images succeed because in a particular socio-historic conjuncture they catch the imagination of particular audiences. To do so, something about the image must address, tap into and mobilise the feelings, moods, aspirations or fantasies of an audience. Stars are stars precisely because they succeed in doing this. Times change and stars of previous eras can come to look archaic as a result. While image analysis is certainly insufficient to understanding the process, it is none the less necessary.

Beckham: a brief case study

It is frequently suggested, by newspapers and by figures in public life, that sport stars should be moral exemplars – role models for the young. When, as is often the case, their behaviour hits the headlines for 'negative' reasons, they are castigated for their failure to set a 'good example'. The concept of sport star as 'role model' though, postulates a crude and over-simplified model of the relation between young people, the media and sport stars. Rather, sport star images involve complex condensations of discourses of masculinity, and morality, shaped by the self-referential and intertextual constructions of celebrity-hood (Andrews, 2001; Whannel, 2001).

When David Beckham emerged as a football star, many factors contributed to his success – his football talent, good looks, and a highly publicised romance with another media star, Victoria Adams (Posh Spice in the pop group, the Spice Girls). He played for a team, Manchester United, that attracted both massive support and considerable loathing, because they are a symbol of the dominance of football by the richest clubs. During Beckham's up and down career, his constant presence in the media provides an interesting case study in celebrity.

100

He first claimed attention with a goal from the halfway line against Wimbledon on August 17, 1996, later described as a 'Goal of the Century'. In summer 1998, a widely publicised photograph of him, on holiday with Victoria, wearing a garment described as 'a sarong', was presented in the tabloid press in terms of deviance from the conventions of masculinity, with hints of his supposed 'emasculation'. His sending off, in England's key match in the World Cup, provided a point of condensation for discourses of morality and fair play in sport, in which national pride became national shame. Beckham became the butt of jokes, many of which featured his supposed dull-wittedness. Part of the terrace hostility to Beckham could be related to the fear of emasculation engendered by a public figure who strays beyond the rigid versions of masculinity favoured in English football culture. However, after a season spent shrugging off the abuse, winning Premiership, FA Cup and European Champions League medals, fathering a child, and marrying Victoria, the story in the popular press became a narrative of redemption and triumph. Yet, as is so often the case with stardom, a hint of sexual ambivalence heightens public fascination. Beckham does 'un-masculine' things; attending fashion events like London Fashion Week fashion show (*Evening Standard*, 15 January 1999). His sartorial adventurousness transgresses the laddish code in which sharp and stylish means Hugo Boss – a little flash but in the solidly 'masculine' tradition of the sharp suit.

Our saturation with media images, and the vastly increased speed of the circulation of information have combined to create the phenomenon of a 'vortex' effect, which Whannel (2002) calls 'vortextuality'. The various media feed off each other and, in an era of electronic and digital information exchange, the speed at which this happens has become very rapid. Public responses from phone, text, and Twitter arrive immediately. Some events come to dominate the headlines to such an extent that it becomes temporarily difficult for columnists and commentators to discuss anything else. They are drawn in, as if by a vortex. The death of Princess Diana, the wedding of 'Becks' and 'Posh', and the death of Michael Jackson constitute examples, each dominating the media for days, to the extent of removing most other issues from the agenda (Whannel, 2010).

The image management of Beckham astutely capitalised on his looks while minimising the exposure of his rather weaker voice. The theme of redemption through love was developed in dramatic fashion in Easter week by *Time Out* (31 March–7 April 1999) which featured David Beckham on the front cover in white trousers and a white see-through shirt in a pose evocative of Christ and the crucifixion, with the caption 'Easter Exclusive: The Resurrection of David Beckham' making the religious reference explicit. Inside, the accompanying article was entitled 'The Gospel according to David' and a subtitle referred to him as 'back from the reputation wilderness' (*Time Out*, 31 March–7 April 1999). It was an image that might have caused controversy if any other star had been featured, but the image of Beckham was proving remarkably resistant to any bad publicity. Stars in the public eye for long enough become larger than life cartoon characters, the narration of their lives taking on the character of a soap opera. The key moments stand out, partly because they are re-circulated in media montage: the last-minute free kick goal against Greece in 2001, securing qualification for the 2002 World Cup; the botched penalty at the 2002 World Cup; Beckham appearing with facial scar and an Alice band, triggering massive curiosity, and the revelation that an angry manager Ferguson had kicked a boot which hit Beckham's face; the subsequent 2003 move to Real Madrid, culminating in a champions medal; the 2007 move to Los Angeles Galaxy and, once again, a few average years culminating in another champions medal; and most recently the flirtation with Paris St Germain, ending in an anti-climatic decision to remain in LA.

Beckham could be regarded as the perfect example of a postmodern star. He represents the dominance of appearance over substance, and his image can, in various playful and sometimes ironic forms, be linked to a wide range of practices and products without significantly changing anything. Postmodernity, though, is a contentious term, assuming different connotations in different contexts. Broadly it refers to the centrality of information and image, the ways in which culture has become increasingly self-reflexive, juxtapositional and parodic; the growing irrelevance of a stable conception of 'reality' and the undermining of established certainties of progress and development. Surface appearances have become central, with substance and authenticity impossible to identify. Postmodern theorists argue that in such a world, the old totalising grand narratives of modernity such as Marxism no longer have explanatory force. In opposition to this view, other theorists (see Giddens, 1990) argue that this period is better characterised as late modernity.

According to postmodern theory, the past two decades have seen the emergence of a world characterised by the rapid exchange of information, the saturation of images and a concern with consumption and identity. This world is epitomised by fragmentation, by the dominance of surface appearance over substance, by a growing self-conscious self-reflexivity permeating all areas of cultural and social life, by pastiche, parody, irony and playfulness. In this context, sporting exchange can be seen as another form of cultural playfulness.

The new electronic media of the late twentieth century – video games, electronic arcade games and computer games – contributed to the secondary circulation of images of sport and sport stars, although secondary circulation has, in the media-saturated environment, become an ambiguous concept. It is no longer always straightforward to distinguish between the primary activity and the spin-off. The popular computer game *PGA Tour Golf* – set up to capitalise on the players tour, incorporates images of and comments from star golfers. The football simulation games, *Pro-Evolution Soccer*, and *FIFA 12* have become ever more 'real' in appearance, with movements, facial appearance, body type, commentary, and camera movements all rendered with growing verisimilitude. Professional footballers not only play these games but also regularly file complaints when they feel the parameters of their virtual selves have underestimated their abilities. There is at least one professional football manager who regularly plays the game *Football Manager*. In visual appearance the distinction between the 'real' game and its simulated version is becoming narrower (see Conway, 2010).

Lara Croft is the world's first virtual star, but may be only paving the way for the emergence of a computerised sports performer, who through digital magic, can be pitted against 'real' performers. Yet, given the apparent public fascination with erratic behaviour, with mis-behaviour, and with the unpredictable, the virtualisation of sport may be an impossible task.

For it is the ways in which, despite the increasing discipline and sophistication of modern scientific coaching, things still do not always go according to plan, that is part of the enduring, and very human, fascination of sport. Despite the commodification of sport, there is always some element of unpredictable spontaneous uncertainty that eludes the marketeers (Whannel, 1994).

CONCLUSION

Sport endeavour, as will be discussed in Chapter 7, on sporting bodies, involves placing the body in jeopardy. The specialist bodies of elite sport are departing from our own, and may indeed come to resemble more closely the fantasy bodies of comic fantasia and simulation game. In the globalised world of contemporary sport, of course, stardom is produced very rapidly through repetition across many different media forms – television, press, magazines, websites, internet chat, social network gossip. The globalising processes of sport in the media are discussed further in Chapter 12. Major events – the Olympics, the World Cup, the Champions League, the Superbowl, Formula One motor racing, and the IPL – have become dominant aspects of media sport in recent years and Chapter 13 examines these 'mega-events'.

ESSAY QUESTIONS

1   Compare and contrast the way the road to sport success is represented in two of the following films: Chariots of Fire, Rocky, Cool Runnings, Raging Bull, Field of Dreams, A League of Their Own.
2   'Winners are celebrated, losers simply disappear.' Discuss whether this is a fair summary of the ways in which television covers sport.
3   'Television has dramatised the role of "The Manager", who is represented as the key figure who shapes the destiny of his team.' Discuss.

EXERCISES

1   Obtain a copy of the Nike advertisement mentioned at the start of this chapter. Do your own analysis, considering image, story, and identity. What do you think are the attributes of live sport that it is attempting to associate with Nike?

2 Build up a case study of images of a currently famous sport star. Analyse the ways in which the star is portrayed, paying close attention to details of setting, background, pose, dress, any accompanying text, and context in which the image appears.
3 Record the build-up and preview part of a live television transmission of a major sporting event. Analyse the themes and issues in order to understand how the audience is drawn in to key narrative questions that the event itself will eventually resolve.
4 Analyse the cutting speed of a live sport event, using a 10-minute sample, and counting the number of separate shots.

FURTHER READING

D. Andrews and S. Jackson (eds), *Sport Stars: The Cultural Politics of Sporting Celebrity* (London: Routledge, 2001).

R. Brookes, *Representing Sport* (London: Arnold, 2000).

G. Whannel, *Media Sport Stars: Masculinities and Moralities* (London: Routledge, 2002).

CHAPTER SEVEN

SPORTING BODIES

DISCIPLINING AND DEFINING NORMALITY

INTRODUCTION

Sport is all about bodies. This might seem to be stating the obvious. All definitions of sport include some kind of physicality; the whole point is to get physical. Sports are organised around and classified by what people do with their bodies. Corporeality may be a prime concern of sporting activity but there are different bodies involved in sport; the athletes in the field, the pool, the ring or the gym, the pitch or track. Some are keeping fit or socialising and others might be competing for the club or nation at the highest international levels. This chapter focuses upon the bodies that engage in sport.

Perhaps not surprisingly, a sociological interest in sport and the physical body has developed in the past twenty-five years (for examples of the different approaches taken and areas of research, ranging from injury and risk to fitness and fatness, see Hall, 1996; Sassatelli, 2000; Young, 2004; Smith Maguire, 2007; Malcolm, 2009; Mansfield, 2009; Pike, 2010; Maguire, 2011). This chapter has a more focused interest, first, in discussing the role of the bodies that take part in understanding sport and, second, to ask what is social about bodies. Sport is a field of enquiry in which enfleshed bodies are central, and has contributed to what has been called 'the corporeal turn' in social theory (Howson, 2005). This chapter examines what is particular about bodies in sport. Sport is also regulated and run by its governing bodies and the two sorts of bodies are closely connected. This chapter presents a discussion of social science research into the body and the social significance of bodies and an introduction to some feminist, Foucauldian and phenomenological theories of the body. It uses two case studies which illustrate these approaches: first, one of gender verification testing and, second, a case study of technological assistance to enhance performance on the track.

The bodies that participate and compete in sport are regulated, for example, through who is allowed to compete and who is not and through the measurement of competition such as times, space, location, record keeping, competence and body size. The bodies that take part regulate themselves in trying to achieve personal best performances or in competition. Is it all about biology, physiology and genetics? To what extent are bodies socially constructed? How do bodies and embodied selves change in relation to social factors? The big questions that are posed by looking at bodies in sport concern the relationship between social and cultural factors and the flesh and between bodies and minds. Sometimes bodies and minds are seen as separate as in the popular entreaty to exercise 'mind over matter'. Sometimes body and mind are one, as is often the case in sport. Physiology and science have focused on flesh and bones and the genetic and biochemical composition of bodies; the social sciences look at the relationship and connections between bodies and what they do, how they are seen and how they are understood and at the points of connection between flesh, culture and social discourses.

Body practices and embodied achievement are fundamental to claims concerning the benefits of sport, but bodies do not provide the objective criteria that the regulatory bodies of sport might claim. Some of the apparent certainties, for example, about gendered bodies are challenged by feminist critiques of the power geometry of sporting classifications. This chapter addresses some of the issues that arise from an over-emphasis upon bodies, the separation of mind and body, and problems linked to the classification and measurement of bodies.

While this chapter challenges the notion that there is a unified body, which can be separated from the mind or self, or which is undifferentiated, the term 'the body' is used as a shorthand way of expressing some of the history of the body and its different meanings. Retaining reference to 'the body' also demonstrates the centrality of corporeality, as the material, living, breathing body of everyday experience, especially in an exploration of differentiation and inequality and thus accommodates 'the corporeal turn' (Howson, 2005).

The 'corporeal turn' refers to the idea that over the past twenty years or so, the body has become a major concern of academic study. Social scientists have expressed a preference for the plural 'bodies' rather than the singular body, because the use of the plural embraces the diversity of different sorts of bodies (Price and Shildrick, 1999). The body and, more especially, bodies have always played a key role in sport and sports studies, although there has been more stress on scientific and medical approaches to the body than upon the social construction of bodies. In sport the materiality of bodies has been mostly the concern of the medical sciences, although psychology has also played an increasingly important role, and their social, cultural and political aspects have been taken for granted. Sport and sporting practices offer a means of understanding the significance of bodies in relation to the relationship between selves, corporeality and the social world (Hargreaves and Vertinsky, 2002).

Bodies cannot be understood without understanding the relationship between embodiment and the wider social world. Bodies are not fixed but change in relation to social forces and transformations and according to how embodied selves live in the world. Bodies change and are shaped by body practices, nutrition and medical interventions, which lead, for example, to muscle development, as well as being subject to different social interpretations and meanings. Some bodies are valued more than others, especially in sport. It is not possible to talk about the body without acknowledging and interrogating what makes bodies different and how bodies are treated and valued differently, and often inequitably, and what sort of explanations can be offered for inequalities that are based on bodily differences.

Bodies are everywhere in Western societies: images of bodies, beautiful bodies, damaged bodies, bodies that can be transformed by medical, technological and pharmaceutical interventions and training regimes, which clearly demonstrates the links between the field of sport and other social worlds; regimes developed within sport are applied to body projects in other fields. Sport also occupies media space and provides material for the proliferation of body images. Even in sport such images are often sexualised and women, in particular, are subject to the same forces of objectification in sport as in other fields (Markula, 2009).

The contemporary Western focus upon the body means that people are routinely exhorted to look after their bodies, for example, through healthy eating, keeping fit and looking good. Increasingly, the promotion of a healthy body, through exercise and healthy eating has become a regulatory strategy of the neo-liberal state; good citizens have healthy bodies and look after themselves through the apparatuses of biopower (Foucault, 1981). Participation in sport is encouraged to further social inclusion and diversity (Woodward, 2007). The body is targeted by the state as a site at which good citizens can be made, suggesting that there is a causal link between the healthy body and the healthy mind (as discussed further in Chapter 9). This link is based on the idea that mind and body are separate and distinct. The proliferation of 'body projects' in Western societies (Giddens, 1991; Shilling, 2008), whereby people are exhorted to take control of their bodies and thus their lives, presupposes that bodies can be shaped and modified by active agency, sometimes expressed as 'mind over matter'.

However, the disciplining of bodies involves varying degrees of control and constraint. Bodies are regulated through the diffuse, heterogeneous and subtle injunctions of 'governmentality'. This concept, deriving from the work of Michel Foucault, is used by Nikolas Rose (1996) to describe the range of social and cultural institutions, which include all the expert medical, psychological and legal advice with which people in liberal democracies are bombarded by the media and is not limited to those of government, to construct good citizens who conform to norms of sexuality, appropriate behaviour and good health and regulate themselves. Governmentality includes guidance on how to care for yourself as a gendered citizen (Richardson, 2000) where assumptions are made about appropriate ways of living your life as a woman or a man.

WHAT IS A BODY?

Bodies are assemblages of breathing, eating, sleeping, reproducing, moving functions; a collection of body parts (Connell, 1995). However, some body parts seem to be accorded more social and political significance than others; as Londa Schiebinger (1993) has pointed out in her studies of the history of science. All bodies here were classified against a standard set by the norm of the European, white male. This is a phenomenon most emphatically expressed in sport, for example, at the 1936 Olympics in Berlin, the so-called 'Nazi Olympics', but also manifest in de Coubertin's early assumptions about white, especially male, supremacy in the Modern Olympic Games (Guttmann, 2005). Bodies come, not only in all shapes and sizes, but bodies are also marked by gender, class, race, ethnicity, generation, ability, disability and sexuality, to mention only some of their distinguishing characteristics. In sport muscles, body mass and size have particular importance although these aspects of bodies are subject to gendered criteria too. Sex is a, if not the, major factor in classificatory systems in sport.

Bodies are central to sport through their maintenance, practices, measurement, successes and failures, but they are never just bodies. In explaining the success or failure of an athlete, it is difficult to extricate the different factors, for example, of confidence, training, nutrition, education, social expectations, affective and emotional aspects which can affect performance, outcomes and experience. One of the most obvious ways in which bodies are classified in sport is by sex; the vast majority of sports have separate competitions and some even have separate rules for women and for men.

MAPPING THE FIELD: SEX, GENDER, FEMINISMS

Not only is sport so often divided in women's sport and men's sport, there is a differential weighting in the value that is given to each. Debates about the sex gender relationship within feminist theory and the social sciences have addressed both the value system in which men's sport has taken precedence over women's and the distinctions between sex as natural and gender as cultural which are closely tied to these values. The separation of sex and gender has been hierarchical and unequal. For example, women have been more closely associated with nature and thus seen as subject to the vagaries and weaknesses of the flesh which determines sex in this division, whereas men have been linked to culture with its connections to the mind and cerebral activities. Thus, in sport, the properties of sex such as the muscular body and body size are seen as advantageous to men but those of women, especially their reproductive capacities are seen as a source of vulnerability. While the mind and the soul might be rated above the body in soul–body, mind–body dualisms, in the sex gender debate, the embodied sex has greater weighting as a determinant of gender. Liz Stanley (1984) described the argument as being one between biological essentialism, which prioritises biological, embodied sex as the determinant of femininity or of masculinity, and *social* constructionism, which focuses on gender as a social, cultural category. This points to the separation between the two concepts, with sex being associated with biology and embodiment and gender with social and cultural practices. There are two issues here. First, sex and gender have been combined, but there is still the assumption that sex as a biological classification is scientific and therefore more certain. Second, where the two have been explicitly disentangled, the influence of sex upon gender has been awarded priority and higher status than any influence gender as a cultural and social construct might have over sex. There is also a normative claim involved in this hierarchy, namely that sex *should* determine gender.

Some second-wave feminists, notably Ann Oakley (1972), have argued that sex and gender were frequently elided to women's disadvantage, whereby cultural expectations of what was appropriate or possible for women were attributed to some biological law. The notion that

women should be relegated to second class citizenship, or even accorded no citizenship status, because of anatomical difference from men, in particular, the possession of a uterus, has a long history. Women have been excluded from activities in the practice of sport (Hargreaves, 1994), as well as membership of sport's ruling bodies, because of their sex, which was claimed to be generative of dire outcomes such as the psychic phenomenon of hysteria. Women have been excluded from sports and continue to run shorter distances, play bouts of less duration and comply with different regimes from men in sport, such as playing off different tees in golf or fighting fewer rounds in boxing, on the basis of physical difference (Woodward, 2007).

Feminists sought to make a distinction between the biological characteristics of the body, the anatomical body and gender as a cultural construct. However, more recently the idea of an oppositional distinction between sex and gender has been challenged, most powerfully by critical feminists such as Judith Butler (1990; 1993) and for many, including the IOC and IAAF, the term 'gender' is largely preferred. The meaning of 'sex' is strongly mediated by cultural understandings that, it is argued, make it impossible to differentiate between sex and gender. The use of gender permits an acknowledgement of this powerful cultural and social mediation (see Price and Shildrick, 1999) but which can transform through the practices of doing sport. Sex, however, allows for a reinstatement of the material enfleshed body (Woodward, 2009, 2012) and avoids the over-emphasis on social construction from which the insistence upon gender suffers. Sex and gender, as Butler argues, are also difficult to disentangle. Sex makes gender and gender makes sex just as the social and the enfleshed are closely enmeshed; bodies are social.

As this chapter shows, the division between sex and gender is not always useful in sport because, first, sex as biological does not yield the certainties we might expect and, second, sex and gender are social and political and inform each other. Bodies are not the same as biology.

DIFFERENT WAYS OF THEORISING BODIES

The corporeal turn provided a way of looking at the importance and relevance of bodies in relation to selves and identities and the intersection of social and enfleshed materialities. A key question concerns finding ways of talking about the body without fixing it as 'a naturally determined object existing outside politics, culture and social change (Fausto-Sterling, 2005: 1495). This has been recognised in sport through the huge expansion of interventions aimed at improving performance, although ideas about what is fixed and cannot or should not be changed endure in relation to sex and disability. The body, although it was for some time an absent presence in academic work, has become central to much of contemporary debate and it is thanks in large part to the insistence by theorists of gender studies such as R.W. Connell (1995), theorists of body studies, including sport, like Nick Crossley (2001), Bryan Turner (1996) and Chris Shilling (2008) and, as we have seen, feminists, from Oakley (1972) to Judith Butler (1993), that the particularities of corporeality have to be addressed. Bodies matter and they matter in specific ways.

Sport poses particular questions and exaggerates some of those posed by the corporeal turn, especially in relation to the constraints of the flesh, on the one hand, and of social forces, on the other. How important are embodied differences in shaping outcomes, in particular, success, in sport or are other social cultural and economic factors as important? If it is possible to exercise agency over body practices, in effect to exercise mind over matter, does this mean that mind and body are separate?

The body may be an increasingly popular focus for social science and sociology of sport research but nonetheless concentrating on the ways in ways bodies shape lives can be problematic for those who have experienced oppression, marginalisation or social exclusion. Feminists and theorists of disability and the politics of race and racism have been wary of too much focus on bodies or embodied experiences because of the risks of biological reductionism and the fear that by stating the importance of the body, they may be reduced to a set of body parts and their experience devalued and allocated to the realm of matter rather than mind. In the history of sport, black athletes have suffered the racialisation of biological theories of racial difference. There are broadly two responses to this. First, the body is a key site for the experience and inscription of differences, for example, of gender, race and disability and thus is a useful focus of analyses of how inequalities are re-constituted through the operation of power; that is, of how and why some differences count and the particular meanings they carry. Second, social theories of the body have highlighted the social construction of embodiment and the ways in which bodies are inscribed with social values which can be challenged and changed.

These two responses have been underpinned by theoretical approaches which draw upon the work of Michel Foucault, with its strong emphasis on the social and cultural regimes through which bodies are made and remade, and phenomenology, drawing on the work of Merleau-Ponty and Simone de Beauvoir, which stresses the importance of lived experience and of being in the world. We briefly outline theses theories in the following sections.

Michel Foucault's discursive bodies

Although few of his own references were to sport, for example, to contests in the Ancient World, Michel Foucault's arguments have been particularly useful in thinking about how sport is used a means of regulating populations. An example is what he calls 'biopolitics', through which the state targets bodies as a means of discipline and regulation (Foucault, 1972; 1981). Foucault also argued that discursive regimes of power bring into being particular types of person, which he calls 'figures', because they become recognised as having substance, for example, in terms of sexuality, the heterosexual couple. Homosexuality is also socially produced through regimes of truth, which are inscribed on bodies. Power functions through bodies by classifying and measuring what bodies do and what they are. Thus, visible differences

110

among people become inscribed with different values, such as are embedded in the racism which still pervades sport, including the scientific racism that attributes particular capacities to black athletes, for example, the ability to box, for Kenyans and Ethiopians to run marathons and for African Caribbean athletes to sprint, all in preference to golf or polo, which are sports associated with white participants. These are social and political properties, not those that reside in bodies exclusively.

Feminist theorists of sport (Markula and Pringle, 2006) have taken up Judith Butler's arguments in *Gender Trouble* (1990), following Michel Foucault's theories that knowledge is produced, rather than revealed (Foucault, 1972, 1981). They have demonstrated how the body *inscribes* rather than *describes* difference; meanings about gender, 'race', 'ethnicity' and disability are produced through the ways in which bodies are inscribed. These meanings are not necessarily or exclusively inherent in the bodies which are so differentiated. However, an over-emphasis on inscription and social construction might suggest that material bodies do not matter; a problem that Butler (1993) attempted to address in *Bodies that Matter*.

While work based on Foucault has been very useful in exploring and explaining the processes through which bodies are produced and reproduced within discourses of sport, that might be less relevant to the material limitations and constraints of the enfleshed self. Although Foucault's work centred on the body, it is in many ways disembodied since the body is always inscribed rather than material and is always subject to regulatory and disciplinary regimes which may be resisted but seem to afford little scope for collective agency beyond a regulation of the self. Analyses of how sporting practices are constructed and enforced, however, offer a challenge to the reactionary claims that it is the particular body which determines the value that is placed upon the person or the activity in sport. An emphasis upon how sport is com-municated and constructed, for example, through media coverage, challenges claims that women's sport is not televised because women's bodies are less powerful than men's (Markula, 2009) or that black and ethnic minority athletes have particular bodies which facilitate running rather than playing golf or polo.

Boxing measures participants by body weight, unlike most sports, but it is not the particularities of the material body that lead to the greater participation in the sport of athletes from migrant groups at particular historical moments. Rather it is the way in which the sport is put into discourse (Foucault, 1981) as a possibility for, usually men, of certain ethnic and class groups at some historical moments (Sammons, 1988; Berkowitz and Ungar, 2009). Women's boxing was 'put into discourse' materially in the ring, and as a sport it was possible to think about it, albeit amidst controversy in 2012. Women in Afghanistan and Iran could conceive of the possibilities as well as the practice of boxing at the London Olympics. Another advantage of Foucault's approach is its engagement with contingency and the specificities of history. Rather than considering that body types are fixed for all time, they are recognised as temporally and spatially specific.

The materiality of bodies is central to sport, however, and sports studies have stressed the ways in which bodies not only matter but also that there is a two-way relationship between the social and the embodied. Bodies can present limitations and constraints not least through injury and the damage which sport can inflict upon them (Hargreaves and Vertinsky, 2002). Theorists of the body in sport have been concerned not only to put the body back into theory (and practice), but also to challenge the ways in which the mind–body split has led to the construction of sporting bodies as material rather than intellectual. The mind–body split has been most effectively interrogated by phenomenological approaches which have particular relevance to sport because of their emphasis on experience and body practices; lived and situated bodies.

Phenomenology: embodiment and experience

Phenomenology, according to Merleau-Ponty (1962: vii), 'tries to give a direct description of our experience as it is, without taking account of its psychological origin and the causal explanation which the scientist, the historian or the sociologist may be able to provide'. Consciousness is the body as lived in a tangible encounter with human, and non-human others. Merleau-Ponty's work has been very influential in the development of theories of 'the body', especially in incorporating agency into a critique of the body. Bourdieu and those who have developed aspects of his work, for example, Nick Crossley (2001) and Loïc Wacquant (1995, 2004), have used the notion of embodiment to locate body practices within material, economic circumstances.

Loïc Wacquant in his ethnographic accounts of a Chicago boxing gym explores some of the ways in which boxers somewhat surprisingly continue to fight even though they have experienced what appears to be significant and painful physical damage. Wacquant uses the idea of embodiment to describe and explain a situation in which mind and body are one and, as is so often the case in sport, there is no time or space for reflection at the point of engagement. Bowlers in cricket, albeit after months of coaching and practice, get their eye in and there is a synthesis between mind and body.

This does not, of course, mean that there is necessarily harmony in this interrelationship. It may never work perfectly and, as with so many other current theories of embodiment, the process is unfinished and incomplete. There are moments in this alliance when we are more preoccupied with the body and others when consciousness takes us up. If you start thinking about a movement, shot or action in sport, you may lose form. The idea of embodiment opens up another possibility for avoiding the binary logic of mind and body and of reinstating the body into the interrelationship between agency and constraint or structural dimensions of experience, even according corporeality a central role, without sacrificing the scope of intentionality and agency which can be exercised by embodied subjects.

Even in those situations where the body might seem to 'take over' and deny the possibility of agency, the notion of embodiment can permit an understanding of what constitutes conscious agency.

One way in which phenomenology has been used is to explain gender differences. Gendered, racialised differences and body practices in sport have often been attributed to corporeal inequalities, relating to size, anatomy, muscle power and stamina and often elided with psychological aspects of competition. The exclusion of women from many sports has often been based on the claim that women's bodies are smaller and weaker. Being 'weaker' may be translated as being less aggressive, for example, less prone to tackle assertively in football or rugby, or less competitive in contact sports like boxing (Woodward, 2007).

Iris Marion Young (2005), whose work was mentioned in Chapter 5, has combined the phenomenological concept of embodiment with Simone de Beauvoir's (1982) notion of the body as a situation to explain the apparent 'remarkable differences' between masculine and feminine body comportment and style of movement and uses the example of 'throwing like a girl' to demonstrate how gendered embodiment is constituted through routine and repeated bodily practices. She examines the practices through which women and girls experience the world through their movement and orientation in spaces by developing specific body competences:

> The young girl acquires many subtle habits of feminine body comportment – walking like a girl, tilting her head like a girl . . . the girl learns actively to hamper her move-ments . . . thus she develops bodily timidity that increases with age. In assuming herself to be a girl, she takes herself to be fragile.
>
> (Young, 2005: 43)

The body is here subject, not object and as such affords the possibility of transformation and of a reconfiguration, for example, through different sets of bodily practices. Femininity is taken in de Beauvoir's (1982) sense of a typical situation of being a woman in a particular society and is thus not fixed, or inherent, or in any sense biological. Rather than being a biological bodily attribute, ways of playing sport are techniques and practices that through repetition become internalised. Consideration of embodiment permits us to think about an alternative to the mind–body division.

> [B]ecause of the concept of embodiment, we can break out of the dualism of the Cartesian legacy, phenomenologically appreciating the intimate and necessary relationship between my sense of myself, my awareness of the integrity of my body and the experience of illness as not simply an attack on my instrumental body but as a radical intrusion into my embodied selfhood.
>
> (Turner, 1992: 167)

Material bodies: sources of certainty

There is a need to engage with the biological dimensions of the body and with what Judith Butler (1993) calls the 'anatomical body', not only because of the importance of the body in shaping experience, especially in sport, but also because of materiality and the diversity of bodies and the embodiment of difference across class, 'race', 'ethnicity', disability, generation and gender, to name but a few aspects of these differences.

The body might seem to offer a source of security and present a bounded self, demarcating one embodied self from another. Thus, the body might offer some fixity in locating a sense of identity. As Pierre Bourdieu (1986) argued, the body is the only tangible manifestation of the person. Sex and gender, as shaped by the physical, largely observable characteristics of the body, are seen as key sources of identity. The visible difference of gender is both a key dimension of classification and a source of troubling anxiety when the classificatory system breaks down, for example, when a person cannot be neatly slotted into one of two genders (Woodward, 2002, 2011). At birth, babies are ascribed a gender. Judith Butler (1993), far from welcoming any such possibilities of certainty, seizes the challenges and subversive potential of uncertainty and suggests that it is only through transgression that the heterosexual matrix, that is the complex sets of cultural practices through which heterosexuality is re-produced and re-configured, can be subverted. Gender is re-produced through iterative acts and is not fixed in the anatomical body. For Butler, there is no distinction between sex and gender; sex too is socially and culturally constructed.

Sporting bodies are not infinitely plastic and malleable; bodies clearly offer limitations to what is possible; injuries, physical disabilities, the impact of ageing and the limits to the physical powers and competence of our bodies restrict our potential and the opportunities to succeed, or even to participate in some sports. These are the constraints of corporeality and of the material body, which constantly remind us that human beings are embodied subjects and demonstrate the necessity of bringing together 'the body' as the object of enquiry and embodied experience as the source of differentiation. The vulnerability as well as the possibilities of flesh unites people in sport. This does not mean that bodies do not and cannot change; there is a much higher degree of plasticity in bodies and the ways in which they are classified as well as levels of achievement than people have thought. Training at altitude can generate improved performance.

The physical features which create the categories of female or male are connected to social, cultural expectations, practices and, since categories and their embodiment change over time, behaviour (Fausto-Sterling, 1992). Thus, being assigned to a specific gender provides a set of ground rules that govern our behaviour, establishing a cornerstone of identity. This is not to deny or underplay the materiality of the body and reduce difference to what is visible. One way in which certainty has been sought in sport is through gender verification testing, to which we now turn.

THE OLYMPICS AND GENDER VERIFICATION

Sport is premised upon a sex gender binary which informs its regulatory framework and the embodied practices of practitioners. There are women's competitions and men's competitions and very few that are mixed, especially at the highest levels. Mixed doubles in tennis is one of the few competitive mixed sports with public recognition, unlike foursomes in golf which are more low status, leisure activities with the high prizes and kudos going especially to top male golfers. Mixed competitions are still based upon the supposed balance of the female–male binary and take difference on board in all its dimensions; enfleshed difference and that of cultural practice and recognition, which means that male athletes top the table in terms of rewards and mixed activities are mostly relegated to the lower echelons of both status and reward (see Chapter 10). However fluid gender categories may be in areas of contemporary Western cultures, in sport they remain firmly entrenched in a clear dichotomy of difference, which is also one which privileges one aspect of the binary, notably that of the male and the attributes of masculinity (Cixous, [1975] 1980).

The International Olympic Committee introduced sex testing in 1968 at the Olympic Games in Mexico City, apparently after claims about the masculine appearance of some competitors. The development of broad shoulders, flat chests and muscular bodies is very likely to have been inevitable as women's events became more competitive with more events and consequent increased participation of women in elite sport: 'The gender polarities long sustained through competitive sport, became blurred as female athletes generally became bigger and stronger' (Wamsley and Pfister, 2005).

The debate about the masculinisation of women athletes had been raging for several decades in the twentieth century, both before and after the institution of gender verification testing and persists in different forms into the twenty-first, although it was greatly intensified during the Cold War period from the early 1950s to the end of the 1980s. On the one hand, women in Eastern Bloc countries had greater freedom to compete in sport and sport was a catalyst for social change (Guttmann, 1988; Riordan and Cantelon, 2003), but, on the other, they were vehicles for Communist ideology. Women played a key role in the making of the Eastern Bloc's sporting success story. Female athletes thus became political tools (Pfister, 2001) as a means of enhancing the role of Eastern Bloc countries in world sport. Some instances are more explicitly politically motivated, like Dora Ratjen, a man who was forced to compete in Hitler's 1936 Olympics and who ultimately lost the gold medal in the women's high jump, having been later found to be Herman Ratjen, a member of the Hitler Youth.

These instances of gender ambiguity are framed within ethical discourses with the implication of cheating and moral transgression. They usually involve either a reassertion of the masculinity to which women mistakenly aspire in sport because they cannot attain it without being masculinised or a sense of pity. More recently, prior to the unification of Germany, in the former East Germany, it is estimated that as many as 10,000 athletes were caught up in the attempt to build a race of superhuman Communist sports heroes using steroids and other performance-enhancing drugs. The shot-putter, Heidi Krieger, was given steroids and contraceptive pills from the age of 16 and she was European champion by the age of 20. Her overdeveloped physique had put a huge amount of pressure on her frame, causing medical problems, while the drugs caused mood swings, depression and resulted in at least one suicide attempt. Later

Krieger underwent gender reassignment surgery claiming that she had been confused about her gender, but felt that the drugs had pushed her over the edge.

The US, Polish-born sprinter Stella Walsh who won gold and silver at the 1932 and 1936 Olympics and set over 100 records, was found at her death to have male genitalia, although she had both male and female chromosomes, a genetic condition known as mosaicism (Schweinbenz and Cronk, 2010).

Rather than the heroic narratives of male athletes' achievements, women's stories seem to have featured tales of enfleshed exploitation. Women remain victims or are corrupt. Women's bodies in these narratives are the target of organised deception and corruption. Sex became a tool for the manipulation of sporting success in a process in which women's bodies were deeply implicated.

The stated aim of gender verification testing was to prevent any man from masquerading as a woman in order to gain advantage in women-only athletic competitions. Gender determination tests were seen as degrading, with female competitors having to submit to humiliating and invasive physical examinations by a series of doctors. Certainty was to be achieved through the common sense of visible difference, but at the expense of women's self-esteem and human dignity. Later the IOC used genetic tests, based on chromosomes. Geneticists criticised the tests, saying that sex is not as simple as X and Y chromosomes, and it is not always easy to ascertain, because, for example, it is thought that around one in 1,600 babies are born with an intersex condition, the general term for people with chromosomal abnormalities (Blackless et al., 2000). It may be physically obvious from birth – babies may have ambiguous reproductive organs, for instance – or it may remain unknown to people all their lives. Human beings may exhibit a variety of chromosomal and physiological characteristics, such as Androgen Insensitivity Syndrome (AIS) when a child is born with XY chromosomes but feminine genitalia, or those with Congenital Adrenal Hyperplasia have XX chromosomes but masculine genitals.

The Spanish hurdler Maria Patino underwent mandatory gender verification testing at the World Student Games in 1985. She was found to have androgen insensitivity which meant she had Y chromosomal material and had small testes inside her body. Patino refused to withdraw or feign injury and was discredited and lost her scholarship. She had lived her life as a woman and, as she told the press after being dismissed, 'If I hadn't been an athlete, my femininity would never have been questioned' (Schweinbenz and Cronk, 2010). The embodied selves caught up in these events are assumed to have some agency and the capacity to make decisions, for example, about whether or not to take the drugs and, if detected, whether or not to withdraw. At the Atlanta Olympic Games in 1996, eight female athletes failed sex tests but all were cleared on appeal; seven were found to have an intersex condition.

There was considerable resistance to gender verification testing from different constituencies which included medical scientists and doctors, all of whom challenged the reliability and validity of such tests. They were also, of course strongly criticised by the women athletes who had been subjected to the tests and on ethical grounds. As a result, by the time of the Sydney Olympic Games in 2000, the IOC had abolished universal sex testing but, as has continued to happen, some women still have to prove they really are women. The IOC, however, was slow to make the decision to abandon the tests.

The IAAF seems to have acted more proactively at this stage in the field of gender testing and at least recognised the diversity of sex gender. In 1990, the IAAF became the first major international sports body to recommend allowing transsexuals to compete, with some restrictions, which were agreed in 2004. Athletes who have sex reassignment surgery before puberty are automatically accepted under the following conditions: their new sex must have all surgical changes completed; they must be legally recognised as their new sex in the country they represent; and they must have had hormone therapy for an extended period of time. For male-to-female transsexuals, this generally means a minimum of two years. Transsexuals, who have had a sex change from male to female, can compete in women's events in the Olympics, as long they wait two years after the operation.

Yet the humiliation of gender testing is evident in several of the high profile cases of recent years. For example, Santhi Soundarajan, a 27-year-old Indian athlete, was stripped of her silver medal for the 800m at the Asian Games in 2006. Soundarajan, who has lived her entire life as a woman, failed a gender test, which included examinations by a gynaecologist, endocrinologist, psychologist and a genetic expert. It appeared likely that she has androgen insensitivity syndrome, where a person has the physical characteristics of a woman but the genetic make-up includes a male chromosome; the trauma of the testing led her to attempt suicide while awaiting the results. Edinanci Silva, the Brazilian judo player, born with both male and female sex organs, had surgery so that she could live and compete as a woman. According to the IOC, this made her eligible to participate in the Games and she competed in Atlanta 1996, Sydney 2000 and Athens in 2004 (Edinanci Silva, 2012).

The IAAF set out its approach in a paper in 2006 (IAAF, 2006) in order to establish a policy and mechanism for managing the issue of gender among participants in women's events. According to this paper, if there is any 'suspicion' or if there is a 'challenge', then the athlete concerned can be asked to attend a medical evaluation before a panel, comprising a gynaecologist, endocrinologist, psychologist, internal medicine specialists and experts on gender/transgender issues. The medical delegate can do an initial check, which could be construed as a pragmatic strategy or a reprise of the focus on visible difference and gendered corporeal characteristics (ibid.).

The legacy of humiliation that accompanied gender verification testing endures in much of the discussion about setting a high degree of certainty about the sex of sporting competitors. One recent illustration of this was manifest in the case of the 800 metre runner Caster Semenya. In May 2010, the International Association of Athletics Federations announced that questions surrounding the gender of the South African 800 metres world champion, Caster Semenya, would be resolved by June 2010. The young athlete had to wait for a resolution of a problem that had been hanging over her since the World Athletics Championship in Berlin in August 2009. Caster Semenya is fast, so fast that other athletes questioned whether she was a woman, leading the IAAF to instigate gender verification tests, albeit in a procedure that had been leaked before the final at the World Athletics Championships in August 2009.

It is hardly surprising that the athlete, especially a runner as she is, has a lean body with muscles; most such athletes do. The body of the athlete poses problems about conventional readings of masculinity and how far it is a feature of the body one inhabits or how far masculinity and femininity are manifestations of the presentation of the self, either in Goffman's sense of a role that is played (Goffman, 1959), or to go further, in Judith Butler's words (Butler, 1990; 1993), sex as well as gender, is performative. The whole thing is socially constructed and there can be no distinctions between sex as biological and gender as socially constructed because the two are inseparable. Either way, performance and appearance are key indicators of gender identity and sporting practice muddies the waters, because loss of body fat, muscle tone and competitive, assertive, even aggressive body practices and comportment all undermine what can be seen as feminine. Such features mean that, especially in media representations of women athletes, there may be claims that they appear masculine, as in the case of Caster Semenya. This presents problems for those who regulate sport. It also raises issues that are the substance of sociological inquiry and suggests some questions. Are gender identities reducible to anatomy or is this confusing flesh and muscle with body practices and what you look like? Could people be the gender they say they are and could an individual state with authority what sex/gender they see themselves as being? Gender identities are made and remade through the interconnections between the inner worlds and lived bodies of individuals and the social worlds we live in and are always situated within the wider field of social systems, values and practices.

Bodies in sport are shaped by sporting practices and these practices shape sport, but bodies are gendered and women in sport have to negotiate racialised, heterosexist stereotypes. Women athletes may feel compelled to present themselves as conventionally feminine in order to avoid such prejudice because sport is often characterised by stereotypes, for example, of heterosexuality and of masculinity. Semenya's raised levels of testosterone may tell us more about what happens to the body of an elite athlete than establishing any certainty about gender categories. Indeed, the IAAF found it so difficult that it took 11 months to decide what Caster Semenya's family had known since her birth and what her own lived experience had told her, namely, that she is a woman (*Telegraph Sport*, 2010).

The debate, especially as manifest in media coverage, invoked expert scientific and medical commentary in its path from claims of unfair practice and descriptions of an athlete with a body variously described as 'manly' and with a 'strikingly musculature physique' to sympathy for defiant resistance to the humiliation of gender verification testing, especially as expressed by the South African sports authorities. Ideas about fair play were invoked with claims that this very fast woman must be a man. There was less coverage of the view that there are global power geometries in play in the subjection of a black South African woman from a poor community to treatment that would not have been given to an athlete from an affluent world

118

understanding sport

power. In all the debates, there has, however, been heavy dependence upon the expert testimony of medical authorities, not only in accessing the certainty of gender identity, but also in treating what may then be seen to be an individual aberration. Such cases are treated as personal and individual troubles with individual solutions, rather than pointing to the social context in which these troubles are experienced. One report suggested that ambiguity may be treated by the use of oestrogen which would increase body fat and, of course, slow her down (*Telegraph Sport*, 2010).

Gender verification tests present a mix of cultural, social and political inequalities which intersect with embodied, enfleshed materialities. Masculinity has not been subject to the same doubts, perhaps because men and masculinity have been seen as the yardstick of normality by which standards and classification of sex are judged, and it can be proved that women are not men. Also women are unlikely to want to masquerade as men in athletic competition because of their enfleshed differences. If there are two sexes, there can be no obfuscation. Establishing criteria by which a person's sex can be incontrovertibly ascertained also suggests that finding certainty and the truth is the morally superior route. The IOC has always insisted that gender verification tests were designed not to differentiate between the sexes but to prevent men pretending to be women and winning unfairly. Ethical questions may have appeared to be paramount but control of women's gender and sexuality also informs these claims.

WHAT'S NORMAL? TECHNOSCIENCE AND THE PROMISE OF CYBORGS

As we have seen, sport is characterised by binaries: the binary logic of sex gender, flesh and the social, winning and losing, nature and culture. These binaries are often underpinned by notions of normality and the 'normal' body, which has frequently been encoded as male, white, able-bodied, heterosexual and middle class. Some of the challenges to assumed norms have been framed within analyses of the developments in science and technology which have subverted ideas of normality and of what is natural. Athletes and their trainers are constantly seeking possibilities of enhanced performance. Some of the most exciting recent research into this has been carried out by feminist technologists and scientists like the biologist Anne Fausto-Sterling (2001), who argues that, not only do sexed categories and sexologists change over time but bodies are gendered in different and contingent ways. For example, in her later work (2005), she interrogates the gendered constitution of the bones which make up the skeleton.

Donna Haraway argues that there is never a separate human, or animal, body entity. Human and machine, human and animal are just two of the distinctions transgressed by cyborg thinking. Haraway takes Simone de Beauvoir's famous dictum that 'one is not born a woman' and translates it into 'bodies are not born; they are made' (1989: 7). Thus, bodies are made in myriad ways, including the merging of humans and machines and of animals and humans. Using the case study of primatology, Haraway suggests that 'the primate body may be read as a map of power' (ibid.: 10). Haraway's boundary creatures are 'animal-human for primate; machine-organic for cyborg; and nature and labor for Oncomouse TM' (2000:140). Corporealisation, that is, the making of bodies, is always mixed up with other things, including technology.

These debates are illustrated in the case of Paralympic athlete, Oscar Pistorius. 'Blade-Runner' was the name given to the white South African runner. His story, as played out in the run-up to the Beijing Olympics and Paralympics in 2008 and Pistorius's re-naming, draws on the title of the film *Blade Runner* (Ridley Scott, 1982). The film concerns the relationship between human and non-human 'replicants', which, or maybe more accurately, who, can be seen as more human than humans. Pistorius's epithet, which invokes the excesses and fantasies of science fiction, derives from the fact that the 21-year-old sprinter is a double amputee who lost both legs below the knees when he was a baby and runs on shock absorbing carbon fibre prosthetics, called cheetah blades. These were designed by the Icelandic company Ossur to store and release energy in order to mimic the reaction of the anatomical foot/ankle joint of able-bodied runners. Cheetah refers to the agility and speed of the animal, but sounds unfortunately like cheater. In 2008, he won the right to be eligible to compete at the Olympic Games in Beijing. The Court of Arbitration for Sport ruled that Pistorius should be allowed to compete against able-bodied athletes. He had competed in two able-bodied athletics meetings in 2007, but the IAAF ruled in January 2008 that his prosthetics qualified as technical aids, which were banned in IAAF-governed sports because they were seen to afford an unfair advantage to the athlete. In the end, he failed to qualify for the Olympics but ran in the Paralympics.

This example of Pistorius is resonant of some of the debates about the rules and regulations that are in place to combat discrimination, but which also construct categories of person, for example, by gender or disability through enfleshed attributes. It also demonstrates the break-down of boundaries. This example has much in common with the Semenya case. The issue is presented as the classification of disability and how regulatory bodies like the IAAF can set the boundaries. This case is also about the question of cheating. Are Pistorius's state of the art blades an enhancement too far that enables him to gain an unfair advantage? Pistorius's experience as a competitive athlete challenges the parameters of the natural body, what might be legitimate means of increasing body competences and achievements in sport, and who judges what we can and what we cannot do. This case has wide repercussions about the nature of performance enhancement in sport which may be more troubling for the bodies that run sport than the bodies who run *in* sport.

CONCLUSION

The aim of this chapter has been to map out the terrain of theorising the body and embodiment and to indicate some of the major problems that have emerged from the process of re-thinking bodies in sport. The problems of focusing on bodies have been framed by different tensions

understanding sport

and different configurations of the status of corporeality. This chapter shows that bodies in sport are social; bodies are not just the concern of medical science and sports trainers. The socially constructed body is haunted by the limiting frailty and materiality of the flesh, creating a tension between biological, anatomical bodies and socially and culturally inscribed bodies. These interconnections between what is social and what is material are reconstituted in the intellectual discussion between the importance of representation and symbolic systems and the experience of lived bodies in phenomenological accounts. The centrality of body practices, which are key to participation in sport, highlights the problem of agency and responsibility in shaping the embodied self that is reflected in the interrelationship between theoretical positions that accommodate self-determination and those that focus upon social, cultural, political apparatuses through which subjects are produced.

The very notion of 'the body' invokes boundaries which postmodernist thinking challenges in diverse ways, demonstrating the impossibility of a bounded self and denying the possibility of a unified subject contained within such a frame.

One of the major problems in developing a theoretical understanding of embodiment is how to provide an adequate explanation of how bodies are social and political while recognising the material properties of flesh; an acknowledgement that athletes are enfleshed selves who can shape their bodies and change sporting practice as well as being shaped by wider social, cultural and political forces. If the body is reinstated, does it mean that athletes can be reduced to their bodies? The body is part of being and becoming human, not its only determinant. The threat of reductionism is one that social critics have engaged with in a variety of ways. Some challenges to reductionism go as far as Butler, following Foucault, to argue that, sex as an example of biological bodies too is gendered and normative. Therefore bodies too are put into place by that which normalises them, which reduces anatomical bodies, like sex, to a category with little meaning outside their social context. Other approaches suggest a more positive engagement with the materiality of bodies in challenging essentialism but retaining recognition of the lived body. Reductionist dangers are shared by those who have experienced exclusion and marginalisation and socially excluded embodied selves who have most strongly resisted them.

Modern sport focuses on the embodied sporting practices that make up the participant bodies in sport through social and cultural practices and the regulatory bodies of sport. The regulatory bodies of sport and the discursive field in which embodied sporting practices are enacted and lived provide a strongly demarcated field, in which bodies are very clearly classified and gender categories are strongly defined, but bodies are extremely difficult to fix by such criteria as are deployed by governing bodies. Bodies interconnect with other technologies and practices and social, cultural and political forces. Bodies can change themselves and the field of sport.

ESSAY QUESTIONS

1 In what ways are bodies socially constructed? How can you demonstrate this, or challenge it using sporting examples?
2 Using the example of sex classifications or those of disability, what does the way in which bodies are categorised tell us about social values?
3 To what extent is it possible to reach certainty about the limits of the body in sport?

EXERCISES

1 List and discuss what you think are the limits of the body in sport. Do each of the factors you list have any social implications or are they all about anatomical bodies?
2 Go to the web page of a sport which you follow and describe images of sporting bodies which appear on the home page and at least four of the sub-sections of the site. Compare the coverage in your group and consider which social, cultural and political factors might be involved in the decisions that have been made.
3 Select an international competition/sporting event. If you chose the Olympics, pick a particular competition and look at the images associated with the coverage of the women's and the men's competitions. Which bodies are present and which are absent? How are these sporting bodies presented?

FURTHER READING

J. Hargreaves and P.A. Vertinsky (eds), *Physical Culture, Power, and the Body* (London: Routledge, 2007).
J. Price and M. Shildrick (eds), *Feminist Theory and the Body: A Reader* (Edinburgh: Edinburgh University Press, 1999).
K. Woodward, *Embodied Sporting Practices: Regulatory and Regulating Sporting Bodies* (Basingstoke: Palgrave, 2009).

CHAPTER EIGHT

SPORT, THE STATE AND POLITICS

INTRODUCTION

It used to be claimed that sport and politics did not mix. This argument no longer holds any credibility and this chapter starts with an explanation of the ways in which sport is necessarily political. It discusses the points of connection between sport and politics and then considers the relationship between the state and sport and the politics of sport policies.

While for at least the past 400 years (for example, when King James I published *The Book of Sports*), the state has sought to intervene in sport and recreation through prohibition, regulation or promotion of various athletic pastimes, it was only in the last quarter of the twentieth century that the political dimensions of sport and leisure, at local, national and international levels, became more widely apparent and discussed. Argument over the connection between sport and politics revolves around two broad viewpoints. There are those who argue that sport is a special form of play and as such should be seen as separate from the 'real world'. Involved in these arguments are ideas such as sport is and should be separate from politics; sport is private and personal rather than public and political; the pursuit of the Olympic ideals is non-political.

While there may still be some people who consider sport and politics to be completely separate entities, it is our view that it is not possible to sustain this belief for long when the historical and contemporary evidence is consulted. Sport (and play) involve rules and regulations that are derived in some way from the 'real world'; sport provides politically usable resources; sport can promote nation-building and international image making; in fact, modern sport has seldom been free of politics (Allison, 1986, 1993).

A brief consideration of the gap between the Olympic ideals ('Olympism') and the social history of the modern Olympic Games since their founding in the last decade of the nineteenth century demonstrates this well (see Tomlinson and Whannel, 1984; Horne and Whannel, 2011, for example). Soon after the conclusion of the first modern Olympics – in Athens in 1896 – the Greeks became involved in a war with Turkey that was fuelled by the pride of hosting the Games. In the aftermath of the First World War (1914–18) and the Russian Revolution

(1917), workers' sports organisations were formed which held workers' sports or 'workers' Olympics' in the 1920s and 1930s as an alternative to the official 'nationalistic' and 'bourgeois' Olympics, as they were perceived (Kruger and Riordan, 1996). The politicisation of the modern Olympics took a quantum leap in 1936 with the staging of the 11th Olympiad in Berlin when Adolf Hitler's Nazi regime was at its strongest. Since the end of the Second World War (1945), being a *nation* in the modern world has come to be signified by two things: belonging to the United Nations and marching in the Opening Ceremony of the Olympic Games. The Olympic Games also became part of the Cold War between the capitalist West and the Soviet bloc countries at this time. Between 1968 and 1988 boycotts on a greater or lesser scale took place at each of the summer Olympics. Even at Atlanta in 1996, the North Koreans did not compete.

Lincoln Allison (1986) has suggested that one of the major reasons why sport is intimately linked with politics and power is because sport creates politically useful resources. Sport has been linked with 'building character' in Britain since the nineteenth century, as we saw in Chapters 1 and 5, and so has often been considered as an agency of political socialisation. In the twentieth century, national governments of many different political persuasions have not been slow to realise the potential of attempting to harness sports to further their particular interests and values. In addition, politicians have increasingly sought to associate themselves and their political parties and policies with the positive image of successful competition often delivered by sports men and women (Monnington, 1993). More generally, John Wilson (1988:149) argues that:

> Regardless of political regime, modern societies now routinely use leisure to make claims for nationhood, to establish the boundaries of their nation-state, to establish an identity for their people, to deny the claims of other peoples for nationhood, to integrate existing conglomerates into national communities and to symbolise and reaffirm hierarchies of power and status among the nations of the world.

He adds (ibid.: 150):

> When we think of leisure in an international context we tend to think of sport . . . It is bureaucratised play, or sport, that is used as a weapon in international conflict, not the more amorphous world of leisure.

Despite the rise of debates about globalisation and the role of sport as both a motor and measure of globalising processes, it is clear that sport still plays a major part in nation building (Rowe, 2003). Nonetheless, as the hosting of sports mega-events, such as the Summer Olympic Games and the FIFA Football World Cup, has grown in significance for host cities, regions and nations, it has become more apparent how nation-based practices can be linked to globalised commercial processes. This has led to discussion of 'corporate nationalisms' (see Silk *et al.*, 2005). The hosting of sports mega-events also raises important regulatory issues connected

124

understanding sport

with sports events. National, regional and municipal governments of hosting locations a now required to respond quickly to the demands of global sport organisations such as FIF/ and the IOC, often passing legislation that circumvents local democratic processes (Horne and Manzenreiter, 2006). These issues are taken up in more detail in Chapter 13.

This chapter does not look in great detail at the organisation and administration of sports. Sports organisations tend to govern themselves, although the state regulates sport. For such information, the reader is advised to consult Houlihan (1991; 1994), Henry (2001), Coghlan and Webb (1990), and Torkildsen (1992). We do, however, examine the political sociology of sport with specific reference to the relationship between the state and sport in Britain. We recognise that just as the state is made up of many different organisations and departmental responsibilities, there is the likelihood of conflicting interests (Houlihan, 2005). First, the question 'what makes sport political?' will be discussed. Then some conceptual clarification will be offered. The final section considers the politics of sports policy in the light of these perspectives.

WHAT MAKES SPORT POLITICAL?

It would be wrong to conclude that the only place to analyse the politics of sport is in central and local government. As suggested already, power exists as much in 'non-political' bodies, such as 'governing bodies' of sport. The very title 'governing body' clearly identifies such an institution as being the context for decision-making (or the exercise of power) that affects people connected with a sport. A few of the questions you might ask about governing bodies as political organisations are: What qualifies as a sport?; What are the rules of a sport?; Who makes and enforces the rules in sport?; Who organises and controls games, meetings, matches and tournaments?; Where will the sports event take place?; Who is eligible to participate in the sport?; and How are rewards distributed to athletes and other organisation members? This approach to power and politics is important when analysing the internal politics of sport. In much of the literature on the politics of sport, however, sport is considered political because it is *ideologically symbolic*. It is not a pure social activity that in some way remains untainted without any of the hallmarks of its social origins. Two principal aspects of this ideological loading are the relationship between different political ideologies and sport and the relationship between nationalism, national identity and sport. These can briefly be considered.

Political ideologies and sport

Political ideologies in Britain can be analysed in many different ways. Simply to identify ideologies with political parties will not suffice, however. Ideologies refer to broader conceptions of the purpose and aims of political parties. They are also more fluid than established party positions. Coalter *et al.* (1988), Henry (2001) and Roche (1993) identified a number of different political ideologies and related these to sport and leisure policy. Coalter identified four 'ideal types' of political perspectives: reluctant collectivism (traditional conservatism and the Liberal Party), Fabianism (old Labourism), anti-collectivism (Thatcherism and the new Right) and Marxism. Henry (2001 48–49) outlined five different political ideologies related to sports policy, largely because he subdivides the Marxist category into the 'new urban Left' and 'structural/scientific Marxism'. Roche (1993) provided probably the most convenient threefold distinction within sports policy. First, he identified the dominant ideology of modern British sport – 'gentlemanly amateurism' – that roughly corresponds with the political ideology of reluctant collectivism and the absence of direct state intervention in sport in Britain for most of the twentieth century. Second, the mid-twentieth-century ideology of welfarism – bringing about a more politicised, professional and bureaucratic approach to sport, especially the creation of the Sports Council – was a hallmark of 'Old Labour' or 'Fabian' policy. Third, in the late twentieth century the twin ideologies of global capitalism and consumerism have influenced sport through ideas such as the free market for sports labour and freedom of contract and these ideas have coincided with the anti-collectivism of the new Right, Thatcherism, or as we now call it in the UK, neo-liberalism. Roche (1993:102) concluded:

> with traditions, professions, organisations and personalities representing at least these three structural waves all currently involved in the struggle for power and authority in sport policy, it is not at all surprising that policy is disorganised.

Table 8.1 illustrates these connections between sports interest, political ideology and political party. In addition to these three ideologies Coalter and Henry also note that Marxist and feminist perspectives on sport policy have been developed that present critical accounts of the role and purpose of sport. These have had much less impact on actual sports policy, but are important to consider in terms of their analytical power.

Table 8.1 Sports interest, ideology and political formation

Sports interest	Ideology	Political formation
Gentlemanly amateurism	Reluctant collectivism	Traditional Conservatism
Corporate welfarism	Fabianism/collectivism	Labour Party
Market anti-collectivism	New right/ Thatcherism/ Neo-liberalism	Elements of both 'New' Labour (1997–2010) *and* Conservative/Liberal Democratic Coalition Government (2010–present)

Nationalism, national identity and sport

The second way in which sport can be seen as overtly political is in its uses to promote national identity. This is not as straightforward as it sounds in the UK, however, since there are complicating factors, not least of which has been devolution to the elected assemblies in Scotland, Wales and Northern Ireland since the 1990s and the subsequent resurgence of identities associated with these parts of the United Kingdom. Polley (1998: 36ff.) argues that many sportspeople in the UK can adopt dual or even triple forms of identity in performing their sport. Hence in the UK it is clear that 'sport has historically provided a key focus for the constituent parts to emphasise "separateness and distinctiveness"' (ibid.: 54). Hence one of the issues in the run-up to the 2012 Olympic Games has been whether or not the 'home nations' would combine as a British team to compete in football, basketball, and other team sport events. Through the maintenance of distinctive sports cultures and structures in the 'submerged' nations of the UK – Scotland, Wales and Northern Ireland – representative sport has provided these countries with the opportunity to be represented as 'full nations' in the wider world of sport. FIFA, the world governing body of association football, actually recognises these and thirteen other football associations of 'countries' that are not recognised as such by the United Nations. The concern is that if it is felt that Britain can play together in certain prestige tournaments, then why could they not do so in all tournaments? This would weaken the case for separate organisations and associations governing the sport in the four nations that comprise the UK. On the international stage or playing field, sport can provide countries with a status out of proportion to their economic, military or political significance. As Polley (ibid.: 62) concludes: 'Sport has offered a popular cultural forum for the power relations between the centre and the margins' in post-war UK politics.

POWER, POLITICS AND THE STATE: A CONCEPTUAL CLARIFICATION

This chapter is mostly concerned with 'big P' politics, that is, with the formal machinery of government and the state. Chapter 9 is concerned with the use of power in a wider social context. The political sociology of sport is interested in both aspects of power. Power here can be defined as:

> the ability of an individual or a social group to pursue a course of action (to make and implement decisions and more broadly to determine the agenda for decision-making) if necessary against the interests, and even against the opposition, of other individuals and groups.
>
> (Bottomore, 1979: 7)

The ability to achieve desired ends despite resistance from others implies that power is best understood as a social relationship. Politics thus involves the clash of values and ideologies and struggles for power between different social groups, as much as formal political party politics. Politics most generally should be understood as the processes through which power is gained and used in social situations. Much of the formal analysis of power and politics is concerned with the actions of government, the opposition parties and the state. A focus on this level of politics alone, however, neglects an important distinction between political *involvement* and political *intervention*. We shall argue that there has been a long-term structural relationship between the state and sport at local, regional, national and international levels. This involvement may not have taken the explicit form of intervention until the latter half of the twentieth century, but it has nonetheless gone on (see Hargreaves (1986) for the nineteenth century and Polley (1998) for examples of this relationship).

The very idea of the state comprises changes, as the following quotation from Stuart Hall (1986: 26) indicates:

> The field of action of the state has altered almost beyond recognition over the last three centuries. The eighteenth century state had no regular police, no standing army, and was based on a highly restrictive male franchise. The nineteenth century state owned no industries, supervised no universal system of education, and was not responsible for national economic policy or a network of welfare provisions.

The state has shifted from being mainly concerned with force to being involved in processes of persuasion – from coercion as the means of securing the maintenance of social order to consent exercised through democratic institutions. As this has occurred, the state has moved since the nineteenth century from being mainly concerned with warfare to welfare and now arguably 'workfare'. McGrew (1992) describes this as the process of the 'civilianisation' of the state. The nature and functions of the state were transformed during the twentieth century through the large scale of activities engaged in by the state and the expansion of functional responsibilities to include welfare and material security of citizens as well as general security and public order. Given the sheer size and complexity of these tasks, it would be over-simplistic to treat the advanced capitalist state (ACS) as some kind of monolithic entity that operates in a unified manner. The state is a highly fragmented and in some senses a de-centred apparatus of rule; despite variations in ACSs in terms of political structures, state forms and welfare provision, they also exhibit common features and similar evolutionary patterns.

The most important factors shaping the growth and development of the modern state in advanced capitalist societies are the development of capitalism as a world economic system and war between nation-states. The state has been formed and continues to develop through a combination of endogenous and exogenous forces, that is, both by internal, national or 'local' forces and external, international and 'global' forces. According to McGrew (1992: 91), 'international economic crises are in many respects the equivalent of war'. According to George Orwell, sport was 'war minus the shooting' (1970 [1945]: 63). The modern state 'has always faced both inwards and outwards; inwards towards society and outwards towards a system of states . . . a complex interplay between endogenous and exogenous processes of change' (McGrew, 1992: 93).

The state in advanced capitalism has to operate in both directions and thus faces decisions about what can be called 'inter-mestic' issues. Simply put, ACSs are subject to globalising forces (Giddens, 1989: 520). While the major internal and external tasks of the state remain to maintain social order and to compete with other states, increasingly the room to manoeuvre over issues is influenced by international developments. While the European welfare state was built on the basis provided by American military and economic hegemony after the Second World War, it was restricted in the 1970s and 1980s as a result of the global economic crisis. In the 1990s the conditions essential to the survival of the welfare state in its conventional form were transformed. In addition international regimes – sets of international rules, norms, procedures, and so on – were established which express the internationalisation of the ACS. Examples of this type of issue in sport include boycotts of international sporting events, spectator control at international football matches and the development of a policy on drugs used to enhance sports performance (see Houlihan, 1991, 1994, 1997). The importance of crowd control at international and domestic football matches can be seen as a good example of where this dual – 'inter-mestic' – focus is required. Crowd trouble at the Italy–England World Cup qualifying match in Rome in October 1997 led to condemnation of the 'mindless hooligans' by some sections of the British and Italian press, but a report critical of the Italian police's tactics by the Football Association met with official agreement. It was probably no coincidence that these events took place as the attempt to establish England as the leading European contender to host the 2006 FIFA World Cup Finals had reached a delicate stage.

It is important to remember that the state is not just 'government'. It refers to a whole apparatus of rule within society – the government, the police, the army, the judiciary, the state-owned industries, etc. It is in essence a public power 'container'. It is the supreme law-making authority within a defined territory. As a result, while the relationship between the state, the market and civil society is important to understand, it is not possible to define the precise boundaries as they change over time and between different societies. The state also includes sub-central (local) government and public and semi-public regulatory commissions and corporations (or quangos; 'quasi autonomous non-governmental organisations') including the British Broadcasting Corporation and the Sports Councils that exist in England, Scotland, Wales and Northern Ireland. Hence our use of the words 'the state' in this book should be understood as shorthand for 'state apparatus' or 'state system'.

To sum up this section, in common with the authors of *Sport in Canadian Society* (Hall *et al*., 1991: 85–87), we consider the role of the state in capitalist countries such as Britain, the USA and Canada to involve the following dimensions: to create or maintain conditions in which capital accumulation can take place; to create or maintain social order or harmony through legitimation; and to retain the monopoly on the legitimate use of violence or coercive force. Capital accumulation, legitimation and coercion summarise the threefold objectives of the state in Britain and underline the breadth of the latter notion compared with a narrow focus on government, which is the hallmark of some studies on politics and sport.

In the past twenty years of social theorising, there has been a move away from grand theory to the 'meso level' of social enquiry in which theories are applied to concrete institutional arrangements and organised collective actors (McLennan, 1995: 39). There is recognition of the need to know how and why particular policies arrive at particular points of time. The notion of the state as 'monolith' is replaced with the state as a 'process', but in which power is unevenly distributed. This view informs the consideration of sports policy to which we now turn (see also the discussion of governance in Chapter 9).

THE POLITICS OF SPORT AND SPORTS POLICY

The following sections deal with the increased role of the state in sport in the past fifty years in Britain, rhetoric and reality in sports policy, the different dimensions of state intervention and involvement in sport, and the politics of sports policy. With respect to sport (and leisure) the increasing role of government since the 1960s has been largely *ad hoc*, leading to the existence of many government departments having an interest and involvement. Through a number of departments, notably the Department of Culture, Media and Sport (CMS, formerly the Department of National Heritage, DNH), the Department of the Environment, Transport and the Regions (DETR, formerly the Department of the Environment, DoE) and the Department for Education and Employment (DfEE), the government is able to exert influence on quasi non-governmental organisations (quangos) and voluntary bodies and trusts such as the Sports Council and the Central Council for Physical Recreation (CCPR) in England and Wales. Territorial responsibilities lie with the Welsh Office, the Department of Education for Northern Ireland (DENI) and the Scottish Office (see Houlihan, 1997: Chapter 3 especially).

As a result, a coherent and systematic government policy towards sport has only recently been attempted in Britain. This is reflected in the fact that until 1997 there had never been a government ministry with 'sport' in the title, although since the 1960s there has been a Minister for Sport. For nearly twenty years the Minister was located in the Department of the Environment (DoE). In 1990 responsibility for sport moved briefly to the Department for Education and Science (now the DfEE). In 1992, the Department of National Heritage became the location for both the minister and the Sport and Recreation Division (SARD) – a group of civil servants responsible for most sport-related policy (Macfarlane, 1986; Coghlan and Webb, 1990). The current Minister for Sport's proper title – 'Parliamentary Under-Secretary of State' within the Department of Culture, Media and Sport – reveals the relatively junior, i.e. non-cabinet or 'third-level', standing of the position. All sports ministers under Margaret Thatcher (1979–91) held this status, while Dennis Howell, Labour's Sports Minister in the 1960s, held a second-level position as a Minister of State.

The first ever Minister for Sport, Lord Hailsham, summed up the prevailing ethos of his appointment in 1962 when he spoke of 'a need, not for a Ministry, but for a focal point under a Minister, for a correct body of doctrine perhaps even a philosophy of Government encouragement' (quoted in Sugden and Bairner, 1993: 96). The main function of the minister was to determine and administer the Sports Council's grant and establish a policy framework for the service. When Labour came to power in 1964, despite being committed to a sports council, a protracted period of negotiation followed. The main difficulty was in establishing the nature of the relationship between a statutory sports council and the Central Council for Physical Recreation (CCPR). Set up in 1935, as the Central Council for Recreation and Training, the CCPR had acted as the main forum for the many national governing bodies of sport and the medical and physical education professions. The problems were a reflection of a desire on the part of the British state to prevent institutions appearing to be state-controlled. A Minister for Sport would be answerable to Parliament, whereas a quasi-independent council, even if appointed by the government, would be outside the parliamentary political process (Whannel, 1983: 91).

When a Conservative government eventually established a statutory and executive Sports Council by Royal Charter in 1971, the underlying tension between the needs of the national governing bodies (the 'elite') and the grass roots remained unresolved. The Sports Council took over many of the functions of the CCPR and most importantly the responsibility for the distribution of funding for sport. The CCPR became an independent forum of sports organisations, with democratic methods of appointment to its ruling body, whereas the Minister for Sport appointed the Sports Council board.

BRITISH SPORT POLICY: RHETORIC AND REALITY

Maurice Roche (1993) noted that the traditional rhetoric in British sports policy comprises two fairly widely espoused ideals that have come to be enshrined in the modern Olympic movement and international sports bodies in general. First, the idea that sport should be engaged in for the love of the game and not for money and, second, that sport ought to be above politics, or that politics should be kept out of sport. Since modern sport – in Britain from the 1960s especially (Whannel, 1986) – has become thoroughly pervaded with both commercialism and politics, an alternative rhetoric about sport has been developed. This utilitarian rhetoric 'provides an alternative set of legitimating ideals concerned with the social utility of sport for promoting such things as public health, social integration and collective morality' (Roche, 1993: 72) – a clear continuation of the nineteenth-century concerns about rational recreation and the 'cult of athleticism'. It was when this second rhetoric was introduced that the associated notions of 'sport for the community' and 'sport for all' were developed as major themes in the development of sport policy.

The traditional rhetoric about sport had its roots in the educational uses of sport in the nineteenth-century British public school system, which was largely responsible for the creation of modern sport as a cultural form and set of institutions. The alternative utilitarian rhetoric, though with some roots in the education sphere, has its main roots in the health promotion of sport by government and the medical establishment in the 1920s and 1930s. The full-blown rhetoric and promotion of sport for its social utility has really only occurred since the late 1950s. At times of apparent national and economic crisis – such as the 1920s and 1930s and the 1970s and the 1980s – the 'problem of enforced leisure' or unemployment has seen state intervention in leisure and sport move forward rather more quickly than at other times (Horne, 1986). As one of us once wrote : 'Nothing loosens the purse strings like panic' (Whannel, 1983: 92).

Roche (1993: 73–74) makes two observations about the sports 'policy community'. The first is that while sport has been presented, in a populist and thus quasi-democratic image, as being 'for all' in post-war campaigns, sports administration and sport policy making certainly have not been 'for all'. He argues that spectators and players have usually been either excluded or discouraged from involvement in the work of sport governing bodies and other policy-making agencies. Despite the rhetoric of 'consultation' and 'representation', in reality, the sports policy community 'has been largely unresponsive to and untouched by democratic ideals and practices' (ibid.: 74). The maintenance of the gentlemanly-amateur or elitist tradition remains reflected in the composition of many of the executive committees of the national governing bodies of sports and the leading forum for their collective voice, the Central Council for Physical Recreation (Whannel, 1983; Hargreaves, 1986). Although in December 2010 the CCPR changed its name to the Sport and Recreation Alliance, it retains this role as the voice of sports governing bodies.

Roche's second point is that the sports policy community has been consistently in a state of 'disorganisation'. Nonetheless, it has still tended to take for granted that it has a lot to offer the wider community. Roche argues that it might be better to adopt a more realistic appraisal of the limitations of sport as well as its vulnerabilities. In short, sport is one of the most 'divided, confused and conflictive policy communities in British politics' (Roche, 1993: 78). Roche makes a powerful case for seeing the sport policy community as an illustration of the tendencies in modern society towards internal over-complexity, in addition to external dependencies and vulnerability to external (especially economic) forces. Endemic system disorganisation and impotent policy making are the result (ibid.:77).

Speaking in 2003, the then UK Minister for Sport Richard Caborn (quoted in the *Guardian*, 26 March 2003, p. 31) complained that:

> There are 400 governing bodies and just 120 odd sports, and that illustrates how hard it is to find out what sports need and want . . . My biggest problem is with the voice of sport, as it doesn't speak with one voice at all.

There are several tensions or contradictions that underpin contemporary sports policy and many stem from this state of disorganisation. One revolves around the dichotomy between social inclusion and social exclusion. Sports policy is focused on both social order and health concerns. A second tension lies in the regulation of more commercialised sport, at a time when the government also wants to encourage markets. This raises issues of access versus commercialisation. A third tension exists between the true benefits and costs of hosting large international sports events. Who really benefits and what are the real costs of staging sports mega-events? We consider some of these questions below and in Chapter 13 (on mega-events

and the Olympic Games, see also Horne and Manzenreiter, 2006, and Horne and Whannel, 2011).

DIMENSIONS OF STATE INVOLVEMENT/INTERVENTION IN SPORT

As we have noted, sport in the United Kingdom has had a highly fragmented organisational structure, it has been underpinned by competing and sometimes conflicting aims and ideologies about the purpose of sport, and the state has not been formally integrated into sports institutions. Nonetheless, governments have increasingly taken sport seriously. As the Sports Council Annual Report for 1982–83 noted: 'The nation lifts its head when our national teams succeed. It also takes to the court, pitch or swimming pool when would-be champions have witnessed their idols demonstrating a high level of sports skill' (cited in Riordan, 1986: 38). Thus, the inspirational value of sports success in terms of nation building has generally been recognised. In the case of post-imperial Britain, with the loss of world-leader status since the 1950s, it has increasingly been assumed that international sports success would help generate patriotism.

Twenty-five years ago, Riordan (1986: 39) noted the gradual transition from the traditional amateur-elitist ethos to a more commercial-professional one in sport in capitalist economies:

> The dominant credo of the former has been that sport should be divorced from politics, government interference and commercialism, professional coaches, sports schools, and the like, and that there should be a firm commitment to the Olympic ideal.

In the UK, an apolitical view of sport has affected the political left-wing for most of the twentieth century (Hargreaves, 1987). Among the mainstream political parties in the UK this view of sport has also held sway – and continues to do so in terms of public debates about a 'golden age' of sport (see Polley, 1998: 1–6, for a discussion of this). Sport was never fully mobilised by the political left in Britain at a time when it was being used in other parts of the world to do precisely that (Kruger and Riordan, 1996). But recognition that sport and politics are related has developed since the 1950s. From a state of covert and informal relations, overt and more formal relations have developed.

Historical studies of the growth of state intervention in sport and leisure in Britain and other advanced capitalist countries suggest that governments have perceived sports policy as a means to an end, rather than an end in itself. A comparison with other countries suggests that national governments may have different goals that they wish to pursue through sports policy. They are nonetheless usually non-sporting goals – nation-building in Canada and the former GDR, and control of the young in France and Britain more generally (Houlihan, 1991: 40–50). The present 'state of play' in sport and leisure policy and institutions bears the legacy of dominant ideas in the nineteenth century as well as a 'conventional wisdom' as to the appropriate division of labour between the voluntary, the public and the commercial sectors of sport and leisure. A comparison between countries suggests that national governments may have different goals, 'few of which relate to the intrinsic benefits and values of sport' (Houlihan, 2002: 195), but they will often attempt to pursue them through sports policy.

From this stance it is possible to see the development of sport and leisure policy in Britain – from 'rational recreation' to the welfare state and 'recreational welfare', via the attack on popular culture and the growth of leisure in the nineteenth century and the development of a mixed economy of leisure in the twentieth – as underpinned by a number of key social concerns. Coalter *et al*. (1988) and Coakley (1998) outlined the range of motives for state involvement in sport in both Britain and the USA (see Table 8.2).

Four factors in particular stand out in explaining the change in the relationship – from informal to formal – between the state, at both central and local level, and sport in Britain since 1945. First, the growth of welfarism and collectivism as the dominant political policy ideology in the post-Second World War period led to calls for greater intervention. This period was to last until the mid-1970s. Second, the state has responded to trends – demographic, economic and social – that have encouraged greater involvement in the provision of sport and leisure facilities, especially for young people. Third, the state has responded to a series of specific crises or events that have beset sport or Britain's sporting accomplishments in the period, for example, a series of significant defeats in international football matches inflicted on England in the 1950s, the emergence of the anti-apartheid campaign using the sports boycott of South Africa as a key tactic in the 1960s and 1970s, and the decision formally to boycott the 1980 Olympic Games held in Moscow in protest at the Soviet Union invasion of Afghanistan. Finally, the growing

Table 8.2 Key concerns of sport and leisure policy in Britain and the USA (nineteenth century onwards)

	United Kingdom	USA
1	Urban deprivation	Safeguard public order
2	Physical health	Maintain and develop fitness and physical abilities of citizens?
3	Moral welfare	Promote the prestige of a community or nation?
4	Social integration, social control and the construction of 'community'	Promote a sense of identity, belonging and unity amongst citizens?
5	Self-improvement	Emphasise values and orientations consistent with dominant political ideology
6	Limits to public provision	Increase citizen support for a political leader and system?
7		Promote general economic development in the community and society

Source: UK adapted from Coalter *et al*. (1988) and USA from Coakley (1998: 403).

economic and social significance of sport has ensured that the state has to intervene in sport. In 1986, sport-related revenues were bringing in to central government £2.4 billion annually. By 1990, sport-related economic activity in Britain (according to the Sports Council, cited in Polley, 1998) constituted £8.27 billion (or 1.7 per cent of GNP), £9.75 billion of consumer expenditure and some 467,000 jobs. This growing economic significance of sport has also coincided with the transformation of sport brought about by the collapse of older sources of revenue and the growth of the sport/media/advertising nexus. These developments are discussed more fully in Chapters 11 and 12.

In an analysis of trends between 1945 and 1990, Peter Bramham identified gradual shifts in the rationale for sport intervention from the 1960s to the 1990s. He noted (1991: 140) that changing rationales for state involvement in sport in Britain 'reflect fundamental concerns about the nature of individual freedom and rights of citizenship'. After the Second World War he identified four predominant rationales:

1   'Traditional pluralism' – with the market and the voluntary sectors to the fore as the major providers of sporting opportunity, and the state in a residual role, stepping in where gaps or 'externalities' occur.
2   'Welfare reform' – with an emphasis on the proactive role of the public sector in meeting the needs of groups disadvantaged in the commercial and voluntary sectors. Sport and recreation came to be seen almost as a 'right of citizenship' – 'as the apex of the framework of the welfare state constructed since the war, with more basic needs having been provided for in earlier stages of development' (ibid.:140).
3   'Managerialist critique of welfare reformism' – stemming from a critique of the approach adopted under 2 above to reach and meet the needs of disadvantaged groups. Alternative approaches to sports provision, for example, community recreation services starting from the grass roots and decentralising service provision, were attempted.
4   'Neo-liberal' – in which the political thinking of the new right informed a departure from the emphasis upon publicly funded provision towards voluntary and commercial sector investment.

Each of these rationales can be related to different stages in the development of sports organisation and sports policy in the UK. The fourth rationale largely continued throughout the 1990s and the first decade of the 2000s despite the election of a Labour government (1997–2010). At the end of the 1990s, a specific sports policy interest of obtaining 'Best Value', associated with the 'Third Way' of the 'New Labour' governments developed. This approach did not make the sports policy community any more cohesive, but it did sustain the domination in sports policy of the combined ideologies of neo-liberalism and consumerism (Green, 2004).

The movement from one rationale to the next is best understood as a response to changes in socio-political and economic conditions, which can also be seen as tempering the full force of each. The highpoint of welfarism came in the mid-1970s when the 1975 Government

White Paper *Sport and Recreation* supported the notion of sport and recreation as a 'need' and a 'right' as a policy intention. As soon as the paper was published, however, economic developments overtook the Labour government. In order to avert a balance of payments crisis, a loan from the International Monetary Fund (IMF) was negotiated. Public expenditure cutbacks were a central condition of the loan and the White Paper's recommendations were not delivered. Interestingly, in the same way the 'neo-liberal' rationale for reducing government support for sport and recreation in the 1980s was restrained by, on the one hand, the recognition of the role of elite sport in contributing to national prestige (Hargreaves, 1986) and, on the other hand, the continued disintegration of social order in the inner cities. Hence Bramham (1991:142) concluded:

> In the late 1980s and early 1990s provision for mass participation is effectively being squeezed out of the public sector . . . while provision for elite sport is being manoeuvred towards private sector funding, leaving a residual public sector concern for physical health promotion and social order.

Sugden and Bairner (1993: 1–9) suggest that the state seeks to exert a degree of influence over sport because sport has come to play an influential part in an individual's socialisation and the construction of notions of community in modern life. They assert that 'the real link between sport and politics is a sociological one'. After Hoberman (1984), sport is seen to have no intrinsic value structure but rather it is a ready and flexible medium through which ideological associations can be relayed: 'despite the idealism of certain sports practitioners and administrators, who cling to the cherished belief that sport is or should be free from politics, historical evidence reveals that this is rarely the case' (Sugden and Bairner, 1993: 10).

It is for this reason that a major underlying reason for growing state intervention in sport in Britain since the 1950s has been the perennial 'youth problem'. The 'Wolfenden gap' identified in the 1950s was about how to get more young people participating in sport. This concern has re-emerged in every decade since although it has been couched in slightly different terms each time (see Coalter, 2007: Chapter 7 especially; Kremer *et al.*, 1997, for a comprehensive discussion of youth and sport in Britain; and Houlihan, 1997: Chapter 7, for a comparison of sports policy for young people in Britain and other advanced capitalist countries).

As sport has increasingly been shaped by neo-liberal discourse and practice, and despite the associated policies of privatisation and withdrawal of state funding more generally, sport has received unprecedented state interest and involvement in different societies (Houlihan, 2002). For example the promotion of sport and the nation through the hosting of sports mega-events has become a key aspect of government policy towards sport, and sport has been enlisted in strategies of urban renewal and regeneration. There has been a shift from promoting 'sport for all' to promoting 'sport for national glory' and this is very well illustrated by the United Kingdom.

Sport has become a most important feature of government intervention and regulation in the UK and this has been reflected in a number of initiatives and publications. The UK Cabinet

Office Strategy Unit document *Game Plan* (2002), for example, identified two main objectives for government in sport and physical activity. First, 'a major increase in participation . . . primarily because of the significant health benefits and to reduce the growing costs of inactivity'. Second, and maybe more importantly, 'a sustainable improvement in international competition, particularly in the sports which matter most to the public, primarily because of the "feelgood factor" associated with winning' (www.strategy.gov.uk/2002/sport/report/sum. htm, accessed 22 April 2003). During the 2005 General Election the Labour Party Manifesto, *Britain Forward Not Back*, was the only one published by the main political parties to specifically mention sport in detail. In Chapter 8, entitled 'Quality of life: Excellence for all', the Labour Party looked 'Forward to Olympic gold, not back to cuts in sport and culture'. While recognising the challenge of broadening participation in sport 'as wide as possible', the manifesto described support for 'the bid to bring the Olympics to London in 2012' as part of a plan to bring 'regeneration to the East End of London', creating sporting, economic and cultural legacies. Since 1999 Scotland has had its own Parliament, with responsibility devolved for certain aspects of government including sport. An amended version of the manifesto in Scotland therefore pointed out that if the bid for the 2012 Olympics were successful, 'it would inspire a generation of sportsmen and women throughout the United Kingdom', and noted that Scottish business had 'already won contracts through the bid process'. In addition, the Labour Party was 'studying plans to bring the Commonwealth Games to Glasgow in 2014', which would 'bring regeneration to the East End of Glasgow and leave lasting sporting, economic and cultural legacies'.

As we hear, parts of major British cities are considered to be in need of renewal, but whether the staging of major sports events in them is going to accomplish this remains debatable. What the true legacy of the 2012 London Summer Olympic and Paralympic Games and the Commonwealth Games in Glasgow in 2014 will be are questions for the future. What is not so debatable is that an uneven balance continues to be present in the politics of sport. In supporting certain sports and events rather than others, governments help to define what is legitimate as opposed to illegitimate sport and leisure practice.

CONCLUSION

Rather than providing a coherent and unified policy for sport, Maurice Roche (1993) argued that the sports policy community in British sport has been little short of a 'disorganised shambles' for much of the post-war period. In this, he shares the conclusions of both pluralists Henry and Houlihan and the Marxist John Hargreaves. This situation reflects the influence of three associated ideologies and the lack of a central organising body for sport. The sports community in Britain has been, and remains, largely a very divided policy community. The three dominant ideologies attached to sport in Britain in the twentieth century – amateurism, welfarism and, since the 1980s, commercialism – continue to co-exist and compete for influence in British sports policy. Different sections of the state, quangos and the national governing bodies of sport all provide different inputs into debates about sport and offer examples of these ideologies. Hence there has been no clearly articulated national sports policy in Britain. Increasingly this pluralistic debate is framed within the wider context of political internationalisation and economic globalisation. Hence there is diversity and no single policy model that best explains sports policy. Policies for sport have had far less influence than might be imagined on sports development and trends in participation and involvement. Interest in sport is divided and reflects the social divisions of society along lines of class, gender, ethnicity, age and impairment. There is a wide gap between the rhetoric and reality of sports participation.

In the past twenty years, government sports policy has developed in a context of the spread of neo-liberal economic ideology and globalisation. This has produced a change in the relationship between sport and the state. Different states use sport for different non-sports ends – economic development and social development, nation building and signalling (branding the nation) and to assist in economic and political liberalisation. As Houlihan (2002: 94) notes, the 'willingness of governments to humble themselves before the IOC and FIFA through lavish hospitality and the strategic deployment of presidents, prime ministers, royalty and super-models, is a reflection of the value that governments place on international sport'. The promotion of sports mega-events – the Olympics and the World Cup especially – in turn relies on two ingredients. On the one hand the media are essential since without the media sports mega-events would not be able to attract the public's attention and corporate sponsorship. On the other hand, without the thousands of volunteers who work for free, the Games would not be able to take place at all. The state constructs what is and what is not legitimate sports practice. The state also creates the framework within which partnerships between local authorities, voluntary sports and commercial organisations operate. The neo-liberal state may have 'less responsibility for direct service delivery' of sport but it has retained, if not actually expanded, its influence because of the other agencies' dependency on state resources (Houlihan, 2002: 200; see also Green and Houlihan, 2004). Hence in contemporary society, the state remains the place to campaign – whether it is over inequalities and social exclusion, the regulation of mega-events, human rights or environmental risks in sport. Sociologists and other social scientists need to continue to study these developments with greater reflexivity; not as cheerleaders, but as critical investigators into the use of sport by the state and corporate interests.

ESSAY QUESTIONS

1   Why has the state become more involved in sport in the past 50 years?
2   'In supporting certain sports and events rather than others, governments help to define what is legitimate as opposed to illegitimate sport and leisure practice.' Discuss.

understanding sport

FURTHER READING

M. Green, 'Changing Policy Priorities for Sport in England: The Emergence of Elite Sport Development as Key Policy Concern', *Leisure Studies*, 23(4) (2004): 365–385 provides an overview of the shift in policy focus from sport for all to sport for national glory.

M. Roche, 'Sport and Community: Rhetoric and Reality in the Development of British Sport Policy', in J. Binfield and J. Stevenson (eds), *Sport, Culture and Politics* (Sheffield: Sheffield Academic Press, 1993), is a concise and astute summary of phases and issues in British sports policy.

CHAPTER NINE

GOVERNANCE AND SPORT

INTRODUCTION

This chapter focuses on governance, as the processes through which rules are made and applied to that sport are efficiently organised and regulated by looking first at how rules are made and who makes them. The Olympic Games offer an example of a sporting regulatory body which has the power to make rules. Second, the chapter looks at what happens when rules are broken, and, finally, at the issues in the contemporary governance of sport and then the possibilities of changing the rules, especially in promoting wider participation and greater equality in sport. As Chapter 8 demonstrated, sport and politics are interconnected. Sport and its practices are situated within wider political and social terrains in which rights and responsibilities are contested and which are marked by power struggles. Sport is big business, so sometimes the stakes are high. Sport also generates its own power struggles and contributes to, as well as reflecting, social and political change. The governance of sport is embedded in the politics of sport because power operates at different levels; through routine and everyday compliance with rules and regulations and through the regulatory practices, which govern sport at local, national and international levels. Sport involves rules: playing by the rules and sometimes breaking the rules. Sport is ruled and governed but rules are also broken and the governance of sport involves measures to limit such transgressions.

This chapter looks at the governance of sport, based upon an understanding of governance as a range of practices which extend across the decisions made by particular governments and the governing bodies of sport at different times, and the routine, everyday practices of people who participate in sport, usually according to the rules, but sometimes who bend the rules to their own, or their team's, advantage. Governance involves the operation of power at different levels and to different degrees and includes a range of mechanisms, some of which generate more power than others. Some of the players in this field have the power to influence and shape outcomes more effectively than others, but change happens when different forces come together in the governance of sport. The chapter identifies the different strands in the governance of sport: governing bodies, legislation, the media, body practices, all of which are specific to time and place and subject to change. The approach taken in this chapter, which can usefully be applied to sport (Cole, 1993; Markula and Pringle, 2006), is one which is based upon an understanding of the governance of sport as multi-dimensional. This approach builds upon a Foucauldian understanding of power as operating diffusely (Foucault, 1981) through diverse relationships which include the practices of the people who play sport, the governing bodies of sport and the wider social, political and cultural terrain. Governance incorporates legislation and the allocation of resources at international, national and more local levels, and the social and cultural values which make up social relations, all of which are subject to and productive of rules. Governing bodies make the rules but they also have to change the rules in response to social and cultural changes.

There are the rules of the game on the field which include conventions of what is allowed and what is not in the culture of sport. Then there are the regulatory bodies which govern sport and the wider framework of legislation and the legitimised practices which, for example, are concerned with promoting widening participation, equal opportunities and fair play, which are embedded in laws such as the UK 2010 Equality Act. This is illustrative of the proliferation of legislation purporting to enhance equality and justice in neo-liberal states. Such practices are also increasingly part of the running of quasi-legal, quasi-autonomous and charitable bodies and routine cultural practices within organisations and institutions which make up contemporary social networks in which sport plays a significant role. Sport is frequently seen as a mechanism for promoting equal opportunities and widening participation (Rowe *et al.*, 2004; Wagg, 2004; Woodward, 2006; Carrington, 2010; Houlihan and Green, 2011).

Sport is particularly wide-ranging in that it plays a significant part in global and local economic networks, involved in so much of the contemporary economic infrastructure, as well as embracing local and community engagement and being an area of social life in which people have enormous personal and psychic investment. Sport is also a commodity: a means of making a living for some and of generating wealth. It also matters to people through the personal and collective attachments which are made, for example, to particular teams and clubs.

Sport is a distinctive field. Embodied practices and specific ways of acting and ways of being are central to sport, as Chapter 7 demonstrated, and sport also has its own regulatory frameworks which set the rules for these embodied practices. Not only are body practices central to sporting projects, sport also has particular features that mark the field out, including its histories and concern with play as well as with competition and cooperation, and the rules which govern sport. Sport is fun but it is also powerfully rule-governed and strongly regulated (Giulianotti, 2005; Guttmann, 2005) and these rules, their making and breaking and transformation are constitutive of the governance of sport. The next section considers the setting of rules, engaging with rules and breaking rules, before going on to examine the governing bodies of the Olympics and the Paralympics. Finally, the discussion focuses on the key players and stakeholders in the making (and breaking) of rules of sport.

WHO MAKES THE RULES?

Sporting regulatory bodies are temporally and spatially situated within different fields and in relation to particular sports. Each sport has its own history and a genealogy which informs the processes through which it is regulated. There are, however, continuities; historically, such bodies have their roots in civil society and have developed through voluntary associations. There are also strong social and cultural continuities, for example, in relation to gendered, racialised inequalities. The governance of sport has developed through the interconnections between different social worlds.

For example, in England, the Football Association (FA) was formed in 1863 to clarify and simplify the range of different sets of rules by which football was played and to attempt to adjudicate in cases of local disagreement, such as the Sheffield clubs who continued to play by their own set of rules into the 1870s. Its stated aims include promoting the development of the game among all ages, backgrounds and abilities in terms of participation and quality to the greatest possible number of people, although it remains largely dominated by white men. The FA regulates the game on and off the field of play. The FA organises senior men's, youth and women's national competitions and England national representative teams in international matches, most notably the men's senior team in the FIFA World Championships and the UEFA European Championships and friendly fixtures. The Women's Football Association was formed in 1969. In spite of the popularity of the women's game (in 1920, 53,000 people watched Dick Kerr's Ladies beat St Helen's, 4–0), the FA banned women from playing on Football League grounds in 1921 because the game was deemed unsuitable for females and ought not to be encouraged. From 1983, the WFA has been affiliated to the FA on the same basis as County Football Associations. The Women's Super League, an eight-team competition, was started in 2011 to promote the women's game. In football, as in most sports, women's participation is regulated by a sub-group of the main regulating body of the men's sport.

In sport, this is often through the relationship between body practices in the field and the regulatory bodies which set boundaries and measure standards. Sport has evolved through a changing relationship between governance and the apparatuses of regulation in sport and routine body practices.

As argued in earlier chapters, sports have histories and are always located within the wider narratives of social, political and cultural life. Sporting bodies are temporally and spatially situated within different fields, ranging from specific bodies, such as the International Olympic Committee (IOC), the International Federation of Association Football or Fédération Internationale de Football Association (FIFA), the Amateur Athletics Association (AAA), the International Association of Athletics Federations (IAAF), the Football Association (FA), the International Cricket Association (ICC), and the World Boxing Association (WBA) to legislative and quasi-governmental bodies and the media which have become particularly powerful in the re-creation and articulation of sport, especially in the media, sport and commercial sponsorship nexus. The governing bodies of sport dictate who can and who

understanding sport

cannot participate and there is a long history of exclusionary practices in the governance of sport. The governing bodies of sport like the IAAF have even been called upon to decide who are women and who are men, as Chapter 7 showed, for example in the case of gender verification. Increasingly the interior as well as the exterior of the body is the focus of the bodies that regulate and discipline sport. DNA is checked to determine the sex of participants in sport, as evident in IOC practices at the Olympic Games, and body fluids are assessed in sport to ascertain whether illegal substances such as performance-enhancing drugs have been consumed in order to comply with the rules of sports regulatory bodies and the wider sphere of governance.

A range of constituencies are involved, each of which is caught up in the power networks which shape what happens in sport and how sport is regulated and constituted. Regulatory bodies prescribe where the sport can be played and by whom, and which body practices are acceptable and which are not. These regulatory bodies in sport determine not only the parameters of what counts as their sport and how they are played, but also some of the relationship between the sport and its spectators.

Rules are embedded in documents like the Olympic Charter, the set of rules governing the Olympic Games and the Olympic Movement, which have to change in response to the transforming social climate. For example, the Olympic Charter, updated in February 2010 (IOC 2010: http://www.olympic.org/Documents/olympic_charter_en.pdf, accessed 30 January 2012) has required additional articles to embrace diverse social relations and widening participation over the past 100 years. For example, the IOC's role has been expanded to 'encourage and support the promotion of women in sport at all levels and in all structures, with a view to implementing the principle of equality of men and women' (http://www.olympic.org/Documents/Reference_documents_Factsheets/Women_in_Olympic_Movement.pdf, accessed 30 January 2012). The IOC has enormous power over the organisation of the Olympics but has to balance the competing interests of different stakeholders.

The media exerted a major force on changes in sport, including shaping and changing the rules of engagement. The media can have enormous influence (Whannel, 2002; Sugden and Tomlinson, 2011) and even change the practices in the field or on the track and in the ring, as happened in boxing with the advent of television broadcasting (Rader, 1984). One of the best examples is that of cricket and fixed over games, especially limited over, Twenty 20 and the Indian Premier League (IPL). The media also popularise sport and bring it into other domains, such as those of celebrity culture (Whannel, 2002). The presence of celebrities is ubiquitous during attempts to gain the right to stage sports events. This was evident in the London 2012 bidding process in Singapore in 2005 when the then Prime Minister Tony Blair flew in for just a few days, and even more so in the bid to stage the men's football World Cups for 2018 or 2022. England was unsuccessful despite the presence of David Beckham in a line-up that included David Cameron, the British Prime Minister at the time and Prince William, the next but one heir to the throne. Celebrity status, like that embodied in David Beckham, lends legitimacy and authenticity through the integration of sports stars into the institutions of the state and the synergies between the fields of sport and of governance more widely.

Sponsors and advertisers specialise in different markets but have both massive economic power and considerable interest in maintaining the credibility of sports events, which has not, however, always prevented them from breaking the rules. Sponsorship can of course be withdrawn from athletes who transgress and break the rules themselves. Professional athletes also play a part, especially in the implementation of rules and even creating new practices. Fans too play a part although this depends in many ways upon the sport. Football fans have challenged profit-motivated global capital embodied in foreign owners which has become hegemonic in the governance of football. The case of FC United in Manchester is instructive, with a structure of governance based on local supporters and serving their interests rather than those of global capital. FC United was formed with the assistance of Supporters Direct and the model of an Industrial Provident Society (IPS) was adopted as the basis on how the club would be structured. A 'one member one vote' ethos runs through the core of the model (FC United Governance, http://www.publications.parliament.uk/pa/cm201011/cmselect/cmcumeds/writev/792/fg55.htm, accessed 30 January 2012). There is, however, diversity and specificity in different places and at different times. Governments, too, as was shown in Chapter 8, play a big part in shaping the governance of sport and the state, and the institutions of state also play key roles through departments of state, like the Department of Media, Culture and Sport (DCMS, http://www.culture.gov.uk/, accessed 30 January 2012).

Governing bodies make the rules of sport, but professional athletes, media companies and spectators all want to have their say. On the playing fields, rules must be interpreted and policed by the referees, umpires and other officials, but players have their own codes and interpretations of rules, especially the rules governing physical contact and personal interaction. How these conflicts are worked out, negotiated, and struggled over, is what is meant by the *process* of governance.

THE GOVERNANCE OF THE GAMES

The Olympics offer an example of the ever increasing complexity of the governance of sport. The Olympic principles are embedded in the Olympic Charter which encompasses a vast range of articles setting out approved principles and practices. The Charter has expanded to accommodate change. The Olympic Charter with its five chapters and 61 articles which comes to 96 pages in the most recent version (at the time of writing), outlines the guidelines and rules of the governance of the Olympic Games, the Olympic movement, and its three main constituents: the International Olympic Committee, the International Federations, and the National Olympic Committees (http://www.olympic.org/Documents/olympic_charter_en.pdf, accessed 30 January 2012). This bureaucratic edifice is both generative and reflexive of contemporary social norms and organisation but resonates with the origins and founding principles of the modern Games and of the principles upon which they were based. What makes the governance of the Olympics distinctive is the explicitly stated ideals and the concept of an Olympic Movement which incorporates and expresses particular sporting values, notably ones that explicitly and emphatically excluded the participation of women, and asserted the values of militaristic, white, aristocratic masculinity (Woodward, 2012). The first Games of the twentieth century in 1904 also included displays of imperialist racism called Anthropology Days (Brownell, 2008) and the modern Games have been marked by racialisation and ethnicisation as well as expressions of resistance, most notably in Mexico in 1968 with the Black Power salutes of John Carlos and Tommie Smith.

The modern Olympics incorporates a vast regulatory system which is a global institution, which may be seen as an 'informal civil institution' and one of the 'less visible aspects of global governance' (Chappelet and Kuhler-Mabbott, 2008: xiii). The governance of the Games includes a network of actors. These are the key players of the IOC itself, the organising committees of particular Games, which are contingent on the host city of course and last only for the duration of those Games, the International Sports Federations, the National Olympic Committees and National Sports Federations. National Olympic Committees (NOCs) are responsible for governing the selection and development of the teams that represent their nation in the Olympic and Paralympic Games (see Horne and Whannel, 2012, Chapter 2).

The Olympic system involves a complex set of processes that have been modified and transformed in light of social and cultural changes, such as the wider participation of women in sport and the implementation of race equality legislation, as well, most notably and most recently, in response to charges of corruption and deception. The Olympic system came late to ethical regulation with an Ethics Commission only being set up in 1999, the same year as the World Anti-Doping Agency (WADA) was established, in a climate of controversy and crisis for the IOC when there was not only media coverage of administrative corruption, but also revelations of drug abuse by athletes and coaches. One of the most significant areas of change has been the establishment of the Paralympics as a parallel organisation with its own system of governance.

PARALYMPICS: NEW SETS OF RULES FOR THE GAMES

The Paralympics were not developed until well after the establishment of the modern Games. Their origins too belong to a particular historical moment when a number of factors combined to create the possibility of such a sporting competition. Militarism, heroic masculinities and embodied sporting practices combine to generate new organisations and practices in the Paralympics too. The Paralympics have gendered roots, having been set up for war veterans at the end of the Second World War, as sport was conventionally attributed to providing therapy for injured military personnel, that is, men who had received injuries in the war.

The Paralympics were set up as parallel to the Olympics, that is, to operate alongside the Summer and Winter Games, rather than be alternate Games. Categories of disability formulated as allowable are broken down into six broad categories. The categories are amputee, Cerebral

145

Palsy, intellectual disability, wheelchair, visually impaired, and 'Others' which includes conditions such as multiple sclerosis and congenital impairments which have different manifestations. Some disabilities have different regulatory bodies, for example the Deaflympics for deaf people (http://www.deaflympics.com/about/, accessed 30 January 2012) and the Special Games (http://www.specialolympics.org/, accessed 29 January 2012) include athletes with intellectual incapacities.

The International Paralympic Committee (IPC) is the global governing body of the Paralympic Movement. The IPC organises the Summer and Winter Paralympic Games, and serves as the International Federation for nine sports, for which it supervises and coordinates the World Championships and other competitions:

> The IPC is committed to enabling Paralympic athletes to achieve sporting excellence and to developing sport opportunities for all persons with a disability from the beginner to elite level. In addition, the IPC aims to promote the Paralympic values, which include courage, determination, inspiration and equality.
> (http://www.paralympic.org/Sport/, accessed 30 January 2012)

The IPC was founded on 22 September 1989, as an international non-profit organisation formed and run by 170 National Paralympic Committees (NPCs) from five regions and four disability-specific international sports federations (IOSDs). The IPC Headquarters and its management team which are located in Bonn, Germany, are described in the contemporary language of diversity politics and the management of social inclusion as having a democratic constitution and structure, made up of elected representatives (http://www.paralympic.org/Sport/, accessed 30 January 2012).

Whereas other international sports organisations for athletes with a disability are either limited to one disability group or to one specific sport, the IPC is an umbrella organisation which represents several sports and disabilities. Social, cultural and medical change have impacted upon the organisation of the Paralympics along with different classificatory systems which have been applied to and created multi-disability competitions, which are included in the Paralympic Games. The Paralympics grew quickly and became important international sport events. The need to govern the Games more efficiently and to speak with a single voice to the IOC resulted in the foundation of the ICC, the International Co-ordination Committee of World Sports Organizations for the Disabled in 1982. Ten years later, the ICC was replaced by the International Paralympic Committee (IPC). The Winter Paralympics in Lillehammer in 1994 were the first Paralympic Games under the management of the IPC, which numbers about 165 member nations. More countries competed at the Beijing 2008 Paralympics (3951 athletes, 146 countries) than in the Munich 1972 Olympic Games. In Beijing, the degree of media coverage was unprecedented in spite of anxieties that were voiced in the media about the status of the Paralympics and disabled athletes prior to the Beijing Games in 2008. With interest in and acceptance for sport for persons with a disability growing, the expansion of the Paralympics is most likely to continue in the future.

When Paralympic sport was introduced in England, in 1948, it was primarily geared towards ex-servicemen injured in the conflicts of the Second World War. Owing to the nature of its inception, there was a notable disparity in the balance of male and female athletes at that time. However, 60 years later, the 2008 Beijing Games still demonstrated a dominance of male athletic participation of almost 2:1, suggesting that gender inequality remains a significant issue.

MAKING THE RULES: KEY PLAYERS

There are seven key players in the making and shaping of rules in sport. First, governing bodies, like the IOC, are central to sports rule making. They will have their own concerns over preserving their own autonomous power to make rules but they must also balance the many competing interests of stakeholders. Second, the media play a key role; television has been a major force in shaping rule changes in sport, to make sport more televisual, to encourage high-scoring games or to create more space for advertising. Parts of the media may also thrive on the controversy that rule disputes generate and they, of course, have considerable power over the course of the debate through their words and images. Third, sponsors and advertisers are engaged in accessing different markets and have different needs in terms of image and presentation; breweries are unlikely to call for a limit to presenting a positive image of drinking, while tennis and golf sponsors making luxury watches would oppose attempts at changing the conventions concerning advertising and display in those sports. In general, sponsors all have an interest in maintaining the credibility and honesty of sports contests. Sponsors rapidly withdraw their support if a sport star invokes hostile public attention, as in the case of golfer Tiger Woods in 2009, who has now been reinstated after the requisite repentance. Sponsors' economic power and influence are potentially immense; this has been illustrated in cases of doping, when sponsorship has been withdrawn from athletes accused of transgression, and even from their sports, with seriously damaging consequences. Fourth, professional athletes are implicated in the governance of sport and how it changes and adapts. Central to the actual interpretation and implementation of rules of all kinds, professional athletes have a range of interests in the process, including protecting their careers, bodies and income as well as creating rules that favour their style of playing. Athletes need to be included in competition to have any chance of succeeding; for those who have been on the margins, for example, women in many sports and disabled athletes, there have to be different strategies to challenge rules and conventions that have excluded them. Fifth, sports fans engage in different routine practices in expressing their support or registering disapproval. In England, the professional foul is still considered unacceptable, while in Italian football crowds respond to last-ditch efforts, even where they result in a red card, with generous applause (Goldblatt, 2007). Last, but not least, governments have invested a great deal in supporting sport, both because of its perceived impact on health and well-being, and because of the desire to act as hosts for international events. They have enormous potential power over all sports authorities, through funding, legislation, scrutiny, combating corruption and the promotion of social inclusion.

Each of these stakeholders in sport implement forces in the processes through which sport is governed. Each element has its own sets of interests, sources of power and ways of exerting influence. How these forces interact and intersect on different occasions shapes the governance of the sport.

RE-MAKING THE RULES

Sport is characterised by rules. The rules we follow tell us we are playing the same games. These rules are universal – or are they? Some players bend the rules and others break them. Sport, as distinguished from organised play, has rules agreed and known in advance to all participants. Without rules, there is neither consistency nor equality. However, this does not guarantee that the rules will be followed unambiguously. The cricketer and commentator Ed Smith describes instances in sport of practices such as, in his own sport of cricket, walking, when a batsman, rather than waiting for the umpire's verdict, would leave the crease because he (Smith's experience only covers the men's game) knew he had nicked the ball; honourable sportsmanship indeed (Smith, 2008). This is not to say that discourses of sporting honour are absent from cricket, as was manifest in the India–England second Test match at Trent Bridge, Nottingham, on the third day on 31 July 2011, when two English batsmen assumed that the last ball before tea was a four and casually set off for the pavilion, only to discover that Ian Bell was in fact technically run out. The Indian captain Mahendra Singh Dhoni ultimately rescinded his appeal in response to the England captain's request. Commentators applauded Dhoni's honourable actions and celebrated what it meant for the game of cricket. The surprise with which this was received, however, is testament to Ed Smith's argument about changing practices of fair play. Smith poses questions about rule breaking and when it might be acceptable to cheat, or even if it is really cheating 'there is the rule book as it's written, a rule book as it is played , and a rule book as it is watched and absorbed in the stands' (Smith, 2008: 120). Practices change; fans might currently be less enthusiastic about their team being honourable and walking in cases where the umpire did not notice, and the opposition did not play by the same rules. Cultural practices and expectations, especially of spectators and promoters, affect the rules and the way sport is played. Some forms of rule breaking, however, are less innocuous and the rules are not always fair and equitable.

The rules and the ethos of sport may stress equity and fair play, none more so than those expressed in the Olympic Movement, but not only are rules often broken, the Olympics have been beset by scandals of corruption, even at the very highest level of their governing body, the IOC (Jennings and Simpson, 1992; Jennings, 1996, Lenskyj, 2000, 2002, 2008) and more recently FIFA (Jennings, 2006; http://news.bbc.co.uk/sport1/hi/football/13598982.stm, accessed 30 January 2012).

Sporting rules, like all forms of rules, have to be formulated, communicated, policed, interpreted and, if necessary, protected by sanctions and punishments. At each and every stage of that process more than one social group or one authority is implicated in the power struggles.

Sport is not always a level playing field and the rules of sport have also served to exclude large numbers of people, or at least made it difficult for them to participate fully. Women have long been excluded from different sports and sporting competitions: women were totally excluded from the first modern Olympics and from many specific events in later Games. Although there was a short demonstration of women's boxing in 1904, it was not until 2012 that the sport was permitted at the Olympics. It was only late in the twentieth century that women's boxing was permitted, with bans not being lifted until the 1970s in most US states (Women Boxing Archive Network, http://www.womenboxing.com/historic.htm, accessed 30 January 2012). The British Board of Boxing Control did not set up a licensing scheme for women until Jane Couch won her landmark case in 1997 (Amateur Boxing Forum, http://blog.abforum.co.uk/women-boxing/womens-boxing-history/, accessed 30 January 2012).

Although there have been enormous changes in the widening participation of women in sport, governance of women's competitions remains largely within the framework of the men's organisations of governance, which precludes change. For example, women's football is governed by the Football Association (FA) and the women's game is a sub-division of the dominant men's game (http://www.thefa.com/, accessed 30 January 2012).

In order to gain recognition, women have had to resist and challenge the constraints of existing, often patriarchal, governance; sometimes they have had to break the rules. The woman credited with doing most for promoting women's track and field athletics, Fanny Blankers-Koen, had to break the rule forbidding women to enter more than three individual events at the 1948 Olympics in order to win four gold medals (100 and 200 metres, 80 metre hurdles and 4 × 100 metres relay). Current debates about the classification of disability are often framed by the parameters of rules, as in the case of the South African athlete Oscar Pistorius (Woodward, 2009) (see Chapter 7). New technologies call into question established rules about the classification of disabilities and what constitutes legitimate enhancement of capacities and performance.

Modern sport is highly structured. First, sports are structured in some ways whether they are played formally or informally; a knockabout on the tennis court or a kickaround in the park or in the street with a make-shift ball and coats for goalposts still follows rules. All sports are governed by either written or unwritten rules; these rules are understood, however rudimentarily, by all who participate. Rules may be embedded in the body practices which make up the sport so that they become taken for granted, or at the other end of the spectrum, they can be highly formalised and complex, requiring considerable expertise to grasp the full range of regulations. Second, most sports are temporally circumscribed, as illustrated by designated time periods such as innings, halves and quarters, or number and time of bouts and rounds, or allocated attempts within a specific time period. Time scales have been adapted in particular instances to prevent indefinitely long sporting encounters and sports have instituted tie-breakers, sudden death playoffs, and shorter versions of selected sports , for example, one-day cricket matches and more recently the development of Twenty-20, Day-Night games. Women often participate for shorter timescales and cover less distance or play fewer sets or games. Third, most sports are spatially circumscribed by the sites of their venues, whether these are arenas, courts, fields, pools, rings, rinks, stadiums, or tracks, with the most privileged, elite athletes accessing the most superior sites. Finally, modern sports tend to be formally administered, whether by local clubs, universities, colleges or schools, professional teams, or sport federations which can be regional, national or international.

BREAKING THE RULES

There is a complex and variable relationship between rules and conventions, formal and informal power. In the range of different groups who have a stake in how the rules are made and how they are interpreted, some of these groups clearly have more influence than others. One of the big questions is how the governing bodies of sport address rule breaking when it extends to corrupt practices, and also who has the power to effect change or initiate actions (Mason et al., 2006).

Match fixing has a long history, often marked by sport's links with gambling, and is usually effected by bribing competitors. One example is the middleweight boxer Jake LaMotta (of the motion picture *Raging Bull* fame) throwing his fight against Billy Fox in 1947. Another is provided by the US 1919 Major League Baseball World Series, during which one of the most well-known gambling conspiracies between players and gamblers, the infamous Black Sox scandal, took place when eight members of the Chicago franchise conspired with gamblers to throw the series. Soccer too has suffered from match fixing, with several examples of Mafia-linked corruption in Italian football as well as the suspension of clubs and the imprisonment of British players for match fixing in France as in the case of Olympique Marseilles (Hill, 2010). Match fixing has been done by teams and clubs that seek to avoid relegation to a lower league or to ensure promotion, and by individuals and clubs to win titles, but all are strongly linked to commercial and financial gain, and many are connected to global gambling networks. Globalisation transgresses legal as well as national boundaries.

The Olympics, with their strong ethos of fair play and amateurism, are not immune from such corruption; the IOC was rife with corrupt practices (Jennings and Simpson, 1992; Jennings, 1996; Lenskyj, 2002), but this came to a head with the 2002 Games at Salt Lake City in Utah when Marc Hodler, an IOC member, broke ranks and revealed that agents had been bribed to vote for cities bidding for the right to host the Games. Salt Lake City, having failed to win their earlier bid to host the Games, realised that they would have to change tactics and offered bribes like everyone else. IOC members and their relatives received benefits from city officials.

The Olympics have been tarnished by the revelations of corruption, which most importantly highlights the need for reform of the governance of sport. Corruption is clearly closely linked to economic factors, given the enormous financial benefits that can accrue from sporting success or, in the case of the Olympics, from hosting such an enormous event, but the desire for economic gain is not the only factor to be addressed. There are cultural and social factors in play too. Corruption takes a variety of forms.

CRISES OF CONFIDENCE AT THE OLYMPIC GAMES

In the run-up to the 2012 London Olympics the IOC president Jacques Rogge was quoted as saying that match fixing and betting were not only embedded in football and cricket but also was a serious risk in Olympic sport. Rogge acknowledged the temptation to cheat among athletes who are not highly paid but attributed cheating to 'human nature' (Rogge, cited in Gibson, 2011: 12). This explanation, which stresses the social processes, gives greater emphasis to the networks and financial systems of gambling which permeate contemporary sport and the processes which facilitate the operation of betting syndicates and the proliferating cultures of gambling rather than prioritising a generic human condition. Temptation has to operate within the wider social field of possibilities and gambling is ubiquitous in the culture of sport.

Doping in sport is a major problem marked by some key moments, which can be categorised by sport and by impact. Some of these key moments in the history of doping in sport have both generated problems and demanded solutions for the governance of sport.

Several of the most memorable examples have taken place at the Tour de France, from Tommy Simpson's 1967 fatal use of amphetamine, which led to limited drug testing in 1968, to the Festina team's use of EPO (erythropoietin) in 1998, when there was evidence of organised doping programmes for entire teams as 400 vials were discovered in the possession of the coach and the Festina team was expelled from the Tour. One of the most dramatic incidents, which also presented a turning point from discourses of concern for the health of the athlete to moral censure expressed in the language of fair play and its converse, cheating, was the case of Ben Johnson, who took anabolic steroids at the 1988 Olympic Games in South Korea. Football has not been immune: Diego Maradona took a cocktail of drugs at the 1994 World Cup. Other footballers have been charged and England's Rio Ferdinand was suspended for 8 months for failing to give a test sample. Public censure has led to stronger anti-doping policies being introduced by all major sports. Drugs such as tretrahydrogestrinone have been developed to evade detection in use as was demonstrated by the case of the English sprinter Dwain Chambers in 2003 (Cashmore, 2005).

Some of the concerns about doping in sport are presented within a medicalised discourse of concern for the athletes involved and the health problems related to drug use. Wider issues relate to the extent of drug abuse and the damage to world sport and the reputation and ethos of sport.

Although individual athletes might gain in the short term, if discovered, they lose on all counts: financially, in their reputation and through banning, making it difficult to recover their position in global sport. Damage is seen to be experienced not only by athletes; drug use can damage sport by toppling heroes from their elevated positions, as in the Ben Johnson case; drugs are bad for business, as well as sport is situated within a profitable global business.

ROOM FOR IMPROVEMENT

The promotion of cohesion and of equality also demands measures to combat corruption. Sunder Katwala argues that sports' governing bodies cannot handle the corruption that is endemic and which has affected every major sport (Katwala, 2002). Governance is seen as both the site of corruption and the solution. Some sporting bodies, notably the IOC, albeit a governing body which has greatly improved its organisation, and FIFA, have become synonymous with the negative aspects of international bureaucracy, corruption and inertia.

Katwala argues that the common thread linking sporting controversies is less a crisis of commercialism than a crisis of governance based on the claim that there is a deep-rooted common governing culture across sport. The aristocratic culture of the elite amateur has been removed to facilitate sport's global transformation, but informal governing structures and closed cultures have largely survived, despite their decreasing ability to cope with the big business of global sport today or with the pressure of an age of accountability. This culture also embedded hegemonic masculinity (Connell, 1997) through personnel, including the same men, rarely if ever women, who dominate the governing bodies of sport such as the IOC and FIFA and the cultural networks of governmentality (Woodward, 2009, 2012).

Katwala argues that only effective sporting governance can deliver the trust of supporters and those employed in the networks of sport. Almost every government around the world commits public resources to sporting infrastructure because of sport's perceived benefits to improving health and education, to creating jobs and preventing crime, and promoting less tangible impacts on social cohesion and the nation's image at home and abroad.

Like all decision-makers today, those governing sport increasingly have to make their decisions under public scrutiny. While multinational corporations are learning to adapt to media and public pressure, those governing sport have frequently failed to do so, as is evident from the scandals that frequently happen around the hosting of major tournaments, such as the Olympic Games and the men's football World Cup. The scandals that may have hit the headlines are nonetheless often individualised and not presented as problems of governance.

Governing sport has become complex. National and international bodies were created to codify the rules, to create the first organised tournaments, to encourage and to facilitate international exchange. But the rapid globalisation and commercialisation of sport involves a whole host of competing interests. Increasingly key questions in governing sport cannot be solved domestically or even by international sporting bodies alone. Effective action on drugs needs unannounced testing during training – that means international agreements on keeping track of athletes to special visa regimes for the IAAF's 'flying squad' drug-testers. The headline controversies feed into a wider debate about whether sporting bodies have the capacity to deal with the new challenges – of agents and player power, the growing role of the courts, with sponsors, new media rights and technological advances, both fair and foul.

152

GOVERNING SPORT IN THE TWENTY-FIRST CENTURY

Sport's governing bodies are independent and autonomous and have sovereignty which they seek to protect, but they are also located within changing societies and cultures. One of the main internal areas of transformation has been to create accountability and transparency (Katwala, 2002).

Katwala suggests that international and national governance of sport is in a parlous state and suggests that the cause of the current crisis is not simply economic. Politics and the practices of governance have failed to keep up with technological and economic change. Sport is governed by self-policing apparatuses and mechanisms, and the autonomy of the governing of sport has meant that it has been resistant to democratic practices and public transparency. The governance of sport remains patriarchal and elitist and has not managed to assimilate social, political and cultural transformations. Thus, the core problems Katwala identifies are:

- lack of transparency in systems of governance;
- failure to achieve accountability;
- the persistence of corruption in terms of bidding, commercial contracts and bribery.

He claims that the standards of governance and openness that are currently the norm in global sport would not be acceptable in the most minimal of democratic polities and legal systems. Another factor is the differential power structures of class, race and gender which are also in play in particular ways in sport. Sport has the capacity to promote elitist practices because sport has its own rules of competition. It is to some extent an inevitable consequence of unaccountable elites who enjoy a favourable and uncritical press and face a fragmented and marginalised opposition constituted by the current miscellany of fan organisations and sports pressure groups. The extent to which these reasons exist depends upon how possible it is to transform the culture and governance of sport.

CHANGING THE RULES OF THE GAME

Reform of international sporting governance is not inevitable but it is possible. Katwala identifies particular aspects of the governance of sport which warrant change and are spaces in which transformations could take place. These include:

- increased transparency, in relation to personnel and the length of their appointments as well as financial accountability and transparency, including disclosure;
- credible ethical frameworks and codes, for example, so that a governing body does not investigate itself in the case of claims of malpractice or corruption;
- recognition that professional sport has to have professional governance;

- improved relationship between professional athletes and the governing bodies of sport;
- giving the fans a voice through consultation as well as communication.

(Katwala, 2002)

All of these suggestions focus on particular aspects of the governance and each is underpinned by power relations which intersect in the governance of sport. Increased transparency challenges the entrenched hegemony of white, male elites. Each of Katwala's suggestions is also based on economic power relations and the specific ways in which global inequalities are played out in sport.

Reform might take place from within sport, but would have to reflect the impacts of globalisation, which so far have not been accommodated in sport, where practices are out of date. Information technologies and the web could promote more democratic practices and give fans a voice rather than being largely used to promote products and gambling. Reform from outside requires intervention from governments whose power has been underestimated. Governments can be the initiators of movements for reform as is evident in the equality, diversity and anti-racism legislation, the implementation of which is increasingly manifest in the field of sport. The alternative would be no change and the continuance of self-interested oligarchies, with existing problems being exacerbated. There could be no resolution of the conflict between values and commercialism, and corruption scandals could escalate.

SPORTING CITIZENS

One example of reform which has had impact, especially in the more routine everyday practices of sport, is the promotion of equality and human rights. Sport has long been the target of government policies which aim to promote 'good citizens' through healthy minds and healthy bodies. This links the enfleshed selves – the bodies that do sport, as discussed in Chapter 7 – and the bodies that organise those activities in the constitution of what may be called good citizens where sport is a device of governance, which promotes social inclusion and compliance. In the often quoted tradition of Juvenal's declaration of the benefits of *mens sana in corpore sano*, a healthy mind in a healthy body, the governance of sport has often targeted the corporeal possibilities of sport as a means to link enfleshed bodies to organising bodies and create physically healthy, fully participatory citizens.

> More people taking part in sport and physical activity at all levels will bring a number of benefits. The report is clear that there is strong systematic evidence of a direct link between regular physical activity and improved health for people of all ages . . . We must get more people playing sport, across the whole population, focusing on the most economically disadvantaged groups, along with school leavers, women and older people.
>
> (DCMS/SU 2002:7)

This UK government report does suggest tensions and contradictions in the ways in which the governance of sport is concerned with providing both opportunities for widening participation, on the one hand, and exercising control over those who might be seen as occupying marginalised or disaffected social positions and who are thus disciplined through sport. This shows how governance is both constraining and enabling. Effective governance has the ability to widen participation, increase equality and to promote fair play through reducing corruption and malpractice, as well as controlling and constraining populations, especially, in the case of sport, of groups such as disaffected young men, who might otherwise be disruptive to society.

Legislation creates different categories of person, classified by race, gender sex, sexuality, disability, special educational needs and generation to name but some of the targets of UK policies. The language of diversity is itself diverse, although in sport in particular, anti-racism has come to embrace a whole range of persons (for example in groups which combat discrimination such as Football Against Racism in Europe, FARE (http://www.farenet.org/) and Kick it Out http://www.kickitout.org/, both accessed 30 January 2012). Those classified as excluded become a broad group including black and ethnic minorities, women, gay, lesbian, bisexual and transgendered people, people with disabilities, disaffected young people, travellers, which make up a very large, majority constituency if all are included (Woodward, 2009).

Policies and practices to widen participation which are based on healthy bodies and healthy minds offer one avenue of change. The promotion of such policies has the ability to make the governance of sport more transparent and more equitable at all levels and in all aspects of governance.

CONCLUSION

The apparatuses of governance in sport manifest ambivalences between the opportunities afforded for greater equity and participation and increased control through the dominance of particular dimensions of power, notably in relation to global capital and the media. Rule making and breaking are part of modern global sport and demonstrate the links between sport and the wider society, as well as what marks out the field of sport from other dimensions of social world practices. Governance incorporates a wide range of different dimensions of power through social, economic and cultural systems, as well as the governing bodies and the political processes through which policies are formally made. Fans, sports stars, practitioners, regulatory bodies and governments are all implicated in the governance of sport, although social divisions and systems intersect in how decisions are made and who has the power to make changes; some stakeholders, such as sponsors and governments, have considerably more power than others. Arguments about how best to resolve the problems of governance also raise questions about how power operates and whether the different stakeholders are able to exercise agency, or whether there are other, more powerful, economic and cultural forces which sweep them away. The continuance of elements of inequality, for example, those based on gender, suggest that this is a far from level playing field. The matter of power and how power operates is central to the debate about the problems of governance in sport.

Aspects of corruption in sport, ranging from bending the rules on the pitch to large-scale fraud and match fixing linked to global gambling networks, demonstrate some of the limitations of the governance of sport. Rule bending by practitioners may be attributed to both economic factors, given the huge rewards that can be gained by those at the highest levels of sport, and cultural shifts across time in what is deemed acceptable or unacceptable behaviour. Some rule bending and even corruption appears to be within the bounds of acceptability, even if it does not comply with traditional notions of honour. Arguably the exploration, analysis and under-standing of cultures of cheating in different sport settings are long overdue. The widespread and multifaceted appearance of cheating suggests that it is not just an unwanted but also an unavoidable epiphenomenon of modern sport deplored by sports associations and the administrative bodies of world sports.

Governance involves the making, breaking and changing of the rules of engagement and provides the mechanisms through which power operates and changes can be made. The rule breaking that is included in the large-scale corruption that has featured in a range of sports – the Olympics, cycling, baseball, football – demonstrates the failure of the management and regulation of sport as a problem of governance. On some occasions it has been lack of regu-latory intervention that has permitted rule breaking, as in the case of the doping scandals that have hit the headlines in almost all sports in some shape or form.

Problems of governance in sport show the links between sport and society; the economics and politics of sport are part of the problem and part of its solution. These problems cannot be attributed to a single cause. For example, corruption is not solely an outcome of commercialism and economic transformation; the vast growth of sponsorship, advertising and media coverage of sport is part of a cultural shift as well as an economic one.

The governance of sport has not always kept up with the changes of globalisation and their economic and political manifestations or with social and cultural changes in the wider arena of social relations. Cultural transformations in sport are interlinked through the networks of globalisation, which open up possibilities of greater transparency, democracy and account-ability in the governance of sport, as well as creating sports celebrities and generating massive financial rewards.

ESSAY QUESTIONS

1   Using the example of the IOC, illustrate the importance of rules and governing bodies for the development of sport. Which factors promote good governance and which militate against it?

2   Outline some of the main causes of a breakdown of confidence in the governance of sport in the twenty-first century. What possibilities are there for change to rectify some of the problems?

EXERCISES

1   Select a sport and find out its governing principles. What forms of governance are in place to secure that the sport's aims can be achieved? Who occupies the key roles in the governing bodies of the sport?
2   Select an example of a situation where rules have been broken or where there has been a crisis of confidence in a sporting governing body. There are examples in the chapter, which range from major issues of corruption in the Olympic Games to individual charges of drug taking, but you could choose any current case. What happened in the case you have chosen? What action could be taken in the governance of the sport and more widely to prevent such an occurrence being repeated?

FURTHER READING

B. Houlihan and M. Green, *Routledge Handbook of Sports Development* (London: Routledge, 2011).
K. Woodward, *Embodied Sporting Practices: Regulatory and Regulating Sporting Bodies* (Basingstoke: Palgrave, 2009).

CHAPTER TEN

THE LABOUR MARKET

INTRODUCTION

This chapter focuses on the place of sport in the economy in relation to the labour market and paid work, through discussion of the specificities of sports work and the synergies between sports work and other aspects of cultural industries and the market economy. Sport presents both particularities that might be seen to be outside other employment regulatory practices, for example, through its emphasis on competition and inclusion of a substantial voluntary sector, but the social position of sports workers, issues of professionalism and labour relations are all part of the wider terrain of a transforming labour market and changing employment practices.

While the effort we expend in keeping fit, working out, or producing the match-winning serve on the municipal tennis court may have little of the innocently playful about it, for most of us – even those who are into 'serious leisure' – for most of the time, sport is a form of recreation or play. For a prominent, and growing, minority of people in Britain, sport is also paid work. Research conducted into *The Economic Value of Sport in England* estimated that the sport sector had outstripped growth in the rest of the economy in the previous twenty years (Sport England, 2010). Over 440,000 people are employed in the sport sector (1.8 per cent of all employment). It was estimated that the sport sector was worth £16.7 billion in 2008 in England alone. The main focus of this chapter, however, is the relatively smaller number of professional sportsmen and sportswomen.

Nearly thirty years ago, Ned Polsky (1985: 98) noted that 'sociology has unduly neglected the study of people who engage in sports or games for their livelihood'. He suggests this has largely been because of the compartmentalisation of work and leisure. There has been little social research into 'the people who work at what most of us play at' (ibid.). This chapter will attempt to correct this imbalance. It primarily concentrates on the working context of professional sport. It will examine careers, working conditions, rewards and costs in the competitive world of professional sport. We will argue that workers in sport and the 'leisure industry', more generally, experience conditions and exhibit strategies similar to other workers in a capitalist labour market.

SPORT, WORK AND THE ECONOMY

It is important to situate our consideration of sports work within an understanding of the changes that have been affecting it for the past forty years. Most notably these transformations involve changes in the social and cultural background and assumptions of administrators of sport, the artificial depression of the costs of sport, the flow of income into mass-spectator professional sports, and the relationship between sports and the mass media, especially television.

Studies of artistic and sport-related occupations, including full-time professional sport, suggest that entering them often requires the ability to break *in*. In order to do this you have to get yourself noticed – either through your teacher or coach at school if they have a contact with the professional game or local sports officials, or by writing directly to the regional branch of your sport's national governing body (Fyfe, 1992: 9). Whichever you do, and whether you play a team or individual sport, you will also have to join a *club*. Here is an illustration of an association footballer breaking into the English professional game:

> From the age of 11 I had been visiting Luton Town for training and coaching sessions. My ambition was to play for my home town team, but even though I ended one season as leading scorer for the youth team, the club didn't keep me on as an apprentice. My dad advised me to get a job and play in my spare time, so I joined Chesham United in the Isthmian League and after leaving school took up an apprenticeship with a local firm as a toolmaker . . . Dad was adamant that I should persevere with my engineering apprenticeship, but the thought that I was just not going to be good enough to earn a full-time living as a professional made me dreadfully depressed.
>
> (Dixon, 1985)

Fortunately for Kerry Dixon, he went on to be capped for England and play for Reading, Chelsea, Southampton and, eventually, Luton Town and Millwall after finishing his apprenticeship. His story reveals the steps that are still necessary to make it into professional football. If a professional club is interested in a young football player – normally aged about 12 or 13 – they will sign him on via Associated Schoolboy or 'S' forms. The agreement will enable him to train at the club two or three times a week but it will restrict the player from playing for any other team. At 16, the club will decide whether or not to sign the player on as a full-time trainee, often as part of Youth Training. As well as practising and playing, trainees have to carry out routine mundane chores, such as cleaning kit, sweeping out changing rooms, etc. At 18 the club will either ask players to sign on full-time or ask them to leave.

There is a considerable amount of wastage at this stage. In his account of the life of Matt Busby and Manchester United, Eamon Dunphy (1991:180–181) recalls the success of United's youth team that had won the 1953 FA Youth Cup final first leg against Wolverhampton Wanderers at Old Trafford, 7–1. The United team for this historic game included Eddie Colman, Duncan Edwards, David Pegg, Liam Whelan and Albert Scanlon who became established first team players. Ronnie Cope played only a single first team game before the Munich air crash (in 1958). Of others in that great youth side, football would hear very little. And that was a vintage year. The failure rate was high. In fact, so good were they that United went on to win the first five ever FA Youth Cups. A glance through the teams shows that most who helped to win the prize never went on to play regular first team football. A few years later, when two 15-year-old Belfast boys arrived in Manchester for a two-week trial, they were so alienated by the initial experience that they returned home after one night. Fortunately for Manchester United (and football), one of them – George Best – was persuaded to return for another try a few weeks later (Dunphy, 1991: 280–281). The situation has not changed fundamentally in terms of the employment relationship in high performance football in Britain since the 1960s.

In 2010, the English Premier League (EPL) and the English Football League (responsible for the Championship and Leagues 1 and 2) estimated that between 60 and 65 per cent of the 700 players offered scholarships (previously referred to as apprenticeships) at the age of 16 were rejected by clubs at the age of 18. Half of those playing with a full-time contract would not be playing professionally at the age of 21, according to the Professional Footballers' Association (PFA) (James, 2010). The opportunities for talented footballers to move around the world have also impacted on the chances of becoming a top-flight player. In the inaugural EPL season, 1992–1993, 71 per cent of players taking part were English. By 2009–2010, the figure had fallen to 38 per cent (ibid.).

The chances of making it to the top in sport in the USA are equally extremely limited. It is useful to refer to Coakley's discussion of the myths and realities behind careers in sport in the USA (1994: 281ff.). While sport can provide satisfying and rewarding careers for some, he argues that there are four important qualifications that need to be made:

1   The number of career opportunities for athletes is severely limited.
2   Career opportunities for athletes (as opposed to coaches, trainers, etc.) are short-term, seldom lasting more than five years.
3   Most career opportunities in sports do not bring much fame or fortune.
4   Opportunities for women, black and other ethnic minorities, older people and disabled people are extremely limited.

Additionally, professional sports careers can be very short-lived, leaving someone with a working life of 30 or even 40 years after their sports career is over. In American football, basketball and baseball average professional careers range from four to seven years in length, but 'this average is deceiving because it obscures the fact that the number of people who play for only 1 or 2 years is far greater than those who play for more than 5 to 7 years' (ibid.: 284).

In Britain, opportunities for making the 'big time' are no more readily available and careers in sport are equally likely to be short-lived. Jobs in sport other than as an active professional sports player include coaching, PE teaching, recreation management, ground staff, sports medicine, sports business, and sports journalism and photography. These do not offer the immediate fame and fortune some professional players receive, but they are attractive occupations for those who want to be involved in sport in some way. The important thing to note is that most of them require the same academic and personal qualifications as many other non-sport related occupations. We will explore these ideas more in the following sections.

REWARDS IN SPORTS WORK

A mythology about the amount of earnings that can be made from sport has developed out of the secrecy shrouding private employment contracts in professional sport and 'shamateurism' in high-performance amateur competitions. The basic wages of sports workers can be augmented by, among other things, bonus payments, prize money, endorsements, benefits and media appearances. Yet reports in the mass media may quite considerably exaggerate the sums involved by, for example, failing to consider the deductions from a lump sum payment (such as the manager's and agent's percentage cut).

High annual earnings also need to be put into the context of total career earnings. The chances of maintaining or improving on the level of income after retirement from a sport are very doubtful. Earnings and conditions vary greatly from sport to sport and within sports. Income, security, length of career and future prospects all differ. Substantial economic inequalities exist between sports workers. Some are at the level of semi-skilled workers, others are paid the same as professionals, better paid skilled workers and small businessmen, while the 'superstars' vie with the income of top company executives and employers.

The largest group of full-time professional athletes in Britain – full-time professional footballers – provide a good illustration of the differentials that now exist in earnings from the sport. While it is a pervasive assumption that professional footballers are now an affluent, relatively homogeneous, occupational group, the reality is quite different. Until the 1960s professional football operated a maximum wage system. It was also underpinned by a code of loyalty to the team almost unthinkable in the present day. So Tom Finney, one of the greatest English players of all time, who spent his whole career at Preston North End, earned £14 a week (£12 in the summer), with a £2 bonus for a win and £1 for a draw throughout the 1950s. Even in 1952 when he was approached by the president of the Italian club Palermo and offered £10,000 to sign for them, with wages of £130 per month, plus bonuses, a villa on the Mediterranean and a car, Finney was persuaded by the club chairman not to leave Preston out of loyalty (Dunphy, 1991:159). At the same time Manchester United players were earning about £750 per year including bonuses. Compared to the rest of the world, wages in British football were very poor and relied upon what Dunphy (ibid.: 158) calls 'the extraordinary psychological confidence trick the Masters had played on their Slaves'.

After the abolition of the maximum wage in 1961, the differentials between different players and teams widened. Fulham was the first club to pay a player (Johnny Haynes) £100 per week. During the 1970s and 1980s players in the English 3rd and 4th Divisions at the lower end of the earnings scale were on wages similar to semi-skilled manual workers. There was a big earnings gap between players in Division 1 and the rest and within Division 1 between the 'stars' and the rest. During the 1970s and 1980s Kevin Keegan regularly made £200,000 per year from salaries, advertising, bonuses and media work. In short, a minority of professional football players can earn a great deal of money each season; the majority earn far less, although still a solid middle-class standard; the rest may be 'comfortable', earning average industrial wages. Chas Critcher (1979: 164) provided a four-part typology of soccer players in relation to the class structure that is worth considering in assessing these changes:

1   traditional/located – part of the respectable working class (e.g. Stanley Matthews, Nat Lofthouse, Albert Finney);
2   transitional/mobile – upwardly mobile working class (e.g. the Charlton brothers, Bobby and Jack);
3   incorporated/embourgeoised – small-scale entrepreneurs (e.g. Bobby Moore);
4   superstars/dislocated – *showbiz/nouveau riche* (e.g. George Best).

How far these distinctions still applied was shown in research carried out by Craig Gurney (1997). While top players in the 1990s, such as Ryan Giggs and Eric Cantona, had been 'commodified and produced as an iconography', most professional footballers have also been subject to the twin processes of what Gurney (1997: 7, 13) calls 'Shearerisation' and 'Gascoingnisation'. Footballers are presented in the mass media as either an undeserving rich elite group or a bunch of notorious, if talented, buffoons, and sometimes both. The result is to project an image of homogeneity in experience and destroy any empathy for football players as *workers*. Gurney used unpublished English Football League data on the average basic weekly wages of players in the four divisions to show the extent of salary differentials in the 1990s. Most of the 3800 professional footballers in England and Wales only earn a little above the average national professional wage. There is a clear divide between players in Premier League teams and the First Division, and between those in the First Division and lower divisions. Up-to-date information about the earnings of Premier League players was not available for Gurney's survey, but in the 1995/ 96 season, basic earnings in Division 1 were twice that in Division 2. By 2006, the average basic pay of EPL players, according to a PFA survey, was £676,000 per year, or £13,000 per week. In the EFL Championship rewards were much less but still considerable: £195,750 (£3764 per week), while in League 1 and League 2 they were £67,850 (£1305) and £49,800 (£954) respectively (Harris, 2009).

Since then, the rewards to EPL players have continued to grow as the revenues coming into the sport through negotiation of exclusive television deals have continued to outstrip most other economic sectors and in turn star players are represented by their agents in contract discussions. One extreme, but also typical, example was what happened in October 2010 after protracted negotiations, which had appeared to include the prospect of Wayne Rooney moving from Manchester United to Manchester City. Wayne Rooney's agent Paul Stretford secured Rooney a doubling of his salary from £90,000 to £180,000 per week! Rooney, often

understanding sport

portrayed by some as an 'anti-Beckham' figure in contemporary British football, is clearly one of the best-paid athletes in the UK today.

In most other professional team sports in Britain the pattern is similar: a small minority at the top securing vast amounts of money a year, some being quite well off, and quite a few struggling. County cricketers, for example, were poorly paid up to the mid-1970s. Now the 230 or so top class players can bring in up to £50,000 per season. The exceptional star player (such as those selected to play for a team in the Indian Premier League (IPL) through auction) is obviously able to improve on this through endorsements and promotional activities. Minor county and league cricket players make considerably less. Table 10.1 illustrates changes at the top of the game in the decade 1999–2009.

A professional footballer's playing career is short, it is mobile and earnings are variable. The average length of a professional footballer's career is calculated to be eight years. Over this limited time the exchange value for the player's 'physical capital' will fluctuate. As Gurney concluded: 'Unless players make investments of cultural, social or economic capital while they are playing, then their "retirement" will be a difficult one' (1997: 11).

Gaining a FIFA Football World Cup Winners medal or an FA Cup Final Winners medal in football is no guarantee of riches as the following examples illustrate. In 2010, Nobby Stiles,

Table 10.1 Rewards in English Professional County Cricket, 1999 and 2009

Reward	1999	2009
Wages: An England International	£70k + bonuses + England match fee (approx. £20k)	£150k + bonuses + Team England Player Partnership income (shared from sponsors)
Wages: A county professional*	£30k + bonuses	£50k + bonuses
Appearances (county appearances by England player)	20 plus	4 or 5
Prize Money: Winners County Championship Division One	£100,000 (out of £182k)	£500,000–£350k for the players, £150k for the county (out of £1.06m)
Prize Money: Winners One-day League Division One§	£53k	£125k
Prize Money: Winners One-day Knockout Trophy§	£53k	£150k
Prize Money: Winners Twenty 20 Cup§	£52k (2003, first year)	£80k

Notes:
* Figures from the Professional Cricketers Association (PCA)
§ various formats and event sponsors
Source: Mitchell (2009).

former Manchester United and England midfield player, became the ninth 1966 England team member to sell his World Cup winners medal through auction as a means of providing for his family. Kevin Beattie, who played for the successful Ipswich Town cup-winning team in 1978, was injured and forced to leave the game prematurely. In the mid-1980s after labouring and sales representative jobs, he was made redundant and offered his cup-winners medal to the local council in order to meet a rates demand and save his family's furniture. Likewise, a few years later when Peter Osgood organised a charity dinner for Southampton's 1976 FA Cup winning team, the guest list included an oil company executive, a publican, a self-employed builder, a grocer, a TV celebrity and racehorse trainer, a chef, and only one football club manager (*Guardian*, 3 November 1990).

The Sunday Times Sport Rich List (Figure 10.1) comprises only current and former sportsmen in Britain and Ireland. Foreign stars playing in the UK and British athletes competing abroad are included as are football managers and racehorse trainers. Women are not included – no British female athlete earned enough to enter the top 100 (golfer Laura Davies was the closest). Seven of the 11 wealthiest sportspeople in the UK and Irish Republic are current and former racing drivers, the 2011 *Sunday Times* Young Sport Rich List suggests (Figure 10.2). Lewis Hamilton (£50m) joined names like Johnny Dumfries [real name John Crichton-Stuart, the Marquess of Bute] (£110m) and Eddie Irvine (£80m) towards the top of list. Hamilton saw his wealth grow by £15m in the past year. In 2010, when the first list of the wealthiest sporting stars in Britain and Ireland was published in *The Sunday Times*, motor racing also dominated the top 15 places.

Top of the *Sunday Times* Sport Rich List for the second year running were two men who kick, or used to kick, a leather ball. Dave Whelan broke his leg while playing for Blackburn Rovers in the 1960 FA Cup final. Though Rovers lost 3–0 and the injury put Whelan's career into decline, he used the £400 compensation he received to start a discount store, which became

1	Dave Whelan (football) £190m
2	David Beckham (football) £135m
3	Sir Tony O'Reilly (rugby union) £120m
4	Johnny Dumfries (motor sport) £110m
5	Lennox Lewis (boxing) £95m
6	Eddie Irvine (motor sport) £80m
7	Jody Scheckter (motor sport) £60m
8	Dave Richards (motor sport) £58m
9=	Lewis Hamilton (motor sport) £50m
9=	David Coulthard (motor sport) £50m
9=	Nigel Mansell (motor sport) £50m
	Source: *The Sunday Times* Sport Rich List, supplement with *The Sunday Times* 15 May, p. 3.

Figure 10.1 *The Sunday Times* Sport Rich List 2011 Top 10

164

```
1        Lewis Hamilton (Motor racing) £50m
2        Jenson Button (Motor racing) £48m
3        Wayne Rooney (Football) £37m
4        Steven Gerrard (Football) £27m
5        John Terry (Football) £23m
6        Andy Murray (Tennis) £22m
7        Luol Deng (Basketball) £19m
8        Joe Cole (Football) £17m
9=       Petr Cech (Football) £16m
9=       Fernando Torres (Football) £16m
11=      Michael Essien (Football) £14m
11=      Carlos Tevez (Football) £14m
13=      Ashley Cole (Football) £13m
13=      Cesc Fabregas (Football) £13m
13=      Ben Gordon (Basketball) £13m
13=      Robbie Keane (Football) £13m
17       Dimitar Berbetov (Football) £12m
18=      Justin Rose (Golf) £10m
18=      James Toseland (Motorcycling) £10m
20       Andrey Arshavin (Football) £9m
         Source: The Sunday Times Sport Rich List, supplement with The Sunday Times 15 May, p. 15
```

Figure 10.2 *The Sunday Times* Young (aged 30 and under) Sport Rich List 2011 Top 20

the JJB chain of sports shops. Now Wigan FC chairman, Dave Whelan was estimated to be worth £190m. In second place is the footballer who manages to combine business with playing in a way no other British athlete can rival: David Beckham. His many sponsorships outstrip his earnings as a player and lead to an estimated wealth of £135m.

Boxer Lennox Lewis (£95m) and former rugby union player Sir Tony O'Reilly were the only other non-racers in the top 11, which saw three men tied in ninth spot. Another big climber was Wayne Rooney, whose fortune increased by £4m to £37m, placing him in 17th place alongside the then England manager Fabio Capello. Others who saw their wealth increase sharply in the past year include Fran Cotton and Steve Smith (both £28m), former rugby players and owners of the Cotton Traders sportswear company, and golfers Colin Montgomerie (£25m) and Luke Donald (£19m). Out of the top 100 richest sportspeople, 51 are associated with football, 14 with motor racing and 11 with golf (BBC News, 2011).

Philip Beresford, compiler of the list, said:

> Motor racing has several factors that combine to make its stars highly rewarded. There are big, often global television audiences and vast commercial interests at stake. And

165

the labour market

unlike football, you only need to pay one or two drivers per team – not 11 or more. For the best drivers that can make salaries and sponsorships huge.

(Woods, 2010)

Motor racing, however, is a winner-take-all sport, with only a handful of entries lower down the list. By contrast, footballers are there in depth, occupying 51 out of the 100 places in 2011. They range from Michael Owen, with £40m, the richest player after Beckham, to Martin O'Neill, the former player turned manager with £10m. In football, it seems, money buys success. It is probably no coincidence that thirteen of the richest young men (under 30 years of age) on the list play have played football, and eight of them (at the time of writing) for either Chelsea or Manchester United.

EQUAL OPPORTUNITIES IN SPORT?

At the end of 2011, there was a controversy when the BBC's annual Sports Personality of the Year show produced a shortlist of ten names containing no female athletes. The BBC defended the shortlist on the grounds that it was compiled in the same way as in the previous five years by the votes of newspapers and magazines. Critics of the shortlist pointed out that several of the magazines that voted were 'lads' mags' that tended to objectify women as page-filling 'eye candy'.

Sarah Gilroy (1997: 109) once suggested that Pierre Bourdieu's notion of 'physical capital' is useful when examining the gendered nature of the body and sport. She argued that 'the exchange value of women's physical capital is very limited' and this helped explain the greater participation rates of men over women in professional sport. Just as female prostitutes have a limited time-span before their bodies lose their 'exchange rate value', she wrote, 'in a similar way, it could be argued that female gymnasts have a limited currency' (ibid.). The reality today, as when Gilroy first made her observations, is that opportunities to take part in professional sports for women in the USA, as well as the UK, are very limited. Women who really want to play professionally have to consider moving abroad.

In the USA there are no professional volleyball or basketball leagues, and hence despite its popularity in North America, women have to come to Europe where professional leagues do exist. The same applies to British women who want to play professional (association) football, although some find opportunities in the North American professional league (and since 2011 the professional FA Women's Super League (WSL) established in England to play in the summer). In many sports, however, the chances for a full-time career are next to none as there are no women's events, teams or leagues.

Jennifer Hargreaves (1994: 203–207) pointed out twenty years ago that apart from a small number of sports – athletics, golf, gymnastics, horse-riding, skiing and tennis – sponsorship deals for women's sports are unusual and in any case are nowhere near as lucrative as those for men's sports. This remains the case today. The WSL was established in 2011 as a summer league to replace the Women's Premier League, which was seen as lacking competitiveness. To help spread the talented players around the WSL operates a salary cap, whereby none of the eight clubs can pay more than four players £20,000 or over per season. This means that even England international football players – such as Sophie Bradley who plays for Lincoln in the WSL – earn only £16,000 per year through their international status and need to maintain a part-time job (in her case in a care home) outside of football (Conn, 2011). More lucrative career opportunities for women remain concentrated in a few sports, notably golf and tennis. Disparities in comparisons of the earnings of individual men and women athletes are evident. Women's sports therefore continue to survive through unpaid labour and various fund-raising activities.

Outside of full-time professional playing, jobs in sport do exist for women. Again, however, there are barriers. West and Brackenridge (1990: 10–12) provided some good illustrations of these twenty years ago. While UK Sports Council statistics have shown that more women than ever before engage in some form of sporting activity, West and Brackenridge argue that 'no commensurate increase has been registered in the numbers of women in positions of power'. Those with the most influential positions in sport tend to be men:

> While the proportion of female athletes attending the Olympic Games increased from 30% in 1980 to 33% in 1988, the number of female officials fell from 33% to 25% . . . In 1988 women constituted just 12% of full members of the British Association of National Coaches (BANC) and 20% of associate members.
>
> (ibid.: 10)

Despite equal opportunity legislation in the USA there has been a noticeable decline in the number of women coaches in the American university system. Few women coaches have been in charge of men's athletic programmes in universities, whereas men are often in charge of coaching women. Where sports have expanded, it has been male coaches who have benefited (ibid.:11). Women in sports work face the same barriers that other women face trying to enter a 'male domain'. They are often seen as unusual and possibly not as competent, for no other reason than their gender.

Despite the rise in fame (and subsequent fall) of Tiger Woods in golf – and large sponsorship and endorsement deals that have come with the success – there are very few black people in the most lucrative individual sports such as golf, tennis and auto racing, or in ice hockey in North America. Track and field athletics offer some opportunities but the rewards for most athletes are relatively small. Even in boxing, many of the most successful black fighters have not been able to retire in comfort or use their sports careers as a stepping stone to others. Yet none of this information appears to influence the career aspirations of many white and especially black school students. One research project with American high school students found that:

As they near (possible) entry into the job market, young blacks are becoming more aware that the rhetoric that 'you can become anything you want to be in America' is, for them, a myth. As the doors for the conventional means of occupational advancement close, many turn to the one industry which has an open door policy with regard to 'good, talented' blacks – the entertainment industry. The many rags-to-riches stories, the testimonies of athletes who now own fine cars, furs and homes, and the (visibility) of super heroes . . . encourages many young men to abandon dreams of success in traditional arenas for a life of basketball, football, or baseball.

(Harris and Hunt, 1984, quoted in Coakley, 1994: 290)

In Britain, sports such as football, boxing, rugby league, horse-racing and speedway continue to offer a possible route of social mobility for white working-class men, while male black athletes tend to be involved in football, boxing and track and field athletics. The largest minority ethnic groups in Britain, Indian, Pakistani and Bangladeshi, continue to be under-represented in most of these team games, prompting some research into the reasons why they are not involved to the same extent (Fleming, 1995).

LABOUR RELATIONS IN SPORT

Sometimes professional athletes will act collectively in order to secure an improvement in their working conditions and salaries. Perhaps as commercialisation in sport increases, players will adopt a greater 'worker consciousness' and the number of strikes and disputes over wages and conditions between management and players will increase. As sport becomes increasingly designed to generate revenues, when people pay to watch them live, or television companies pay to broadcast them, athletes become part of the entertainment industry (Coakley, 1994: 317ff.). This has consequences for their legal status and rights, which has been the most controversial issue in professional team sport in Britain and North America since the 1960s (Beamish, 1993). Here are two examples, from North America and Britain, of struggles over the *social relations of sports production*.

The reserve system and free agency in North America

Until the mid-1970s, professional athletes in team sports in the USA and Canada had little or no legal power to control their own careers. They were subject to a set of employee restrictions known as the *reserve system* which began in baseball in 1879. It virtually bound a player to one team in perpetuity:

They could play only for the team drafting (selecting) them. They could neither pick the team they wanted to play for, nor control when and to whom they might be traded (transferred) even when their contracts expired. They were obliged to sign contracts forcing them to agree to forfeit rights to control their careers.

Basically professional athletes in team sports in the USA in the 1960s and 1970s were the property of whoever owned the team. It enabled owners to set salaries relatively low and prevented players from being able to sell their abilities to the team that would give them the best deal in terms of money and playing/working conditions. The owners had a greater degree of control over their players/workers than in any other business in the USA.

Professional athletes had often objected to the reserve system, but in the 1970s players' unions and organisations were established which helped to challenge the system through the courts. In 1976, the courts ruled that players had the right to become free agents – to accept contracts from other teams when their contracts expired. This led to a great increase in the salaries of baseball and basketball players in the 1970s and 1980s. In the NFL (football) and NHL (ice hockey) team owners managed to avoid the effects of the legal change through negotiating restrictions on free agency with the players' associations. In 1992, these restrictions were challenged, with hockey players gaining some concessions and the NFL agreeing to let football players become free agents after being in the league for five years.

The growth of players' unions and associations since the 1970s has given them a collective strength that previously only the team owners possessed. They have been able to gain greater control over their salaries and working conditions – with the latter being more at issue than money. It has not been easy to keep players organised (Beamish, 1988). Owners have not looked kindly upon players who act as union representatives. A strike, which could last for a whole season, might cost a player 20 per cent of his or her total income as a professional player. During the 1987 NFL strike, owners signed non-union players to take the place of those taking part in the action.

The issue of incomes in sport is confused by the attention that the highest paid athletes receive. Salaries actually vary widely within and between sports in the UK and in the USA. Many professional athletes in the USA do not receive incomes much greater than those of other workers. Coakley (1994: 321) cites figures that show that in 1993 the salaries of players with the 158 minor league baseball teams ranged from $1,200 to $3,000 (£750–£1880) per month. As their jobs are seasonal, they do not always get paid for twelve months of the year. This pattern is similar for other professional sports including men's and women's basketball, American football, ice hockey, soccer and volleyball. Of course since the 1970s, some athletes have been able to draw enormous salaries. A few established baseball players have signed contracts worth around $7 million per year (£4.38 million) in the 1990s and some young basketball players have signed contracts worth several million dollars. Current average salaries in the NBA, NFL, NHL and MLB can compare favourably with those paid to other entertainers in the television, film and music industry.

The football labour market in England

The labour market in British sport is equally distinguished from other markets for labour by the special restrictions imposed on the sale and mobility of labour. As in the USA, the freedom of labour to choose one's own employer is restricted and professional athletes face increased dependence on the owners and controllers of sport. So, for example, county cricketers must obtain permission to register with another county, while in football, rugby league and speedway, players can be bought and sold by their employers. Employers remain in the position of being able to choose the next employer of a current employee. This was illustrated in 2010–2011 when Manchester City did not want to let Craig Bellamy play for a rival team in the English Premier League (EPL) and allowed him to play instead for Championship side Cardiff City.

The English Football League Clubs used to operate a *retain and transfer system* similar to the reserve system in the USA. In 1963, the retain and transfer system was dramatically modified following the successful claim for damages made by George Eastham against his club Newcastle United. Under the retain and transfer system that then operated, a professional footballer signed a contract with his club for one or two years. At the end of the contract the players were not free to move to another club under the jurisdiction of the Football League or the FA unless the directors of the club gave permission. When a contract came to an end under the retention system, either a player could register again with the same club or the club might give notice of retention with an offer of a minimum wage of £418 a year. There was no maximum period of retention and the player remained a member of his club and could not play for any other.

In June 1960, George Eastham had refused to re-sign the contract that Newcastle offered him. He was supported in his legal action by the players' 'union', the Professional Footballers' Association. The retain and transfer scheme was found to be in restraint of trade and was modified in the players' favour. At the end of a contract a player is either given a 'free transfer' or retained on terms that are as good as in his previous contract and put on the transfer list at some negotiable fee.

Before 1961, the footballers' market was also governed by a maximum wage regulation. The threat of a strike (led by Jimmy Hill and the Professional Footballers Association – PFA) removed this restraint and changed the whole shape of the league. Those clubs in large centres of population could now exploit their economic power and induce the most talented players to their sides (Corry *et al.*, 1993). An interesting exception to this rule, at least until the 1980s, was Manchester United. Five years after the abolition of the maximum wage, in 1966, no Manchester United player was close to earning the £100 per week that Tommy Trinder, the chairman of Fulham, had awarded to Johnny Haynes. 'The going rate at Old Trafford was half that amount, the club's renewed preeminence notwithstanding' (Dunphy, 1991:301).

Until 1995, players could still only move from one club to another if a transfer fee, or at least terms for the transfer, had been agreed. Those who wished to leave a club against its wishes

understanding sport

were at a disadvantage. Transfer requests made in writing lost a player approximately 5 per cent of the agreed fee, which was his by right if he was transferred at a club's behest. On the other hand, a player's refusal to comply with a transfer might hinder his chances of selection for the team. A manager might decide to transfer a player but not always to the highest bidder – especially if a transfer to a rival in the same division might rebound upon their chances of promotion or a championship (Dunphy, 1991: 297). The virtual abolition of the old-style retain and transfer system saw the rise of agents negotiating terms of employment and salaries for the top players and the practice of sales of players just at the end of their contracts. This was given yet another boost in December 1995 by the Bosman judgment.

The Bosman judgment refers to a ruling made by the Court of Justice of the European Communities (the 'European Court') on 15 December 1995 in proceedings between the former Belgian football player Jean-Marc Bosman, the Belgian Football Association, RC Liège, US Dunkerque and the Union of European Football Associations (UEFA) about the interpretation of Articles 48, 85 and 86 of the EEC Treaty. It enforced two changes that have affected all professional European football players. First, it abolished the legality of all foreign player restrictions or 'nationality clauses' on European Union (EU) citizen players anywhere within the EU. Second, it confirmed the right of an EU citizen player to move free of any transfer fee to another country within the EU on the expiry of his contract (see Parrish and McArdle, 2004, for further details).

As with the example from North America, it would seem that sportsmen only go on strike when they become free agents. In the USA, up until the mid-1970s, baseball players were tied to their clubs even when out of contract. Until the Bosman ruling made the practice illegal, European footballers were tied to their clubs in the same way. When the judgment was made, nearly every national football association in the EU enforced tight restrictions on the use of foreign players. The judgment's impact has been made more rapid by the growth of television's interest in football and the increased spectacularisation of the game. The ruling has enhanced quality at the highest club level but may be enforcing less enthusiasm and skill at the national team level. Clubs in Italy, Spain, England and Germany can now pack their squads with limitless numbers of foreign players which may have a detrimental effect on the national team. At the time of the ruling, former Spurs and German international Jürgen Klinsmann said: 'The Bosman verdict is great for the superstars but I'm not sure how good it is, in the long run, for the run-of-the-mill professionals' (quoted in *World Soccer*, February 1997, p. 20). Another effect of the Bosman case is that players with the big clubs can demand more pay in return for committing themselves to longer contracts. In 1996, for example, the then Brazilian World Footballer of the Year, 20-year-old Ronaldo, was able to secure a contract worth £2.5 million a year for nine and a half years with Barcelona.

Changes to the regulatory frameworks within which professional and elite level sport is conducted, such as the Bosman case, have led to new developments in the movement and migration of elite athletes (Gardiner and Welch, 2000). Research interest in the movement of elite athletes within and between nations has grown in the past twenty-five years as a recent edited collection testifies (Maguire and Falcous, 2011). Although sports geographers were the first to monitor the geographical variations in migratory flows of athletes (Bale, 1984, 1991), sociologists and social historians, among others, have been quick to take up the challenge of considering the implications of athletic talent migration for various sports (e.g. Bale and Maguire, 1994a, 1994b; Maguire, 1999; Lianfranchi and Taylor, 2001; Obel, 2001; Magee and Sugden, 2002).

Research into sport and migration has focused on three themes: first, the impact of athletic talent migration on both host countries and donor countries, on the role of intermediaries such as sports agents, and the effect on sports fans and the athletes themselves; second, the responses of nationally based governing bodies of sport and sports associations to athletic talent migration; and third, the implications of athletic talent migration for conceptions of identity in regions and nations.

The decision in the Bosman court case in 1995 reflected a wider attempt to abolish transfer fees as part of an effort to remove all obstacles to the freedom of movement of labour in European Union member states. Many European football clubs have come to depend on transfer fees as compensation for the scouting, training and development of junior players. Some are also concerned that now 'star' players will have even more bargaining power, and local loyalties will diminish even further in importance for players. Nationally developed players may no longer represent the route to success for teams, and there are also implications for coaching, training and national sides. Similar concerns, for example, have been expressed about the growth in the number of Japanese baseball players in the Major League Baseball (MLB) since Nomo Hideo joined the Los Angeles Dodgers in 1995 (see Hirai, 2001). To date, however, there has been less sustained academic analysis of the mobility of non-Western sports stars, including those from Asia and Africa. In the case of Africa, work by Bale (2004), Bale and Sang (1996) and Darby (2000, 2001) has contributed to our understanding of the migration of football players and athletes. In Australasia, Hall (2000) has discussed the impact of the sports 'brawn drain' on football in Australia, and Obel (2001) has considered the response of the NZ Rugby Football Union (NZRFU) to player migration. With a few exceptions (for example, Klein, 1994; Chiba, 2004; Carter, 2011), academic interest in sports labour migration among professional baseball leagues in the Pacific-rim countries has been quite limited.

As journalist Simon Kuper noted in the *Financial Times* (31 October) in 2010, 'Pundits rhapsodize about the old days, when players often spent their entire careers at one club, but that was because clubs could then simply forbid them to move. No longer.' If the Bosman judgment has enhanced quality at the highest club level and the showbiz aspects of football, at the lower reaches of the game the only certainty seems to be that there will be more uncertainty. Bosman has won his fellow players freedom of movement between European clubs, but sociological research supports the argument that a modern form of slavery still exists in association football. Working in sport also has other peculiarities. As Stone once noted:

172

It would seem to be readily apparent that the occupation is one in which the work cycle differs from that of most other occupations. Specifically, the worker has a relatively short productive work life, and generally his occupational experience does not qualify him for any other skill.

(Stone, 1970: 20)

Roderick (2006) explores several of the themes touched upon in this chapter by looking at the precarious careers and routine working culture of professional footballers in England.

INDIVIDUAL SPORTS

Much praise was given to Luke Donald, the English professional golfer, when he finished top of both the European and US money lists for golf in 2011. For this unique achievement he was rewarded with prize money totalling in excess of £8.4 million. Yet athletes in individual sports, such as boxing, tennis, track and field athletics and golf, seldom share a common legal status with those in team sports, and seldom share one with other individual athletes. Their situation depends upon what they must do in order to train and qualify for competition in their sport. Few sports people can pay for the training needed to attain professional level skills without outside assistance. In boxing a fighter must have a recognised agent or manager. Participation in golf and tennis tournaments usually requires prior membership of a professional organisation. Track and field meetings often have an official selection committee that issues invitations to take part. In these ways the legal status of individual athletes is shaped by the particular agreement they reach with their sponsor or other persons or groups needed for participation.

Because most people who want to work in sport do not possess the income necessary to attain the skill levels required to engage in it full-time, they usually have to enter into a contractual relationship which requires them to give up some control over their lives and future rewards from the sport in return for the help needed to become professional. This is another way in which *class relations* enter into the work world of sport. Athletes pass a degree of control over their lives to another person or group of persons in order to continue their sport beyond amateur performance levels.

Yet this leads, as Hargreaves (1986: 127) puts it, to the situation where most sports workers are in a *contradictory class position*:

> In common with working-class people they are employees selling their labour, experiencing insecurity and subject to the authority of employers and officials. But in terms of levels of earnings, work satisfaction, autonomy in the work task and future prospects, most are clearly closer to the middle and upper levels of society.

Another way in which top sports workers appear to join the social and economic elite is in their support of the capitalist ideal through their function as heroes and role models. The celebrity star system turned George (Best) into 'Georgie' in the 1960s, Paul Gascoigne into 'Gazza' in the 1990s (Dunphy, 1991: 299; Hamilton, 1993) and David Beckham into 'Becks' in the 2000s (Cashmore, 2002; Whannel, 2002). In so doing, they are made to perform

> the role of sales staff, not only for particular products and organisations, but for a way of life as such. When stars' performances and appearances endorse products and business organisations they simultaneously endorse the system of production and consumption and the ideals associated with it.
>
> (Hargreaves, 1986: 129)

While there are risks attached to the use of certain sports celebrities to endorse products, sporting performance can outweigh any problems associated with traditional considerations of marketability. Hence manufacturers Nike used tennis players John McEnroe, and Andre Agassi, and football players Ian Wright and Eric Cantona to sell sports shoes in the 1990s and 2000s. Through association with such 'rebels', 'bad boys' and 'anti-heroes', the link between the company's slogan to 'Just Do It' and the footwear was actually enhanced. This is not to say that transgressions of more widely held social values by sport stars can always lead them to maintain their sponsorship value. Tiger Woods lost countless millions in sponsorship after his marital infidelities were revealed, Thierry Henry lost creditability after his 'hand ball' during a World Cup qualifying match against the Republic of Ireland cost the Irish team a place in the 2010 finals. Agassi (2009) revealed in his autobiography details of drug use that would have damaged his reputation had they been known at the time of his peak of fame. It is likely that other sports stars will continue to be involved in controversies as, for example, the use of Twitter grows and reveals aspects of their personal lives not publishable in the mainstream media.

CONCLUSION

One development associated with changes in high performance sport is the greater pro-fessionalisation – and unionisation – of sport workers. The rise of player militancy and the recognition of the need for collective organisation vis-à-vis owners and controllers have seen the growth of professional associations among sports workers, such as the Professional Footballers Association, the Cricketers Association, the Professional Golfers Association, the Association of Lawn Tennis Professionals, the Jockeys Association and the International Athletes Club. The emergence of these organisations, and professionalisation in general, can be understood 'as a strategy designed, among other things, to limit and control the supply of entrants to an occupation in order to safeguard or enhance its market value' (Parkin, 1979: 54).

Six characteristics have been identified with an occupational claim to be a profession: (1) a body of theoretical knowledge; (2) education and training; (3) examinations; (4) code of conduct; (5) 'service to the public'; and (6) the existence of a professional association. Yet sport workers are not professionals in the conventional sense – they exercise virtually no control over entry to their jobs, they have no monopoly over knowledge, they cannot lay down standards of work, and they cannot control the labour process. In this respect, the market for sports labour remains close to the capitalist ideal of a free market, and with freedom of movement secured, players' thoughts have turned to what they might achieve from collective action. As journalist David Runciman (1996) puts it:

> Free agency meant that what had once been a highly artificial market in baseball players' salaries became a truly competitive one, with the top performers able to command undreamt of sums and the journeymen pros merely unheard of ones. To meet this demand, the clubs had to find new sources of income, which they duly did, in merchandising and multi-million-dollar (and eventually multi-billion-dollar) TV deals. But far from making everyone happy, all this money made everyone extremely insecure.

Along with insecurity comes the transformation of relationships between sport workers and their employers, and sport workers and their fans. We consider some of these developments in Chapters 11 and 12.

ESSAY QUESTIONS

1 To what extent are professional sportsmen and sportswomen members of the working class?
2 Using material from this chapter (and the rest of the book), write a critical review of an autobiography written by a sport celebrity.

EXERCISES

1 Outline the division of labour in a non-professional sports club or society that you are familiar with. Compare this with the division of labour in a professional sports club. What functions do the officials serve? Who is responsible for upholding the rules and/or punishing offenders? Is anyone in the organisation irreplaceable? Where does the power lie?
2 Outline and discuss the occupational culture of any one professional sport using different theoretical perspectives on sport as work.

FURTHER READING

J. Hargreaves, *Sport, Power and Culture: A Social and Historical Analysis of Popular Sports in Britain* (Cambridge: Polity Press, 1986), presents a classic consideration of 'The Social Position of Sports Workers' in a sub-section of Chapter 6.

M. Roderick, *The Work of Professional Football: A Labour of Love?* (London: Routledge, 2006), a sociological insight into the world of professional football as work.

M. Trescothick, *Coming Back to Me* (London: HarperCollins, 2008) discusses the stresses encountered while playing in top-flight cricket.

CHAPTER ELEVEN

SPORT, COMMERCIALISATION AND COMMODIFICATION

INTRODUCTION

As a social practice, sport occupies a contradictory position. On the one hand, it is associated with spare time, leisure, exercise and doing things for fun. On the other, it has become a multi-million dollar industry, with huge rewards for top performers, and a branch of both the entertainment and leisure industries. Clearly sport is part of the economic system and a potential means of generating profit. Yet so many of its key institutions, still marked by the formation of modern sport in the nineteenth century, are not simple examples of capitalist entrepreneurship. Readers of this book in the twenty-first century may be puzzled that commercialisation is even an issue – it appears taken for granted that sport is thoroughly commercialised. Yet for much of the period between 1960 and 2000, commercialisation was a key preoccupation both of sports administrators who sought to accelerate or to resist commercialisation, and of cultural commentators who were frequently critical of the commercialisation of sport. Equally, any readers younger than 40 may well be puzzled that the issue of amateurism remained such a crucial element in sport organisation right up till the 1980s. Yet these themes were central to the tensions and contradictions that underpinned the dramatic transformations of elite sport between 1965 and 1995. This chapter contains, first, an account of the economic development of sport and its transformation since the 1960s, then a review of analytic perspectives upon this development, and finally an outline of economic processes and relations in sport that require further investigation.

THE ECONOMIC DEVELOPMENT OF SPORT

Before the 1860s, sporting practices did not involve the systematic and regularised institutionalising of economic relations. Certainly there were plenty of instances of the exchange of money. Working-class cricketers were rewarded for their performance by country squires, boxers, pedestrian runners and jockeys could gain from their excellence, and substantial sums changed hands in gambling. The aristocracy and the squirearchy played a significant role as patrons (Malcolmson, 1973). Cricket, golf and horse-racing all developed institutional bodies, aristocratic in form and style, that were formed in the eighteenth century and functioned as *de facto* governing bodies (the Marylebone Cricket Club, the Jockey Club and the Royal and Ancient Club of St Andrews, see Mortimer, 1958; Cousins, 1975; Brookes, 1978). However, the public performance of sport did not typically involve the regular and routinised exchange of money.

As noted in Chapter 1, from the 1840s, the new public schools became the seedbed of a cult of athleticism. Traditional team games were appropriated, transformed and codified, and an ideology of fair play developed (Dunning, 1971; McIntosh, 1979; Mangan, 1981). Yet there was still no organised form of professionalised sport that we would recognise as such. Around the world, there were thriving cultures of informal or ritualised sport, but it was only with the emergence of organised regulatory bodies and the power of imperial countries like Britain and France to extend these organisation forms beyond national boundaries, that modern organised sport began to take shape. The following paragraphs briefly sketch economic developments in relation to sport from the mid-nineteenth century onward.

1860–1890

From the 1860s, a complex process of transformation began, which saw the emergence of nationally agreed rules, governing bodies, competitions and trophies, spectator sport, professional sport and the amateur/professional distinction. The growth of rail travel and inter-school competition required nationally agreed rules and governing bodies. The amateur/professional distinction emerged from the need of the middle class to mark social distinctions, and the working class became marginalised from sport organisation (Whannel, 1983; Mason, 1988). The concept of the amateur, and dominance of sport organisation by a bourgeois elite had a profound impact on the nature of sport governance.

By 1860, the old rural traditions of sporting events at local fairs and festivals, sustained by squirearchical patronage, had been in decline for several decades. The enclosure of common land and other agricultural change, industrialisation and rural de-population, and a retreat into insularity among the rural gentry all played a part in this decline (Malcolmson, 1973). Living conditions in the new industrial towns left little space, time or resources for informal leisure cultures to flourish, although the very existence of such cultures was a tribute to the resilience of subordinate classes in the teeth of brutal exploitation. The long working week, lack of public open space, Sabbatarianism preserving Sunday as the Lord's Day, and the clamp-down on cruel sports during the first half of the nineteenth century constituted major limitations on the leisure of popular classes (Bailey, 1978; Cunningham, 1980; Holt, 1989).

From the 1860s, a whole series of governing bodies came into being, consolidating the power of the male Victorian middle class to define the shape that sport was taking (see Table 11.1). New competitions such as the Open Golf Championship (1860) were established. Cricket's County Championship was started in 1873 as a compromise between the country house

Table 11.1 The formation of the national governing bodies of British sport

Sport	Date of formation
Football	1863
Swimming	1869
Rugby	1871
Cycling	1878
Rowing	1879
Skating	1879
Athletics	1880
Boxing	1881
Hockey	1886
Tennis	1886
Skiing	1903

game, dominated by the socially exclusive rural gentry, and the professional touring teams seen as too vulgar and commercial (Brookes, 1978). The Football Association established its Challenge Cup in 1871. Boxing's Queensberry Rules were established in 1867 (Butler, 1972; Carpenter, 1982; Brailsford, 1989) and the first Wimbledon championship was in 1877 (Brady, 1959; Robertson, 1977). In rowing and athletics, concerted attempts were made to exclude working-class competitors, resulting in the establishment of the concept of the amateur, who could receive no payment, prize, reward or compensation for sporting involvement. The athletics authorities outlawed professional athletics, which became marginalised, and this established a model many other sports sought to emulate.

However, the growth of working-class sport, and resultant pressure for broken time payments put pressure on the ethos of amateurism. The Football Association compromised to retain control, allowing the establishment of a professional Football League in 1888; while in refusing any compromise, the Rugby authorities precipitated a split, the northern clubs breaking away to form Rugby League in 1895 (Dunning and Sheard, 1976). Other sports like tennis and athletics were successful in outlawing and marginalising professionalism. The last decades of the nineteenth century saw the emergence and development of regular entry-fee paying spectator sport, and in effect the commencement of commercialisation in the modern sense.

1890–1914

Between 1890 and 1914, a commercialisation of society and a more sophisticated com-modification of cultural forms was underway. Spectator sport was becoming established as a significant element in the national culture (Dobbs, 1973). Department stores and chain stores were established. The launch of the *Daily Mail* in 1896 ushered in the era of the mass circu-lation popular press. Advertising grew rapidly. In sport, there was substantial investment in sports stadia (Inglis, 1983), the sporting press emerged and thrived (Mason, 1993), and sporting goods and equipment businesses began to develop. International governing bodies (IOC, FIFA, IAAF, ILTF, etc.) were established and the number of regular international competitions grew. A sport star system began to become more central, with cricketer W.G. Grace, in his later years, one of the biggest figures, in every sense. Regardless of the amateur code, sport at its elite level was already taking on some of the characteristics of business. It had an income, and an eye to the balance sheet. Most sport organisations were decisively not businesses in form, structure or aspiration. However, around the cultural activity of sport, a wide variety of entrepreneurial activities were beginning to develop.

1918–1939

During the inter-war era, the cinema became the dominant medium, and radio and television were established (Richards, 1984; Scannell and Cardiff, 1991). Film newsreels enabled audiences to see moving images of sporting events, while radio brought live sport into the home and enabled the establishment of new shared national rituals, such as the King or Queen's Christmas Message, Cup Final Day, the Boat Race and Last Night of the Proms. The percentage of households with radio rose from 10 per cent in 1924 to 71 per cent in 1938.

A distinction developed between spectator sports that could, potentially, sustain a professional dimension, and those that did not attract significant spectators and remained leisure activities. The power of traditional governing bodies, however, placed considerable restrictions on this process, especially in the case of sports such as athletics and tennis where professionalism was not permitted. Average First Division football crowds, which had been around 16,000 before the First World War, had risen to over 30,000 by 1938. Gambling grew rapidly, fuelled by the introduction of greyhound racing in the late 1920s and football pools at the start of the 1930s. The introduction of greyhound racing was a great popular success. Sixty-two companies were set up in 1927 alone and the following year a governing body, the National Greyhound Racing Association, was established. By 1931 there were around 18 million admissions. The launch of football pools was an even bigger success with around 6 million punters by the mid-1930s. Illegal off-course betting may have had a turnover of as much as £400 million annually in the inter-war period.

Sport became more commercialised, but compared to other cultural leisure forms like cinema, sport was still comparatively un-commercialised and indeed its distinctive institutions often exhibited a striking resistance to commerce. They functioned as organisational bureaucracies, with a redistributive function, but had less entrepreneurial dynamism than many other elements of the leisure industry.

1945–1962

At the end of the Second World War there was a period of enormous appetite for public entertainment. Cinemas, dance halls, public houses and sporting events all attracted exceptionally large crowds. However, during the 1950s, the old communal public forms of entertainment – pubs, cinemas, dance halls and sporting venues – suffered from competition with the growth of television and other forms of domestic entertainment (hi-fi record players, etc.) and activity (DIY, etc.). The increase in car ownership, enabling greater mobility, benefited other activities – day trips to the countryside, seaside or relatives – rather than sport. Three processes were striking: (1) a growing affluence; (2) the rise of private, familial and domestic spheres as sites of consumption; and (3) the decline of traditional working-class communities (Cohen, 1972).

Ironically, the growth of television was seen by sport as a threat. There was, however, the beginning of an increase in the tempo of commercialisation, which was most visible in football. Charles Critcher argues that a transformative trend commenced in the 1950s, at least in football, in which the major factors were the growth of professionalisation, spectacularisation, internationalisation and commercialisation (Critcher, 1979).

1962–1980

The combination of the growth of jet travel, television coverage and commercial sponsorship triggered a transformation of sport in the 1960s. Television, sponsorship, advertising and merchandising are still, together and separately, the dynamic force underpinning the commercialisation of sport. Technological improvements in television, the addition of a second BBC television channel in 1964, and the banning of television cigarette advertising in 1965 triggered a revolution in which sponsorship revenue became crucial, and television coverage became vital for obtaining sponsorship (Whannel, 1986).

The transformation of sport by television and sponsorship between 1965 and 1985 was dramatic. Television at the start of the 1960s provided a grainy black and white image. By 1980, high quality live colour pictures were being relayed around the world by satellite, augmented by slow motion action replay. Sponsorship was a major source of revenue for the elite level of sport. Sports agents became rich and powerful by intervening to manage relations between stars, managers, governing bodies, promoters, television executives and sponsoring companies. Amateurism was heading for terminal decline, as the brakes came off commercialisation. Made for television and tailored for television events proliferated, the sports shoe, clothing and equipment businesses mushroomed. The 1968 Copyright Act enabled the patenting of distinctive shirt designs and triggered the extraordinary growth of the replica clothing business and associated merchandise (Chaplin, 1991).

The impetus for the transformation of sport came from opportunist and maverick entrepreneurs who established themselves as sports agents, and who constituted the mediation point between sport organisations, sport stars, television, sponsors and advertisers (see Wilson, 1988; Aris, 1990; Stoddart, 1990). Jack Kramer, Kerry Packer, Mark McCormack, Horst Dassler of Adidas and Rupert Murdoch of News Corporation are key figures in this process. Kramer's professional tennis circuit sowed the seeds of professionalisation in tennis. McCormack's skilful handling of the earning power of the three top golfers of the 1960s and 1970s, Arnold Palmer, Jack Nicklaus and Gary Player, provided the foundation of his business empire, International Management Group, with its television subsidiary TWI. Packer had the economic power to challenge the previously cosy relationship between cricket and television, and his own World Series Cricket ushered in floodlit cricket, coloured clothing, hard-sell advertising, more cameras, more close-ups and more replays (see Bonney, 1980; Haigh 1993). Dassler taught the leading world governing bodies, like FIFA and the IOC, how to exploit television advertising and sponsorship, through his company ISL. Murdoch's Sky Television has been the driving force behind the transformation of football in England since the 1990s.

1980–1990

Sport became an international television spectacle, producing vast earnings for elite performers and strengthening the power of sports agents, and in the process traditional authority was undermined (Gruneau, 1997). Horst Dassler of Adidas was the key dynamic force, working with FIFA president, Joao Havelange, to transform the marketing of the World Cup and with IOC President Juan Antonio Samaranch to introduce global sponsorship to the Olympic Games. Sponsorship was limited to specific product categories and with exclusive world rights in each category sold to the highest bidder. This triggered a competitive bidding process between corporations such as Pepsi and Coca Cola, helping to maximise the amounts raised.

The growing global visibility of major sport was of considerable appeal to advertisers. The 1984 Olympic Games made over $100m from sponsorship, ten times that made in previous Games. In the USA, only the McDonald's logo (recognised by 100 per cent of respondents) was more recognisable than the five rings of the Olympics (recognised by 99 per cent). Almost half of people interviewed in the USA, Singapore, Portugal, and West Germany, thought the Olympic rings indicated that a product was of good quality (Wilson, 1988: 28). Merchandising became a key part of sports promotion. Corporate hospitality accounts for an ever greater portion of seats at major events – almost 25 per cent of seats for the 1998 World Cup went to sponsors and corporate entertainment. One significant feature of the media sport industry is the convergence of interests between sports promotion, television, advertising, sponsorship, and merchandising. While ticket allocation is shrouded in a degree of uncertainty, it seems likely that at least 25 per cent of seats for the major events of the 2012 Olympic Games will be reserved for the Olympic Family and its corporate friends.

The commodification process seeks to maximise sponsorship, advertising and merchandising revenue. Snooker capitalised on its television success during the 1980s with new tournaments, new sponsors and expansion into new markets (see Burn, 1986). Television was the shop window that allowed the promotion of sporting spectacles like American football to new markets (see Maguire, 1990). The global reach of television and the economic power of the USA encouraged an Americanisation of the form, content and styles of sport television around the world (McKay and Miller, 1991). However, the process of bringing together an audience for new, imported or Americanised sporting spectacle was complex. Long-established sporting cultures are embedded in lived experiences with their own histories, rooted in national cultures. Transplanting cultural experiences is a problematic and uneven process, as the short history of professional basketball in Britain suggests (see Maguire, 1988).

1990–2010

In 1990, although the Internet had become established, the digital revolution had hardly begun. Television subscription channels for sport in the United Kingdom grew slowly at first, hampered by slow dish sales and competition between two providers, BSB and Sky (see Chippendale and Franks, 1991). However, once Sky Television, into which BSB was 'merged', had the field to itself, the rapidly growing revenue from the pay-per-channel services began to give satellite television enhanced scope to obtain the rights to major events. Barnett (1990) has drawn attention to the rising power of satellite television, and to the shift from broadcasting as a public service towards broadcasting as a commodity to be chosen and purchased. The launch of digital television and growth of pay-per-view transmission of major football matches and other big events provided a significant new impetus to the commodification of sport. The economic basis of subscription channels is that even a modest subscriber base can produce substantial revenues. There are three factors however that, to date, have prevented all sport disappearing onto BSkyB or other pay-per-channel outlets. First, government legislation protects a select list of 'national events' which have to be screened on free-to-view terrestrial channels. Second, given the relatively low viewing figures for Sky's football, and other sports, the sponsors prefer to retain access to the larger terrestrial audience and are happy for highlights rights to remain with BBC or ITV. Third, alienating the non-subscriber audience completely would not be in Sky's interests.

Since 1990, as media content of all kinds became digitalised, the Internet became central to the distribution of media content. Multiple channel television and deregulation have paved the way for the replacement of analogue television by digital television. Sport channels, with new access to extra channels, widescreen, high definition and 3D transmission have benefited. Although the convergence of the technologies of television and computing has been slower than predicted, it seems likely that more sport will be available on the Internet. Given ownership of its own rights a sport club with a global recognition can sell live games globally through its own website (see Rowe, 2011, for a discussion of media developments). Globalising processes (discussed more fully in Chapter 12) have ensured that the promotional culture, with its brands and iconic celebrities, has become one of the dynamic driving forces in the commercialisation and commodification of sport.

SPORT CELEBRITIES: COMMODIFYING THE SELF

Baudrillard's discussion of the political economy of the sign (1972) drew attention to the rising significance of the symbolic value of goods, which he regarded as eclipsing their use value. The convergence of sport stardom and the celebrity culture has fostered an objectification of the body and a commodification of the self. The intensity of media attention paid to major sporting events produces a vortextual effect that draws people in, builds an audience, and greatly enhances the economic opportunities associated with television rights, sponsorship, corporate entertainment and marketing (Whannel, 2002). Top stars now utilise the services of whole platoons of 'cultural intermediaries' – public relations advisors, image consultants, personal shoppers, and marketeers (Featherstone, 1991). The appearances of such stars on the media are carefully planned to link to promotional opportunities for books, clothing, films, personal appearances. Michael Jordan and David Beckham are two of those who have most successfully accomplished the branding of the self. Brand Beckham, skilfully managed, has branded himself and become his own symbolic form, available at a price to attach to your product, whether it is designer sunglasses or a major football team (see Cashmore, 1994).

The symbolic form, though, is not entirely in the control of those who seek to transform symbolic capital back into financial capital. Image is inherently unstable. Note the prevalence of style guides which divide the world into the cool and the uncool; the hip and the not-hip; that divide celebrities into heroes and zeroes; or that constantly pose the questions like 'What's Hot? What's Not?' The saturation of culture with image and celebrity demands turnover, innovation, and the thrill of the new; and so old celebrities must constantly be jettisoned to make way for new ones. The process whereby a star loses their lustre is a mysterious one – an ill-judged remark, a poorly chosen outfit, being caught by photographers on a bad hair day – all can precipitate a draining away of public enthusiasm. Hence football player Paul Gascoigne went from being the focal point of 'Gazzamania' to 'sad, fat, clown' in a matter of months; rugby player Johnny Wilkinson won a nation's attention, but had no desire to be a marketing tool; only the complete lack of British competition kept Tim Henman, despite his inherent dullness, at the epicentre of tennis fandom, until Andy Murray arrived. The trajectories of stars like Tiger Woods, Mike Tyson, Denis Rodman, Paula Radcliffe, and Michael Schumacher serve to illustrate that public image is a complex and unpredictable form, that is always uncertain, and can never be completely controlled. Modern media culture cannot be understood without analysing the complex interplay of symbolic form and economic relationship.

POLITICAL ECONOMIES OF SPORT

There is a substantial degree of agreement that commercialisation is a striking feature of modern sport, and broad agreement as to the main features of the subsequent transformations of sport, which have been well documented (Aris, 1990; Barnett, 1990; Hofmann and Greenberg, 1989; Wilson, 1988) There are various interpretations that can be offered, from the perspectives of modernisation, conservatism, functionalism and Marxism. Guttmann's

184

stress in *From Ritual to Record*, on specialisation, rationalisation, quantification and the quest for records suggests that the commercialisation of sport is a logical outcome of the development of a modernised rationalised society (Guttmann, 1978). Functionalist analyses emphasise the function of the commercialisation of sport in boosting facilities, providing a means of entertainment and integration, a model of reward for achievement and a system of incentives (Coakley, 1978; Gratton and Taylor, 1986, 1987, 1991). In opposition to both the 'inevitability of modernisation' and functional pragmatism, a conservative perspective contrasts the 'corruption' of modern sport with the supposed greater purity of sport and its more Corinthian and amateur ideals. This form of cultural conservatism usually involves establishing a contrast between a generalised decline of the present and a superior past (see Lasch, 1980; Allison, 1986, 1993).

From a Marxist perspective, the commercialisation of sport provides another rich example of the tendency of capital to seek out and penetrate new areas of society in which profits can be generated. One can distinguish between some early Marxist-inspired critiques of sport that were interesting and provocative, whilst also being somewhat one-dimensional and prone to a crude economic reductionism (Hoch, 1972; Vinnai, 1976; Brohm, 1978) and the greater sophistication of some more recent accounts (Gruneau, 1983; Hargreaves, 1986). Jean-Marie Brohm (1978) argued that modern sport is directly linked to the interests of capital. One problem with this argument is that from the 1950s sport in communist societies increasingly took a similar form. Brohm says this is because such societies were not genuinely communist but rather state capitalist, but this is an over-simplified explanation for a complex phenomenon in which sport developed a globalised character. Brohm rightly draws attention to the ways in which sport is governed by the principles of competition, and record, and by the precise measurement of space, time and output. For Brohm, sport is the rational organisation of human output, and in a most useful formulation he calls sport the 'Taylorisation of the body'; in other words the scientific means for producing maximum output from the human body. This gives him a means of applying the principle of labour power and surplus value to athletic performance.

In *Sport, Power and Culture*, John Hargreaves (1986) sketches five different forms that the relation between sport and capital can assume within commercialisation. The first is profit-maximising, with examples being professional boxing and horse-racing. However, as Hargreaves points out, many sports have no real aspirations to make profits and simply hope to break even. Thus the second form of relationship is the attempt to remain financially viable through various survival strategies such as fund raising. The third form of relationship sees sport stimulating the accumulation of capital indirectly, providing a market for goods and services. So sport helps to produce the sports equipment, clothing and gambling industries. In the fourth relationship, sport aids capital accumulation indirectly, by offering opportunities for advertising and sponsorship. Finally, sport attracts a degree of investment for non-economic reasons. Directors of football clubs are often motivated by prestige, desire to have local influence or to use the club for corporate entertaining. Of course, economic and non-economic motives often overlap and in practice several of these relationships can be at work simultaneously.

Hargreaves (1986) sums up the process whereby through commercialism sport has become a central component of national culture in the following terms:

- Without the cult of athleticism there would be no organised sports.
- Without rational recreation and athletic missionising, organised sport would not have penetrated and become a part of working-class culture.
- Without the popularity of sport among sub-groups, and their move into some amateur-gentleman controlled sports, the commercial development of sport could not have happened.
- Without mass sport, the political elite would have not had this field for articulating the national interest.

While commodification is of central value in analysing sport and culture, it is important to pay close attention to the multiple levels in which it occurs, to the unevenness, the lack of fit, the discontinuities, the tensions, the contradictions, and to remember that, at the heart of the process lies a set of relations between the performative spectacle, and the gaze of the spectator which can never be totally subsumed by commodity, and remains on occasion to offer the sublime and transcendent moment (see Whannel, 1994b).

The concept of the commodity form presupposes the construction of an object or service that can be traded, through the abstract system of equivalence of money, in order that surplus value may be extracted in the form of profit. Who buys sport? The cash-nexus intervenes in numerous ways. People buy tickets, season tickets, executive boxes and hospitality packages. They also purchase television sets, digital boxes and satellite decoders; and may rent access to dedicated sport channels. They may buy newspapers for the sport sections, or dedicated sports magazines. Some also purchase sport merchandise; most notably replica shirts. This is not the only source of revenue for sport, of course. Television companies pay huge sums to acquire rights. Sponsors and advertisers pay, but sometimes they are buying from a sports club or stadium owner, sometimes from a club, and sometimes from a governing body. There has risen a whole new tier of expertise – sport agents, sponsorship brokers, event managers, public relations consultants, who also make money from sport; albeit in and through another set of economic relations.

If the customer appears in diverse forms, so too does the vendor. Who is 'selling' sport? Sport clubs and stadium owners sell admission, at a variety of price levels. Catering is often franchised, with clubs and/or stadia taking a cut. Merchandising may be in the hands of a club, a governing body or a licensed retailer. Television companies are both buying and selling sport. Commentators and experts sell their expertise, to television, who purchase it to enhance the value and audience appeal of their product. Sponsors and advertisers buy sport in order to boost sales, and in doing so are investing in image association.

Clearly there is not one simple 'commodity' here but rather a whole set of overlapping commodities, embedded in a diverse but linked set of economic relations. Equally, we are not dealing with a simple unitary commodified object, but rather a complex set of objects, practices, processes and symbolic forms, which all too easily become condensed together in the category 'sport'. We are never simply dealing with monetary capital, but also with cultural capital, with symbolic value, with icons, with stars, with narratives and with discourses.

Signification has its own history, sedimented common sense, popular memories, cultural sensibilities, structures of feeling. Adherence to and involvement in the processes of sports spectatorship have their own historically shaped and formed sensibilities, in which the shared memories, values and commitments continue to form and re-form the experience of 'consuming' sport. When people purchase 'sport', what are they purchasing? At the level of basic economics, people buy entrance to a stadium, or subscribe to a sports channel, in order to view a spectacle.

They do not, however, generally acquire a commodity that can be traded, sold on. They do acquire a form of sporting cultural capital, and they also undergo an experience; of excitement, involvement, passion, emotional peaks and troughs. Welsh comedian, poet and rugby fan Max Boyce's poem which features the line 'I know, cos I was *there*' expresses the importance of the situated experience of the unpredictable live event. These experiences may be intricately linked to a commodity, but are not themselves reducible to a commodity form. They may, of course, seek to embed the memory, the traces of the experience in the form of merchandise – souvenir programmes, replica shirts, and posters, but these commodities are not the experience, but rather indices that mark and identify the memory of the 'being-there-ness' of experience.

Why do television companies buy rights? Why 'do' sport? The most obvious answer is of course that they wish to win audiences, although apart from a few major events, sport is not an especially prominent means of winning audiences. In the case of companies who make their own revenue from selling advertising, it may seem that the sporting commodity is simply 'sold on'. However, as Dallas Smythe pointed out, advertisers are not buying the programmes, they are buying audiences – in short they are buying us (see Smythe, 1977, 1978; Murdock, 1978; Jhally, 1982). The programmes, from this perspective, are not the commodity, but simply the means of producing the commodity of audiences. We, the viewers, are the commodity which advertisers purchase. This provocative re-focusing of analysis offered by Smythe gives us much purchase on an advertising-based television channel, but does not account effectively for public service broadcasting or subscription television.

ADVERTISING AND PROMOTIONAL CULTURE

The economic relations through which the new professionals of the sports world – sport agents, sponsorship brokers, event managers, and public relations consultants – intervene in sport, add another dimension. Their income is usually based on receiving percentages of the revenue they can generate for their client, or of the size of the rights payments they negotiate. On a simple level, they are selling their negotiating skills. This skill involves the inflation of value, or to put it another way, the ability to increase surplus value. In an era in which symbolic value, as Baudrillard has argued, has eclipsed use value, such skills can gain very large rewards (Baudrillard, 1972).

All these forms of economic relation depend ultimately upon the performativity of sport – the spectacle is initially not an object but a process. Indeed, it is an unpredictable and unscripted process, and therein precisely lies its specific appeal. The capitalisation of sport involves exactly the process of transforming this process into commodity forms. This, however, is not a single simple or unitary process, but a complex layering of economic relations, which do not neatly work together. At the cultural level, the tensions and contradictions are even more apparent.

We can examine this using two examples: online gambling and the Olympic Games. Online gaming has extended the lure of betting beyond the walls of the casino and now hails a global audience. Gambling is a highly profitable form, offering one of the few commodities in which people will pay for the mere possibility of a return, and have to accept that they may well pay out for no gain. Online gambling is widely advertised, frequently accompanied with sexualised images of showgirls and female croupiers. There is a direct link to online betting sites on the top page of almost every English professional football club website. Spread betting, a model derived from city trading, long established in the USA, has extended its reach to other parts of the world. With its technological base and city trader image, such forms of gambling constitute an addition to the repertoire of toys for the boys, or at least toys for the heterosexual boys. Rather like the mythologised heroin dealer at the school gate, from whom the first taste was always free, the online poker sites offer free taster games, and then cash floats to start you off. Once registered, if you fail to play, regular email invitations will come your way. Gambling is an inevitable process of attrition: in the long run the players lose and the house wins. As a means of getting the audience to meet the full cost of the entertainment and provide the profit, online gaming is a perfect media form. This is another instance of capital seeking new areas to penetrate. The moment, only a few years ago, when the Internet was being proclaimed by some as a wonderful new collectivised and socialised space where free interaction could take place already seems a long time ago. Sport gambling constitutes an interface between deviance and criminality, as the growing incidence of attempts to fix the outcome of sporting events illustrates. Indeed, security experts now regard such attempts as a greater threat to the 'integrity' of the Olympic Games than the use of performance-enhancing drugs.

The Olympic Games has never been innocent of commerce, but the extent to which marketing has moved from periphery to core in the past thirty years is remarkable. The strategies and styles of marketing have become globalised. The marketing strategy for the Beijing Olympics used a rhetoric and structure virtually indistinguishable from that employed in Athens 2004, Sydney 2000 or Atlanta 1996. It is instructive to examine the language of the *Beijing 2008 Marketing Plan Launch*. Two things are striking. First, the systematic global marketing of the Olympic Games and its symbols to corporate sponsors, still controversial in the mid-1980s (see Whannel, 1994b), has become absolutely routinised and taken for granted. Second, despite the unique and extraordinary character of China, a dynamic market economy presided over by an authoritarian communist state, there was virtually nothing culturally distinct about the language, which could have emanated from any corporate marketing culture anywhere in the world.

The IOC President Jacques Rogge called the Games 'an unprecedented marketing opportunity for China' which would 'provide a unique global platform, a powerful international stage for building brands and market share'. The Chairman of the IOC Marketing Commission proclaimed that 'we expect the power of this enduring marketing partnership to reach new heights and generate a new level of benefits . . . in 2008 the unity of humanity will reach a new crescendo'. The President of the Chinese Olympic Committee asserted that 'successful marketing is a vital guarantee for the success of an Olympic Games'. The President of the Beijing Organising Committee outlined the way that 'the unique format of the marketing operations of the Olympic Games and its global brand impact will provide an effective way for Chinese enterprises to raise their international reputation and credibility and for Chinese products to move to the world'. The Mayor of Beijing declared that 'preparations for the Beijing 2008 Olympics have created a very favorable environment for the development of Chinese enterprises and provided a new driving force for enterprises to enter international market' (Beijing 2008 Marketing Plan).

The symbolic force of Olympism is condensed into one of the world's most recognised logos and the Marketing Plan commented that 'The power of Olympic Marketing starts with the fundamental value of the symbol of the five rings' (Beijing 2008: 23). Never was Baudrillard's (1972) assertion about the rise of symbolic value more applicable. Staging an Olympic Games enables a further condensation of the image of city and of country onto the five-ring symbol. The Marketing Plan referred to

> The Powerhouse combination of Beijing 2008: an integration of Brand China, Brand Beijing, the COC and Chinese Olympic Team . . . showcase the heritage, the culture and the spirit of its people . . . an unrivalled marketing platform for building the national brand, and clearly communicating the image of China . . . the full integration of Brand China into Beijing 2008 will infuse the Games with cohesive expressive and emotive brand attributes essential to the overall success of the event and its marketing programmes.
>
> (ibid.: 35)

Indeed, this relationship provided a promotional dream, linking city, country, idealism and enterprise:

> In short, Beijing 2008 represents the full potential of Brand China, Brand Beijing and the Chinese Olympic team which are joined as seamless components in the unmatched long-term marketing platform offered by the Games.
>
> (ibid.: 39)

In this discourse, the Olympic Games has become 'an unrivalled marketing platform from which to build an unmatched competitive advantage by maximising the power of the Olympic Image' (ibid.: 59). The Games provides sponsors with 'powerful opportunities to reach consumers in a multitude of ways' and as a bonus:

> By supporting Olympic athletes, sponsors also demonstrate a commitment to noble and enduring values, convey good corporate citizenship, and communicate a dedication to success, excellence and goodwill.
>
> (ibid.: 59)

The discourse offers its readers, potential sponsors, a flattering self-image of their benevolent role: 'sponsors intimately communicate their commitment to the Olympic ideals, the Games, the athletes while helping to enhance the lives of consumers everywhere' (ibid.: 63). The stakeholders of the Olympic family are univocal in their performance of a unified and unifying discourse, suturing together Olympism and enterprise, goodwill and profit, identity and brand. This, then, is the new Olympic spirit.

ECONOMIC RELATIONS

While there has been an extensive debate about commercialisation in sport, it has focused on the issue of commodification of elite sport. A full and comprehensive political economy of sport has yet to be elaborated. Such analysis would need to attend to a range of aspects of the economic process – the question of ownership and control, the nature of economic relations within the sports business, the process of production and relations of production, sports labour power and the production of surplus value. We need to clarify what in modern sport constitutes the product, who are the workers, who the owners, who are the customers, what precisely are the relations between them, and what the nature of sport consumption is. In the following concluding section we map out some of the key research questions, concerning ownership and control, the process of production, labour relations, and commodity exchange that could be explored in the next decade.

Ownership and control

What is the 'sports business'? Clearly this term now denotes a wide range of economic activities and institutions, many of them only connected by sets of economic relations. Television companies, sponsors, agents, promoters, governing bodies and performers are all part of the sports business but occupy distinctly different places within it. Who owns it, who controls it, and what distinctions can be made between owners and controllers? How much consolidation, vertical integration, horizontal integration has there been? How much diversification?

The label 'sport' covers complex sets of cultural practices and institutions, and the ownership of sport is therefore no simple question. The infrastructure of sport – tracks, courses, pitches, pools and stadia – has the character of a mixed economy. Public ownership, predominantly at local level, and private ownership are both common. The competitions and organisational forms of sport could be said to be the 'property' of the various governing bodies, but only by virtue of authority vested in them by their constituent members. Individual performers are, in some sports, the property of their clubs, in others, the property of managers, and, in still others, they are free agents. As in other forms of business, ownership and control are not the same. Owners do not necessarily exert sole control and enterprises can be, in part, controlled by those who have no share in ownership.

Governing bodies notionally control their sports, but such control can only be exerted if it reflects the wishes of their constituent parts, or members. The interests of such members can diverge and, where possible, governing bodies have to engineer compromise. On occasion this is impossible. Smaller football clubs have an interest in the continued redistribution of television revenue; the major clubs would prefer to retain it for themselves. It was the inability of the Football League to produce a compromise formula that led to the breakaway Premier League. Television, advertisers and sponsors all exert powerful influences on the ways in which sports are controlled. Horse-racing provides an example of the complexities. Racecourses have a variety of owners, most of whom are limited companies. Horses are predominantly in the hands of affluent individuals. They are looked after by training establishments, also private businesses. Television companies and the betting industry exert a significant influence on the organisation of racing, without having any ownership stake in it. Not surprisingly then, tensions between those who notionally own sport and those who seek to control it are common.

Labour and profit

As discussed in Chapter 10, there clearly are relationships between management and labour involved in the sports business. Top stars earn millions, while some sports performers may be rewarded massively, modestly or, in amateur sport, not at all, but substantial areas of sporting labour are poorly paid and involve relatively low levels of skill – ticket collecting, stewarding, shop workers. Other tasks – groundsman, stable girl – involve possibly greater skill but are still low reward. As a work-force, workers in the sports industry are poorly organised – there is a broad and divisive division of labour with little in common between the roles. Top stars, on the other hand, in conjunction with their agents, can now wield substantial power. However, managers and owners in sports like soccer still exert considerable power to hire and fire in abrupt ways that would not be possible in many other industries (see Beamish, 1988, 1993; Maguire, 1990; Bale and Maguire, 1993). The Olympic Games, which generates large revenues, is nevertheless reliant on the unpaid labour of thousands of volunteers.

The production process and the product

Analysis of the sports process of production reveals a contradiction. The sports performance is transient, and unpredictable, and this is precisely what gives sport much of its appeal. Paradoxically, though, it has to be turned into a product, an object, in order to be marketed. In turning it into a commodity, there is the need to guarantee its quality. Inevitably some of the uncertainty must be sacrificed. The process of commodification threatens the very value of the performance precisely as it tries to cash in on the value (Whannel, 1994b). So if the sports performance is the product, who is the producer? To what extent is it merely the athletes, or is it also the coaches, the promoters, the agents and the television producers? More systematic analysis is needed of the cash nexus here – who is paying who to do what?

ALTERNATIVES AND RESISTANCES

Emergent sports that become commercialised, systematised and marketed, such as beach volleyball, nevertheless still continue to exist in casualised and simplified forms. Beach volleyball has acquired an organised and competitive form but is still played, for fun, on the beach. In other words, the sport has been characterised by a remorseless transformation of casual leisure into serious leisure, but also by retention of the values of casual, informal and spontaneous play and indeed by forms of resistance to commercial incorporation. The collection *Understanding Lifestyle Sports*, edited by Belinda Wheaton (2004), explores some of these issues in fascinating detail. One of the hardest tasks for any analysis of sport is to retain recognition of the different and distinct levels and cultural contexts, not just of different sports but also of the same sports in different settings. Indeed, it is precisely the cultural specificities of actual sporting practices that provide the character, the flavour and texture of the experience of sport. The very specific nuances provided by the setting, the milieu, the distinctive rituals, habits, manners and forms of slang of participants and spectators constitute the embedded and localised meanings. One reason that cultural critics of the sports business are hostile to the processes of commercialisation is that it is this very embedded, localised, richness that tends to disappear in the more homogenous globalised and mediated forms that dominate 'sport' today. We turn to these developments in the next chapter.

ESSAY QUESTIONS

1   'Major sports could function perfectly successfully without sponsorship.' Discuss.
2   Is it correct to assert that the only sports that can succeed financially are those that work well on television? Discuss with reference to examples from two of the following: badminton, golf, cricket, squash, motor racing, show jumping, boxing.

3   Compare and contrast the relatively free market structure of the English Premier League (Football) in which clubs have a large degree of autonomy with the centrally controlled structure of the National Football League (American Football).

EXERCISES

1   Choose three football clubs and try to find out who owns them and what other business interests those people have.
2   Record sample 10-minute spells of live transmission of three different sports. Devise a means of analysing which company advertisements are visible, and how long for.
3   Which sports have the biggest audiences on television? (You will find there are different ways of assessing this, which you will need to research.)

FURTHER READING

A. Billings, *Olympic Media: Inside the Biggest Show on Television* (London: Routledge, 2008).
S. Jackson and D. Andrews, *Sports, Culture and Advertising: Identities, Commodities and the Politics of Representation* (London: Routledge, 2004).
T. Slack (ed.) *The Commercialisation of Sport* (London: Routledge, 2004).

CHAPTER TWELVE

GLOBAL TRANSFORMATIONS

INTRODUCTION

The development of sport, and the economic processes underlying it, cannot be understood without some examination of the impact of globalisation. As David Rowe (2011: 3) notes: 'The passage of sport under modernity from village green . . . to global village . . . has not only involved the mutation of sport but also profoundly affected the societies and cultures that have housed and received it.' That is, as this book and other recent writers argue (Giulianotti and Robertson 2009; Marjoribanks and Farquharson, 2012), sport can be conceived of as both a motor and a measure of social change.

Globalisation is a broad process in which markets, trade, labour relations and culture have attained global dimensions; the forms of organisation that connect them have a global character. During the development of these processes (and views differ about how long ago the processes commenced) the influence of nation-states has, some argue, declined. Global trade, of course, is not new, and its development was closely related to colonialism, the development of the European empires, and the subsequent rise of the USA. Many of the forces and relations suggested by the term 'globalisation' have been around for a long time. However, four significant developments have contributed to the identification of globalisation as a relatively novel process:

1   Major corporations have moved from being multi-national to *transnational*, and as such have moved beyond the point at which they can be easily controlled by individual nation-states. (Note, for example, the power of the major banking groups to resist regulatory mechanisms proposed by nation-states.)
2   De-regulation has fostered a much greater *international division of labour* in which production can more readily be relocated wherever wage rates are low, legal protection for workers are minimal, and trade unions are weak or illegal.
3   A *postmodern consumer culture* has fostered a market for branded goods that tend to have a high profit margin.
4   The unprecedented global *mobility* of people during the twentieth century has had an

understanding sport

impact on the reconstruction of markets around the cultures that have emerged from diasporas and the formation of new hybrid identities.

More than ten years ago British sociologist Anthony Giddens warned against exaggerating corporate power, or underestimating the continuing power of the nation-state, but nevertheless expressed the impact of globalisation in stark terms when he pointed out that:

> In the new global electronic economy, fund managers, banks, corporations, as well as millions of individual investors, can transfer vast amounts of capital from one side of the world to another at the click of a mouse. As they do so, they can destabilise what might have seemed rock-solid economies – as happened in the events in Asia [in the late 1990s].
>
> (Giddens, 2002: 9)

We now know that the whole world is susceptible to great economic instability and the economic credit crisis since 2008 was in some way related to this interconnectedness or 'connectivity'. While it is clear that globalising processes have been underway, that their impact has been dramatic, and they have had transformative effects, most notably in South East Asia, they have not led to a weakening of the established centres of corporate power, or any transfer of wealth from rich to poor, in fact, the reverse appears to be the case. This is not to say that the various impacts of globalising processes do not have contradictory effects. The rise of globalising processes and weakening powers of nation-states have stimulated the growth of strong local and regional identities. The growing significance of the 'hollowed out' corporation, of franchising, and of sub-contracting, has given rise to a new stronger entrepreneurial class in many developing countries, producing new localised forms of the circulation of capital, that in turn produce new localised modes of consumption. As Rowe (2011: 9) also notes: 'The idea that the global is a single, irreversible, consistent process is disempowering.'

This chapter focuses on key developments in global transformations and their impact on sport and the role of sport in global transformations. First, we consider interpretations of globalisation. Then we consider how sport developed in the midst of the growth of other international organisations. The third section focuses attention on the growth of the mass media's relationship to sport as this is the main way that sport as cultural practice has been globalised. Next, we reflect on sport as globalised practice. Finally, we consider the opportunities these developments have given for resistance to globalisation. What forms of local response are there to globalising processes and what is the relation of local and global, which some argue have produced a new cultural form, 'glocalisation'? How should we view the politics of globalisation?

INTERPRETING GLOBALISING PROCESSES

The concept of globalisation and its impact have become key issues in social analysis, raising a number of questions. How significant are globalising processes given that, as some would argue, economies are still largely rooted in, and managed by, nation-states? When is the key period of emergence of a globalised social order? World trade, it could be argued, has its roots in the great explorations of the fifteenth century. The empires of the Spanish, Portuguese and Dutch laid the foundations of colonial exploitation, subsequently pursued by the French and to most dramatic effect, the British. Karl Marx and his co-author Frederic Engels were keenly aware of globalising processes, as is evident in *The Communist Manifesto*, written in 1848. Robertson (1992) suggests the late nineteenth century as the take-off point for globalisation, while others regard globalisation as a much more recent process, for some as recently as the 1990s. For some, it represents the triumph of capitalism and neo-liberal economics. For America's neo-conservatives, it involves the establishment of a new world order. Optimistic analyses look forward to a 'flat world', where inequalities will be ironed out. More pessimistic accounts view it as imposing a cultural homogenisation, a McDonaldisation or Disney-fication of the world. Still others view globalisation as an intensification of capitalist exploitation, or a threat to the environment, which must be resisted. There are those who reject the term and suggest we talk of globalising processes rather than globalisation (see Jones, 2010, for an overview of different key thinkers on globalisation).

Historian Eric Hobsbawm (1994) suggests that the key transition begins from the 1960s. The post-Second World War Western world, he argues, is characterised by a consensus that the aim of rising production, full employment, industrialisation, growing foreign trade, and modernisation could be achieved by systematic government control, management of mixed economies, and co-operation with organised labour movements, so long as they were not Communist. There was a growing internationalisation. Between 1965 and 1990, the percentage of exported goods doubled. However, Hobsbawm argues, the world economy remained international rather than transnational until an increasingly transnational economy began to emerge, from the 1960s onwards. This new transnational world economy had 'no specifiable territorial base or limits, which determined, or rather sets limits to, what even the economies of very large and powerful states can do' (Hobsbawm, 1994: 273).

The new transnationalisation involved the emergence of transnational firms, the growing significance of offshore finance, and a new international division of labour. The USA, Hobsbawm suggests, was the first country to experience the effects of these large sums of unattached capital that circulated the globe looking for quick profits, but by the early 1990s even joint action by leading central banks proved impotent. There was a growing tendency for enterprises to free themselves from the controls of the traditional nation-state. The volume of Third World manufacturing rose dramatically from the 1980s, producing a new international division of labour (ibid.: 273–277).

Paradoxically, with the developing power of globalising processes, social practices like sport become *both more marginal and yet more central* in one and the same move. In terms of the great forces shaping the world, such as the dynamic tensions between local and global; the search for authenticity in the context of postmodern culture; the contradictions of a world based on growth and consumption situated on a planet with finite and diminishing resources;

the scientific and technological capacity for destruction seemingly outstripping the moral and political authority to control it; sport, like many other social practices, does indeed seem small, epiphenomenal and marginal to the big issues of the epoch. Yet the greater cultural visibility of these apparently marginal social practices is striking.

In the television era, of course, global sporting rituals become symbolic events of considerable cultural visibility. The spread of jet travel from the 1960s made international sporting competition much more practical, boosting European football competition, for example. Major sport events offer an ideal commodity for international television. Television has high first copy costs, but very low replication costs. Having made a programme, the costs of extending it to further audiences around the globe are, by comparison, minimal. This has two main effects. First, there is a strong impulse to export television programmes where possible, as any extra overseas sales provide extra revenues at minimal cost. Second, because the consequent extra costs are small, the price to the purchaser can be relatively elastic, reducing according to the financial scale of the market. This applies to popular American television successes, from *I Love Lucy* to *Dallas*, that have been re-sold around the world over the years. Sport is an even more readily exportable cultural form, because localism can easily be built in by dubbed commentary in local languages.

THE GLOBALISING MEDIA SPORT INDUSTRIES

In the field of sport, it has been the combination of the emergence of a world media system, the development of transnational corporations, and the foundation of an international sport system that has given the sports business its global character. In the nineteenth century there were not yet many global organisations, or organisations with global aspirations. Interestingly, it was in connection with sport that many of the earliest international organisations were formed. As far as globalisation in sport is concerned, then, it can be argued that the crucial take-off period was between 1870 and 1930. Table 12.1 highlights some of these key developments in the context of the emergence of other international organisations.

International sporting contact developed rapidly between the twentieth century's two world wars, but just as the spread of the railways helped produce national sport in the mid-nineteenth century, so it was jet travel that gave a major boost to international sport in the post-Second World War period. The growth of sport internationally in turn helped the growth of the sport clothing and equipment industry, led by British firms like Slazenger, Lilywhites, Dunlop and Wilson. The development of the sports business from the 1970s required a whole new category of professionals – international lawyers, corporate accountants, financial advisers and management consultants. These developments served to further weaken traditional amateur paternalism and fostered the growth of entrepreneurship.

As discussed in Chapter 6, most people, generally, consume sport through its various forms of representation. Far more people watch sport on television and/or read about it in the papers

Table 12.1 The formation of international organisations, 1851–1945

	Sports Organisation	General Organisations
1851		International Sanitary Conference
1861	First English cricket side to tour Australia	
1863		International Committee of the Red Cross
1864		First Geneva Convention
1864		International Workingman's Association
1872	First International Association Football Match	
1874		Universal Postal Union
1875		International Bureau of Weights and Measures
1881	International Federation of Gymnastics formed	
1886	International Rugby Football Board formed	
1892	International Rowing Federation formed	
1894	International Olympic Committee formed	
1896	First modern Olympic Games	
1899		First Hague Convention
1900	Union Cycliste Internationale formed	
1904	FIFA, world governing body of football formed	
1906	FINA: International Swimming Federation formed	
1909	Imperial Cricket Conference	
1912	IAAF (Athletics) formed	
1913	ITLF (Tennis) formed	
1919		League of Nations
1919		International Federation of Red Cross and Red Crescent Societies
1920		World Organisation of the Scout Movement
1930	First FIFA Football World Cup	
1945		World Bank
1945		International Monetary Fund
1945		United Nations

than attend as live spectators. As the modern mass media develop, our relationship with sport has been transformed. The earliest sporting tales were spread by word of mouth, which was augmented by written accounts as the print media developed. New sport magazines and guides began to appear in the mid-nineteenth century (Herd, 1952: 221; Bowen, 1970: 118–119; Goldlust, 1987: 69; Mason, 1988: 47–48).

In the 1870s and 1880s in a period that Boorstin (1961) calls 'the graphic revolution', there were a series of technological innovations in image production, such as dry plate photography (1873), the telephone (1876) and roll film (1884). The first newspaper sport department was established in1883 and the first sports section in 1895 (McChesney, 1989: 53).

The introduction of cinema, from the late 1890s, brought movement and hence sporting action to the audience for the first time (Aldgate, 1979: 17). The introduction of sound at the

understanding sport

end of the 1920s encouraged investment in new cinemas (ibid.: x). From the 1920s, radio brought the excitement and drama of the immediacy and uncertainty of sport into the home. After the Second World War, television combined the spectacle of the moving image with the immediacy and domestic reach of radio and in the process would transform sport. In 1950, there were only 5 million television sets in the world, and only the UK, the USA and the USSR had established television systems. Television was launched in Australia in 1956, the year of the Melbourne Olympics. By 1966, 81 per cent of British households, and 93 per cent of US ones had television (Chandler, 1988: 175). By 1970, there were 250 million sets in 130 countries, and television spread rapidly in Africa, Asia and Latin America (Green, 1972).

Newspapers had to adjust to the new electronic media. After the destruction of the power of the print unions during the 1980s in the UK, the introduction of computer-based typesetting and layout and colour printing accelerated the drift away from traditional page layout and towards a collage style in which headlines and photo displays came to dominate. This in turn heightened the force and impact of stories about easily recognised star figures. The once clear division between public and private spheres became blurred, and areas of life once resolutely private are now in the public domain. Much of the new sensation, scandal and gossip that has become a staple of tabloid content has featured sport stars, and has contributed both to a public fascination with personality and private life of sporting celebrities; and to the construction of discourses of moral censure.

Advertising, sponsorship, product endorsement, and corporate hospitality have played a role in the transformation and commodification of sport, through their influence on the presentation both of events, and of individual stars. Television's need for sports with audience appeal, combined with the needs of the advertising industry to find figures with market appeal and dynamic images with positive connotations, have combined to make top sport stars extremely wealthy and highly visible. However, it took television, and the globalisation of sport, to turn sport stars into hot properties from a marketing point of view.

At the start of the 1990s, Sky Television was losing around £1 million a week, and English football was only just recovering from two decades of problems with crowd behaviour, the Bradford fire, the Heysel Stadium incident and the Hillsborough stadium disaster. By the end of the decade, football was earning hundreds of millions of pounds in rights payments from television, its new chic appeal had forced almost all papers to launch massive football-dominated sport supplements, and a highly profitable Sky was making more and more inroads into BBC's diminishing sport portfolio.

The deregulation of rights negotiation allowed television channels to acquire the rights to the European games of specific clubs, and competition between the five terrestrial channels and Sky meant that there was more live football on television than ever before. The establishment of the English Premier League, and re-vamping of the European Cup as the Champions League, the introduction of all-seat stadia, and the importation of glamorous foreign stars increased the spectacularisation of football. New, more affluent customers were attracted, admission prices rose dramatically, grounds filled up. The cost and the need at many clubs to purchase season tickets to ensure access inevitably excluded poorer supporters. The new, more affluent football following attracted a new range of sport magazines. The rapid growth in pubs and bars featuring football fostered a whole new communal culture of television sport spectatorship. Major matches in the European Champions League attracted considerable attention, around the world. The digital revolution has accelerated these changes. More money will flood into football, and more games will be available, and although some will be pay-per-view, others will be available on the Internet. The combination of the growth of satellite television, sport in pubs and bars, sport supplements in papers, the launch of new sport magazines, the global reach of the English Premier League and the European Champions League, and the extension of the fame of top sport stars beyond the confines of the sport pages has placed sport in a more central position in cultural life globally.

TELEVISION, SPORT AND THE GLOBALISED AUDIENCE

When trying to understand globalising processes in sport, the World Cup and the Olympic Games are prime instances and in both cases the event has been closely linked to global marketing (see Chapter 13 for further discussion of mega-events). Sport as a television commodity has a major advantage – for the most part, it crosses language and cultural barriers relatively easily. Where sports are already understood, followed and consumed in many countries, all that is necessary is the dubbing on of a new commentary (in the case of live broadcasts, local language commentaries are provided either at origin or locally). So a major international sport event provides an ideal marketing medium for a corporation wishing to market globally. It used to be the case that relatively few corporations did market globally, and even now the sports market tends to be dominated by familiar names – Coca-Cola, McDonald's. However, digitalisation now allows the superimposition of localised advertising on globally transmitted live events, giving advertising space sellers the best of both worlds – global and local advertising. The concept of virtual advertising was basically designed for sport (Jackson *et al.*, 2005: 5). The global distribution of the star teams and individuals who to large degree are still based in the so-called 'developed' world has in turn been a major factor in the growth of the merchandising markets that have boosted the finances of the New York Yankees, Real Madrid, Manchester United and the other giants of corporatised sport.

Global sport offers great opportunities for global marketing and the advertising strategies of large corporations are increasingly equipped to exploit this opportunity. The ten largest advertising agencies now have offices in more than 50 different countries with the largest global firm, McCann Erickson, having over 200 offices in 130 countries (ibid.: 4). Branding is not new. In the 1950s, advertisers understood that they were selling image as well as product (see Packard, 1957). But the growing sophistication of advertising and promotion, and a heightened understanding of the market and patterns of consumption together contributed to the tendency, identified by Baudrillard, for symbolic value to become the dominant characteristic of the commodity. At the same time, a number of key structural changes were

altering the way that many big corporations functioned. The growth of a globalised post-Fordist mode of production gave rise to what has become called the 'hollowed out' corporation – based on centralised design and marketing but reduced manufacturing workforce, extensive sub-contracting, and casualisation of production, and a franchising of retailing. This, as Naomi Klein (2000) has pointed out, left corporations free to focus on production of image and identity, as embodied in logos and brands. Klein refers to the 'seemingly innocuous' idea developed by management theorists in the mid-1980s: that corporations should produce brands rather than products. Traditional corporations came to be seen as too large. The new corporations were based more on brand, image and design; examples include Nike, Microsoft, Tommy Hilfiger, and Intel. Trade liberalisation and labour law reform made it easier to outsource production.

Secondary marketing (spin-off products) became another means by which the commercial potential of brands could be exploited. Brand and image enhanced the value of secondary merchandising, especially to children. Klein points out that the companies that exited the early 1990s slump running were the ones that opted for marketing over cheapness – Nike, Apple, the Body Shop, Calvin Klein, Disney, Levis and Starbucks. For these companies the ostensible product was a mere filler for the real product – the brand. Some companies, of course, had always understood that they were selling brands – Coke, Pepsi, McDonald's, Burger King, and Disney. In the late 1980s and early 1990s Gap, IKEA, the Body Shop and Starbucks spread like wildfire. 'Brands not products' became the rallying cry for a marketing renaissance led by a new breed of companies that saw themselves as meaning brokers instead of product producers (Klein, 2000).

Since 1990, many corporations have been attempting to free themselves from manufacturing to focus on design and promotion. Klein points out that anyone can manufacture a product to order, and such tasks can be farmed out to contractors and subcontractors whose only concern is filling the order on time and under budget, ideally in the Third World, where labour is cheap, laws lax, and tax breaks available (ibid.). According to the 2005 *Fortune* Global Forum, the sports industry has become a major factor in wealth generation in China, which is now the world's largest producer and exporter of footwear. Shoes are the number one export commodity in Chinese light industry. In 2004, China exported 6 billion pairs of shoes which earned US$156.2 billion in foreign currency (*China Pictorial*, July 2005, p. 6). Ironically, in 2005, a film was released in China about a football team, Africa United, composed mainly of Africans and playing in a Beijing local amateur league. It was called *African Boots in Beijing* (*That's Beijing*, 16 July 2005, p. 47). The Chinese Government signed a contract with American Major League Baseball (MLB) to help develop China's baseball league through player and coach exchanges (*That's Beijing*, 16 July 2005, p. 25). Basketball, though, has been the real growth sport – note the success of the enormous Chinese basketball player Yao Ming in the USA. His success has helped basketball rival football in popularity in China.

GLOBALISING SPORT

Modern globalised sport is the product of the jet, television and corporate capitalism. In 1950, only Great Britain, the USA and the USSR had television. Since the early 1970s, television has spread rapidly to Africa, Asia and Latin America. The media system increasingly prompted international exchange in sport and this partly retained the traditional character of cultural imperialism. American television had a massive advantage in that the high production values and spectacular appearance of a sport like American football could make a profitable economic return in the North American market alone. This meant that American football, like much of American television, could be sold very cheaply around the world, undercutting local production while still making a profit (Whannel, 1986). However, sport from other countries now contributes to the export trade – Australian Rules, sumo, and the Tour de France have all found a space and an audience on British television (see also Boyle and Blain, 1991).

American television has assumed an awesome cultural and economic power, with its companies bidding astronomic sums for the rights to the Superbowl and the Olympic Games. The American television rights for the 1992 Winter and Summer Games cost American television more than US$600 million. US television pays for the Olympics, and plays a major role in influencing how it is run, exerting a subtle, indirect, but major influence on the layout of the site and stadia, the nature of ceremonies and the choice and timing of events.

Arguably sport has been an important element in globalising processes since the late nineteenth century. Many of the first international modes of organisation, such as the IOC, the IAAF, FIFA and the ILTF were sporting bodies. And yet in a world dominated by and in many ways defined by media imagery, it is in no small part sport that drives television – it is one of the primary forms pushing the commodification of television – it sells dishes, it sells subscriptions, and it is, apart from movies, the only viable pay-per-view form of television. In a world in which the power and authority of the United Nations have been considerably reduced, the major events of sport (the Olympic Games, the World Cup) constitute instances of the very limited number of institutions through which we define ourselves as a global collectivity.

In a consumer culture in which, despite apparent endless variety, innovations and transformations, there is also a perceptible uniformity and predictability about commodities, sport also offers intensity, excitement and unpredictability (Horne, 2006). Even though frequently derided for being over-competitive, and rife with cheating, drug abuse and gamesmanship, sport is arguably one of the least destructive forms of contestation we have. Therefore, one cannot really examine globalising processes without taking sport into account. In terms of the global and the local, sport is one of the most visible and prominent commodity forms in which these tensions are played out. Shirts and hats proclaiming Manchester United, Brazil, New York Yankees, and David Beckham are seen around the world, while the intensity of anger among Manchester United fans over the takeover of Manchester United by Malcolm Glazer provided a graphic and theatrical playing out of local–global tensions.

The spectacularisation of top-level sport on television, enabled by the growing technological command of image production and distribution, is a key part of the commodification process (Morris and Nydahl, 1985). Major sporting events win and hold enormous audiences, and have become global events. They serve to condense complex symbolic systems – of politics, nationalism, gender, race and aspiration (see Real, 1975; Wenner, 1989). The ceremonies and rituals surrounding the Olympic Games are in themselves a rich and complex field, juggling the needs of television for a comprehensible spectacle, the desire of Olympics organisers to demonstrate their munificence, the pressure to advertise a national culture, and the need to draw on aspects of the history, heritage and traditions of the host country, not necessarily easily read by the global TV audience (Tomlinson, 1996). The production of spectacle on this scale is necessarily laden with ideology. (See Wren-Lewis and Clarke, 1983; Gruneau, 1989; Tomlinson, 1989; Whannel, 1994; for more broad-ranging collections on the Olympics and the media, see McPhail and Jackson, 1989 and Spa *et al.*, 1995.)

The International Olympic Committee has the benefit of an instantly recognisable and highly marketable symbol, which signifies internationalism, excellence and the purity of Greek idealism. Perversely, the prohibition of advertising in the Olympic arena gives the symbol the aura of being above commerce and hence greatly increases its commercial value. This gives a clue to the resolution of a paradox at the heart of sport. Sport is capable of generating substantial profits although the key institutions were not formed as commercial endeavours. Yet, increasingly, beneath the cloak of traditional amateurism, they are reshaping themselves according to the nature and opportunities of the marketplace.

Gruneau (1997) charts this re-shaping in the context of Canadian sports, emphasising the realignment between public, private and voluntary subsidisation of the spectacle of sport and the market. His examples include budget cuts in government-funded community recreation programmes, leading to contracting out and partnerships; commercial sponsorship of sports programmes in the voluntary sector; cuts in school sports programmes and reliance on fund-raising; erosion of state funding to national amateur sports, and the need to search for corporate sponsorship.

Throughout, government policies in Canada were guided more and more by a new rhetoric of privatisation, deregulation and economic 'competitiveness'. Gruneau states that 'the market has responded by infusing sport at virtually all levels with the spectacular promotional logic of a media-based and increasingly transntional, consumer culture' (ibid.: 4).

North American leagues are attempting to expand globally in various ways:

- satellite and cable channels relay American sport to Asia and Europe;
- merchandising team logos and the global products of teams;
- global marketing of sportswear and shoes;
- staging of exhibition games outside North America;
- sponsorship of other professional teams transnationally.

Gruneau asserts that, 'In today's society of the spectacle, virtually every cultural event, indeed every public communication, has come to have promotional messages and public relations purposes built into it.'

Like the Olympics, Wimbledon tennis is efficient at trading upon its image. Ticket sales are only 20 per cent of income, with 60 per cent coming from television, and 20 per cent from other sources (Wilson, 1988). Rejecting title sponsorship, competition sponsorship and arena ads, which could be worth £5–10 million, the Wimbledon authorities accepted the prompting of agent IMG to concentrate on marketing and licensing the name and the logo. They market clothes, shoes, wallets, belts, luggage, bone china, preserves, sheets, blankets, towels, stationary and calendars with the Wimbledon brand (ibid.).

Exporting sports became a significant trend in the 1980s. American football, Australian Rules, sumo, and cricket have targeted new potential markets. Baseball has a long-term strategy for marketing the game in Europe, snooker is established in Thailand, Hong Kong, Malaysia, Singapore, Brazil and China. Attempts continue, however, to establish a European American Football League and FIFA still waits for signs that the association game of football has caught on more fully in North America (Sugden and Tomlinson, 1998).

RESISTANCES 1: AMERICAN AND OTHER EXCEPTIONALISMS

Joseph Maguire (1999) acknowledges the profound changes of globalisation, and that this to some degree displaces the nation as a unit of analysis, but argues that globalisation cannot be regarded as simply a path to homogenisation. He emphasises the tendency towards diminishing contrasts and increasing varieties. Maguire, drawing on Pieterse (1997), suggests a multidimensional and open-ended process, geographically wide and historically deep, which emphasises the flows between the West and the non-West, the creolisation of cultural forms, and the hybridisation of cultural identities.

Alan Bairner (2001) reviews some of the problems posed by theories of globalisation. He cites Holton (1998) that the key idea of globalisation is the single interdependent world and suggests that while globalisation is regarded as both positive and negative, both interpretations see it as inevitable and all-consuming. Bairner suggests that the forces of globalisation also produce reactions and resiliencies. He suggests using a single key dichotomy, Appadurai's (1990) concept of a tension between cultural homogenisation and heterogenisation. Bairner warns that the tendency to equate globalisation with the triumphant march of world capitalism and indeed with the hegemonic domination of American cultural forms, takes an overhomogenous view of America, and discounts patterns of overt resistance to Americanisation, especially in Islamic countries.

In sport, as with other cultural forms, there can be different degrees of resistance to globalising processes. Societies with long-established local sporting traditions are often resistant to adopting with any great enthusiasm sporting imports. The USA, with its own well-established dominant television sports of American Football, baseball, ice hockey and basketball, has been resistant to the importation of association football, and Formula One motor racing. America's own sports, with the arguable exception of basketball, have met with mixed success in their attempts to build a more global market. Australian Football and Japanese sumo have tended to be seen as exotic novelties in other countries and have not built significant audiences. On the other hand, with the exception of North America, football has succeeded in becoming virtually *the* global game. The FIFA World Cup held in 2010 in South Africa certainly con- solidated its position throughout Africa. Television coverage of the English Premier League and the European Champions League has gained large audiences in South-east Asia, particularly in China and Malaysia. Even in India, the EPL is rapidly building an audience. This television audience in India or Malaysia , however, is not triggering any great interest in local football. China and Japan remain the Asian countries with the most significant football development. Nor is the sports business driven entirely by Western countries. The fastest growing and one of the most successful sport competitions of recent decades is the Indian Premier League (IPL) in cricket (see Rowe, 2011: 108–112, for a useful overview of the redirection of global flows brought about by the IPL).

The economic rise of the 'BRIC' countries (Brazil, Russia, India and China) that are newly developing their economic power has prompted revisionism among some global theorists. It is notable, for example, that following a successful Olympics in China and the FIFA World Cup in South Africa, both events will be held in Rio de Janeiro in 2016 and 2014 respectively while Russia will act as host for the 2014 Winter Olympic Games in Sochi and the FIFA World Cup finals in 2018 (on BRIC's hosting of mega events, see Curi *et al.*, 2011, and Rowe, 2011: 112–114).

RESISTANCES 2: ALTERNATIVE RESPONSES TO GLOBALISATION

With developments such as these, there may be a need to 'de-Westernise' our perspectives on globalising processes. For Western scholars writing in the twenty-first century it takes a considerable effort of intellectual repositioning to reverse the picture, and to look at it from outside the Western context. Globalisation is only a currently fashionable label for a set of processes that have a long history. Imperial adventures, colonial invasion, the slave trade, the ordering and regulation of world trade, and the migration of people all look very different as processes when viewed from the position of the colonised. Theories of postmodern culture can seem a very metropolitan and Western phenomenon, which portray a mediascape constructed in the image factories of the (Western) culture industries. Yet the complacent assumptions of the Western metropolitan intellectual are frequently misplaced.

Anthony King (1991) argues that the image of modern Western metropolitan cities as being in the vanguard of multicultural diversity and postmodernism does not hold up; at the start of the twentieth century, the great colonial port cities – Singapore, Hong Kong, Calcutta and Rio – were far more diverse and indeed were more accurate precursors of the twenty-first century than the great Western cities such as London and Paris. Globalisation *now* cannot really be understood without a consideration of colonialism *then*. Culture is being made and remade by processes that constantly link past and present, core and periphery, margin and centre in ways that re-juxtapose, reconfigure and hybridise these terms.

This picture is complicated by the fact that, as already asserted, sport also has resistances to globalisation – by no means all sports can be readily exported. Football, motor racing, athletics, golf and tennis are among the most readily exportable, yet 'soccer' still struggles to make significant inroads in the USA. American basketball has managed to build a global following, thanks largely to the marketing efforts of Nike around the iconic figure of Michael Jordan (see Andrews, 2001). Rugby Union, despite vigorous development strategies, remains largely rooted in the white Commonwealth countries, while outside the old British Empire, cricket is barely heard of, far less understood. The diversity of sports and their cultural embeddedness might reasonably be seen as a strength rather than a weakness, and only the perverse distortions of international marketing have managed to present this resistance to importation as a problem that must be overcome by more energetic promotion. Miller *et al.* (2001: 10) emphasise the continued dominant position of what they call the US–Western Europe–Japan triad in the economics of sport, pointing out that the three areas are responsible for well over 90 per cent of the money paid for Olympic television rights in 2000. They argue that the nation-state has lost its potency and relevance, but instead assert that in a globalising context, analysis must both encompass and transcend individual nation-states (ibid.: 22).

One way in which this can be done is through attention to the histories of social activism around and within sport and sports mega-events, such as the Olympic Games. For example, Christian Tagsold (2011) demonstrates that although there were almost no critical voices raised against the Olympics and its uses by the Japanese state in the 1950s and 1960s, when Tokyo's 1964 Summer Olympics heralded the return of Japan to international society, during the city of Nagoya's bid for the 1988 Summer Olympics, broad-based citizens groups emerged in protest against their city's bid. The protest groups argued that the Games would be a wasteful expenditure of public money and would cause ecological problems. Calling into question the ideals of the Olympic Games themselves, this was 'probably the first popular anti-Olympic movement in Asia' (Tagsold, 2011). The anti-Olympic movement was not the main reason for the failure of Nagoya's bid, since Seoul, the only other competitor for host city, arguably were better at lobbying and playing the political power games within the Olympic movement. Nonetheless, the anti-Olympic movement formed in reaction to the city's bid laid the grounds for some of the principles used in subsequent arguments against hosting or staging mega-events, whether it is the Olympics, FIFA Football World Cups or World Expos, in other cities around the world.

Relatedly, Harvey *et al.* (2009) have recently explored the idea of alterglobalisation in relation to sport. While much has been written about globalisation and anti-globalisation processes and dynamics in general, it is the political and economic domains that have generated the most attention because it may be argued that the political and economic forms drive the changes

in the other categories. Harvey *et al.* argue, however, that a multiplicity of processes of globalisation are important for the understanding of this complex phenomenon. This is particularly the case for the understanding of alterglobalisation, as the global movements associated with it strive for political, social, and cultural as well as economic change. Alterglobalisation is a multifaceted form of resistance to neo-liberal globalisation that emerged with the first World Social Forum in Porto Allegre, Brazil, in 2001. Since then, global social movements, as well as a myriad of non-governmental organisations, have been active at the local and the global levels in advocating more humane globalisation. Alterglobalisation refers to the large spectrum of global social movements that present themselves as supporting new forms of globalisation, urging that values of democracy, justice, environmental protection, and human rights be put ahead of purely economic concerns.

Harvey *et al.* (2009) outline a framework for the study of the influence of alterglobalisation on sport and pose questions such as: What forms do the movements challenging the world sports order take today? Does an alterglobalisation movement exist in sport? What alternative models of sport do they propose? Alterglobalisation champions global social movements, but what do global social movements mean exactly and what makes them so different from other forms of social movements? Harvey *et al.* argue that new global social movements aim to change society not just in economic ways, but also in various social, cultural, identity and political aspects and identified the following under the label of global social movements: civil rights; ecological issues; women's rights; anti-racist movement; peace campaigns; lesbian, gay, bisexual, transsexual and queer rights; human security; workers' rights; children's rights; aboriginal rights and general internationalism.

Harvey *et al.* argue that the current hegemonic global sport order is based on fully commodified sport, that is, a form where sport is prominently an exchange value, is monopolised by multinational corporations in the manufacturing and professional sectors of the sport industrial cluster, and is governed by a supra-national authority, the International Olympic Committee (IOC) and the largest international federations' globocracy (Nelson, 2002). For some, this global sport world order constitutes the sport branch of the current supranational 'Empire' that dominates the world, as described by Hardt and Negri (2000).

Since the first half of the 1990s, however, contestation and resistance to globalisation have expanded to form a vast, loosely connected, international network of resistant groups, sporting and otherwise, that have coalesced around the notion of anti-globalisation and, more recently, the concept of alterglobalisation. Harvey *et al.* draw a distinction between non-sport organisations that use sport to achieve broader social changes or try to change sport and its institutions, and sport organisations that seek to achieve social change or socially progressive transformation of sports forms, sports competitions and sports organisations broadly. In line with the diversity and fluidity of alterglobalisation initiatives, they recognise that, in practice, individuals, groups and agencies may link, overlap and shift around between two or more of the categories; nonetheless, they argue that this distinction is useful for the purposes of analysis.

Their work highlights two alterglobalisation-related responses involving both sport and non-sport organisations: *reformists* who attempt to modify sport and/or produce difference in existing sport institutions and organisations; and *transformists* who seek to produce alternative sport forms within different sport organisations. In short, the impact on sport of global social movements/alterglobalisation can be both the modification of existing social relations, and/or the production of alternative social relations.

CONCLUSION: ALTERNATIVE WAYS OF THEORISING SPORT AND GLOBALISATION

There are other ways of examining global processes (Jones, 2010). The terms transnationalism and cosmopolitanism are often evoked in the context of globalisation, yet each has different inflections. Transnationalism suggests a form of corporation that has transcended national belongingness, but also a new form of cultural product – transnational cinema, for example, that works across themes, images and motifs that are not so much the product of a national sensibility, but rather the product of a diasporic and hybridised cultural context. Modern cricket has been transformed by modes of dress and presentation once regarded as 'Americanised', yet in localised inflection they have become integral to the modern game. The IPL is somehow not simply Indian in character, any more than it is simply British, and certainly not simply 'Americanised'.

The term cosmopolitan, often linked with metropolitan, typically celebrates the diversity, and consequent hybridities of modern urban life, in which, in food, in music, in film, in art, new creative fusions flourish. As such, it appeared to link globalising processes with a positive image of modernity, in which go-ahead enterprise-based, dynamic and progressive cities are contrasted with the backward, traditional, conservative and inward-looking rural world. Ironically, this is actually how the Athenians of Ancient Greece perceived things too.

Despite these diverse modes of theorising, there is general agreement that globalising processes are at work. Some regard this as a new phenomenon transcending the established structures of nation-states, seen as of declining relevance. Others see the process as a continuation of established patterns of cultural imperialism. For many analysts, globalising processes in sport are closely linked to Americanisation (Maguire, 1991). Whannel (1986) regards international television sport as a form of Western cultural imperialism. Jean Harvey and François Houle (1994) argue that globalisation is an alternative to Americanisation and imperialism, not a form of it. Maguire (1990), in discussing the spread of American football to England, points out, with reference to soccer, that cultural exchange is not always a one-way process. US dominance has been challenged by Europe and Japan. Guttmann (1991) says globalisation is just part of modernisation, while McKay and Miller (1991) and McKay *et al.* (1993) say that the globalisation of capital is a key part of the process. Rowe *et al.* (1994) also remind us of the complexities of international cultural exchange.

208

understanding sport

In order to comprehend the reach of international images and markets it is necessary to move beyond the simple logic of cultural domination and towards a more multi-directional concept of the flow of global traffic, in people, goods and services. Complex cultural trajectories intertwine. Scottish engineers, Spanish and Italian immigrants and Argentinean masculinity produced a particular context for football during the early part of the century, and seventy years later, in the 1980s and 1990s, Argentinean footballer Diego Maradona cuts a swathe through Spain and Italy before the road to coke-fuelled celebritydom, physical collapse, rehabilitation in Cuba and resurrection back home as a television star.

The popular image of the English, through their Empire, spreading sport around the world, is an over-simplification – it is more complex than that. Indigenous modes of play have been coming into contact with forms of culture brought by invading empires since the Romans. The imperial colonising forces of Holland, France, Spain and England all have had an impact on this process. The codification and reification of team games framed by muscular Christianity were the distinctive English contribution. The public school ethos fed into the work of muscular Christians (priests and missionaries, civil servants and diplomats, and army officers), all of whom channelled English sports into the British Empire. Football, though, tended to spread via engineers and traders and became most strongly established outside the British Empire. Arguably, this process involved not so much imposition of games as of rules, governance and authority (see Chapter 9). Here, though, France played at least as significant a role, being to the fore in the establishment of the IOC and FIFA, among other key bodies. From the perspective of the colonised countries, the very dominance by a foreign power meant that on the symbolic terrain of sport, playing the colonial masters at their old game and beating them became a politically charged ritual.

As noted earlier, Klein (2000) identified the growing importance of the logo in contemporary capitalism. Until the early1970s, logos on clothes were generally hidden from view. In the late 1970s, the country club wear of the 1950s became mass style. Ralph Lauren's Polo horseman and Izod Lacoste's alligator escaped from the golf course and scurried into the streets. By the mid-1980s Lacoste and Ralph Lauren were joined by Calvin Klein, Esprit and in Canada, Roots. The logo itself was growing in size, especially in the case of Tommy Hilfiger (Klein 2000). Manchester United, Real Madrid, the New York Yankees, the NBA, the MLB and the NFL have all been working hard, with varying degrees of success, to promote and develop their brands. The logo, Klein argued, becomes central. It is part of a shift from an image to a lived reality. The effect is to marginalise the host culture and foreground the brand as the star. One impact of the permeation of globalising processes by branded commodities is a heightened re-configuring of identities. Giddens suggests that:

> In more traditional situations, a sense of self is sustained largely through the stability of the social positions of individuals in the community. Where tradition lapses, and lifestyle choice prevails, the self isn't exempt. Self-identity has to be created, and recreated on a more active basis than before.
>
> (2002: 47)

Branded clothes constitute primary materials used in order to express self-identity, but identities are also re-made in the context of histories, traditions, and movements. The processes of diaspora, migration and hybridity are not new; on the contrary, they have marked the process of human interaction, exchange and contestation since the beginnings of trade. However, the shrinking of the globe by technology, the ease and speed of travel, the instantaneity of electronic communication, the perfect replication of digitalisation, and the nature of access to the 'back catalogues' of cultural production have bestowed a greater complexity. Sport with its stars, its brands and its dramatic action beamed worldwide, has become an integral element in the complex cultural and economic processes that constitute the contemporary global transformations of the social order.

ESSAY QUESTIONS

1   According to David Rowe (2011: 10), 'Diverse twenty-first century mobilities disturb and reconfigure established relationships between places, people, objects and organisational units.' Critically assess the way this impacts on any one sport.
2   Select any sport other than association football and discuss its development in relation to two theories of globalisation.

EXERCISE

1   Read Harvey et al. (2009). In groups identify: (i) two other non-sport organisations that use sport to achieve broader social changes or try to change sport and its institutions; and (ii) two other sport organisations that seek to achieve social change or socially progressive transformation of sports forms, sports competitions and sports organisations broadly.

FURTHER READING

R. Giulianotti and R. Robertson, *Globalization and Football* (London: Sage, 2009) outlines a sociological account of the growth, spread and continuing global interest in the so-called 'world's game'.

D. Rowe, *Global Media Sport: Flows, Forms and Futures* (London: Bloomsbury, 2011). Academic; this book provides an excellent overview of developments in the relationship between sport and media in many of its contemporary globalised forms.

CHAPTER THIRTEEN

SPORT SPACES, SITES AND EVENTS

INTRODUCTION

This chapter looks at both the phenomena of sporting spectacles and mega-events, and at the sites at which they are enacted. International sporting spectacles, such as the Olympics and the FIFA men's and women's World Cups, are illustrative of the interconnections between the media, commercial investment, and sporting identifications that are deeply implicated in particular spaces. They also demonstrate the connections and relationalities between sporting practices, their representations, and the architecture of sporting spaces and places. The chapter concludes with a commentary and questions concerning the relationship between sporting mega-events and the more routinised sporting activities and practices of the national and local sport culture.

Events like the Olympic Games, the World Cup Final, tournament and other sports mega-events, act as socio-cultural reference points, and reveal both the appeal and elusiveness of sport. In the age of global television, moreover, the ability of major sports events to shape and project images of the host city or nation, both domestically and globally, makes them a highly attractive instrument for political and economic elites. It is in this context that the pursuit of hosting sports mega-events has become an increasingly popular strategy of governments, corporations, and civic 'boosters' world-wide, who argue that major economic, developmental, political, and socio-cultural benefits will flow from them (Horne and Manzenreiter, 2006; Tomlinson and Young, 2006). Numerous studies and reports have fuelled the popular belief that sport has a positive impact on the local community and the regional economy, acting as a generator of national and local economic and social development. Economically it has been viewed as an industry around which cities can devise urban regeneration strategies. Socially it has been viewed as a tool for the development of urban communities, the reduction of social exclusion and crime, and the articulation of a society's collective identity. In reflecting on the successful bid for the London 2012 Olympics, the then Prime Minister of the UK, Tony Blair, promised a 'magical and memorable Games' that would 'do justice to the great Olympic ideals' (Lee, 2006: xiv). Blair had visited Athens prior to the bid deadline and wrote in a bid promotional leaflet: 'I visited Athens for the 2004 Olympic Games and returned convinced that hosting the Games could bring unparalleled social and economic benefits to the United Kingdom' (London 2012, 2004). Of course, this statement was made several years before the 2008 economic recession, but to cite the Athens model as an inspiration can be seen as a short-term, even naïve view, one that nevertheless continues to be used in the rhetoric and rationale underpinning cities' and nations' attempts to stage the highest-profile events.

It is revealing to compare this established and persisting view of sports mega-events with conclusions derived from a study of the effects and outcomes of the 2010 Vancouver Winter Olympics (Schmidt, 2007; Shaw, 2008). The Olympics are shown to be in large part a tool used by business corporations and governments (local, regional and sometimes national) to develop spaces of cities or the countryside. They permit corporate land grabs by developers. Several major construction projects took place in association with the 2010 Winter Games: the building of the Canada Line railway link connecting the airport and downtown Vancouver, the athletes' village, and a convention centre; developments in the Callaghan Valley west of Whistler (the main skiing area where the Olympic snowsport events took place); and the building of an extension to the 'Sea to Sky Highway' through Eagleridge Bluffs, in West Vancouver, to enable faster automobile transportation between Vancouver and Whistler. The view of one critic was that it was a disaster for any city on the planet to host the Olympics. Host city populations face increased taxes to pay for the 'party'. The poor and the homeless face criminalisation and/or eviction as downtown areas are gentrified, creating potentially more lucrative property markets and environments appealing to more affluent visitors or full-time residents. The hosting of such a mega-event skews all other economic and social priorities and constitutes a loss of opportunity to do other things with the public resources that have been spent on the Games. The IOC markets sport as a product, pays no taxes, and demands full compliance with its exacting terms and conditions, including government guarantees about meeting financial shortfalls. The end results are 'fat-cat' projects and media spectacles benefiting mostly the corporations that sponsor the Games, the property developers that receive public subsidies, and the IOC that secures millions of dollars from television corporations and global sponsors. The passion and enthusiasm of Vancouver's inhabitants, and other Canadian citizens, should not be ignored or underestimated, but the lasting legacy of the event may be the profits ensured by the business and entrepreneurial elites.

Sports mega-events have the following principal characteristics: (1) they are large-scale; (2) they have dramatic character, popular mass appeal, and international significance; and (3) they produce significant consequences for the host (city or nation), not least the attraction of global media attention (Horne and Manzenreiter, 2006; Tomlinson and Young, 2006). It is essential to look critically at the assumptions, beliefs and misrepresentations – the 'unknown knowns' – of sports mega-events (Horne, 2007a) – that are often suppressed or even repressed. Clearly when considering sport spaces, sites and events, such as the Olympic Games, the role and impartiality of the researcher are called into question. We would emphasise the importance of continuing to ask difficult questions about the hosting of sports mega-events (Sugden and Tomlinson ,1998; Horne and Whannel, 2012). Among the questions that this chapter will attempt to answer therefore are: Why do governments and cities compete for the right to host major international sporting events?; What are the commercial underpinnings of hosting such events?; How do Olympic 'boosters' and 'sceptics' portray the 'legacies', economic and otherwise, that are proclaimed for the Games?; What is the relationship between hosting an event and the wider sporting culture of a country and/or nation? We consider each of these questions in what follows.

WHY DO GOVERNMENTS AND CITIES WANT TO HOST SPORTS MEGA-EVENTS?

The attraction of hosting an Olympic Games (or another sports mega-event) is possibly greater today than ever before. It is widely assumed that hosting an Olympic Games represents an extraordinary economic opportunity for host cities (and nations), justifying the investment of large sums of public money. Yet this view has only developed in the past thirty years. Hosting the 1976 Summer Olympics resulted in huge losses and debts for the city of Montreal. The debt incurred on the interest for the loans to build what turned out to be largely 'white elephant' sports infrastructure was only finally paid off in November 2006 – costing the Montreal taxpayers well over CA$2 billion in capital and interest costs, without anything like commensurate benefits. Rather than experiencing a post-Olympic boom, the economy of Montreal in the mid-1970s went into a steep decline that would last for almost two decades. No wonder then that when the decision by the IOC on the host for the 1984 Summer Games took place, there was – once a barely credible bid from Tehran had been withdrawn – only Los Angeles bidding to host the event (Whitson and Horne, 2006). The Los Angeles bidding team was able to negotiate its own terms in securing the Games (Tomlinson, 2005c, 2012): it sponsored the Olympic torch relay for the first time, permitted the branding of facilities, used the opening and closing ceremonies as a vehicle for its Cold War ideological messages, and along with an IOC searching successfully for new levels of sponsorship helped transform the political economy (and so supersede the amateur ethos) of the Olympics.

Today established cities in advanced capitalist societies and cities in developing economies alike weigh up the possibility of hosting the Olympic Games. At the time of writing, the hosts for the next four Olympic Games (2012, 2014, 2016 and 2018) are known and five cities are set to submit 'bid books' for the Summer Olympic Games of 2020 (see Table 13.1). Depending on the stage in the cycle of staging and bidding to host an Olympics then at least three or four cities are anticipating hosting an Olympics and others are waiting their turn. The change in the allure of hosting the Olympics has partly come about because of the success that the LA Games appeared to be – in terms of making a substantial financial surplus or profit of over US$220 million, laying a solid economic foundation for a support system for athletes in the USA, and putting on a television spectacular involving many of the world's athletes. The attraction of hosting has also come about because of changes that the International Olympic Committee (IOC) has made to the process of selecting cities following investigative journalists' revelations of insider corruption in the 1980s and 1990s (see Simson and Jennings, 1992, and the website, www.transparencyinsport.org, accessed 15 May 2012).

Table 13.1 Summer and Winter Olympic Games* hosts, 1960–2020

| Year | Summer Games | | Winter Games | |
	Place	Country	Place	Country
1960	Rome	Italy	Squaw Valley	United States
1964	Tokyo	Japan	Innsbruck	Austria
1968	Mexico City	Mexico	Grenoble	France
1972	Munich	West Germany	Sapporo	Japan
1976	Montreal	Canada	Innsbruck	Austria
1980	Moscow	Soviet Union	Lake Placid	United States
1984	Los Angeles	United States	Sarajevo	Yugoslavia
1988	Seoul	South Korea	Calgary	Canada
1992	Barcelona	Spain	Albertville	France
1994			Lillehammer**	Norway
1996	Atlanta	United States		
1998			Nagano	Japan
2000	Sydney	Australia		
2002			Salt Lake City	United States
2004	Athens	Greece		
2006			Turin	Italy
2008	Beijing	China		
2010			Vancouver	Canada
2012	London	United Kingdom		
2014			Sochi	Russia
2016	Rio de Janeiro	Brazil		
2018			Pyeong Chang	South Korea
2020	Decision due at IOC session in Buenos Aires, September 2013: [candidate cities Baku, Doha, Istanbul, Madrid, or Tokyo]			

Notes * Since 2000 the Paralympic Games has been staged at the same venue as the Summer and Winter Olympic Games

**From 1994 Summer and Winter Games have been staged in different years, allowing US TV to spread the burden of raising advertising revenue over two years.

(Sources: adapted from Whannel, 1992; Toohey and Veal, 2000; www.olympic.org (accessed 19 December 2011).

Consideration of the sports mega-events staged or to be staged in the BRIC countries – Brazil, Russia, India and China – reveals several of the underlying tensions that emerge when a sports mega-event is staged outside the advanced urban centres of the northern hemisphere and also provides the chance to reflect on the role of the media in the construction of a culture of consumption which surrounds such events.

Table 13.2 The population size of the four BRICs

Country	Population
Federal Republic of Brazil (B)	193 million
Russian Federation (R)	141 million
Republic of India (I)	1.15 billion
People's Republic of China (C)	1.3 billion

The acronym 'BRICs' was coined in 2001 by the British Goldman Sachs economic consultant Jim O'Neill (2001). It has since become a common umbrella term in business, media, academic and government rhetoric about the future potential of these 'emerging giants', in particular the threat or opportunity that these economies present to the developed world. The BRICs can be seen as the West's/North's imagining of a new East/South with geo-political status and power to rival the developed world. Indeed, much BRICs discourse echoes Cold War rhetoric. Global political economy also seems to develop sporting metaphors – for example, the so-called 'next 11' are the eleven nations thought to be the biggest emerging economies after the four BRICs, and talked of as an emerging line-up: they include South Korea, Mexico, South Africa, Egypt, Indonesia, Vietnam, Chile and Argentina.

The development of BRICs discourse took place in the wake of the 9/11 attack in the USA and the growing recognition of the complexity of economic globalisation. Arguably, and possibly counter-intuitively, the attack on the World Trade Center in Manhattan prompted the search for new conceptualisations of globalisation beyond Americanisation. Another assumption underpinning the BRICs' discourse is that, with such large populations, these countries will develop even bigger economies to rival if not challenge the countries in the G7/G8. By 2009, the BRICs' share of global GDP collectively had reached 15 per cent.

In the context of neo-liberal globalisation, nation-states use sport for different non-sports ends: economic development and social development, nation building and signalling (branding the nation) and to assist in economic and political liberalisation. The allure of sports mega-events relates to their economic, political and symbolic potential. Looking back to the Beijing Summer Olympic Games in 2008, and the Delhi Commonwealth Games in 2010, and projecting forward to the Sochi Winter Olympic Games in 2014 in Russia and the Brazil FIFA World Cup Finals in 2014 and Summer Olympic Games in 2016 reveals the importance of specific social, economic and political contexts for understanding the impacts and outcomes of hosting sports mega-events.

As can be seen in Table 13.3, estimations of the costs of the hosting of these mega-events confirm that these are indeed very large-scale and expensive projects. Delhi in 2010 staged the most expensive Commonwealth Games ever. The estimated cost of the 2014 Winter Olympic Games is three times the cost of any previous Winter Olympics.

Table 13.3 BRICs and sports mega-events, 2008–2018

Year of event	Location (Country)	Event	Host status awarded	Cost
2008	Beijing (China)	Summer Olympic and Paralympic Games	2001	$US 15–40 billion
2010	Delhi (India)	Commonwealth Games	2003	$US 6.8 billion
2014	Sochi (Russia) 7–23 February Coastal zone: Sochi Mountain zone: Krasnaya Polyana	Winter Olympic Games	2007	$US 14 billion
2014	Brazil	FIFA World Cup Finals	2007	$US 12 billion
2016	Rio de Janeiro 5–21 August 7–18 Sept. Paralympic Games	Summer Olympic and Paralympic Games	2009	$US 14.4 billion
2018	Russia	FIFA World Cup Finals	2010	

To represent these four countries as a completely unified group, however, is not without problems. For example, it belies each country's own set of economic, social and political relations, both intra-nationally and with their regional neighbours and the developed world, and potentially masks the socio-historical cross-border exchanges that encouraged their emergence. There are many differences between, say, the experience of Russia when part of the Soviet Union between 1917 and 1989, and Brazil under its military dictatorship from the mid-1960s to mid-1980s, for example. Nonetheless, relations between them and other developing economies and economic regions are highly instructive when it comes to considering sports mega-events today.

For example, much of the funding – and, indeed, the labour – to build the stadia for the 2007 Cricket World Cup held in the Caribbean (referred to as the 'West Indies' in cricket parlance) came from two of the BRICs. The Indian government contributed to building Guyana's Providence Stadium, constructed by the Indian firm Shapoorji Paloonji Company at a cost of $25 million. Money and labour from the People's Republic of China (PRC) helped build stands and pavilions in Grenada and Jamaica, as well as Antigua's stadium, and most of the funding for the reconstruction of Queen's Park Stadium in Grenada came from China (see Horne, 2007b, for details). China has also contributed massively to the building of the sports infrastructure in several African countries and is developing a substantial investment programme in Brazil.

Staging the world's largest sports events creates similar challenges for the four BRICs as for other more established regions and countries. Four immediate challenges are: consumption, construction, containment and communication. These give rise to a series of related questions, as follows.

1   *Consumption*: Sport and sports mega-events have become an increasingly central rather than peripheral cultural form in the growth and spread of capitalist consumer cultures – including tourism, consumerisation, and global visitor destinations (Horne, 2006). This creates a potential set of issues about *under-consumption*. Are the 'Games' as popular as the official rhetoric claims, or as the bidding teams hope?

2   *Construction*: Designing, building, engineering, and then sustaining 'iconic' facilities are all part of the cost of hosting sports mega-events. These projects prompt the traditional questions: will the facilities be ready on time? At the stated costs? And of adequate standard? Will the facilities be more a form of monumentalism than a contribution to the communities where they are built?

3   *Containment*: Security and surveillance technologies connected with sports mega-events were a developing market before 9/11. Social control and surveillance measures associated with sports mega-events have grown since (Giulianotti and Klauser, 2010; Sugden, 2012). As with other major sports events in South America, new processes and technologies in public surveillance and security will be evident during the two mega-events to be held in Brazil (McLeod-Roberts, 2007). This raises among other questions the issues of: for whom are the measures being introduced? And who is being subject to increasing surveillance? (On developments in China ahead of the Beijing Olympic Games, see Klein, 2008.)

4   *Communication*: Mega-events involve both reaching the global audience and managing the message conveyed. This is no simple matter, as the message is also relayed to local, national, and global audiences and constituencies (Tomlinson, 2005b). Harm to national reputation is a potential risk, given the vast television audiences. What happens if/when things go wrong? Media professionals can be unforgiving if first impressions are negative, as Atlanta learned at its 1996 Summer Games when transport arrangements were inadequate, and a bomb explosion in an urban park sent nervous waves across the city and the world. Journalists and broadcasters have been equally unforgiving at events in BRIC locations. The perils of media coverage from the South to the North/East to the West have been apparent for several decades, for example, at the Olympic Games in Mexico 1968 and Moscow 1980. Maintaining a good image can be difficult. Dimeo and Kay (2004) have demonstrated developing countries run several risks when hosting large events, not least of which is being portrayed negatively in the global media. Coverage of events in developing nations is always prone to negative responses when something goes wrong. It is clear, for example, that the Delhi 2010 organisers' objectives were beset by the same contradictions that have confronted many previous hosts of large-scale sports events. Some examples of British newspaper headlines during the 2010 Commonwealth Games provide an illustration of the print media response: 'Empty Delhi. Credibility takes a dive'

(*Guardian*, 11 October, p. 24); 'It's just not cricket: Indians stay away from costly Games' (*Guardian*, 6 October, p. 17); and 'Sexual athletes: condoms block Delhi Games drains' (*Guardian*, 8 October, p. 17).

As regards one of the future mega-events in Brazil, barely had the 2010 FIFA World Cup Finals in South Africa been concluded, when a British newspaper reported that:

> With just 47 months until the next World Cup, the press is back on phase one of the World Cup reporting cycle: predicting the next tournament will be a security disaster staged in unbuilt grounds in unready cities, all of it run as a sweaty private cabal for FIFA's personal gain.
>
> (*Observer*, 18 July 2010, available at: http://www.guardian.co.uk/ football/2010/jul/18/fifa-world-cup-sepp-blatter [accessed 29 March 2011])

Research into sports mega-events can provide insights into the main dynamics of contemporary capitalist consumer culture. Sports mega-events have been largely developed by undemocratic organisations, often with anarchic decision-making and a lack of transparency, and more often serving the interests of global flows of finance, technology and imagery than local communities. In this respect, they represent a shift of public funds to private interests and in many ways reflect policies underpinning contemporary 'disaster capitalism' informed by the 'shock doctrine' (Klein, 2007). Using a crisis, or in this case a transformative sport spectacle, to re-shape urban space and the economy in the interests of business can be seen as part of the same strategy but instead this time using 'shock and awe' in the service of 'celebration capitalism' (Boykoff, 2011; Hayes and Horne, 2011).

The strategy of hosting events, sporting and otherwise, has become popular among both developed and emerging economies because it offers two prospects difficult to obtain in any other way: (1) the ability to respond to external pressures for global competitiveness, at the risk of heightening internal inequalities; and (2) a chance to reinforce collective identity, at the risk of damaging international reputation if things go wrong and the foreign media negatively report the event (Black and van der Westhuizen, 2004). Research on sports mega-events throughout the world has demonstrated that the benefits of staging them tend to be overestimated and the costs tend to be underestimated (for example, see several of the contributions to Horne and Manzenreiter, 2006). Additionally as British journalist David Runciman (2010) wrote in advance of the 2010 FIFA World Cup Finals:

> In reality, sports tournaments rarely do much to transform the fortunes of the countries that host them – at least not for the better – let alone change the fate of whole continents. But they can tell us a lot about where power really lies.

Other journalists suggest that hosts would be better off playing down the 'legacy' aspects, for example, 'Hosts need to understand what a World Cup is: a party. It leaves nothing behind except a hangover, good memories and a large bill' (Kuper, 2010: 2). Certainly the 'legacies' for countries hosting sports mega-events recently have included: consumerisation and increased reliance on China for construction (the 2007 West Indies Cricket World Cup); debates over the unequal distribution of benefits (the 2010 South Africa FIFA World Cup Finals); and environmental conflicts (the 2010 Vancouver Winter Olympic Games). In the case of the 2012 London Summer Olympic Games, newly built 'Westfield Stratford City', billed as Europe's largest shopping mall, promises to be the gateway to the Games for 70–80 per cent of potential spectators and is likely to be a clearer legacy than any of the facilities on the Olympic Park for several years to come: shopping, not sport, may be the activity to benefit most from the event.

Sports mega-events have also come in recent years to be seen as potential catalysts for sustainable social and economic development in developing economies and sport as a means of meeting international development goals (Darnell, 2010). In this ideological climate Curi et al. (2011: 14) have recently suggested that a 'BRIC-way to organise sport mega-events' may come to dominate the Olympics in the near future. If this is the case – and given the success of Russia in winning the right to host the 2018 FIFA Football World Cup Finals in December 2010 – then the issues identified here will certainly require further social scientific investigation and scrutiny.

WHAT ARE THE COMMERCIAL UNDERPINNINGS OF HOSTING SPORTS MEGA-EVENTS?

The major inducement to engage in Olympic hosting now as opposed to the 1980s is of course financial – the sponsorship and television rights money that the IOC has negotiated largely covers most of the *operating* costs of the Olympic Games – between US$2–2.5 billion for the Summer 'edition'. The Games attract vast television audiences – the 2008 Beijing Olympics drew an estimated cumulative global television audience of 4.7 billion over the 17 days of competition, according to market research firm Nielsen. Such estimated audience figures have to be treated with caution, as we have noted elsewhere in this book, but Nielsen's estimate surpassed the 3.9 billion viewers for the Athens Games in 2004 and the 3.6 billion who watched the 2000 event in Sydney. The 2008 Beijing Olympics was also the most-viewed event in US television history – according to Nielsen, 211 million viewers watched at least some of the first 16 days of Olympic coverage on US network NBC.

Large television audiences have meant that television corporations and broadcasting unions have been prepared to pay increasing sums of money for exclusive coverage of the Olympics. This income to the IOC has helped it to offset the operational costs of the Games. Hence in future, alongside cities like Paris, London, New York, Chicago, Madrid and Beijing, smaller cities, for example Copenhagen (Denmark), and those in the 'Global South', such as Durban (South Africa) and Delhi (India), will now consider bidding for the Summer Olympic Games. Acting as host to the IOC's Congress (Copenhagen 2009, Durban 2011, Buenos Aires 2013) or one of the 'lower order' sports mega-events (Delhi hosted the Commonwealth Games in 2010) is also considered as a way of leveraging support for a subsequent Olympics bid.

In addition to broadcast partnerships, for the past 25 years, the IOC has operated the TOP (The Olympic Partner) worldwide sponsorship programme and the IOC official supplier and licensing programme (see Table 13.4). Since 1985, when the TOP programme started (Tomlinson, 2005c, 2012a), the financial health of the IOC has been secured by the first two sources – television rights payments and global sponsorship deals. As an article in *The Economist* put it, ahead of the Atlanta Summer Olympics in 1996: 'The zillion dollar Games' have developed because 'the power of corporate hype linked with global television is a marvellous machine for promoting sports'. Television rights accounted, in the economic cycle to 2008, for slightly more than 53 per cent of IOC revenue and it is likely that television income will continue to increase. Television income for the 2010 and 2012 Games is already assured at US$3.8 billion, an increase of 40 per cent on the US$2.6 billion the IOC received for the 2006 and 2008 Games.

Table 13.4 TOP sponsors (The Olympic Programme/Partner Programme), 1988–2012

TOP 1 1988 Seoul	TOP 2 1992 Barcelona	TOP 3 1996 Atlanta	TOP 4 2000 Sydney	TOP 5 2004 Athens	TOP 6 2008 Beijing	TOP 7 2012 London
Coca-Cola	Coca-Cola	Coca-Cola	Coca-Cola	Coca-Cola	Coca-Cola	Coca-Cola
Kodak	Kodak	Kodak	Kodak	Kodak	Kodak	
Sports Illustrated/ Time	Sports Illustrated/ Time	Time Inc.	Time Inc.	Time Inc.		
VISA	VISA	VISA	VISA	VISA	VISA	VISA
	Bausch & Lomb	Bausch & Lomb				
		Xerox	Xerox	Xerox		
Brother	Brother					
3M	3M					
Federal Express	United States Postal Service (USPS)	United Parcel Service (UPS)	United Parcel Service (UPS)			
Matsushita (Panasonic)	Matsushita (Panasonic)	Matsushita (Panasonic)	Matsushita (Panasonic)	Panasonic	Panasonic	Panasonic
	Ricoh					
	Mars					
		IBM	IBM			

John Hancock	John Hancock	John Hancock	John Hancock	
	Samsung	Samsung	Samsung	Samsung
	McDonald's	McDonald's	McDonald's	McDonald's
		Swatch	Swatch	
		Atos Origin	Sema*	Atos Origin
			General Electric	General Electric
			Lenovo	
				Acer
				Dow
				Omega
			Procter & Gamble	

Note: * Sema is the computer services division of Atos Origin.
Sources: de Moragas Spa *et al.* (1995: 29);Toohey and Veal (2000).

The IOC refers to its financial operations in terms of an 'Olympic quadrennium' – a four-year period (from 1 January–31 December). The latest one for which accounts have been made available (2005–2008) generated a total of more than US$5.4 billion in revenue (IOC, 2011). The IOC distributes approximately 90 per cent of Olympic marketing revenue to organisations throughout the Olympic Movement to support the staging of the Olympic Games and to promote the worldwide development of sport and retains the rest to cover operational and administrative costs of governing the Olympic Movement. The IOC provides TOP programme contributions and Olympic broadcast revenue to the Organising Committees of the Olympic Games (OCOGs) to support the staging of the Olympic Games and Olympic Winter Games. Long-term broadcast and sponsorship programmes enable the IOC to provide the majority of the OCOGs' operational budget well in advance of the Games, with revenues effectively guaranteed prior to the selection of the host city. The two OCOGs of each Olympic quadren-nium share approximately 50 per cent of TOP programme revenue and value-in-kind contributions, with approximately 30 per cent provided to the summer OCOG and 20 per cent provided to the winter OCOG. During the 2005–2008 Olympic quadrennium, for exam-ple, the Torino (Turin) 2006 Organising Committee received US$406 million in broadcast revenue from the IOC, and the Beijing 2008 Organising Committee received US$851 million. The OCOGs, in turn, generate substantial revenue from the domestic marketing programmes that they manage within their host country, including domestic sponsorship, ticketing and licensing. National Olympic Committees (NOCs) – of which there are over 200 – receive financial support for the training and development of Olympic teams and Olympic athletes. The IOC distributes TOP programme revenue to each of the NOCs throughout the world. The

IOC provided approximately US$370 million to NOCs for the 2005–2008 quadrennium. The World Football Governing Body FIFA reported, for its 2007–10 four-year cycle, revenue amounting to US$4189 million; its expenditure was $US3558 million, leaving $US631 million dollars to play with.

HOW DO MEGA-EVENT 'BOOSTERS' AND 'SCEPTICS' PORTRAY THE 'LEGACIES', ECONOMIC AND OTHERWISE, THAT ARE PROCLAIMED FOR THE EVENTS?

Although there appear to have been many positive developments since the Los Angeles Olympics, several academics and sports people at the time (see the contributors to Tomlinson and Whannel, 1984) and since have been critical of the increasing commercialisation of the Games and the likely impact this has had on the event. These commentators have been portrayed as 'gloom merchants' and 'naysayers' by some of those involved with the Olympics and associated sports federations, but the criticisms are not voiced solely by people who want to put an end to the Olympics. Commerce comprises not just the elite body of Olympic sponsors. With the increasing involvement of powerful global brands as Olympic sponsors has come attendant commercial rights legislation – to provide exclusivity to their association with the Olympic symbols (the interlocked rings, the name of the Games, etc.) and avoid 'ambush marketing' which the corporations pay millions of dollars to obtain; and this has been seen as overly restrictive by smaller businesses and organisations. The Olympic Games also provides a major attraction to sponsors at a national level and thus drains resources away from other non-Olympic sports and cultural activities during the build-up to the event. Criticisms of the IOC as an organisation have also had some impact on its practices.

The IOC remains a private organisation, which only accepts invited members. The voting membership of the IOC currently consists of slightly more than 110 people, including the President Jacques Rogge, but only about 15 of these are women and active athletes. The IOC contains several members of royal families and corporate leaders and people holding an executive or senior leadership position within an IF or a NOC. It thus remains subject to accusations of lack of transparency while it claims to be a movement and a 'family' based on a philosophy beyond politics. Alongside the myths and ideology of Olympism – with elements such as the creed, the motto and the flame often borrowed from Christianity – it is not surprising that quasi-religious claims are often made such as upholding the 'spirit' of the Games. Critics prefer to portray the Olympics nowadays as an 'industry', a 'machine' and even a 'disease' that creates a blight on the cities and their populations that act as its hosts.

In the build-up to the London 2012 Olympic and Paralympic Games to be held in July and August 2012, numerous news stories related to it captured the headlines in the UK media. Concerns over spiralling costs reappeared as it was announced that the number of security guards required had been a 'finger in the air exercise' and the figure had more than doubled to 23,700. More military personnel were to be deployed in total than for the Afghanistan campaign. When it was revealed that Olympic TOP sponsor Dow Chemical would also provide LOCOG with the polyester and polyethylene wrap for the Olympic Stadium, there was an outcry as Dow owns the company Union Carbide that was responsible for a toxic gas disaster in Bhopal in 1984. The threat of an Olympic boycott by India was reported. Then despite record investment and legacy promises attached to the 2012 Games, it was reported that the Active People Survey had found that public participation in sports had fallen. Regular participation had declined for young people and women especially. Local people involved in the social disturbances that occurred in London during August 2011 were also reported as recognising the social disparity that existed between their situation and the large sums of money spent on the event.

ARCHITECTURE AND SPORT SPACE

Despite criticisms, the allure of hosting sports mega-events has increased greatly in the past twenty-five years. One of the notable features accompanying the race to host mega-events is the building of iconic, one-off, architectural structures. Journalist and architectural critic Deyan Sudjic (2005: 326) suggests that architecture 'is constantly about . . . power, glory, spectacle, memory, identity', while it always changes in form. That this is as true for the buildings and facilities underpinning sport and sports mega-events as it is for other construction projects can be seen through a brief examination of selected buildings designed for the summer Olympic Games (see Table 13.5).

The role of architects in the creation of memorable Olympic infrastructures has not been analysed much until relatively recently. This may partly be to do with the fact that while stadia built prior to 1984 included the well-received Tokyo and Munich projects, it also included Montreal that stands out as one of the most negative examples of contemporary architectural ambition. The complex design and ambitious *grand projet* left the city with an enormous debt, only paid off completely over thirty years later in November 2006 (http://www.cbc.ca/canada/

Table 13.5 Examples of selected Olympic Games and architects

Olympic Games	Architect
Tokyo 1964	Tange Kenzo (Yoyogi National Gymnasium, Tokyo)
Munich 1972	Gunter Behnisch and Frei Otto (Olympiastadion, Munich)
Montreal 1976	Roger Taillibert (Montreal Stadium)
Sydney 2000	Bligh Lobb Sports Architecture (Stadium Australia, Sydney)
Athens 2004	Santiago Calatrava Valls (Olympic Sports Complex, Athens)
Beijing 2008	Jacques Herzog/Pierre de Meuron (Beijing National Stadium)
London 2012	HOK Sport/ Populous™ with McAlpine (Olympic Stadium); Zaha Hadid (Aquatics Centre)

montreal/story/2006/12/19/qc-olympicstadium.html, accessed 15 January 2007; see also Whitson and Horne, 2006).

It is clear that the Olympic Games and other sports mega-events have long provided opportunities for nations to signal emergence or their re-emergence on the international stage. While there are and can only be a few 'global cities', attempts to promote locations has become common in the past twenty years. Whether as new hubs for business and finance or as tourist destinations, cities increasingly are building and utilising iconic architecture and urban spaces to flag their presence in the world. Sports mega-events play their part in this competition for global promotion and branding.

The hosting of a major event enables symbolic as well as material nation building to take place. Short (2004: 68ff.) identifies four modalities of global cities: (1) transportation hubs and networks; (2) global cultures and cosmopolitanism; (3) global imaginings and place marketing; and (4) global spectacles, signature architects and cosmopolitan urban semiotics. The Summer Olympic Games is 'the mega-event with the ability to create, reinforce and consolidate global city status' (ibid.: 108) as it combines these modalities. The Summer Olympics are 'global spectacles, national campaigns and city enterprises' at one and the same time (ibid.: 86).

Globally, the IOC, prompted by concerns about its environmental impact, wavering public opinion in the light of corruption revelations and interest in the amorphous concepts of 'legacy' and 'sustainability' that developed in the 1990s, has helped shape the environment in which the change in the role of architecture and stadium architects in sport has taken place. Concerns about legacy have been the focus of one IOC conference and transfer of knowledge has become a vital part of the organisation of Olympic events. The related concern with 'sustainability' has existed since 1994 when the IOC adopted the environment as the third pillar of the Olympic Movement.

Sklair (2006, 2005) argues that 'starchitects' assist what he calls the Transnational Capitalist Class (TCC) through the construction of transnationally attractive consumption spaces and the production of Iconic Architectural (IA) forms. Since the 1980s, starchitects have been invited to build iconic buildings and consumption spaces and the ideological role of these reflects other processes going on in cities. This includes the re-imagining/imagineering of cities as consumption centres, rather than centres of production; the building of urban entertainment destinations (UEDs) and other themed environments; and the construction of spaces for the consumption of experiential commodities, such as sports and recreational events, concerts and other commercial gatherings, which include stadia or 'tradiums' often increasingly named after a sponsor rather than their location in the city (Rutheiser, 1996). Saunders (2005: viii) suggests: 'Spectacle is the primary manifestation of the commodification or commercialization of design.' This has involved a simulated de-McDonaldisation in some places and the creation of ballparks as theme parks (Ritzer and Stillman, 2001).

As already noted, some sociologists have already responded to these developments critically. A persistently relevant way of understanding how space and/or place make sport so important a cultural form – on its various levels and scales of participation and performance – is available

understanding sport

in the works of geographer John Bale (2003), who has adapted the concept topophilia to the study of the location and cultural meaning of sport. Deriving from the Greek words for place and love, topophilia describes the powerful emotional attachments that people can have to a place, location or site (Tuan, 1974). Attachment to and affection for sport places, particularly those imbued with traditional meanings that can be sustained, upheld, and reproduced, are emphasised in Bale's work and have had a particular influence on how the relocation of the stadium impacts upon established spectator communities.

In North America, however, journalist Dave Zirin has identified the building of iconic sports and leisure spaces as a poor 'substitute for anything resembling an urban policy in this country' (Zirin, 2009: 262). He describes the way that the Louisiana Superdome became a shelter for 30,000 of New Orleans' poorest residents left homeless by the effects of Hurricane Katrina in August 2005. Built from public funds 30 years earlier, it would normally have been beyond their means to enter the arena. The homeless people were then moved on from there to the Houston Astrodome in Texas, not to government housing, public shelters or somewhere nearer to their devastated homes. Zirin (ibid.: 262) argues: 'Stadiums are sporting shrines to the dogma of trickle-down economics.' Some $16 billion of US public money has been spent on stadium construction and upkeep in the previous decade. Despite evidence to the contrary that they function as financial cash cows, 'the domes keep coming' (ibid.), however. The opening of two new baseball arenas in 2009 in New York, Citi Field (New York Mets) and the new Yankee Stadium (New York Yankees) – the latter the most expensive sport stadium in the world (ahead of the new Wembley Stadium in London) – testifies to the continuing lure of sports facilities (Cornwell, 2009).

In the UK, Inglis (2000, 2005) identifies two moments when sport stadium architecture under-went fundamental change – at the end of the nineteenth century and the end of the twentieth century. The 'local' stimulus to the most recent shift in Britain has been the sustained investment in the infrastructure of football stadia in England, Wales, and to a lesser extent Scotland, since the publication of the Taylor Report (1990) into the Hillsborough Stadium disaster in 1989 that recommended, among other things, the move toward all-seat football stadia. One of the first fruits of this tragic stimulus was the Alfred McAlpine (now Galpharm) Stadium built in Huddersfield, designed by Rod Sheard, which became the first sports venue to win a Royal Institute of British Architects (RIBA) 'building of the year' award in 1995. As we have seen, following the merger of Sheard's Lobb Partnership and HOK in 1999, Sheard and HOK Sport (and now known as Populous™) have become even more prominent in promoting sports architecture. On this more local level, far from the profile and aspirations of mega-event managers and entrepreneurs, sport facilities can combine the dynamism of the new – the technology of stadium design – with the values and various passions of tradition – the emotions of the fan or the loyal supporter. Names might change – in soccer, Arsenal's Emirates, Bolton's Reebok, and Brighton's American Express Community stadia – but meanings, memories and values can be sustained in the new environment.

The 2012 Olympic Games has had an extensive influence on architecture in the UK in the past seven years. Sport-related projects, as well as in the mega-event form, may become more important for architects as they look to diversify in the sectors in which they operate. In doing so, architects will be drawn even more into urban, spatial, politics. Bélanger (2009) identifies several contradictory and contested features of the urban sport spectacle that architects can become enmeshed in as they produce (trans)national sport spaces. First, the paradox of distinctiveness is that if everywhere has iconic architecture, then there is a global sameness to the pursuit of distinction. This can lead to the creation of unspectacular spectacles, or the predictable monotony of the spectacular in commodified space, as geographer David Harvey once argued was the case with respect to postmodernist architecture (see Merrifield, 2002, especially pp. 144–155). Second, there are various urban narratives, imaginaries and themes that can create a division between, in architectural as well as other terms, the spectacular global and the vernacular local. This in turn can lead to spectacular local resistance to and/or negotiation with the global spectacle through novel uses and vernacular appropriation of the built environment (Stevens, 2007). Third, the production of consumption spaces, such as the new-made-to-look-old nostalgic baseball parks in the USA (such as Camden Yards in Baltimore or PNC Park in Pittsburgh) uses collective memory to reformulate a new consumerised public sphere. Yet as spaces, sports stadia are both public and private – both popular and disciplining, intimate as well as commercial. They are shaped by public meanings and form the basis of popular memories, including at times of disaster, becoming the forum for cultures of commemoration. Hence Belanger alerts us to the ever-present gap between capital's intentions and the use-values of spectacular urban sport spaces.

CONCLUSION

We noted earlier, in Chapter 4, that alongside the expanding profile of the elite one-off Olympic event in London, England, in the build-up to the 2012 Summer Games, adult participation rates in that country have been in decline. One of the claims that many event-bidders make is that the big event will boost participation and bring new generations of young people into the sport culture of the city, region or country. But a closer look at trends and developments in hosting cities and societies suggests that this is a bogus claim, at best a well-intentioned misapprehension. Admiring a great athlete does not mean that all young people will seek to emulate the athlete's achievements. Many are happy to follow Dame Kelly Holmes's musings on Twitter, but with no aspirations to dedicate themselves to the track and the competitive sport ethos. Sport stars are for the most part celebrities rather than role models, and apart from some dramatic cases having sustained impact beyond the national – gymnastics after the achievements of the USSR's Olga Korbut and Romania's Nadia Comaneci in the 1970s – the 'podium policies' adopted in medal-chasing approaches do not automatically translate into increased participation; interest and increased enthusiasm perhaps, but not sustained sporting activity. Behind the headline-grabbing large-scale events, garnering the 300 million plus television viewers worldwide for Barcelona versus Manchester United in the UEFA Champions League final at Wembley in 2011 (Tomlinson, 2012b), Britain's sport culture remains an intriguing mix of the watchers and the physically active, the old and the new, the popular and the elite, the accessible and the inaccessible. The polo-playing privileged play on undisturbed in the calm of southern England's Cowdray Park; the Wimbledon crowd gathers for its summer ritual at tennis's oldest tournament; football's traditional male fan base is complemented by more women in the all-seater stadium; the village cricket team perpetuates an image of old England; the Irish, Scottish and Welsh national rugby sides question any notion of the national UK sport culture. British sport continues to be a mosaic of activities marking social differences but in some forms creating cultural harmony and collective social meaning. Who you watch and shout for, with whom (if anyone) you choose to play, is a complex outcome of a range of interconnected influences, including the classic sociological influences of social class, income, gender, age, and disability, and the inevitable obduracy of the historical. Spectacle and thrill may be conjured in the local park in a scratch small-sided soccer game; the most hyped mega-event spectacle can produce the dullest most routinised encounter, of both competitive teams and their followers. This is the beauty, seduction and socio-cultural importance of sport, in its infinite and unpredictable varieties.

ESSAY QUESTIONS

1   'When fans develop an attachment to and affection for sport places they can be manipulated by owners of sports teams and events.' Discuss.
2   Why has 'legacy' become so important for the hosts of sports mega-events and transnational sports bodies such as the IOC and FIFA?

EXERCISES

1   Find out who were the architects of the stadium used by your local or favourite football, rugby or cricket team. How many other sports facilities have they built in the UK and/or elsewhere in the world?
2   Debate the proposition that 'It's better to be a sceptic than a booster when it comes to hosting sports mega-events anywhere in the world'.

FURTHER READING

J. Horne and W. Manzenreiter (eds), *Sports Mega-events: Social Scientific Analyses of a Global Phenomenon* (Oxford: Blackwell, 2006).
A. Tomlinson, and C. Young (eds), *National Identity and Global Sports Events: Culture, Politics and Spectacle in the Olympics and the Football World Cup* (Albany, NY: SUNY, 2006).

CHAPTER FOURTEEN

CONCLUSION

METHODS FOR UNDERSTANDING SPORT CULTURE

INTRODUCTION

In understanding and researching sport, socio-cultural approaches in sport studies have generated some distinctive methodologies, which have made significant interventions and contributions to particular spheres of social investigation; these include studies of mega-events, globalisation processes, body cultures, public rhetoric and ideologies, governance processes, and integrated studies of the production and consumption of the spectacle. This conclusion briefly reflects upon selected aspects of the philosophy of science as applied to the analysis of sport culture, and then considers methodological issues in the context of sport history and media studies, before looking at how particular methods have been used by socio-cultural researchers focusing primarily upon the meaning of sport and its cultural significance in contemporary societies.

The aim of this chapter is, then, to stimulate or provoke students of sport to think critically about and problematise research methods, to recognise both that the choice and use of particular methods are not a neutral or solely technical decision, and that the knowledge produced in the socio-cultural analysis of sport can in itself embody a form of agency, shaping cultures and futures. We offer here not so much a 'how-to' manual on research methods, but rather a way of understanding the implications of an informed, and reflective, choice of methods. In doing this, we do the following:

1   Acknowledge the centrality of methods in producing knowledge that is potentially trans-
    formative and responsive to social change.
2   Demonstrate the relationship between theories and methodologies and methods and
    show how theoretical approaches inform and are shaped by methods.
3   Explore methods in the context of what is particular about sport and sporting activities in
    all their manifestations, including the affects of sport and the relationship between affect
    and sensation.
4   Explore some of the particularities of adopting different methodologies to research in
    sport, for example, in relation to access, immersion, insider/outsider status and ways of

being inside, and the advantages and limitations of quantitative approaches and large-scale surveys and questionnaires, especially in recording social change.

5   Consider what the study of sport can contribute to the wider field of methods and methodologies.

METHODS, METHODOLOGY, INTERPRETATION

Methodology is the theory of methods; methods are the techniques that are adopted for the study of chosen phenomena, in both past and present time, across both time and space, often chosen in relation to an overall methodological position or stance. Throughout this book we have drawn upon a range of empirical sources – from surveys to documents, trend data to focused observation, industry data to interviews, oral histories to questionnaires – to illuminate the nature of sport culture, and have, where appropriate, commented upon the relationship between concepts, theories, and analytical techniques employed in the reported studies. In this chapter we ask readers both to think back over some of the sources that we have quoted and used as knowledge, and to contextualise that knowledge in relationship to debates in the philosophy of science and what are sometimes called the paradigm wars, after the influential work of Thomas Kuhn (1962).

Often confused with the particular experimental research methods or fieldwork techniques employed in a study, the term 'methodology' refers to the theory of or rationale for the methods and analytical techniques that are chosen for a study. These include consideration of the wider questions generated by the philosophy of science: How is evidence gathered?; What is the relationship of the researcher to, say, the sport subculture under study?; What is the role of the researcher in the fieldwork setting?; Is a value-free, neutral socio-cultural analysis possible?; What is the status of the knowledge generated in the study?; How do the experiences and views of the researcher – as, say, an experienced and knowledgeable sports performer or enthusiast, as well as a trained social observer or social scientist – relate to the sport subculture s/he is studying?; Should socio-cultural studies be replicable or even verifiable?

Methods themselves are products of the social world, but the knowledge that they generate reproduces or reshapes elements of that world. Some approaches have begun to claim that it is as important to study the 'social life of methods' as it is to absorb the findings and results of research studies, as these latter are no more than the product of the methods that have generated them. As CRESC researchers John Law and Evelyn Ruppert have put it:

> Methods aren't a neutral toolkit that can simply be picked up and put down. Indeed, they aren't narrowly methodological. The technicalities are important but we're making a bolder claim: we're saying that research methods are vital *players* in the social world: that they help to *create* society. And we want to know how.
> (http://www.cresc.ac.uk/our-research/cross-theme-research/social-life-of-methods, accessed 15 May 2012)

Prior to consideration of some of the most influential methodological strategies that have shaped knowledge in sport studies, it is important to recognise the currents of intellectual history and the ways of thinking that have framed dominant approaches in the study of sport. The socio-cultural study of sport has been developed on the basis of a primarily interpretive analytical approach, in contrast to a positivist approach. In positivism, the systematic study of society depended upon the application of the methods and procedures of the natural sciences to the study of social reality and the social world, in generating testable hypotheses and establishing facts as a basis for explanations. In contrast, interpretivism (Bryman, 2000: 13), as

> an alternative to the positivist orthodoxy . . . is predicated upon the view that a strategy is required that respects the differences between people and the objects of the natural sciences and therefore requires the social scientist to grasp the subjective meaning of social action.

It is such subjective meanings that make sport culture so significant in contemporary societies and communities, and the methods that have best illuminated this significance are qualitative ones within an interpretivist framework.

We need nevertheless to generate quantitative data, on participation, audiences, finances, in order to understand sport, and so to adopt an interpretivist approach is not to reject quantitative data or approaches. A perfectly valid study of, say, the motivations, performance and culture of a group of veteran distance runners could include the objectives of both explanation and understanding, using robust physical measures of performance, questionnaires on the runners' reasons for and perceived benefits of running, and observation of the subculture of the group. Such multi-method work in an integrated study renders traditional splits between, say, quantitative and qualitative researchers, potentially obsolete. Also, as in Scott Fleming's (1995) study of sport in the lives of young South Asians, a quantitative questionnaire can be used to identify broad attitudes and activity trends, and a qualitative methodology combining participant observation and in-depth interviews used to explore the meanings and experiences in more depth. Such studies on the whole adopt an inductive process, in which researchers weave between theory and analysis, moving from the particular to the general: observation and findings lead to interpretation and theory, and in the iterative process there is a 'weaving back and forth between data and theory' (Bryman, 2004, p. 10). Deduction, going from the general theory to the particular case/experimental question, is the terrain of the scientist, setting up the controlled experiment in the environmental chamber or on the treadmill; induction is for the socio-cultural researcher or social scientist, observing and revising and refining as the research progresses. Although these approaches – the deductive/quantitative versus the interpretive/qualitative – are often seen as an either/or dichotomy, it would be a mistake to think that the accomplished researcher adopts one of these approaches only. But it is undeniable that qualitative researchers have come to be major players in the socio-cultural analysis of sport, influenced by various strands of interpretive theory and method. Qualitative

research has been particularly valuable in exploring the sphere of the cultural, the meanings and values underlying sport, and in earmarking the characteristics of sport culture that constitute its distinctiveness and social significance. We now consider approaches and debates within historical work on sport, and in media studies, prior to reflecting on the distinctiveness of sport and then highlighting specific methodological themes and topics that have concerned socio-cultural researchers of sport.

HISTORIES

In Chapters 1 and 2 we showed how historical processes and dynamics shaped the sport culture of modern Britain, and in Chapter 3 we raised the question of how historians and sociologists might give different weight to theories, concepts and evidence. Histories of sport have taken various forms, from the dislocated minutely detailed accounts of the actions of sportsmen and women, through to the overarching theorisation of sport as an increasingly important dimension of modernity. Somewhere in between, social and/or cultural historians have illuminated the nature of sporting institutions and practices in particular times and places. What has bound together the work of disparate researchers with deep-rooted methodological differences has been an interest in the balance of continuity and change in the histories of sport culture, and a concern with the analysis of determining influences, including the motors of socio-cultural change. For such an analysis, in the telling of the historical story of the emergence and growth of sport in all its varied forms in Britain and other societies and cultures, a rigorous attention to empirical sources remains essential. Documents and records (written and visual) – diaries, minute-books, correspondence, club and society ephemera, contemporary observations, company accounts, government policies, official statistics – are vital to the understanding of the historical role of sport culture in the making of a society. Social observers and journalists have been invaluable in providing disinterested accounts of sport in a cultural or socio-historical context.

Of course, the historian's sources do not speak for themselves; they demand careful and scrupulous, and as far as possible objective and balanced, interpretation. It is in this sphere that historically-inclined social scientists such as Douglas Booth have challenged the more traditional historical analyses of some sport historians. In the name of a radicalised or post-modern history, and following Alan Munslow's general model in *Deconstructing History* (1997), Booth's *The Field: Truth and Fiction in Sport History* (2005) has provoked extensive debate among historians and sociologists alike. The hugely influential historian of sport, Allen Guttmann (2005), reviewed Booth's book and questioned in elegant and convincing fashion his classification and characterisation of sport historians: reconstructionists; constructionists; and deconstructionists. The first are said by Booth to operate on an essentially a-theoretical level, drawing out, as an all but natural process, narratives of the history of sport from their purportedly truth-telling sources and archives: these reconstructionists are said to deal with unique events rather than patterns, individuals not collectivities. Constructionists are said to recognise that historical understanding needs theories, and that any historical interpretation is to some degree provisional: the constructionist critically interrogates his or her own analysis, but aspires to generalisations about collective behaviour. The deconstructionist claims that history is an endless series of subjective interpretations, trading in multiple truths, and amplifies the importance of history and historical materials as discourse. The uses made of history in this book have been in the main what Booth would call of a *reconstructionist* tenor. Society has remade sport at different periods and sport has contributed in turn to the remaking of cultures and societies. This has allowed us to make generalisations about the paths, directions, and trajectories that sport has taken: from amateurism to professionalism; from the national to the international and the global (and back); from a deeply-rooted patriarchal base to a more open and accessible – though still far from egalitarian – cultural form; from formal character-building team games to, in Bourdieu's term, *les sports californiennes*; from sport as fun to sport as self-improvement. And in understanding these processes it would be unacceptable to ignore the forms of discourse through which the different forms of sport culture have been generated, promoted, represented, consumed, and contested. We could go on from example to example. But the point that is most important here is that to box a critical socio-cultural analysis in as an either/or of the Munslow/Booth taxonomy is flawed thinking and argument. We need to analyse discourses in history, and histories in discourse: not history as discourse. An adequate historical grasp of sport culture needs competing theories, an interest in trends and social collectivities, and sensitivity to the discourses that have sustained and sometimes challenged particular models and cases of sport culture. We need to grasp the nature and significance of events; recognise historical conjunctures when things change or are challenged; and contextualise our understanding in the *longue dureé* of the enduring life of societies (Tomlinson and Young, 2011). This book is based on an openness to empirical sources of any kind, all critically assessed, and used not to peddle singular interpretations, but to offer informed interpretations based upon evidence, bolstered by concepts and theory.

MEDIA ANALYSIS

A contemporary socio-cultural analysis of sport is to some extent a default form of media studies. Top-level sport is watched on traditional and new media by countless more people than see it in the flesh or encounter it live. Sport participation is a seriously minority activity, as we have demonstrated in Chapter 4. The 'did-you-see' of sporting gossip relates to the different media through which most sports followers have gained their knowledge. We have shown in several chapters in this book how the forms of representation of sport have grown in scale and sophistication. No study of sport culture can fail to recognise the need for semiological analysis of the meaning-making processes of sport, and analysis of the ideological processes that are at work in the sport media. In this, one must beware the misreadings or excesses of influential commentators. The Italian academic, Umberto Eco, in a magazine/newspaper essay written in 1969 (Eco, 1986), wrote of sports activity as a form of 'waste', labelling 'the athlete as monster' in the centre of forms of 'play' that are mere 'spectacle for

understanding sport

others'. He claimed too that the boundaries between doing sport and merely talking about it have become blurred:

> Since chatter about sport gives the illusion of interest in sport, the notion of *practicing sport* becomes confused with that of *talking sport*; the chatterer thinks himself an athlete and is no longer aware that he doesn't engage in sport.

Eco is no fan of sport, and hardly the objective observer, calling his essays in this genre his 'invectives against sport'. 'And if sport equals "Waste"', for Eco, 'sports chatter is the glorification of Waste, and therefore the maximum point of Consumption'. In the extraordinary expansion and escalation of new media and social media, Eco would no doubt damn sport anew: but this would ignore the generative collective cultural agency and achievement underlying gossip, chatter and everyday discourse on sport. His dismissal of sport is hermetically sealed, not of the observable and everyday world, and hermeneutically blind. His conclusion may well have some currency, but remains a mere postulation unless informed by adequate observation and analysis of the forms, places and styles of sport chatter. Rigorous analysis of sport media, sport journalism, sport discourses, indeed all forms of representation of sport, is a central platform of analytical work in a socio-cultural approach. In the production and consumption of sport, media processes are critical, and an understanding of them is a core element in any depth hermeneutical analysis of sport culture.

The depth hermeneutic is an integrated method for the study of cultural phenomena, in which different phases in the production, construction and consumption of a cultural or sporting form or practice are recognised, but can be studied in an inter-related fashion. First articulated in communication and media studies, the depth hermeneutic was fully formulated by John B. Thompson (*Ideology and Modern Culture*: *Critical Social Theory in the Era of Mass Communication*, 1990), as a way of linking 'different types of analysis' on 'the path of interpretation'. In relation to a sporting event, a depth hermeneutic approach would study, first, the circumstances of social production of the event (for instance, its organisational structures, its funding, its cultural or political genesis); second, the constructed product itself, its dominant themes and motifs and its essentially performed context, often in the form of lived ritualised performances as well as artefacts – this would take the form of a formal/discursive analysis of the features, patterns and relationships characterising the event; and finally the method would be concerned with, in Thompson's words, 'the creative construction of meaning . . . an interpretive explication of what is represented or what is said'; it would explore the modes and varieties of reception and interpretation of the event, how it is consumed and in what ways meanings and understandings are generated in that act of consumption. Full depth hermeneutic studies can be daunting, requiring teams of experienced researchers competent in a variety of research techniques. The attraction of the method is clear though, offering analysis of the sport and its meanings at all phases from production to consumption, including the (theoretically) limitless cycles of interpretation. In the making, consuming, and remaking of sport culture, the role of the media is absolutely central, and a depth hermeneutic approach provides a framework for recognising the different levels and effects of the sport media in a socio-cultural analysis. We now pause to reflect upon the specificities of sport itself and the challenges that this poses to the researcher.

THE PUZZLE OF SPORT

Sport is sometimes claimed to be a separate, relatively autonomous sphere of human culture and endeavour, but this book has demonstrated how sports culture is a social construction. It is embedded in economics and produced in part by political processes. Sports are part of global society but at the same time personal passions. There is something distinct and powerful in the way that sport is part of the cultural industries, but also fuels identity formation and provides a source of deep emotion for those engaging in sport activity and events – competitors and onlookers alike. But sports culture does not merely reflect wider social, political and economic forces and processes: sport in turn produces culture. It does so in at least the three following ways. First, the core dynamic of sport produces winners and losers in distinctly public forms, with associated rewards and recognition. Second, sport privileges particular physical assets and qualities, and in so doing perpetuates sexual differences and division: in sport, more than in any other cultural sphere, men and women are kept apart and separately categorised. Third, sport generates uniquely passionate forms of following in communities and societies, stimulating levels of commitment – to your village or national team, to your local hero or global superstar. The analysis offered in this book has shown in many ways this capacity of sport to define culture and make the social, and to provide experiences, emotions and feelings – affects – of a special kind for countless people. This is the puzzle of sport, its simultaneous ordinariness and memorability.

Special moments in sport live long in the individual and the collective memory. The big mega-events of sport are not just watched at the time: they are replayed in gossip and argument in families and workplaces, pubs and clubs, contested and debated in the social media. Sporting moments are made and remade in a continuing dialogue and endless cycle of human interactions and interpretations. Given these distinctive features of sports culture, are there research methods and methodologies best fitted to a socio-cultural analysis? Is there something so distinctive about sports cultures that particular methodological frameworks and/or methods are needed to research them? We do not attempt to answer these questions here but pose them as an additional seminar exercise, perhaps especially when planning research projects into socio-cultural aspects of sport.

As previously stated, the aim of this final chapter has not been to outline a how-to research manual; nor is it a comprehensive review of methods and methodology in socio-cultural sport studies. For such directions and overviews, readers and students are referred to the extensive literature in the field in monographs and guides to research (see, for example, Andrews *et al.*, 2005; Gratton and Jones, 2010; Atkinson, 2011) as well as the dramatically expanded field of journals and research periodicals. All such journals will include methods sections or descriptions of the methodological base of the studies in their published articles. Readers and students are advised to read these closely, to interrogate the basis of the evidence presented, and the arguments generated on the basis of the data and the evidence.

Rather than offering a how-to approach to researching sport, this conclusion has sought to make the case for an evaluative, pluralistic, methodological reflexivity in the interdisciplinary, critical sport studies scholar. Our main contention in this methodological debate is that sport is a field of study in which knowledge production of particular socio-cultural dimensions is shaped by the relationship between those who produce this knowledge and the subjects and objects of research.

CONCLUSION

Sport shares much with other fields of inquiry, such as family life and intimacy, work, the judiciary, the military and religious communities, in each of which social, economic, political and cultural relations are made and re-made, but it is also distinctive in many ways. Sport is marked by strong emotions and passionate commitment which operate at the local level of communities and in the international arena; it combines routine everyday participation with global media coverage of mega-events. Sport is part of global flows of knowledge and capital; it is big business. In a world in which knowledge is a key resource and motor for change, sport is specifically concerned with bodies and body practices which are increasingly subjected to technologies that extend the possibilities of athletic achievement measured and assessed by ever more sophisticated techniques.

Sport networks operate in particular ways; they may often be based on kinship ties, but sporting affiliations work in different ways. Sport can cut across social divisions and it can reinforce or shape them. Sport provides a reinstatement of social divisions and cultural values and it challenges them by forging new opportunities. Sport also raises particular questions about how the researcher can get inside this field. Sport provides a rich field where so many different forces are in play: personal identifications, emotion, community ties, social inequalities, divisions and opportunities.

This book has shown that a socio-cultural analysis of sport has enhanced understanding of (at least) the following areas: bodies; public culture/mega-events; consumption; gender/sexuality; cultural continuities; and socio-cultural change. It is arguable that a sociologist of the family, or of a religious sect, or a factory/company, might also throw light on many of these wider sociological themes. But the contours of the sport culture, embracing too the passions and affiliations that sport generates among not just fans and competitors, but also many of its scholars and researchers, are conducive to particular forms of analysis such as those outlined in this commentary and throughout the review of research we have attempted to provide in this book. This book has argued the case for a specifically socio-cultural analysis of sport. We hope that readers will find it a valuable guide for understanding, via hermeneutic methods and other methodologies, the meaningful, purposeful, and changing cultural practices and values that characterise sport in modern Britain and contemporary culture.

BIBLIOGRAPHY

1 INDUSTRIAL SOCIETY, SOCIAL CHANGE AND SPORTS CULTURE

Bailey, P. (1978) *Leisure and Class in Victorian England: Rational Recreation and the Contest for Control, 1830–1885*, London: Routledge & Kegan Paul.

Balfour, A.J. (1912) *Arthur James Balfour as Philosopher and Thinker: A Collection of the More Important and Interesting Passages in his Non-political Writings, Speeches and Addresses, 1879–1912*, selected and arranged by W.M. Short, London: Longmans, Green.

Bamford, T.W. (1967) *Rise of the Public Schools: A Study of Boys' Public Boarding Schools in England and Wales from 1837 to the Present Day*, London: Nelson.

Brailsford, D. (1991) *Sport, Time and Society: The British at Play*, London and New York: Routledge.

Clark, A. (1991 [1961]) *The Donkeys*, London: Pimlico.

Clarke, G. and Webb, I.M. (2005) 'Wilkie, Dorette (1867–1930)', *Oxford Dictionary of National Biography*, Oxford University Press, available at: http://www.oxforddnb.com/view/article/63387 (accessed 7 Feb. 2012).

Cunningham, H. (1980) *Leisure in the Industrial Revolution c.1780–c.1880*, London: Croom Helm.

De S. Honey, J.R. (1977) *Tom Brown's Universe: The Development of the English Public School in the Nineteenth Century*, New York: Quadrangle/The New York Times Book Co.

DNH (Department of National Heritage) (1995) *Sport: Raising the Game*, London: Department of National Heritage.

Dobbs, B. (1973) *Edwardians at Play: Sport 1890–1914*, London: Pelham Books.

Dunning, E. and Sheard, K. (1979) *Barbarians, Gentlemen and Players: A Sociological Study of the Development of Rugby Football*, New York: New York University Press.

Giddens, A. (1982) *Sociology: A Brief but Critical Introduction*, London: Macmillan.

Golby, J.M. and Purdue, A.W. (1984) *The Civilisation of the Crowd: Popular Culture in England, 1750–1900*, London: Batsford Academic and Educational.

Griffin, E. (2005) *England's Revelry: A History of Popular Sports and Pastimes 1600–1830*, Oxford: Oxford University Press.

Gruneau, R. (1983) *Class, Sports, and Social Development*, Amherst, MA: University of Massachusetts Press.

Guttmann, A. (1978) *From Ritual to Record: The Nature of Modern Sports*, New York: Columbia University Press.

Guttmann, A. (1986) *Sports Spectators*, New York: Columbia University Press.

Guttmann, A. (2004) *Sports: The First Five Millennia*, Amherst, MA: University of Massachusetts Press.

Haley, B. (1978) *The Healthy Body and Victorian Culture*, New Haven, CT: Harvard University Press.

Hargreaves, Jennifer (1994) *Sporting Females: Critical Issues in the History and Sociology of Women's Sports*, London: Routledge.

Hargreaves, John (1982) 'Sport, Culture and Ideology', in Jennifer Hargreaves (ed.), *Sport, Culture and Ideology*, London: Routledge & Kegan Paul.

Hargreaves, John (1986) *Sport, Power and Culture: A Social and Historical Analysis of Popular Sports in Britain*, Cambridge: Polity Press.

Harris, J. (1993) *Private Lives, Public Spirit: A Social History of Britain, 1870–1914*, Oxford: Oxford University Press.

Holt, R. (1989) *Sport and the British: A Modern History*, Oxford: Oxford University Press.

Horne, J., Lingard, R., Weiner, G. and Forbes, J. (2011) 'Capitalizing on Sport: Sport, Physical Education and Multiple Capitals in Scottish Independent Schools', *British Journal of Sociology of Education*, 32: 861–879.

Kalton, G. (1966) *The Public Schools: A Factual Survey of Headmasters' Conference Schools in England and Wales*, London: Longmans.

Kanitkar, H. (1994) '"Real True Boys": Moulding the Cadets of Imperialism', in A. Cornwall and N. Lindisfarne (eds), *Dislocating Masculinity: Comparative Ethnographies*, London: Routledge.

Kumar, K. (1978) *Prophecy and Progress: The Sociology of Industrial and Postindustrial Society*, Harmondsworth: Penguin Books.

McIntosh, P. (1979) *Fair Play: Ethics in Sport and Education*, London: Heinemann.

Maguire, J. (1986) 'Images of Manliness and Competing Ways of Living in Late Victorian and Edwardian Britain', *British Journal of Sports History*, 3: 191–215.

Malcolmson, R. (1973) *Popular Recreations in English Society, 1700–1850*, Cambridge: Cambridge University Press.

Mangan, J.A. (1981) *Athleticism in the Victorian and Edwardian Public School: The Emergence and Consolidation of an Educational Ideology*, Cambridge: Cambridge University Press.

Mangan, J.A. (1986) *The Games Ethic and Imperialism: Aspects of the Diffusion of an Ideal*, London: Viking.

Mangan, J.A. (ed.) (1992) *The Cultural Bond: Sport, Empire, Society*, London: Frank Cass.

Mason, T. (1996) 'Football, Sport of the North', in J. Hill and J. Williams (eds), *Sport and Identity in the North of England*, Keele: Keele University Press.

Secondary Heads Association (1994) *Enquiry into the Provision of Physical Education in Schools 1994*, London: Secondary Heads Association.

Stedman-Jones, G. (1983) 'Working-class Culture and Working-Class Politics in London: 1870–1900: Notes on the Remaking of a Working Class', in *Languages of Class: Studies in English Working-Class History, 1832–1982*, Cambridge: Cambridge University Press.

Thompson, E.P. (1967) 'Time, Work-Discipline, and Industrial Capitalism', *Past and Present*, 38: 56–97.

Thompson, E.P. (1968) *The Making of the English Working Class*, Harmondsworth: Penguin Books.

Tomlinson, A. (1992) 'Shifting Patterns of Working-class Leisure: The Case of Knur and Spel', *Sociology of Sport Journal*, 9: 192–206.

Tomlinson, A. and Young, C. (2010) 'Sport in History: Challenging the *Communis Opinio*', *Journal of Sport History*, 37: 5–17.

Toynbee, A. (1967) 'The Classical Definition of the Industrial Revolution' (1884), in P.A.M. Taylor (ed.), *The Industrial Revolution in Britain: Triumph or Disaster?*, Boston: D.C. Heath.

Wakeford, J. (1969) *The Cloistered Elite: A Sociological Analysis of the English Public Boarding School*, London: Macmillan.

Walvin, J. (1975) *The People's Game: A Social History of English Football*, London: Allen Lane.

Webb, I. (1979) 'The History of Chelsea College of Physical Education', unpublished doctoral thesis, Department of Education, University of Leicester.

Wilkinson, R. (1964) *The Prefects: British Leadership and the Public School Tradition: A Comparative Study in the Making of Rulers*, London: Oxford University Press.

Young, D. (1984) *The Olympic Myth of Greek Amateur Athletics*, Chicago: Ares Publishers Inc.

2 CASE STUDIES IN THE GROWTH OF MODERN SPORTS

Bailey, P. (1978) *Leisure and Class in Victorian England: Rational Recreation and the Contest for Control, 1830–1885*, London: Routledge & Kegan Paul.

Bale, J. (1989) *Sports Geography*, London: E & FN Spon.

BBC Radio 4 (1998) *Analysis* (presented by David Walker), 1 June.

Brookes, C. (1978) *English Cricket: The Game and its Players through the Ages*, London: Weidenfeld and Nicolson.

Channel 4 (1986) *Take the Money and Run*, in *Open the Box* series, Programme Researcher Garry Whannel, Producer Michael Jackson, Director Mike Dibb, Beat Productions and BFI Education for Channel 4, Channel 4 Television Co., Ltd, broadcast 2 June.

Cousins, G. (1975) *Golf in Britain: A Social History from the Beginnings to the Present Day*, London: Routledge & Kegan Paul.

Crump, J. (1989) 'Athletics', in T. Mason (ed.), *Sport in Britain: A Social History*, Cambridge: Cambridge University Press.

Downes, S. and Mackay, D. (1996) *Running Scared: How Athletics Lost Its Innocence*, Edinburgh: Mainstream Publishing.

Gruneau, R. (1983) *Class, Sport and Social Development*, Amherst, MA: University of Massachusetts Press.

Hall, S. (1986) 'Popular Culture and the State', in T. Bennett, C. Mercer and J. Woollacott (eds), *Popular Culture and Social Relations*, Milton Keynes: Open University Press.

Hargreaves, Jennifer (1994) *Sporting Females: Critical Issues in the History and Sociology of Women's Sports*, London: Routledge.

Hargreaves, John (1986) *Sport, Power and Culture: A Social and Historical Analysis of Popular Sports in Britain*, Cambridge: Polity Press.

Harris, J. (1993) *Private Lives, Public Spirit: A Social History of Britain, 1870–1914*, Harmondsworth: Penguin.

Holt, R. (1989) *Sport and the British: A Modern History*, Oxford: Oxford University Press.

Holt, R. and Tomlinson, A. (1994) 'Sport and Leisure', in D. Kavanagh and A.Seldon (eds), *The Major Effect*, London: Macmillan.

Horne, J., Tomlinson, A. and Whannel, G. (1999) *Understanding Sport: An Introduction to the Sociological and Cultural Analysis of Sport*, London: E & FN Spon.

Howat, G.M.D. (2004) 'Grace, William Gilbert [W. G.] (1848–1915)', *Oxford Dictionary of National Biography*, Oxford University Press, 2004; online edn, Jan 2011. Available at: http://www.oxforddnb.com/view/article/33500 (accessed 7 Feb 2012).

Luckes, D. (1994) 'Cricket, Commercialism and the Media, with Particular Reference to the Effects of the Packer Revolution of 1977', unpublished M.Phil. thesis, Chelsea School Research Centre, University of Brighton.

Malcolm, D., Gemmell, J. and Mehta, N. (eds) (2010) *The Changing Face of Cricket: From Imperial to Global Game*, London: Routledge.

Mason, T. (ed.) (1989) *Sport in Britain: A Social History*, Cambridge: Cambridge University Press.

Midwinter, E. (1981) *W.G. Grace: His Life and Times*, London: George Allen & Unwin.

Sandiford, K.A.P. (1994) *Cricket and the Victorians*, Aldershot: Scolar Press.

Szymanski, S. (2010) 'The Rise of the Indian Premier League', seminar presentation, Judge Business School, Cambridge.

238

Tomlinson, A. (1984) 'Physical Education, Sport and Sociology: The Current State and the Way Forward', in I. Glaister (ed.), *Physical Education, Sport and Leisure: Sociological Perspectives*, London: NATFHE (National Association of Teachers in Further and Higher Education).

Tomlinson, A. (2011) *The World Atlas of Sport: Who Plays What, Where, and Why*, Brighton and Oxford: Myriad Editions/New Internationalist.

Tomlinson, A. (2012) 'Lording it: London and the Getting of the Games', in J. Sugden and A. Tomlinson (eds), *Watching the Olympics: Politics, Power and Representation*, London: Routledge.

Whannel, G. (1983) *Blowing the Whistle: The Politics of Sport*, London: Pluto Press.

Whannel, G. (1986) 'The Unholy Alliance: Notes on Television and the Re-making of British Sport, 1965–1985', *Leisure Studies*, 5: 22–37.

Williams, J. (1989) 'Cricket', in T. Mason (ed.), *Sport in Britain: A Social History*, Cambridge: Cambridge University Press.

3 DEBATES, INTERPRETATIONS, THEORIES

Bailey, P. (1978) *Leisure and Class in Victorian England: Rational Recreation and the Contest for Control, 1830–1885*, London: Routledge & Kegan Paul.

Bairner, A. (ed.) (2005) *Sport and the Irish: Histories, Identities, Issues*, Dublin: University College Dublin Press.

Bhaskar, R. (1993) 'Materialism', in W. Outhwaite and T. Bottomore (eds), *The Blackwell Dictionary of Twentieth Century Social Thought*, Oxford: Basil Blackwell.

Clarke, J. and Critcher, C. (1985) *The Devil Makes Work: Leisure in Capitalist Britain*, London: Macmillan.

Cunningham, H. (1980) *Leisure In the Industrial Revolution, c.1780–c.1880*, London: Croom Helm.

Delves, A. (1981) 'Popular Recreation and Social Conflict in Derby, 1800–1850', in E. Yeo and S. Yeo (eds), *Popular Culture and Class Conflict, 1590–1914: Explorations in the History of Labour and Leisure*, Brighton: Harvester.

Dunning, E. and Sheard, K. (1979) *Barbarians, Gentlemen and Players: A Sociological Study of the Development of Rugby*, New York: New York University Press.

Elias, N. (1978a) *What is Sociology?*, London: Hutchinson.

Elias, N. (1978b [1939]) *The History of Manners: The Civilising Process*, vol. 1, Oxford: Basil Blackwell.

Elias, N. and Dunning, E. (1986) *Quest for Excitement: Sport and Leisure in the Civilizing Process*, Oxford: Basil Blackwell.

Giddens, A. (1982) *Sociology: A Brief but Critical Introduction*, London: Macmillan.

Giulianotti, R. (ed.) (2004) *Sport and Modern Social Theorists*, London: Palgrave Macmillan.

Golby, J.M. and Purdue, A.W. (1984) *The Civilisation of the Crowd: Popular Culture in England, 1750–1900*, London: Batsford Academic and Educational.

Guttmann, A. (1978) *From Ritual to Record: The Nature of Modern Sports*, New York: Columbia University Press.

Hall, S. (1986) 'Popular Culture and the State', in T. Bennett , C. Mercer and J. Woollacott (eds), *Popular Culture and Social Relations*, Milton Keynes: Open University Press.

Hargreaves, John (1986) *Sport, Power and Culture: A Social and Historical Analysis of Popular Sports in Britain*, Cambridge: Polity Press.

Harrison, B. (1971) *Drink and the Victorians: The Temperance Question in England, 1815–1872*, London: Faber.

Holt, R. (1989) *Sport and the British: A Modern History*, Oxford: Oxford University Press.

Holt, R. (1994) 'King across the Border: Denis Law and Scottish Football', in G. Jarvie and G. Walker (eds), *Scottish Sport in the Making of the Nation: Ninety-Minute Patriots?*, Leicester: Leicester University Press.

Horne, J. and Jary, D. (1987) 'The Figurational Sociology of Sport and Leisure of Elias and Dunning: An Exposition and a Critique', in J. Horne, D. Jary and A. Tomlinson (eds), *Sport, Leisure and Social Relations*, London: Routledge & Kegan Paul.

Horne, J. and Jary, D. (1994) 'The Figurational Sociology of Sport and Leisure Revisited', in I. Henry (ed.), *Leisure: Modernity, Postmodernity and Lifestyles*, Eastbourne: Leisure Studies Association (Publication No. 48).

Hughson, J., Inglis, D. and Free, M. (2005) *The Uses of Sport*, London: Routledge.

Jarvie, G. and Maguire, J. (1994) *Sport and Leisure in Social Thought*, London: Routledge.

Jarvie, G. and Walker, G. (eds) (1994) *Scottish Sport in the Making of the Nation: Ninety-Minute Patriots?*, Leicester: Leicester University Press.

Johnes, M. (2005) *A History of Sport in Wales*, Cardiff: University of Wales Press.

Malcolmson, R.W. (1973) *Popular Recreations in English Society, 1700–1850*, Cambridge: Cambridge University Press.

Malcolmson, R.W. (1984) 'Sports in Society: A Historical Perspective', *The British Journal of Sports History*, 1: 60–71.

Mason, T. (1988) *Sport in Britain*, London: Faber and Faber.

Mason, T. (1995) *Passion of the People? Football in South America*, London: Verso.

Mills, C.W. (1970) *The Sociological Imagination*, Harmondsworth: Penguin.

Polley, M. (2008) 'History and Sport', in B. Houlihan (ed.) *Sport and Society*, 2nd edn, London: Routledge.

Rojek, C. (ed.) (1989) *Leisure for Leisure?*, London: Macmillan.

Storch, R.D. (1976) 'The Policeman as Domestic Missionary: Urban Discipline and Popular Culture in Northern England, 1850–1880', *Journal of Social History*, 9: 481–509.

Tomlinson, A. (1996) 'Olympic Spectacle: Opening Ceremonies and Some Paradoxes of Globalization', *Media Culture & Society*, 18: 583–602.

4 SOCIAL STRATIFICATION AND SOCIAL DIVISION IN SPORT

Abrams, M. (1995) 'Leisure Time Use by the Elderly and Leisure Provision for the Elderly', in C. Critcher, P. Bramham and A. Tomlinson (eds), *Sociology of Leisure: A Reader*, London: E & FN Spon.

Bourdieu, P. (1978) 'Sport and Social Class', *Social Science Information*, 17: 819–840.

Bourdieu, P. (1986) *Distinction: A Social Critique of the Judgement of Taste*, London: Routledge & Kegan Paul.

Burdsey, D. (2007) *British Asians and Football: Culture, Identity, Exclusion*, London: Routledge.

Carrington, B. (1997) 'Community, Identity and Sport: An Exploration of the Significance of Sport within Black Communities', paper presented at the British Sociological Association Annual Conference, 'Power/Resistance', University of York, April.

Carrington, B. (2002) 'Sport, Masculinity and Black Cultural Resistance', in J. Sugden and A. Tomlinson (eds), *Power Games: A Critical Sociology of Sport*, London: Routledge.

Carrington, B. (2010) *Race, Sport and Politics: The Sporting Black Diaspora*, London: Sage.

Cashmore, E. (1982) *Black Sportsmen*, London: Routledge.

Cashmore, E. (1990) *Making Sense of Sport*, London: Routledge.

Central Statistical Office (CSO) (1993) *Social Trends 23, 1993 Edition*, London: HMSO.

Central Statistical Office (CSO) (1996) *Social Trends 26, 1996 Edition*, London: HMSO.

Collins, M. with Kay, T. (2003) *Sport and Social Exclusion*, London: Routledge.

Connell, R.W. (1983) *Which Way is Up? Essays on Sex, Class and Culture*, Sydney: Allen & Unwin.

Connell, R.W. (1995) *Masculinities*, Cambridge: Polity Press.

Corrigan, P. (1979) *Schooling the Smash Street Kids*, London: Macmillan.

Dahrendorf, R. (1979) *Life Chances: Approaches to Social and Political Theory*, Chicago: University of Chicago Press.

Davidoff, L. (1986) *The Best Circles: Society Etiquette and the Season*, London: The Cresset Library.

Deem, R. (1986) *All Work and No Play?*, Milton Keynes: Open University Press.

Denis, N., Henriques, F. and Slaughter, C. (1995) 'Leisure in Ashton', in C. Critcher, P. Bramham and A. Tomlinson (eds), *Sociology of Leisure: A Reader*, London: E & FN Spon.

Elias, N. (1986) 'An Essay on Sport and Violence', in N. Elias and E. Dunning, *Quest for Excitement: Sport and Leisure in the Civilizing Process*, Oxford: Basil Blackwell.

Elias, N. (1993) *Time: An Essay*, Oxford: Basil Blackwell.

Fleming, S. (1995) *'Home and Away': Sport and South Asian Male Youth*, Aldershot: Avebury.

Fleming, S. and Tomlinson, A. (1996) 'Football, Racism and Xenophobia in England (1): Europe and the old England', in U. Merkel and W. Tokarski (eds), *Racism and Xenophobia in European Football*, Aachen: Meyer & Meyer.

Flintoff, A., Scraton, S. and Bramham, P. (1995) 'Stepping into Aerobics?', in G. McFee, W. Murphy and G. Whannel (eds), *Leisure Cultures: Values, Genders, Lifestyles*, Brighton: Leisure Studies Association.

Fox, K. and Rickards, L. (2004) *Sport and Leisure: Results from the Sport and Leisure Module of the 2002 General Household Survey*, London: TSO.

Garland, J. and Rowe, M. (1996) 'Football, Racism and Xenophobia in England (2): Challenging Racism and Xenophobia', in U. Merkel and W. Tokarski (eds), *Racism and Xenophobia in European Football*, Aachen: Meyer & Meyer.

Green, E., Hebron, S. and Woodward, D. (1990) *Women's Leisure: What Leisure?*, London: Macmillan.

Grusky, D.B. (1993) 'Social Stratification', in W. Outhwaite and T. Bottomore (eds), *The Blackwell Dictionary of Twentieth-century Social Thought*, Oxford: Blackwell.

Hall, M.A. (1996) *Feminism and Sporting Bodies: Essays on Theory and Practice*, Champaign, IL: Human Kinetics.

Hargreaves, Jennifer (1994) *Sporting Females: Critical Issues in the History and Sociology of Women's Sports*, London: Routledge.

Hargreaves, John (1986) *Sport, Power and Culture: A Social and Historical Analysis of Popular Sports in Britain*, Cambridge: Polity Press.

Hodges, H.M. (1964) *Social Stratification: Class in America*, Cambridge, MA: Schenkman.

Horne, J. (1996) 'Kicking Racism out of Soccer in England and Scotland', *Journal of Sport and Social Issues*, 20: 45–68.

Howkins, A. and Lowerson, J. (1979) *Trends in Leisure, 1919–1939*, London: Sports Council and Social Science Research Council.

Imray, L. and Middleton, A. (1983) 'Public and Private: Marking the Boundaries', in E. Gamarnikow, D. Morgan, J. Purvis and D. Taylorson (eds), *The Public and the Private*, London: Heinemann Educational Books.

Itzkowitz, D.C. (1977) *Peculiar Privilege: A Social History of English Fox-hunting, 1753–1885*, Hassocks: Harvester.

Kew, S. (1979) *Ethnic Groups and Leisure*, London: Sports Council and Social Science Research Council.

Limb, M., Matthews, H. and Vujakovic, P. (1995) 'Disabling Countryside: An Investigation of Wheelchair Users' Experiences of Informal Recreation', in S. Fleming, M. Talbot and

A. Tomlinson (eds), *Policy and Politics in Sport, Physical Education and Leisure*, Eastbourne: Leisure Studies Association.

Long, J., Carrington, B. and Spracklen, K. (1996) 'The Cultural Production and Reproduction of Racial Stereotypes in Sport: A Case Study of Rugby League', paper presented at British Sociological Annual Conference, 'Worlds of the Future Ethnicity, Nationalism and Globalization', University of Reading, April.

Long, J. and Wimbush, E. (1979) *Leisure and the Over 50s*, London: Sports Council and Social Science Research Council.

Manning, F. (1973) *Black Clubs in Bermuda: Ethnography of a Play World*, Ithaca, NY: Cornell University Press.

Marshall, G. (ed.) (1994) *The Concise Oxford Dictionary of Sociology*, Oxford: Oxford University Press.

Middleton, A. (1986) 'Public and Private: Marking the Boundaries', in P. Lowe, T. Bradley and S. Wright (eds), *Deprivation and Welfare in Rural Areas*, Norwich: Geo Books.

OED (Oxford English Dictionary) (1979) *The Compact Edition of the Oxford English Dictionary*, London: Book Club Associates.

Office of Population Censuses and Surveys (OPCS) (1995) *General Household Survey 1993: An Inter-departmental Survey Carried Out by OPCS between April 1993 and March 1994*, Social Survey Division (K. Foster, B. Jackson, M. Thomas, P. Hunter and N. Bennett), London: HMSO.

Parkin, F. (1976) 'Strategies of Social Closure in Class Formation', in F. Parkin (ed.), *The Social Analysis of Class Structure*, London: Tavistock.

Prendergast, S. (1978) 'Stoolball: the Pursuit of Vertigo?', *Women's Studies International Quarterly*, 1: 15–26.

Ravenscroft, N. (2004) 'Sport and Local Delivery', in Sport England, *Driving Up Participation: The Challenge for Sport (Academic Review Papers Commissioned by Sport England as Contextual Analysis to Inform the Preparation of the Framework for Sport in England)*, London: Sport England.

Rowe, N. (2004) 'Introduction', in Sport England, *Driving Up Participation: The Challenge for Sport (Academic Review Papers Commissioned by Sport England as Contextual Analysis to Inform the Preparation of the Framework for Sport in England)*, London: Sport England.

Salisbury, J. and Jackson, D. (1996) *Challenging Macho Values: Practical Ways of Working with Adolescent Boys*, London: The Falmer Press.

Saunders, P. (1997) 'Social Mobility in Britain: An Empirical Evaluation of Two Competing Explanations', *Sociology*, 31: 261–288.

Scraton, S. (1995) 'Boys Muscle in Where Angels Fear to Tread': Girls' Sub-cultures and Physical Activities', in C. Critcher, P. Bramham and A. Tomlinson (eds), *Sociology of Leisure: A Reader*, London: E & FN Spon.

Scraton, S. and Flintoff, A. (eds) (2002) *Gender and Sport: A Reader*, London: Routledge.

Scraton, S. and Watson, B. (eds) (2000) *Sport, Leisure Identities and Gendered Spaces*, Eastbourne: Leisure Studies Association.

Sport England (2006) *Active People Survey Headline Results: Sport by Sport Fact Sheet*, London: Sport England.

Sport England (2012) *Active People 5, Participation: Once a Week for 30 Minutes at Moderate Intensity*, 04_Sport factsheet_APS5.pdf, (accessed 5 February 2012).

Sporting Equals (2007) *Briefing Paper: Ethnic Minorities and Physical Activity in the North West*, available at: http://www.oldham.nhs.uk/LinkClick.aspx?fileticket=6byvrJTZvjg%3D&tabid =190&language=en-US (accessed 15 May 2012).

Sports Council and Women's Sports Foundation (1992) *Women and Sport: The Information Pack*, London: Sports Council.

Spracklen, K. (1995) 'Playing the Ball, or the Uses of League: Class, Masculinity and Rugby: A Case Study of Sudthorpe', in G. McFee, W. Murphy and G. Whannel (eds), *Leisure Cultures: Values, Genders, Lifestyles*, Brighton: Leisure Studies Association.

Sugden, J. and Tomlinson, A. (2000) 'Theorizing Sport, Social Class and Status', in J. Coakley and E. Dunning (eds), *The Handbook of Sport and Society*, London: Sage.

Sugden, J. and Tomlinson, A. (2010) 'What Beckham Had for Breakfast: The Rolling Menu of 24/7 Sports News', in S. Cushion and J. Lewis (eds), *The Rise of 24-Hour News Television: Global Perspectives*, Oxford: Peter Lang.

Talbot, M. (1988) 'Their Own Worst Enemy? Women and Leisure Provision', in E. Wimbush and M. Talbot (eds), *Relative Freedoms: Women and Leisure*, Milton Keynes: Open University Press.

Thomas, N. and Smith, A. (2009) *Disability, Sport and Society: An Introduction*, London: Routledge.

Thompson, L. (1997) 'The Girls Done Good', *Guardian*, 2, Monday, 5 May, pp. 2–3.

Tomlinson, A. (1986) 'Playing Away from Home: Leisure, Access and Exclusion', in P. Golding (ed.), *Poverty and Exclusion*, London: Child Poverty Action Group.

Tomlinson, A. (1997) 'Ideologies of Physicality, Masculinity and Femininity: Comments on *Roy of the Rovers* and the Women's Fitness Boom' in A. Tomlinson (ed.), *Gender, Sport and Leisure: Continuities and Challenges*, Aachen: Meyer & Meyer.

Tomlinson, A. (2007) 'Sport and Social Class', in G. Ritzer (ed.), *The Blackwell Encyclopedia of Sociology, SE–ST*, vol. 9, Oxford: Blackwell.

Tomlinson, A., Ravenscroft, N., Wheaton, B., and Gilchrist, P. (2005) *Lifestyle Sports and National Sport Policy: An Agenda for Research*, London: Sport England.

Tomlinson, A. and Yorganci, I. (1997) 'Male Coach/Female Athlete Relations: Gender and Power Relations in Competitive Sport', *Journal of Sport and Social Issues*, 21: 134–155.

Turner, B.S. (1988) *Status*, Milton Keynes: Open University Press.

Urry, J. (1989) 'Social Class in Britain', in M. Cole (ed.), *The Social Contexts of Schooling*, London: The Falmer Press.

Veblen, T. (1953 [1899]) *The Theory of the Leisure Class: An Economic Study of Institutions*, New York: Mentor.

Verma, G.K., Macdonald, A., Darby, D.S., and Carroll, R. (1991) *Sport and Recreation with Special Reference to Ethnic Minorities: Final Report*, (July), Manchester: University of Manchester, School of Education/Centre for Ethnic Studies in Education.

Waddington, D., Wykes, M. and Critcher, C. (1991) *Split at the Seams? Community, Continuity and Change after the 1984–5 Coal Dispute*, Milton Keynes: Open University Press.

Wesolowski, W. and Slomczynski, K.M. (1993) 'Class', in W. Outhwaite and T. Bottomore (eds), *The Blackwell Dictionary of Twentieth-century Social Thought*, Oxford: Blackwell.

Whannel, G. (1983) *Blowing the Whistle: The Politics of Sport*, London: Pluto Press.

Wheaton, B. (ed.) (2004) *Understanding Lifestyle Sports: Consumption, Identity and Difference*, London: Routledge.

Wheaton, B. and Tomlinson, A. (1998) 'The Changing Gender Order in Sport? The Case of Windsurfing Subcultures', *Journal of Sport and Social Issues*, 22: 252–274.

White, A., Mayglothing, R. and Carr, C. (n.d.) *The Dedicated Few: The Social World of Women Coaches in Britain in the 1980s*, Chichester: West Sussex Institute of Higher Education.

Whitson, D. (2002) 'The Embodiment of Gender: Discipline, Domination, and Empowerment', in S. Scraton and A. Flintoff (eds) *Gender and Sport: A Reader*, London: Routledge.

Williams, R. (1977a) *Marxism and Literature*, Oxford: Oxford University Press.

Williams, R. (1977b) 'Literature in Society', in H. Schiff (ed.), *Contemporary Approaches to English Studies*, London: Heinemann.

Willis, P. (1977) *Learning to Labour: How Working Class Kids Get Working Class Jobs*, Farnborough: Saxon House.

Wimbush, E. and Talbot, M. (eds) (1988) *Relative Freedoms: Women and Leisure*, Milton Keynes: Open University Press.

Woods, R. (1994) 'Today's Older Consumers: An Emerging Third Age of Personal Fulfilment or a Wasted Era of Frustrated Possibilities?', in Henley Centre, *Leisure Futures*, Vol. 1, London: The Henley Centre for Forecasting, pp. 5–10.

5 THE SOCIAL CONSTRUCTION OF IDENTITY AND CULTURAL REPRODUCTION

Belotti, E. (1975) *Little Girls*, London: Writers and Readers.

Bennett, T., Emmison, M. and Frow, J. (1999) *Accounting for Tastes: Australian Everyday Cultures* Cambridge: Cambridge University Press.

Bennett, T., Savage, M., Silva, E., Warde, A., Gayo-Cal, M. and Wright, D. (2009) *Culture, Class, Distinction*, London: Routledge.

Bishop, J. and Hoggett, P. (1986) *Organising Around Enthusiasms: Mutual Aid in Leisure*, London: Comedia/Routledge.

Boslooper, T. and Hayes, M. (1973) *The Femininity Game*, New York: Skein & Day.

Bourdieu, P. (1978) 'Sport and Social Class', *Social Science Information*, 6: 819–840.

Bourdieu, P. (1984) *Distinction: A Social Critique of the Judgement of Taste*, London: Routledge.

Bourdieu, P. (1990) *In Other Words: Essays Toward a Reflexive Sociology*, London: Sage.

Bourdieu P. (2000) 'Social Space and Symbolic Space', in D. Robbins (ed.), *Pierre Bourdieu*, Vol. 4, London: Sage, pp. 3–16.

Byrne, E. (1983) *Women and Education*, London: Tavistock.

Coakley, J. (1993) 'Sport and Socialisation', in J. O.Holloszey (ed.), *Exercise and Sport Sciences Reviews*, Vol. 21, New York: Williams & Wilkins, pp. 169–200.

Coakley, J. (1994) *Sport in Society: Issues and Controversies*, St Louis, IL: Mosby.

Coakley, J. and Donnelly, P. (1999) *Inside Sports: Using Sociology to Understand Athletes and Sport Experiences*, London: Routledge.

Coakley, J. and Pike, E. (2009) *Sports in Society*, London: McGraw-Hill.

Coakley, J. and White, A. (1992) 'Making Decisions: Gender and Sport Participation Among British Adolescents', *Sociology of Sport Journal*, 9: 20–35.

Coalter, F. (1987) 'Sport and Delinquency', unpublished manuscript cited in D. Robins (1990).

Connell, R.W. (1983) *Which Way is Up? Essays on Sex, Class and Culture*, Sydney: Allen & Unwin.

Connell, R.W. (1987) *Gender and Power: Society, the Person and Sexual Politics*, Cambridge: Polity Press.

Connell, R.W. (1995) *Masculinities*, Cambridge: Polity Press.

Defrance, J. (1995) 'The Anthropological Sociology of Pierre Bourdieu', *Sociology of Sport Journal*, 12(2): 121–131.

Dixon, B. (1977a) *Catching Them Young*, vol. 1: *Sex, Race and Class in Children's Fiction*, London: Pluto.

Dixon, B. (1977b) *Catching Them Young*, vol. 2: *Political Ideas in Children's Fiction*, London: Pluto.

Dixon, B. (1990) *Playing Them False: A Study of Children's Toys, Games and Puzzles*, Stoke-on-Trent: Trentham Books.

Donnelly, P. (1985) 'Sport Subcultures', *Exercise and Sport Science Review*, 13: 539–578.

Donnelly, P. and Young, K. (1988) 'The Construction and Confirmation of Identity in Sport Subcultures', *Sociology of Sport Journal*, 5:. 223–240.

Dunne, M. (1982) 'An Introduction to Some of the Images of Sport in Girls' Comics and Magazines' in M. Green and C. Jenkins (eds), *Sporting Fictions*, Birmingham: Centre for Contemporary Cultural Studies/Department of Physical Education, University of Birmingham.

Fleming, S. (1995) *'Home and Away': Sport and South Asian Male Youth*, Aldershot: Avebury.

Fraser, E. (1987) 'Teenage Girls Reading *Jackie*', *Media, Culture & Society*, 10: 407–425.

Giulianotti, R. (2005) *Sport: A Critical Sociology*, Cambridge: Polity Press.

Gunter, B. (1986) *Television and Sex-role Stereotyping*, London: Libby/Independent Broadcasting Authority.

Habermas, J. (1972) *Knowledge and Human Interests*, London: Heinemann.

Hall, S. (1992) 'The Question of Cultural Identity', in S. Hall, D. Held and T. McGrew (eds), *Modernity and its Futures,* Cambridge: Cambridge University Press, pp. 273–325.

Hargreaves, J. (1994) *Sporting Females: Critical Issues in the History and Sociology of Women's Sports*, London: Routledge.

Horne, J. (2006) *Sport in Consumer Culture*, Basingstoke: Palgrave.

Horne, J, Tomlinson, A. and Whannel, G. (1999) *Understanding Sport*, London: E & FN Spon.

Howe, P. (1999) 'Professionalism Commercialism and the Rugby Club: From Embryo to Infant at Pontypridd RFC', in T. Chandler and J. Nauright (eds) *The Rugby World: Race, Gender, Commerce and the Rugby Union,* London: Frank Cass.

Howe, P. (2001) 'An Ethnography of Pain and Injury in Professional Rugby Union: The Case of Pontypridd RFC', *International Review for the Sociology of Sport*, 36(3): 289–303.

Hughes, R. and Coakley, J. (1991) 'Positive Deviance Among Athletes: The Implications of Over-conformity to the Sport Ethic', *Sociology of Sport Journal*, 8: 307–325.

Jarvie, G. and Maguire, J. (1994) *Sport and Leisure in Social Thought*, London: Routledge.

Jenks, C. (ed.) (1998) *Core Sociological Dichotomies*, London: Sage.

Keillor, G. (1994) *The Book of Guys*, London: Faber and Faber.

Kremer, J. and Scully, D. (1994) *Psychology in Sport*, London: Taylor & Francis.

Lee, M. (1986) 'Moral and Social Growth Through Sport: The Coach's Role', in G. Gleeson (ed.), *The Growing Child in Competitive Sport*, London: Hodder & Stoughton.

Leonard, W.M. II (1984) *A Sociological Perspective of Sport*, Minneapolis: Burgess.

McCormack, J. and Chalip, L. (1988) 'Sport as Socialisation: A Critique of Methodological Premises', *The Social Science Journal*, 25: 83–92.

McPherson, B., Curtis, J. and Loy, J. (1989) *The Social Significance of Sport*, Champaign, IL: Human Kinetics.

McRobbie, A. (1991) *Feminism and Youth Culture*, London: Macmillan.

Mead, M. (1977 [1935]) *Sex and Temperament in Three Primitive Societies*, 2nd edn, London: Routledge & Kegan Paul.

Murphy, W. and Whannel, G. (eds) *Leisure Cultures: Values, Genders, Lifestyles*, University of Brighton, Eastbourne: Leisure Studies Association.

Philips, D. (1995) 'White Boots and Ballet Shoes: Girls Growing Up in the 1950s', in G. McFee, W. Murphy and G. Whannel (eds), *Leisure Cultures: Values, Genders, Lifestyles*, University of Brighton, Eastbourne: Leisure Studies Association.

Roberts, K. and Brodie, D. (1992) *Inner-city Sport: Who Plays, and What are the Benefits?* Voorthuizen: Giordano Bruno.

Robins, D. (1990) *Sport as Prevention: The Role of Sport in Crime Prevention Programmes Aimed at Young People*, Oxford: University of Oxford, Centre for Criminological Research, Occasional Paper 12.

Sabo, D. and Jansen, S.C. (1992) 'Images of Men in Sport Media: The Social Reproduction of Gender Order', in S. Craig (ed.), *Men, Masculinity and the Media*, London: Sage.

Scraton, S. (1987) 'Boys Muscle in Where Angels Fear to Tread': Girls' Sub-cultures and Physical Activities', in J. Horne, D. Jary and A. Tomlinson (eds), *Sport, Leisure and Social Relations*, London: Routledge & Kegan Paul.

Scraton, S. (1992) *Shaping Up to Womanhood*, Milton Keynes: Open University Press.

Stanworth, M. (1980) *Gender and Schooling*, London: Women's Research and Resources Centre.

Stevenson, C. (1975) 'Socialisation Effects of Participation in Sport: A Critical Review of Research', *Research Quarterly*, 46: 287–302.

Stevenson, C. (1985) 'College Athletics and "Character": The Decline and Fall of Socialisation Research', in D. Chu, J.O. Segrave and B.J. Becker (eds), *Sport and Higher Education*, Champaign, IL: Human Kinetics.

Stevenson, C. (1990) 'The Early Careers of International Athletes', *Sociology of Sport Journal*, 7: 238–253.

Sugden, J. and Bairner, A. (1993) *Sport, Sectarianism and Society in a Divided Ireland*, Leicester: Leicester University Press.

Tomlinson, A. (1995) 'Ideologies of Physicality, Masculinity and Femininity: Comments on *Roy of the Rovers* and the Women's Fitness Boom', in A. Tomlinson (ed.), *Gender, Sport and Leisure: Continuities and Challenges*, Brighton University: Chelsea School Research Centre, Topic Report 4.

Tomlinson, A. (2004) 'Pierre Bourdieu and the Sociological Study of Sport: Habitus, Capital and Field', in R. Giulianotti (ed.) *Sport and Modern Social Theorists*, Basingstoke: Palgrave, pp. 161–172.

Tuchman, G. (1978) 'The Symbolic Annihilation of Women by the Mass Media', in G. Tuchman (ed.) *Hearth and Home: Images of Women in the Mass Media*, New York: Oxford University Press.

Wacquant, L. (1995) 'Pugs at Work', *Body & Society*, 1(1): 65–93.

Wacquant, L. (2007) *Body & Soul: Notebooks of an Apprentice Boxer*, Oxford: Oxford University Press.

Watson, B. (2008) 'Identity', in D. Kirk, C. Cooke, A. Flintoff and J. McKenna (eds), *Key Concepts in Sport and Exercise Sciences*, London: Sage, pp. 140–143.

Whannel, G. (1995) 'Sport Stars, Youth and Morality in the Print Media', in G. McFee, W. Murphy and G. Whannel (eds), *Leisure Cultures: Values, Genders, Lifestyles*, Brighton: Leisure Studies Association.

Wheaton, B. (ed.) (2004) *Understanding Lifestyle Sport*, London: Routledge.

White, A. and Coakley, J. (1986) *Making Decisions: The Response of Young People in the Medway Towns to the 'Ever Thought of Sport?' Campaign*, London: Greater London and South East Region Sports Council.

Wolfenden Report (1960) *Sport and the Community*, London: Central Council for Physical Recreation.

Young, I.M. (1980) 'Throwing Like a Girl: A Phenomenology of Feminine Body Comportment, Motility and Spatiality', *Human Studies*, 3: 137–156.

Young, K., White, R, and McTeer, W. (1994) 'Body Talk: Male Athletes Reflect on Sport, Injury and Pain', *Sociology of Sport Journal*, 11: 175–194.

6 SPORT AND REPRESENTATION

Anderson, B. (1983) *Imagined Communities*, London: Verso.

Andrews, D. (2001) 'Michael Jordan: Corporate Sport and Postmodern Celebrityhood', in D. Andrews and S. Jackson (eds), *Sport Stars: The Cultural Politics of Sporting Celebrity*, London: Routledge.

Barnett, S. (1990) *Games and Sets: The Changing Face of Sport on Television*, London: BFI.

Birrell, S. and Loy, J. (1979) 'Media Sport: Hot and Cool', *International Review of Sport Sociology*, 14(1): 5–18.

Blain, N., Boyle, R. and O'Donnell, H. (1993) *Sport and National Identity in the European Media*, Leicester: Leicester University Press.

Bolla, P.A. (1990) 'Media Images of Women and Leisure: An Analysis of Magazine Ads, 1964–87', *Leisure Studies*, 9(3): 241–252.

Bown, G. (1981) '2000 Million Televiewers', unpublished thesis, Royal College of Arts, London.

Brennan, C. (1995) 'Lillehammer as Seen by the Media', *Citius, Altius, Fortius*, 3(1): 32–33.

Bryant, J., Comiskey, P. and Zillmann, D. (1977) 'Drama in Sports Commentary', *Journal of Communication*, 27(3): 140–149.

Buscombe, E. (ed.) (1975) *Football on Television*, London: BFI.

Cantelon, H. and Gruneau, R.S (1988) 'The Production of Sport for Television', in J. Harvey and H. Cantelon (eds.) *Not Just a Game*, Ottawa: University of Ottawa Press.

Carrington, B. (2010) *Race, Sport and Politics: The Sporting Black Diaspora*, London: Sage.

Cashmore, E. (1982) *Black Sportsmen*, London: RKP.

Chandler, J. (1988) *Television and National Sport*, Chicago: University of Illinois Press.

Clarke, A. and Clarke, J. (1982) *Sport Culture and Ideology*, London: RKP.

Colley, I. and Davies, G. (1982) 'Kissed by History: Football as TV Drama', in *Sporting Fictions*, London: CCCS.

Conway, S. (2010) '"It's in the Game" and "Above the Game": An Analysis of the Users of Sports Videogames', *Convergence: The International Journal of Research into new Media Technologies*, Special Issue on Sport in New Media Cultures, 16(3).

Cook, P. (1982) 'Masculinity in Crisis', *Screen*, 23(3/4): 39–46.

Crawford, S. (1991) 'The Black Actor as Athlete and Mover: An Historical Analysis of Stereotypes, Distortions and Bravura Performances in American Action Films', in *Canadian Journal of History of Sport*, 22(2): 23–33.

Crawford, S.A.G.M. (1992) 'Birth of the Modern Sport Spectacular: The Real Madrid and Eintracht Frankfurt European Cup Final of 1960', *International Journal of the History of Sport*, 9(3): 433–438.

Critcher, C. (1979) 'Football Since the War', in J. Clarke, C. Critcher and R. Johnson (eds), *Working Class Culture: Studies in History and Theory*, London: Hutchinson.

Daney, S. (1978) 'Coup d'Envoi: Le sport dans la télévision', *Cahiers du Cinéma*, 292: 39–40.

Duncan, M. C. and Hasbrook, C.A. (1988) 'Denial of Power in Televised Women's Sports', *Sociology of Sport Journal*, 5(1):1–21.

Dunne, M. (1982) 'Introduction to Some of the Images of Sport in Girls' Comics and Magazines', in C. Jenkins and M. Green (eds), *Sporting Fictions*, Birmingham: Birmingham University PE Dept and CCCS.

Dyer, K. F. (1982) *Catching up the Men*, London: Junction.

Fleming, S. (1991) 'Sport, Schooling and Asian Male Youth Culture', in *Sport, Racism and Ethnicity*, London: Falmer.

Fleming, S. (1994) 'Sport and South Asian Youth: The Perils of "False Universalism"', *Leisure Studies*, 13(3).

Geraghty, C., Simpson, P. and Whannel, G. (1986) 'Tunnel Vision: Television's World Cup', in A. Tomlinson and G. Whannel (eds), *Off The Ball: The Football World Cup*, London: Pluto, pp. 20–35.

Giddens, A. (1990) *The Consequences of Modernity*, Cambridge: Polity Press.

Gilroy, P. (1990) 'Frank Bruno or Salman Rushdie', *Media Education*, 14:14–18.

Goldlust, J. (1987) *Playing for Keeps: Sport, the Media and Society*, Melbourne: Longman.

Gruneau, R. (1989) 'Making Spectacles: A Case Study in Television Sports Production', in L. Wenner (ed.), *Media Sports and Society*, Newbury Park, CA: Sage.

Halbert, C. and Latimer, M. (1994) 'Battling Gendered Language: An Analysis of the Language

Used by Sports Commentators in a Televised Co-Ed Tennis Tournament', *Sociology of Sport Journal*, 11: 309–329.

Hargreaves, Jennifer (1994) *Sporting Females*, London: Routledge.

Higgs, C.T. and Weiller, K.H. (1994) 'Gender Bias and the 1992 Summer Olympic Games: An Analysis of Television Coverage', *Journal of Sport and Social Issues*, 18(3): 234–246.

Hill, J. (1994) 'Reading the Stars: A Postmodernist Approach to Sports History', *The Sports Historian*, 14: 45–55.

Hobsbawm, E. and Ranger, T. (eds) (1983) *The Invention of Tradition*, Cambridge: Cambridge University Press.

Holt, R., Mangan, J.A. and Lanfranchi, P. (eds) (1996) *European Heroes: Myth, Identity and Sport*, London: Frank Cass.

Horne, J. and Bentley, C. (1989) 'Women's Magazines, Fitness Chic and the Construction of Lifestyles', in *Leisure Health and Wellbeing*, Leeds: LSA.

Hrycaiko, D. *et al*. (1978) *Sport Physical Activity and TV Role Models*, Ottawa: CAHPER.

Jarvie, G. (1991) *Highland Games: The Making of the Myth*, Edinburgh: Edinburgh University Press.

Klein, A.M. (1990) 'Little Big Man: Hustling, Gender, Narcissism and Body-building Sub-culture', in M. Messner and D. Sabo (eds), *Sport, Men and the Gender Order*, Champaign, IL: Human Kinetics.

Lawrence, G. and Rowe, D. (eds) (1987) *Power Play: The Commercialisation of Australian Sport*, Sydney: Hale and Iremonger.

Leath, V.M. and Lumpkin, A. (1992) 'An Analysis of Sportswomen on the Covers and in the Feature Articles of *Women's Sport And Fitness* Magazine, 1975–89', *Journal of Sport and Social Issues*, 16(2): 121–126.

MacNeil, M. (1988) 'Active Women, Media Representations and Ideology', in J. Harvey and H. Cantelon (eds) *Not Just a Game*, Ottawa: University of Ottawa Press.

McPhail, T. and Jackson, R. (eds) (1989) *The Olympic Movement and the Mass Media*, Calgary: Hurford Enterprises.

Maguire, Joseph (1988) 'Race and Position Assignment in English Soccer: Ethnicity and Sport', *Sociology of Sport Journal*, 5: 257–269.

Majors, R. (1990) 'The Cool Pose', in M. Messner and D. Sabo (eds), *Sport, Men and the Gender Order*, Champaign, IL: Human Kinetics.

Messner, M. (1993) *Power at Play: Sports and the Problem of Masculinity*, Boston: Beacon.

Miller, L. and Penz, O. (1991) 'Talking Bodies: Female Body-Builders Colonise a Male Preserve', *Quest*, 43: 148–163.

Miller, T. (1989) 'Sport Media and Masculinity', in D. Rowe and G. Lawrence (eds), *Sport and Leisure*, Sydney: Harcourt Brace Jovanovich.

Morris, B.S and Nydahl, J. (1985) 'Sports Spectacle as Drama: Image, Language and Technology', *Journal of Popular Culture*, 18(4): 101–110.

Neale, S. (1982) '*Chariots of Fire*: Images of Men', *Screen*, 23(3/4): 47–53.

Nocker, G. and Klein, M. (1980) 'Top-level Athletes and Idols', *International Review of Sport Sociology*, 15: 5–21.

Nowell-Smith, G. (1978) 'Television – Football – The World', *Screen*, 19(4): 45–59.

O'Donnell, H. (1994) 'Mapping the Mythical: A Geo-politics of National Sporting Stereotypes', *Discourse and Society*, 5: 345–380.

Peters, R. (1976) *Television Coverage of Sport*, Birmingham: CCCS.

Poulantzas, N. (1973) *Political Power and Social Classes*, London: New Left Books.

Rader, B.G. (1984) *In Its Own Image: How TV Has Transformed Sports*, New York: Free Press.

Real, M. (1975) 'Superbowl: Mythic Spectacle', *Journal of Communication*, 25: 31–43.

Real, M. (1989) 'Super Bowl Versus World Cup Soccer: A Cultural-Structural Comparison', in L. Wenner (ed.), *Media Sports and Society*, London: Sage.

248

Rowe, D. and Lawrence, G. (1989) *Sport and Leisure: Trends in Australian Popular Culture*, Sydney: Harcourt Brace Jovanovich.

Sabo, D. and Jansen S.C. (1992) 'Images of Men in Sports Media: The Social Reproduction of Gender Order', in D. Craig (ed.), *Men, Masculinity and the Media*, London: Sage, pp. 169–184.

Sabo, D., Jansen, S.C., Tate, D., Duncan, M.C. and Leggett, S. (1996) 'Televising International Sport: Race, Ethnicity and Nationalistic Bias', *Journal of Sport and Social Issues*, 20(1).

Shifflett, B. and Revelle, R. (1994) 'Gender Equity in Sports Media Coverage: A Review of the NCAA News', *Journal of Sport and Social Issues*, 18(2): 144–150.

Téléciné (1978) 'Sport et télévision, *Téléciné*, 22: 6–19.

Tomlinson, A. (1996) 'Olympic Spectacle: Opening Ceremonies and Some Paradoxes of Globalisation', *Media, Culture & Society*, 18(4).

Tomlinson, A. (1999) 'Staging the Spectacle: Reflections on Olympic and World Cup Ceremonies', *Soundings*, no. 13, London: Lawrence and Wishart.

Van de Berg, L.R. and Trujillo, N. (1989) 'The Rhetoric of Winning and Losing: The American Dream and America's Team', in L. Wenner (ed.) *Media, Sports and Society*, London: Sage.

Wenner, L. (1989) *Media, Sports and Society*, London: Sage.

Wenner, L. (1995) 'The Good, the Bad and the Ugly: Race, Sport and the Public Eye', *Journal of Sport and Social Issues*, 19(3): 227–231.

Whannel, G. (1982) 'Narrative and Television Sport: The Coe and Ovett Story', in C. Jenkins and M. Green (eds), *Sporting Fictions*, Birmingham: CCCS, pp. 209–230.

Whannel, G. (1983) *Blowing the Whistle: The Politics of Sport*, London: Pluto.

Whannel, G. (1992) *Fields in Vision: Television Sport and Cultural Transformation*, London: Routledge.

Whannel, G. (1993) 'No Room for Uncertainty: Gridiron Masculinity in *North Dallas Forty*', in P. Kirkham and J. Thumin (eds), *You Tarzan: Masculinity, Movies and Men*, London: Lawrence and Wishart, pp200–211.

Whannel, G. (1994) 'Sport and Popular Culture: The Temporary Triumph of Process over Product', *Innovation in Social Sciences Research*, 6(3): 341–350.

Whannel, G. (1995a) 'Sport, National Identities and the Case of Big Jack', *Critical Survey*, 7(2): 158–164.

Whannel, G. (1995b) 'Sport Stars, Youth and Morality in the Print Media', in G. McFee, W. Murphy and G. Whannel (eds), *Leisure Cultures: Values, Genders, Lifestyles*, Brighton: Leisure Studies Association, pp. 121–136.

Whannel, G. (2001) 'Punishment, Redemption and Celebration in the Popular Press: The Case of David Beckham', in D. Andrews and S. Jackson (eds), *Sport Stars: The Cultural Politics of Sporting Celebrity*, London: Routledge, pp. 138–150.

Whannel, G. (2002) *Media Sport Stars, Masculinities and Moralities*, London: Routledge.

Whannel, G. (2010) 'News, Celebrity and Vortextuality: A Study of the Media Coverage of the Jackson Verdict', *Cultural Politics*, 6(1): 65–84.

Williams, C. L., Lawrence, G. and Rowe, D. (1987) 'Patriarchy, Media and Sport', in G. Lawrence and D. Rowe (eds), *Power Play*, Sydney: Hale and Iremonger.

Williams, J. and Taylor, R. (1994) 'Boys Keep Swinging: Masculinity and Football Culture, in England', in T. Newburn and E. Stanko (eds), *Just Boys Doing Business: Men, Masculinities and Crime*, London: Routledge, pp. 214–233.

Willis, P. (1982) 'Women in Sport in Ideology', in J. Hargreaves (ed.), *Sport, Culture and Ideology*, London: Routledge & Kegan Paul.

Wonsek, P.L. (1992) 'College Basketball on Television: A Study of Racism in the Media', *Media, Culture & Society* , 14(3): 449–462.

Wren-Lewis, J. and Clarke, A. (1983) 'The World Cup: A Political football?', *Theory, Culture & Society*, 1: 123–132.

Yeates, H. (1992) 'Women, the Media and Football Violence', *Social Alternatives*, 11(1): 17–20.

Young, K. (1986) 'The Killing Field: Themes in Mass Media Responses to the Heysel Stadium Riot', *International Review for the Sociology of Sport*, 21: 253–267.

7 SPORTING BODIES: DISCIPLINING AND DEFINING NORMALITY

Beauvoir, S. de (1982 [1952]) *The Second Sex*, trans. H.M. Parshey, New York: Vintage.

Berkowitz, M. and Ungar, R. (2009) *Fighting Back? Jewish and Black Boxers in Britain*, London: Department of Hebrew and Jewish Studies, University College London.

Blackless, M., Charuvastra, A., Derryck, A, Fausto-Sterling, A., Lauzanne, K, and Lee, E. (2000) 'How Sexually Dimorphic Are We? Review and Synthesis.' *American Journal of Human Biology* ,12: 151–166.

Bourdieu, P. (1984) *The Logic of Practice*, Oxford: Blackwell.

Bourdieu, P. (1986) *Distinction: A Social Critique of the Judgement of Taste*, trans R. Nice, Cambridge, MA: Harvard University Press.

Butler, J. (1990) *Gender Trouble: Feminism and the Subversion of Identity*, London: Routledge.

Butler, J. (1993) *Bodies That Matter: On the Discursive Limits of Sex*, London: Routledge.

Cixous, H. (1980 [1975]) 'Sorties', in E. Marks and I. de Courteviron (eds), *New French Feminisms: An Anthology*, Amherst, MA: University of Massachusetts Press.

Connell, R.W. (1995) *Masculinities*, Oxford: Blackwell.

Crossley, N. (2001) *The Social Body: Habit, Identity and Desire*, London: Sage.

Edinanci, S. (2012) http://www.intersexualite.org/Edinanci_Silva.html (accessed 15 May 2012).

Fausto-Sterling, A. (1992) *Myths of Gender; Biological Theories about Women and Men*, 2nd edn, New York: Basic Books.

Fausto-Sterling, A. (2001) *Sexing the Body. Gender Politics in the Constructions of Sexuality*, New York: Basic Books.

Fausto-Sterling, A. (2005) 'The Bare Bones of Sex', *Signs: Journal of Women in Culture and Society*, 30(21): 1491–1527.

Foucault, M. (1972) *The Archaeology of Knowledge and the Discourse of Language*, London: Pantheon.

Foucault, M. (1981) *The History of Sexuality*, Vol. 1, Harmondsworth: Penguin.

Fraser, M. and Greco, M. (eds) (2005) *The Body: A Reader*, London: Routledge.

Giddens, A. (1991) *Modernity and Self-Identity*, Cambridge: Polity Press.

Goffman, E. (1959) *The Presentation of Self in Everyday Life*, New York: Random House.

Grosz, E. (1994) *Volatile Bodies: Towards a Corporeal Feminism*, Bloomington, IN: Indiana University Press.

Guttmann, A. (2005) *Sport in the First Five Millennia*, Amherst, MA: University of Massachusetts Press.

Hall, A. (1996) *Feminism and Sporting Bodies: Essays on Theory and Practice*, Champaign, IL: Human Kinetics.

Haraway, D. (2000) *How Like a Leaf: An Interview with Thyrza Nichols Goodeve*, London: Routledge.

Haraway, D. (1985) 'A Manifesto for Cyborgs: Science Technology and Socialist Feminism in the 1980s', *Socialist Review*, 80: 65–107.

Haraway, D. (1989) 'The Biopolitics of Postmodern Bodies: Determinations of Self in Immune System Discourse', *differences: A Journal of Feminist Cultural Studies* 1: 3–43.

Hargreaves, J. (1994) *Sporting Females*, London: Routledge.

Hargreaves, J. and Vertinsky, P. (eds) (2002) *Physical Culture, Power and the Body*, London: Routledge.

Howson, A. (2005) *Embodying Gender*, London: Sage.

IAAF (2006) 'Gender Verification', available at: http://www.iaaf.org/mm/document/imported/36983.pdf (accessed 15 May 2012).

Irigaray, L. (1985) *Speculum of the Other Woman*, trans. G.C. Gill, Ithaca, NY: Cornell University Press.

Kessler, S. (1998) *Lessons from the Intersexed*, Rutgers, NJ: Rutgers University Press.

Maguire, J. (2011) 'Body Matters: Theories of the Body and the Study of Sport Cultures', *Sport in Society*, 14: 927–936.

Malcolm, D. (2009) 'Medical Uncertainty and Clinician-Athlete Relations: The Management of Concussion Injuries in Rugby Union', *Sociology of Sport Journal*, 26: 191–210.

Mansfield, L. (2009) 'Contemplating Fatness in the Fitness Field', in C. Tomrley and A. Kaloski Naylor (eds), *Fat Studies in the UK*, York: Raw Nerve Books, pp. 128–133.

Markula, P. (2009) *Olympic Women and the Media: International Perspectives*, London: Palgrave.

Markula, P. and Pringle R. (2006) *Foucault, Sport and Exercise: Power Knowledge and Transforming the Self*, London: Routledge.

Merleau-Ponty, M. (1962) *Phenomenology of Perception*, trans. C. Smith, London: Routledge.

Moi, T. (1999) *What is a Woman?: And Other Essays*, Oxford: Oxford University Press.

Novas, C. and Rose, N. (2000) 'Genetic Risk and the Birth of the Somatic Individual', *Economy and Society*, 29: 485–513.

Oakley, A. (1972) *Sex, Gender and Society*, London: Temple Smith.

Pfister, G. (2001) 'Breaking Bounds: Alice Profé, Radical and Emancipationist', in J.A Mangan and Fan Hong (eds), *Freeing the Female Body: Inspirational Icons*, London: Frank Cass, p. 98–118.

Pike, E. (2010) 'Growing Old (Dis)Gracefully?: The Gender/Ageing/Exercise Nexus', in E. Kennedy and P. Markula (eds), *Women and Exercise: The Body, Health and Consumerism*, London: Routledge.

Price, J. and Shildrick, M. (1999) *Feminist Theory and the Body: A Reader*, Edinburgh: Edinburgh University Press.

Richardson, D. (2000) *Rethinking Sexuality*, London: Sage.

Riordan, J. and Cantelon, H. (2003)'The Soviet Union and Eastern Europe', in J. Riordan and A. Kruger (eds), *European Cultures in Sport: Examining the Nations and Regions*, London: Intellect Books, pp. 89–102.

Rose, N. (1996) *Inventing our Selves*, Cambridge: Cambridge University Press.

Sammons, J. (1988) *Beyond the Ring. The Role of Boxing in American Society*, Chicago: University of Illinois Press.

Sassatelli, R. (2000) 'The Commercialization of Discipline: Keep-Fit Culture and Its Values', *Journal of Modern Italian Studies*, 5: 396–411.

Schiebinger, L. (1993) *Gender in the Making of Modern Science*, Boston: Beacon Books.

Schweinbenz, A.N. and Cronk, A. (2010) 'Femininity Control at the Olympic Games', *Third Space*, 9(2), available at: http://www.thirdspace.ca/journal/article/viewArticle/schweinbenzcronk/329 (accessed 15 May 2012).

Shilling, C. (1997) *Identity and Difference*, London: Sage.

Shilling, C. (2008) *Changing Bodies: Habit, Crisis and Creativity*, London: Sage.

Smith Maguire, J. (2007) *Fit for Consumption: Sociology and the Business of Fitness*, London: Routledge.

Stanley, L. (1984) 'Should "Sex" Really be "Gender", or "Gender" Really Be "Sex"?' in R. Anderson and W. Sharrock (eds), *Applied Sociology*, London: Allen and Unwin.

Telegraph Sport (2010) Available at: http://www.telegraph.co.uk/sport/othersports/athletics/7873240/Caster-Semenya-given-all-clear-after-gender-test-row.html (accessed 15 May 2012).

Turner, B. (1992) *Regulating Bodies: Essays in Medical Sociology*, London: Routledge.

Turner, B. (1996) *The Body and Society: Explorations in Social Theory*, London: Sage.

Wacquant, L (1995) 'The Pugilistic Point of View: How Boxers Feel about their Trade', *Theory and Society*, 24(4): 489–535.

Wacquant, L (2004) *Body and Soul: Notebooks of an Apprentice Boxer*, Oxford: Oxford University Press.

Wamsley, K.B. and Pfister, G. (2005) 'Olympic Men and Women: The Politics of Gender in the Modern Games', in K. Young and K.B. Wamsley (eds), *Global Olympic Historical and Social Studies of the Modern Games: Research in the Sociology of Sport*, Vol. 3 New York: Elsevier, pp. 103–125.

Woodward, K. (2002) *Understanding Identity*, London: Bloomsbury.

Woodward, K. (2007) *Boxing, Masculinity and Identity: The 'I' of the Tiger*, London: Routledge.

Woodward, K. (2009) *Embodied Sporting Practices: Regulating and Regulatory Bodies*, Basingstoke: Palgrave.

Woodward, K. (2011) *Gender*, Bristol: Policy Press.

Woodward, K. (2012) *Sex, Power and the Games*, Basingstoke: Palgrave.

Young, I.M. (2005) *On Female Body Experience. 'Throwing Like a Girl' and Other Essays*, Oxford: Oxford University Press.

Young, K. (ed.) (2004) *Sporting Bodies, Damaged Selves: Sociological Studies of Sports-Related Injury*. London: Elsevier.

8 SPORT, THE STATE AND POLITICS

Allison, L. (ed.) (1986) *The Politics of Sport*, Manchester: Manchester University Press. Allison, L. (ed.) (1993) *The Changing Politics of Sport*, Manchester: Manchester University Press.

Bottomore, T. (1979) *Political Sociology*, London: Hutchinson.

Bramham, P. (1991) 'Explanations of the Organisation of Sport in British Society', *International Review for the Sociology of Sport*, 26: 139–154.

Cabinet Office Strategy Unit (2002) *Game Plan*, London: The Cabinet Office.

Coakley, J. (1998) *Sport in Society: Issues and Controversies*, 6th edn, Boston: McGraw-Hill.

Coalter, F. (2007) *A Wider Social Role for Sport: Who's Keeping the Score?* London: Routledge.

Coalter, R, with Long, J. and Duffield, B. (1988) *Recreational Welfare*, Aldershot: Gower.

Coghlan, J. and Webb, I. (1990) *Sport and British Politics Since 1960*, London: The Falmer Press.

Giddens, A. (1989) *Sociology*, Cambridge: Polity Press.

Green, M. (2004) 'Changing Policy Priorities for Sport in England: The Emergence of Elite Sport Development as Key Policy Concern', *Leisure* Studies, 23(4): 365–385.

Green, M. and Houlihan, B. (2004) 'Advocacy Coalitions and Elite Sport Policy Change in Canada and the United Kingdom', *International Review for the Sociology of Sport*, 39(4): 387–403.

Hall, A., Slack, T., Smith, G. and Whitson, D. (1991) *Sport in Canadian Society*, Toronto: McClelland & Stewart.

Hall, S. (1986) 'Popular Culture and the State', in T. Bennett, C. Mercer and J. Woollacott (eds), *Popular Culture and Social Relations*, Milton Keynes: Open University Press.

Hargreaves, J. (1986) *Sport, Power and Culture: A Social and Historical Analysis of Popular Sports in Britain*, Cambridge: Polity Press.

Hargreaves, J. (1987) 'The Outflanking of Socialist Sport in Britain, 1880–1980', talk given at 'Images of Sport', British Society of Sports History Conference, South Glamorgan Institute of Higher Education, Cardiff, September.

Henry, I. (2001) *The Politics of Leisure Policy*, London: Macmillan.

Hoberman, J. (1984) *Sport and Political Ideology*, London: Heinemann.

Horne, J. (1986) '"Enforced Leisure" and Compulsory Games in the 1930s: An Exploration of the

Social Control of Spare Time', in F. Coalter (ed.), *The Politics of Leisure*, Eastbourne: Leisure Studies Association.

Horne, J. and Manzenreiter, W. (2006) 'An Introduction to the Sociology of Sports Mega-Events', in J. Horne and W. Manzenreiter (eds), *Sports Mega-Events: Social Scientific Analyses of a Global Phenomenon*, Oxford: Blackwell, pp. 1–24.

Horne, J. and Whannel, G. (2011) *Understanding the Olympics*, London: Routledge.

Houlihan, B. (1991) *The Government and Politics of Sport*, London: Routledge.

Houlihan, B. (1994) *Sport and International Politics*, London: Harvester Wheatsheaf.

Houlihan, B. (1997) *Sport, Policy and Politics*, London: Routledge.

Houlihan, B. (2002) 'Political Involvement in Sport, Physical Education and Recreation', in A. Laker (ed.) *The Sociology of Sport and Physical Education* London: Routledge, pp. 190–210.

Houlihan, B. (2005) 'Public Sector Sport Policy: Developing a Framework for Analysis', *International Review for the Sociology of Sport*, 40(2): 163–185.

Kremer, J., Trew, K. and Ogle, S. (eds) (1997) *Young People's Involvement in Sport*, London: Routledge.

Kruger, A. and Riordan, J. (eds) (1996) *The Story of Worker Sport*, Champaign, IL: Human Kinetics.

Macfarlane, N. (1986) *Sport and Politics: A World Divided*, London: Collins Willow.

McGrew, A. (1992) 'The State in Advanced Capitalist Societies', in J. Allen, P. Braham and P. Lewis (eds), *Political and Economic Forms of Modernity*, Cambridge: Polity Press.

McLennan, G. (1995) *Pluralism*, Milton Keynes: Open University Press.

Monnington, T. (1993) 'Politicians and Sport: Uses and Abuses', in L. Allison (ed.), *The Changing Politics of Sport*, Manchester: Manchester University Press.

Orwell, G. (1970 [1945]) 'The Sporting Spirit', in *The Collected Essays, Journalism and Letters of George Orwell*, Vol. 4, Harmondsworth: Penguin Books, pp. 61–64.

Polley, M. (1998) *Moving the Goalposts: A History of Sport and Society since 1945*, London: Routledge.

Riordan, J. (1986) 'Politics of Elite Sport in East and West', in G. Redmond (ed.), *Sport and Politics*, Champaign, IL: Human Kinetics.

Roche, M. (1993) 'Sport and Community: Rhetoric and Reality in the Development of British Sport Policy', in J. Binfield and J. Stevenson (eds), *Sport, Culture and Politics*, Sheffield: Sheffield Academic Press.

Rowe, D. (2003) 'Sport and the Repudiation of the Global' *International Review for the Sociology of Sport*, 38(3): 281–294.

Silk, M., Andrews, D. and Cole, C. (eds) (2005) *Sport and Corporate Nationalisms*, Oxford: Berg.

Sports Council (1983) *Sports Council Annual Report*, London: Sports Council.

Sugden, J. and Bairner, A. (1993) *Sport, Sectarianism and Society in a Divided Ireland*, Leicester: Leicester University Press.

Tomlinson, A. (1996) 'Olympic Spectacle: Opening Ceremonies and Some Paradoxes of Globalization', *Media, Culture & Society*, 18: 583–602.

Tomlinson, A. and Whannel, G. (eds) (1984) *Five Ring Circus: Money, Power and Politics at the Olympic Games*, London: Pluto Press.

Torkildsen, G. (1992) *Leisure and Recreation Management*, London: E & FN Spon.

Whannel, G. (1983) *Blowing the Whistle: The Politics of Sport*, London: Pluto Press.

Whannel, G. (1986) 'The Unholy Alliance: Notes on Television and the Re-making of British Sport, 1965–1985', *Leisure Studies*, 5: 22–37.

Wilson, J. (1988) *Politics and Leisure*, London: Unwin Hyman.

Anderson, E. and McCormack, M. (2010) 'Intersectionality, Critical Race Theory and American Sporting Oppression: Examining Black and Gay Male Athletes', *Journal of Homosexuality*, 57: 949–967.

Brownell, S (2008) *The 1904 Anthropology Days and Olympic Games: Sport, Race, and American Imperialism*, Lincoln, NB: University of Nebraska Press.

Carrington, B. (2010) *Race, Sport and Politics: The Sporting Black Diaspora*, London: Sage.

Cashmore, E. (2005) *Making Sense of Sports*, 4th edn, London: Routledge.

Chappelet, J.L. and Kuhler-Mabbott, B.K. (2008) *The International Olympic Committee and the Olympic System: The Governance of World Sport*, London: Routledge.

Cole, C.L. (1993) 'Resisting the Canon: Feminist Cultural Studies, Sport and Technologies of the Body', *Journal of Sport and Social Issues*, 17(2): 77–97.

Connell, R.W. (1997) 'Change among the Gatekeepers: Men, Masculinities and Gender Inequality in the Global Arena', *Signs: Journal of Women in Culture and Society*, 30(31): 1801–1825.

DCMS/SU (2002) *Game Plan: A Strategy for Delivering Government's Sport and Physical Activity Objectives*, London: Cabinet Office.

Foucault, M. (1981) *The History of Sexuality:* Volume 1: *An Introduction*, trans. R. Hurley, Harmondsworth: Penguin.

Gibson, O. (2011) 'IOC Leader Lauds London as 2012 Preparations Enter Final Straight', *Guardian*, 26 July, pp. 12–13.

Giulianotti, R. (2005) *Sport a Critical Sociology*, Cambridge: Polity Press.

Goldblatt, D. (2007) *The Ball Is Round: A Global History of Soccer*, London: Riverhead Trade.

Guttmann, A. (2005) *Sport: The First Five Millennia*, Amherst, MA: University of Massachusetts Press.

Hill, D. (2010) *The Fix: Soccer and Organised Crime*, Toronto: McClelland and Stewart.

Horne, J. (2011) 'Sport and Lifestyle', in P. Bramham and S. Wagg (eds), *The New Politics of Leisure and Pleasure*, Basingstoke: Palgrave, pp. 211–224.

Horne, J. and Whannel, G. (2012) *Understanding the Olympics*, London: Routledge.

Houlihan, B. (2008) 'Doping and Sport', in B. Houlihan (ed.), *Sport and Society: A Student Introduction*, 2nd edn, London: Sage.

Houlihan, B. and Green, M. (2011) *Routledge Handbook of Sports Development*, London: Routledge.

Jennings, A. (1996) *The New Lords of the Rings: Olympic Corruption and How to Buy Gold Medals*, London: Pocket Books.

Jennings, A. (2006) *FOUL! The Secret World of FIFA: Bribes, Vote Rigging and Ticket Scandals*, London: HarperCollins.

Jennings, A. and Simpson, V. (1992) *The Lords of the Rings*, Toronto: Stoddart.

Katwala, S. (2002) *Democratising Global Sport*, London: Foreign Policy Centre.

Lenskyj, H. (2000) *Inside the Olympics Industry: Power, Politics and Activism*, Albany, NY: State University of New York Press.

Lenskyj, H. (2002) *The Best Ever Olympics: Social Impacts of Sydney 2000*, Albany, NY: State University of New York Press.

Lenskyj, H. (2008) *Olympic Industry Resistance: Challenging Olympic Power and Propaganda*, Albany, NY: State University of New York Press.

Markula, P. (2006) 'Technologies of the Self', *Sociology of Sport Journal*, 20: 87–107.

Markula, P. and Pringle, R. (2006) *Foucault, Sport and Exercise: Power, Knowledge and Transforming the Self*. New York and London: Routledge.

Mason, D.S., Thibault, L. and Misener, L. (2006) 'An Agency Perspective on Corruption in Sport: The Case of the International Olympics Committee', *Journal of Sport Management*, 20: 52–73.

Rader, B.G. (1984) *In Its Own Image: How Television Has Transformed Sports*, London: Free Press.

Rowe, N., Adams, R. and Beasley, N. (2004) 'Driving Up Participation in Sport: The Social Context, the Trends, the Prospects and the Challenges' in Sport England, *Driving Up Participation: The Challenge for Sport*, London: Sport England.

Smith, E. (2008) *What Sport Tells Us About Life: Bradman's Average, Zidane's Kiss and Other Sporting Lessons*, London: Viking.

Sugden, J. and Tomlinson, A. (eds) (2011) *Watching the Olympics: Politics, Power and Representation*, London: Routledge.

Wagg, S. (ed.) (2004) *British Football and Social Exclusion*, London: Routledge.

Whannel, G. (2002) *Media Sport Stars: Masculinities and Moralities*, London and New York: Routledge.

Woodward, K. (2006) *Boxing, Masculinity and Identity: The 'I' of the Tiger*, London: Routledge.

Woodward, K. (2009) *Embodied Sporting Practices: Regulating and Regulatory Bodies*, Basingstoke: Palgrave Macmillan.

Woodward, K. (2012) *Sex, Power and the Games*, Basingstoke: Palgrave Macmillan.

10 THE LABOUR MARKET

Agassi, A. (2009) *Open: An Autobiography*, New York: Knopf.

Bale, J. (1984) *Sport and Place: A Geography of Sport in England, Scotland and Wales*. London: Hurst.

Bale, J. (1991) *The Brawn Drain: Foreign Student-Athletes in American Universities*, Urbana, IL: University of Illinois Press.

Bale, J. (2004) 'Three Geographies of African Footballer Migration: Patterns, Problems and Postcoloniality', in G. Armstrong and R. Giulianotti (eds) *Football in Africa: Conflict, Conciliation and Community*, Basingstoke: Palgrave.

Bale, J. and Maguire, J. (eds) (1994a) *The Global Sports Arena*, London: Frank Cass.

Bale J. and Maguire, J. (1994b) 'Sports Labour Migration in the Global Arena', in J. Bale and J. Maguire (eds), *The Global Sports Arena: Athletic Talent Migration in an Interdependent World*, London: Frank Cass, pp. 1–21.

Bale, J. and Sang, J. (1996) *Kenyan Running: Movement Change, Geography and Global Change*, London: Frank Cass.

Beamish, R. (1988) 'The Political Economy of Professional Sport', in J. Harvey and H. Cantelon (eds), *Not Just a Game: Essays in Canadian Sport Sociology*, Ottawa: Ottawa University Press.

Beamish, R. (1993) 'Labor Relations in Sport: Central Issues in their Emergence and Structure in High-performance Sport', in A. Ingham and J. Loy (eds), *Sport in Social Development*, Champaign, IL: Human Kinetics.

BBC News (2011) 'Motor Racing Dominates Sport's Rich list', available at: http://www.bbc.co.uk/news/business-13404429 (accessed 18 May 2011).

Carter, T. (2011) *In Foreign Fields: The Politics and Experiences of Transnational Sport Migration*, London: Pluto.

Cashmore, E. (2002) *Beckham*, Cambridge: Polity Press.

Chiba, N. (2004) 'Pacific Professional Baseball Leagues and Migratory Patterns and Trends: 1995–1999', *Journal of Sport and Social Issues*, 28(2): 193–211.

Coakley, J. (1994) *Sport in Society: Issues and Controversies*, St Louis, IL: Mosby.

Conn, D. (2011) 'Summer Start and Hopes of a Better Time for Women's Super League', *Guardian*, 'Sport', 11 July.

Corry, D. and Williamson, P. with S. Moore (1993) *A Game Without Vision: The Crisis in English Football*, London: Institute for Public Policy Research.

Critcher, C. (1979) 'Football since the War', in J. Clarke, C. Critcher and R. Johnson (eds), *Working Class Culture: Studies in History and Theory*, London: Hutchinson, pp. 161–184.

Darby, P. (2000) 'The New Scramble for Africa: African Football Labour Migration to Europe', *European Sports History Review*, 3: 217–44.

Darby, P. (2001) *Africa, Football and FIFA*, London: Frank Cass.

Dixon, K. (1985) *Kerry: The Autobiography*, London: Macdonald/Queen Anne Press.

Dunphy, E. (1991) *A Strange Kind of Glory: Sir Matt Busby and Manchester United*, London: Heinemann.

Fleming, S. (1995) *'Home and Away': Sport and South Asian Male Youth*, Aldershot: Avebury.

Fyfe, L. (1992) *Careers in Sport*, London: Kogan Page.

Gardiner, S. and Welch, R. (2000) 'Show Me the Money': Regulation of the Migration of Professional Sportsmen in post-Bosman Europe', in A. Caiger and S. Gardiner (eds), *Professional Sport in the European Union: Regulation and Reregulation*, The Hague: T.M.C. Asser Press, pp. 107–126.

Gilroy, S. (1997) 'Working on the Body: Links between Physical Activity and Social Power', in G. Clarke and B. Humberstone (eds), *Researching Women and Sport*, Basingstoke: Macmillan.

Gurney, C. (1997) 'Football(er)s Coming Home: A Case Study of Housing Histories, Labour Market Histories and Propinquital Relationships of Male Professional Footballers', unpublished paper, presented at the British Sociological Association Annual Conference, University of York, April.

Hall, M. (2000) *The Away Game: The Inside Story of Australian Footballers in Europe*, Sydney: Harper Sports.

Hamilton, I. (1993) 'Gazza Agonistes', *Granta No. 45*, London: Penguin Books, pp. 9– 125.

Hargreaves, Jennifer (1994) *Sporting Females: Critical Issues in the History and Sociology of Women's Sports*, London: Routledge.

Hargreaves, John (1986) *Sport, Power and Culture: A Social and Historical Analysis of Popular Sports in Britain*, Cambridge: Polity Press.

Harris, N. (2009) 'Pitch Battle', *Guardian*, 'Work' section, 8 August, pp. 1–2.

Harris, O. and Hunt, L. (1984) 'Race and Sports Involvement: Some Implications of Sports for Black and White Youth', paper presented at the AAHPERD Conference, Anaheim, CA.

Hirai, H. (2001) 'Hideo Nomo: Pioneer or Defector?' in D. Andrews and S. Jackson (eds), *Sport Stars,* London: Routledge, pp. 187–200.

James, S. (2010) 'A Game of Two Careers', *Guardian*, 'Work' section, 12 June, pp. 1–2.

Klein, A. (1994) 'Trans-Nationalism, Labour Migration and Latin American Baseball', in J. Bale and J. Maguire (eds), *The Global Sports Arena: Athletic Talent Migration in an Interdependent World*, London: Frank Cass, pp. 183–205.

Kuper, S. (2010) 'Inside Wayne's World', *Financial Times*, 'Life & Arts' section, 30–31 October, p. 19.

Lanfranchi, P. and Taylor, M. (2001) *Moving with the Ball: The Migration of Professional Footballers*, Oxford: Berg.

McGovern, P. (2002) 'Globalization or Internationalization? Foreign Footballers in the English League, 1946–95,' *Sociology*, 36(1): 23–42.

Magee, J. and Sugden, J. (2002) 'The World at Their Feet': Professional Football And International Labor Migration', *Journal of Sport and Social Issues*, 26(4): 421–437.

Maguire, J. (1999) *Global Sport*, Cambridge: Polity Press.

Maguire, J. (2004) 'Sport Labor Migration Research Revisited', *Journal of Sport and Social Issues*, 28(4): 477–482.

Maguire, J. and Falcous, M. (eds) (2011) *Sport and Migration: Borders, Boundaries and Crossings*, London: Routledge.

Mitchell, K. (2009) 'Flintoff and Fame Will Not Disturb the County Game', *Observer* Sport section, 20 September, p. 14.

Obel, C. (2001) 'National Responses to the Migration of Players and Coaches in the Sport of Rugby Union', in Koh Eunha *et al.* (eds), *Proceedings of the 1st World Congress of Sociology of Sport*, Seoul: Organizing Committee for the 1st World Congress of Sociology of Sport, pp. 533–542.

Parkin, F. (1979) *Marxism and Class Analysis: A Bourgeois Critique*, London: Tavistock.

Parrish, R. and McArdle, D. (2004) 'Beyond Bosman: The European Union's Influence Upon Professional Athletes' Freedom of Movement', *Sport in Society*, 7(4): 403–419.

Polsky, N. (1985) *Hustlers, Beats and Others*, New York: Doubleday Anchor.

Roderick, M.J. (2006) *The Work of Professional Football: A Labour of Love?*, London: Routledge.

Runciman, D. (1996) 'Striker Force', *Guardian*, 20 August.

Sport England (2010) *The Economic Value of Sport in England*, London: Sport Industry Research Centre [SIRC]/Sport England.

Stone, G. (1970) 'American Sports: Play and Display', in E. Dunning (ed.), *The Sociology of Sport*, London: Frank Cass.

West, A. and Brackenridge, C. (1990) *A Report on the Issues Relating to Women's Lives as Sports Coaches in the United Kingdom, 1989/90*, Sheffield: Sheffield City Polytechnic/ PAVIC Publications.

Woods, R. (2010) '*The Sunday Times* Sport Rich List: Racing Drivers Have Formula to Build Fortunes', available at: http://business.timesonline.co.uk/tol/business/specials/rich_list/article7114071.ece (accessed 18 May 2011).

11 SPORT, COMMERCIALISATION AND COMMODIFICATION

Allison, L. (ed.) (1986) *The Politics of Sport*, Manchester: Manchester University Press.

Allison, L. (ed.) (1993) *The Changing Politics of Sport*, Manchester: Manchester University Press.

Aris, S. (1990) *Sportsbiz: Inside the Sports Business*, London: Hutchinson.

Bailey, P. (1978) *Leisure and Class in Victorian England*, London: Routledge & Kegan Paul.

Bale, J. and Maguire, J. (eds) (1993) *The Global Arena: Sports Talent Migration in an Interdependent World*, Leicester: Leicester University Press.

Barnett, S. (1990) *Games and Sets: The Changing Face of Sport on Television*, London: BFI.

Baudrillard, J. (1972) *Pour une Critique de l'Économie Politique du Signe*, Paris: Gallimard.

Beamish, R. (1988) 'The Political Economy of Professional Sport', in J. Harvey and H. Cantelon (eds), *Not Just a Game*, Ottawa: University of Ottawa Press.

Beamish, R. (1993) 'Labour Relations in Sport: Central Issues in Their Emergence and Structure in High-Performance Sport', in *Sport and Social Development*, London: Human Kinetics.

Beijing Olympic Organising Committee (2008) *Beijing 2008 Marketing Plan*, Beijing, China: Beijing Olympic Organising Committee.

Bonney, B. (1980) *Packer and Televised Cricket*, Sydney: NSW Institute of Technology.

Brady, M. (1959) *The Centre Court Story*, London: Sportsmans Book Club.

Brailsford, D. (1989) *Bareknuckles: A Social History of Prizefighting*, Cambridge: Lutterworth Press.

Brookes, C. (1978) *English Cricket*, London: Weidenfeld and Nicolson.

Brohm, J-M. (1978) *Sport: A Prison of Measured Time*, London: Ink Links.

Burn, G. (1986) *Pocket Money*, London: Heinemann.

Butler, F. (1972) *A History of Boxing in Britain*, London: Arthur Barker.

Carpenter, H. (1982) *Boxing: An Illustrated History*, London: Collins.

Cashmore, E. (2004) *Beckham*, Cambridge: Polity Press.

Chaplin, D. (1991) 'History of English Football Equipment', unpublished dissertation, RIHE, London.

Chippendale, P. and Franks, S. (1991) *Dished: The Rise and Fall of British Satellite Broadcasting*, London: Simon & Schuster.

Cohen, P. (1972) 'Sub-cultural Conflict and Working Class Community', in *Working Papers in Cultural Studies*, no. 2, Birmingham: CCCS.

Coakley, J. (1978) *Sport in Society: Issues and Controversies*, St Louis: C. V. Mosby.

Cousins, G. (1975) *Golf in Britain*, London: RKP.

Critcher, C. (1979) 'Football Since the War', in J. Clarke, C. Critcher and R. Johnson (eds), *Working Class Culture*, London: Hutchinson.

Cunningham, H. (1980) *Leisure in the Industrial Revolution*, London: Croom Helm.

Dobbs, B. (1973) *Edwardians at Play: Sport, 1890–1914*, London: Pelham Books.

Dunning, E. (ed.) (1971) *The Sociology of Sport*, London: Cass.

Dunning, E. and Sheard, K. (1976) 'The Bifurcation of Rugby Union and Rugby League', *International Review of Sport Sociology*, 11: 2.

Featherstone, M. (1991) *Consumer Culture and Postmodernism*, London: Sage.

Gratton, C. and Taylor, P. (1986) *Sport and Recreation: An Economic Analysis*, London: E & FN Spon.

Gratton, C. and Taylor, P. (1987) *Leisure in Britain*, Letchworth: Leisure Publications.

Gratton, C. and Taylor, P. (1991) *Government and the Economics of Sport*, London: Longman.

Gruneau, R. (1983) *Class, Sports and Social Development*, Amherst, MA: University of Massachusetts Press.

Gruneau, R. (1997) 'Canadian Sport in the Society of the Spectacle', paper presented at 'How Sport Can Change the World', conference of the Japanese Society for the Sociology of Sport, Ritsumeikan University, Kyoto, Japan, 27–28 March.

Guttmann, A. (1978) *From Ritual to Record*, London: Columbia University Press.

Haigh, G. (1993) *The Cricket Wars: The Inside Story of Kerry Packer's World Series Cricket*, Melbourne: Text Publishing Company.

Hargreaves, J. (1986) *Sport Power and Culture*, London: Polity Press.

Hoch, P. (1972) *Rip Off the Big Game: The Exploitation of Sports by the Power Elite*, New York: Anchor Books.

Horne, J. (2006) *Sport in Consumer Culture*, Basingstoke: Palgrave.

Holt, R. (1989) *Sport and the British: A Modern History*, Oxford: Oxford University Press.

Hofmann, D. and Greenberg, M. (1989) *Sport$biz*, Champaign, IL: Human Kinetics.

Inglis, S. (1983) *The Football Grounds of England and Wales*, London: Collins.

Jhally, S. (1982) 'Probing the Blindspot: The Audience Commodity', *Canadian Journal of Political and Social Theory*, 6(1–2):. 204–210.

Lasch, C. (1980) *Culture of Narcissism*, London: Abacus.

McIntosh, P. (1979) *Fair Play*, London: Heinemann.

McKay, J. and Miller, T (1991) 'From Old Boys to Men and Women of the Corporation: The Americanisation and Commodification of Australian Sport', *Sociology of Sport Journal*, 8: 86–94.

Maguire, J. (1988) 'Race and Position Assignment in English Soccer: Ethnicity and Sport', *Sociology of Sport Journal*, 5: 257–269.

Maguire, J. (1990) 'More than a Sporting Touchdown: The Making of American Football in England, 1982–1990', *Sociology of Sport Journal*, 7: 213–237.

Malcolmson, R.W. (1973) *Popular Recreations in English Society, 1700–1850*, Cambridge: Cambridge University Press.

Mangan, J.A. (1981) *Athleticism in the Victorian and Edwardian Public School*, London: Cambridge University Press.

Mason, T. (1988) *Sport in Britain*, London: Faber and Faber.

Mason, T. (1993) 'All the Winners and the Half Times', *The Sports Historian (The Journal of the British Society of Sports History)*, 13 May, pp. 3–12.

Mortimer, R. (1958) *The Jockey Club*, London: Cassell.

Murdock, G. (1978) 'Blindspots about Western Marxism: A Reply to Dallas Smythe', *Canadian Journal of Political and Social Theory*, 12(2): 109–119.

Richards, J. (1984) *The Age of the Dream Palace: Cinema and Society in Britain, 1930–39*, London: Routledge & Kegan Paul.

Robertson, M. (1977) *Wimbledon, 1877–1977*, London: Arthur Barker.

Rowe, D. (2011) *Global Media Sport: Flows, Forms and Futures*, London: Bloomsbury Academic.

Scannell, P. and Cardiff, D. (1991) *A Social History of British Broadcasting*, Vol. 1, *1922–39*, Oxford: Basil Blackwell.

Smythe, D. (1977) 'Communications: Blindspot of Western Marxism', *Canadian Journal of Political and Social Theory*, 12(3): 1–27.

Smythe, D. (1978) 'Rejoinder to Graham Murdock', *Canadian Journal of Political and Social Theory*, 12(2): 120–129.

Stoddart, B. (1990) 'Wide World of Golf', *Sociology of Sport Journal*, 7(4); 378–388.

Vinnai, G. (1976) *Football Mania,* London: Ocean Books.

Whannel, G. (1983) *Blowing the Whistle: The Politics of Sport*, London: Pluto.

Whannel, G. (1986) 'The Unholy Alliance: Notes on Television and the Re-Making of British Sport', *Leisure Studies*, 5(2): 22–37.

Whannel, G. (1994) 'Profiting by the Presence of Ideals: Sponsorship and Olympism', in *International Olympic Academy: 32nd Session*, Olympia, Greece: International Olympic Academy, pp. 89–93.

Whannel, G. (2002) *Media Sport Stars: Masculinities and Moralities*, London: Routledge.

Wheaton, B. (ed.) (2004) *Understanding Lifestyle Sport: Consumption, Identity and Difference*, London: Routledge.

Wilson, N. (1988) *The Sports Business*, London: Piatkus.

12 GLOBAL TRANSFORMATIONS

Aldgate, A. (1979) *Cinema and History: British Newsreels and the Spanish Civil War*, London: Scolar.

Andrews, D. (ed.) (2001) *Michael Jordan, Inc.* Albany, NY: State University of New York Press.

Appadurai, A. (1990) 'Disjuncture and Difference in the Global Cultural Economy', *Public Culture*, 2(2).

Bairner, A. (2001) *Sport, Nationalism and Globalization*, Albany, NY: State University of New York (SUNY) Press.

Boorstin, D. (1961) *The Image*, Harmondsworth: Penguin.

Bowen, R. (1970) *Cricket*, London: Eyre and Spottiswoode.

Boyle, R. and Blain, N. (1991) 'Footprints on the Field: TV Sport, Delivery Systems and National Culture in a Changing Europe', paper presented at the International Television Studies conference, London: Institute of Education, University of London.

Chandler, J. (1988) *Television and National Sport*, Chicago: University of Illinois Press.

Curi, M., Knijnik, J. and Mascarenhas, G. (2011) 'The Pan American Games in Rio de Janeiro 2007: Consequences of a Sport Mega-Event on a BRIC Country', *International Review for the Sociology of Sport*, 46(2): 140–156.

Giddens, A. (2002) *Runaway World*, 2nd edn, London: Profile.

Giulianotti, R. and Robertson, R. (2009) *Globalization and Football* , London: Sage.

259

Goldlust, J. (1987) *Playing for Keeps: Sport, the Media and Society*, Melbourne: Longman.

Green, T. (1972) *The Universal Eye: The World of Television*, New York: Stein and Day.

Gruneau, R. (1989) 'Making Spectacles: A Case Study in Television Sports Production', in L. Wenner (ed.) *Media, Sports and Society*, Newbury Park, CA: Sage.

Gruneau, R. (1997) 'Canadian Sport in the Society of the Spectacle', paper presented at 'How Sport Can Change the World', international conference of the Japanese Society for the Sociology of Sport, Ritsumeikan University, Kyoto, Japan.

Guttmann, A. (1991) 'Sport Diffusion: A Response to Maguire and the Americanisation Commentaries', *Sociology of Sport Journal*, 11: 337–355.

Hardt, M. and Negri, A. (2000) *Empire*, Cambridge, MA: Harvard University Press.

Harvey, J., Horne, J. and Safai, P. (2009) 'Alterglobalization, Global Social Movements, and the Possibility of Political Transformation through Sport', *Sociology of Sport Journal*, 26(3): 383–403.

Harvey, J. and Houle, F. (1994) 'Sport, World Economy, Global Culture and New Social Movements', *Sociology of Sport Journal*, 11: 337–355.

Herd, H. (1952) *The March of Journalism*, London: George Allen and Unwin

Hobsbawm, E. (1994) *Age of Extremes: The Short Twentieth Century, 1914–1991*, London: Michael Joseph.

Holt, R. (1996) 'Cricket and Englishness: The Batsman as Hero', *International Journal of the History of Sport*, 13.

Holton, R.J. (1998) *Globalization and the Nation-state*, Basingstoke: Macmillan.

Horne, J. (2006) *Sport in Consumer Culture*, Basingstoke: Palgrave.

Jackson, S.J. and Andrews, D.L. (eds) (2005) *Sport, Culture and Advertising: Identities, Commodities and the Politics of Representation*, London: Routledge.

Jackson, S., Andrews, D. and Scherer, J. (2005) 'Introduction: The Contemporary Landscape of Advertising', in S. Jackson and D. Andrews (eds) *Sport, Culture and Advertising: Identities, Commodities and the Politics of Representation*, London: Routledge.

Jones, A. (2010) *Globalization: Key Thinkers* Cambridge: Polity Press.

Kidd, B. (1987) 'Sports and Masculinity', in M. Kaufman (ed.) *Beyond Patriarchy: Essays by Men on Pleasure, Power and Change*, Toronto: Oxford University Press, pp. 250–261.

King, A.D. (ed.) (1991) *Culture, Globalization and the World-System*, Basingstoke: Macmillan.

Klein, N. (2000) *No Logo*, London: Flamingo.

McChesney, R.W. (1989) 'Media Made Sport: A History of Sports Coverage in the USA', in L. Wenner (ed.) *Media, Sports and Society*, London: Sage.

McKay, J., Lawrence, G., Miller, T. and Rowe, D. (1993) 'Globalisation and Australian Sport', *Sport Science Review*, 2: 10–28.

McKay, J. and Miller, T. (1991) 'From Old Boys to Men and Women of the Corporation: The Americanisation and Commodification of Australian Sport', *Sociology of Sport Journal*, 8: 86–94.

McPhail, T. and Jackson, R. (eds) (1989) *The Olympic Movement and the Mass Media: Past, Present and Future Issues*, Calgary: Hurford.

Maguire, J. (1990) 'More than a Sporting Touchdown: The Making of American Football in England, 1982–1990', *Sociology of Sport Journal*, 7:. 213–237.

Maguire, J. (1991) 'The Media–Sport Production Complex: The Case of American Football in Western European Societies', *European Journal of Communication*, 6: 315–335.

Maguire, J. (1999) *Global Sport*, Cambridge: Polity Press.

Marjoribanks, T. and Farquharson, K. (2012) *Sport and Society in the Global Age*, Basingstoke: Palgrave.

Marlow, J. (1982) 'Popular Culture, Pugilism and Pickwick', *Journal of Popular Culture*, 15.

Marx, K. and Engels, F. (1848) *The Manifesto of the Communist Party*, London: Lawrence and Wishart.

Mason, T. (1988) *Sport in Britain*, London: Faber and Faber.

Miller, T., Lawrence, G., McKay, J. and Rowe, D. (2001) *Globalization and Sport*, London: Sage.

Morris, B.S. and Nydahl, J. (1985) 'Sports Spectacle as Drama: Image, Language and Technology', *Journal of Popular Culture*, 18: 101–110.

Nelson, D. (2002) 'Globocracy', *International Politics*, 39: 245–250.

Packard, V. (1957) *The Hidden Persuaders*, New York: McKay.

Pieterse, J. (1997) 'Going Global: Futures of Capitalism', *Development and Change*, 28: 367–382.

Real, M. (1975) 'Super Bowl: Mythic Spectacle', *Journal of Communication*, 25: 31–43.

Robertson, R. (1992) *Globalization*, London: Sage.

Rowe, D. (2011) *Global Media Sport: Flows, Forms and Futures*, London: Bloomsbury Academic.

Rowe, D., Lawrence, G., Miller, T. and McKay, J. (1994) 'Global Sport? Core Concern and Peripheral Vision', *Media, Culture & Society*, 16: 661–676.

Shipley, S. (1989) 'Boxing', in T. Mason (ed.) *Sport in Britain: A Social History*, Cambridge: Cambridge University Press.

Spa, M. de Moragas, Rivenburgh, N. and Larson, J. (1995) *Television in the Olympics*, Luton: John Libbey.

Sugden, J. and Tomlinson, A. (1998) *FIFA and the Contest for World Football* Cambridge: Polity Press.

Tagsold, C. (2011) 'The Tokyo Olympics', in W.W. Kelly and S.Brownell (eds) *The Olympics in East Asia: Nationalism, Regionalism, and Globalism on the Center Stage of World Sports*. New Haven, CT: Council on East Asian Studies, Yale University.

Tomlinson, A. (1989) 'Representation, Ideology and the Olympic Games: A Reading of the Opening and Closing Ceremonies of the 1984 Olympics', in T. McPhail and R. Jackson (eds) *The Olympic Movement and the Mass Media: Past, Present and Future Issues*, Calgary: Hurford.

Tomlinson, A. (1996) 'Olympic Spectacle: Opening Ceremonies and Some Paradoxes of Globalization', *Media, Culture & Society*, 18(4): 583–602.

Wenner, L. (ed.) (1989) *Media, Sport and Society*, Newbury Park, CA: Sage.

Whannel, G. (1986) '"The Unholy Alliance": Notes on Television and the Re-making of British Sport, 1965–1985', *Leisure Studies*, 5(1): 22–37.

Whannel, G. (1994) 'Profiting by the Presence of Ideals: Sponsorship and Olympism', in *International Olympic Academy, 32nd Session*, Olympia, Greece: International Olympic Academy.

Wilson, N. (1988) *The Sports Business*, London: Piatkus.

Wren-Lewis, J. and Clarke, A. (1983) 'The World Cup: A Political Football?', *Theory, Culture & Society*, 1: 123–132.

13 SPORT SPACES, SITES AND EVENTS

Bale, J. (2003) *Sporting Geographies*, 2nd edn, London: Routledge.

Bélanger, A. (2009) 'The Urban Sport Spectacle: Towards A Critical Political Economy of Sports', in B. Carrington and I. McDonald (eds), *Marxism, Cultural Studies and Sport*, London: Routledge, pp. 51– 67.

Black, D. and van der Westhuizen, J. (2004) ‚The Allure of Global Games for "Semi-Peripheral" Polities and Spaces: A Research Agenda', *Third World Quarterly*, 25(7): 1195–1214.

Boykoff, J. (2011) 'The Anti-Olympics', *New Left Review*, 2nd Series, No. 67, January– February.

Cornwell, R. (2009) 'Yield of Dreams', *Independent*, 17 April, p. 48.

Curi, M., Knijnik, J. and Mascarenhas, G. (2011) 'The Pan American Games in Rio de Janeiro 2007:

261

bibliography

Consequences of a Sport Mega-Event on a BRIC Country', *International Review for the Sociology of Sport*, 46: 140–156.

Darnell, S. (2010) 'Mega Sport for All? Assessing the Development Promises of Rio 2016', in R. Barney, J. Forsyth and M. Heine (eds), *Rethinking Matters Olympic: Investigations into the Socio-Cultural Study of the Modern Olympic Movement*, 10th International Symposium for Olympic Research, London: Ontario, pp. 498–507.

Dimeo, P. and Kay, J. (2004) 'Major Sports Events: Image Projection and the Problems of "Semi-Periphery": A Case Study of the 1996 South Asia Cricket World Cup', *Third World Quarterly*, 25(7): 1263–1276.

Giulianotti, R. and Klauser, F. (2010) 'Security Governance and Sport Mega-Events: Toward an Interdisciplinary Research Agenda', *Journal of Sport and Social Issues*, 34(1): 49–61.

Harvey, J., Horne, J. and Safai, P. (2009) 'Alterglobalization, Global Social Movements, and the Possibility of Political Transformation through Sport', *Sociology of Sport Journal*, 26(3): 383–403.

Hayes, G. and Horne, J. (2011) 'Sustainable Development, Shock and Awe? London 2012 and Civil Society', *Sociology*, 45(5).

Horne, J. (2006) *Sport in Consumer Culture*, Basingstoke: Palgrave.

Horne, J. (2007a) 'The Four "Knowns" of Sports Mega-Events', *Leisure Studies*, 26(1).

Horne, J. (2007b) 'World Cup Cricket and Caribbean Aspirations: From Nello to Mello', *North American Congress on Latin America (NACLA) Report on the Americas*, 40(4): 10–14.

Horne, J. (2010) 'Cricket in Consumer Culture: Notes on the 2007 Cricket World Cup', *American Behavioral Scientist*.

Horne, J. and Manzenreiter, W. (2006) 'An Introduction to the Sociology of Sports Mega-events', in J. Horne and W. Manzenreiter (eds), *Sports Mega-events: Social Scientific Analyses of a Global Phenomenon*, Oxford: Blackwell, pp. 1–24.

Horne, J. and Whannel, G. (2012) *Understanding the Olympics*, London: Routledge.

Inglis, S. (2000) *Sightlines: A Stadium Odyssey*, London: Yellow Jersey.

Inglis, S. (2005) *Engineering Archie: Archibald Leitch, Football Ground Designer*, London: English Heritage/HOK.

IOC (2011) *Olympic Marketing Fact File 2011 Edition*, Lausanne: International Olympic Committee.

Jennings, A. (1996) *The New Lords of the Rings*, London: Simon & Schuster.

Jennings, A. (2006) *Foul*, London: Harper Sport.

Klein, N. (2007) *The Shock Doctrine*, London: Allen Lane.

Klein, N. (2008) 'The Olympics: Unveiling Police State 2.0', *The Huffington Post*, available online: available at: http://www.huffingtonpost.com/naomi-klein/the-olympics-unveiling-po_b_117403.html (accessed 30 October 2010).

Kuper, S. (2010) 'Life and Arts' Section, *Financial Times*, 30/31 October, p. 2.

Lee, M. (2006) *The Race for the 2012 Olympics: The Inside Story of How London Won the Bid*, London: Virgin.

Lenskyj, H. (2008) *Olympic Industry Resistance*, Albany, NY: State University of New York Press.

London 2012 (2004) *Backing the Bid: The UK's Games*, London: London 2012 Nations and Regions Group, available at: http://www.london2012.com/documents/bid-publications/ backing-the-bid.pdf (accessed 7 February 2012).

McLeod-Roberts, L. (2007) 'Paramilitary Games', *NACLA Report on the Americas*, 40(4): 20–25.

McNeill, D. (2009) *The Global Architect*, London: Routledge.

Merrifield, A. (2002) *Metromarxism: A Marxist Tale of the City*, New York: Routledge.

Observer (2010) 'Planet Sport', 18 July, available at: http://www.guardian.co.uk/football/2010/jul/18/fifa-world-cup-sepp-blatter (accessed 29 March 2011).

O'Neill, J. (2001) 'Building Better Global Economic BRICs', *Goldman Sachs, Global Economics Paper No: 66*, 30 November.

Ritzer, G. and Stillman, T. (2001) 'The Postmodern Ballpark as a Leisure Setting: Enchantment and Simulated De-McDonaldization', *Leisure Sciences*, 23(2): 99–113.

Roche, M. (2000) *Mega-Events and Modernity*, London: Routledge.

Runciman, D. (2010) 'Football's Goldmine', *Guardian*, 'Review' section, 22 May, pp. 2–3.

Rutheiser, C. (1996) *Imagineering Atlanta: The Politics of Space in the City of Dreams*, New York and London: Verso.

Saunders, W. (2005) 'Preface', in W. Saunders (ed.), *Commodification and Spectacle in Architecture*, Minneapolis: University of Minnesota Press, pp. vii–viii.

Schmidt, C. (2007) 'Five Ring Circus: The Untold Story of the Vancouver 2010 Games' (documentary film), available from www.TheFiveRingCircus.com.

Shaw, C. (2008) *Five Ring Circus: Myths and Realities of the Olympic Games*, Gabriola Island, BC: New Society Publishers.

Short, J.R. (2004) *Global Metropolitan: Globalizing Cities in a Capitalist World*, London: Routledge.

Simson, V. and Jennings, A. (1992) *The Lords of the Rings: Power, Money and Drugs in the Modern Olympics*, London: Simon & Schuster.

Sklair, L. (2005) 'The Transnational Capitalist Class and Contemporary Architecture in Globalizing Cities', *International Journal of Urban and Regional Research*, 29(3): 485–500.

Sklair, L. (2006) 'Iconic Architecture and Capitalist Globalization', *City*, 10(1): 21–47.

Stevens, Q. (2007) *The Ludic City: Exploring the Potential of Public Spaces*, London: Routledge.

Sudjic, D. (2005) *The Edifice Complex: How the Rich and Powerful Shape the World*, London: Penguin.

Sugden, J. (2012) 'Watched by the Games: Surveillance and Security at the Olympics', in J. Sugden and A. Tomlinson (eds), *Watching the Olympics: Politics, Power and Representation*, London: Routledge, pp. 228–241.

Sugden, J. and Tomlinson, A. (1998) *FIFA and the Contest for World Football: Who Rules the Peoples' Game?* Cambridge: Polity Press.

Taylor Report (1990) *The Hillsborough Stadium Disaster 15 April 1989: Final Report of the Inquiry by the Rt Hon Lord Justice Taylor*, London: HMSO.

Tomlinson, A. (2005a) 'Olympic Survivals', in L. Allison (ed.) *The Global Politics of Sport: The Role of Global Institutions in Sport*, London: Routledge.

Tomlinson, A. (2005b) 'Picturing the Winter Olympics: The Opening Ceremonies of Nagano (Japan) 1998 and Salt Lake City (USA) 2002', *Tourism Culture & Communication*, 5: 83–92.

Tomlinson, A. (2005c) 'The Commercialisation of the Olympics: Cities, Corporations and the Olympic Commodity', in K. Young and K. Wamsley (eds), *Global Olympics: Historical and Sociological Studies of the Modern Games*, New York: Elsevier, pp. 179–200.

Tomlinson, A. (2012a) 'The Making – and Unmaking? – of the Corporate Olympic Class', in H. Lenskyj and S. Wagg (eds), *The Palgrave Handbook of Olympic Studies*, Basingstoke: Palgrave.

Tomlinson, A. (2012b) 'Introduction', in J. Novick, H. Richards and R. Steen (eds) *Cambridge Companion to Football*, Cambridge: Cambridge University Press (forthcoming).

Tomlinson, A. and Whannel. G. (eds) (1984) *Five-Ring Circus*, London: Pluto.

Tomlinson, A. and Young, C. (eds) (2006) *National Identity and Global Sports Events: Culture, Politics and Spectacle in the Olympics and the Football World Cup*, Albany, NY: SUNY.

Toohey, K. and Veal, T. (2000) *The Olympic Games: A Social Science Perspective*, Oxford: CABI, p. 108; available at: www.olympic.org (accessed 19 December 2011).

Tuan Yi-Fu (1974) *Topophilia: A Study of Environmental Perceptions, Attitudes, and Values*, Englewood Cliffs, NJ: Prentice-Hall.

Wainwright, M. (2008) 'The Happy Architect', *Guardian*, Society Guardian section, 19 November, pp. 1–2.

Whitson, D. and Horne, J. (2006) 'Underestimated Costs and Overestimated Benefits? Comparing the Impact of Sports Mega-Events in Canada and Japan', in J. Horne and W. Manzenreiter (eds), *Sports Mega-Events*, Oxford: Blackwell/Sociological Review Monograph, pp. 73–89.

Zirin, D. (2009) *A People's History of Sports in the United States: 250 Years of Politics, Protest, People and Play*, New York: The New Press.

14 CONCLUSION: METHODS FOR UNDERSTANDING SPORT CULTURE

Andrews, D., Mason, D. and Silk, M. (eds) (2005) *Qualitative Methods in Sports Studies*, Oxford: Berg.

Atkinson, M. (2011) *Key Concepts in Sport and Exercise Research Methods*, London: Sage.

Booth, D. (2005) *The Field: Truth and Fiction in Sport History*, London: Routledge.

Bryman, A. (2004) *Social Research Methods*, 2nd edn, Oxford: Oxford University Press.

Eco, U. (1986) *Travels in Hyper Reality*, London: Harcourt Brace Jovanovich.

Fleming, S. (1995) *Home and Away: Sport and South Asian Male Youth*, Aldershot: Avebury.

Gratton, C. and Jones, I. (2010) *Research Methods for Sport Studies*, 2nd edn, London: Routledge.

Guttmann, A. (2005) 'Straw Men in Imaginary Boxes', *Journal of Sport History*, 32: 395–400.

Kuhn, T. (1962) *The Structure of Scientific Revolutions*, Chicago: University of Chicago Press.

Munslow, A. (1997) *Deconstructing History*, London: Routledge.

Thompson, J.B. (1990) *Ideology and Modern Culture*: *Critical Social Theory in the Era of Mass Communication*, Cambridge: Polity Press.

Tomlinson, A. and Young, C. (2011) 'Sport in Modern European History: Trajectories, Constellations, Conjunctures', *Journal of Historical Sociology*, 24: 409–427.

INDEX

265

266

extreme sports 91

fair play 147, 149, 154
Falcous, M. 172
fans 143, 146–7, 153
Farquharson, K. 194
Fausto-Sterling, A. 109, 114, 119
FC United 143
Featherstone, M. 184
femininity 59, 72–3, 91, 93, 113, 118
feminism 60, 92–3, 106, 108–11, 119
Ferdinand, Rio 150
Festina Team scandal 150
FIFA 125, 127, 129, 141, 147, 151, 180, 182, 202, 204, 209, 222; World Cup Finals (men's) 23, 129, 150, 182, 205, 211, 215, 218–19; World Cup Winners' medals 162–3
FIFA 12 computer game 102
figurational sociology 40–3
Finney, Tom 160
fitness activities 60
fitness chic 90, 93
Fleming, S. 61–2, 85, 96, 168, 230
Flintoff, A. 30, 56, 59–60
folk sports 1–2, 18–19, 25, 38–48, 178; structural properties 6–8
football: as career 158–65, 170–3; class 54–5; commercialisation 180–3, 191; fans 143, 146; folk form 2, 38–48; and globalisation 199–201, 205–6, 209; governance 143, 146, 149–50; politics 129; representation 93, 95, 100–2; in schools 54–5; social change 2, 10, 13–14; theoretical frameworks 38–48
Football Against Racism in Europe 154
Football Association 141, 148, 179; cup finals 158–9, 163, 179
football clubs 158–60, 163–5, 170–1, 202
Fortune Global Forum (2005) 201
Foucault, Michel 82, 107, 110–12, 121, 140
Fox, Billy 149
France 98, 133, 149–50, 178, 196, 202, 209
Fraser, E. 74
free agency 168–9, 175
functionalism 79, 184–5
funding 136, 186, 202–4, 216, 220–1
Fyfe, L. 158

gambling 149–50, 180, 185, 191
Game Plan (Cabinet Office Strategy Unit) 136
Gardiner, S. 171
Garland, J. 62
Gascoigne, Paul 174, 184
gaze theory 41, 56, 62, 92–4, 186

gender issues 11–12, 30–2, 38, 46, 56–61, 69–70, 234; bodies 106–7, 111–13; constructed 109; and governance 141–2, 144, 146, 148; representation 91–4; and sex 108–9, 114–19, 121; socialisation 71–4; and sports work 165, 167; verification 114–19
Geraghty, C. 89
Germany 24, 41, 50, 89, 97–8, 115, 145, 172, 182
Gibson, O. 150
Giddens, A. 4, 48, 102, 107, 129, 195, 209
Giggs, Ryan 161
Gilroy, P. 96
Gilroy, Sarah 165
Giulianotti, R. 40, 83, 140, 194, 210, 217
Glazer, Malcolm 202
globalisation 32, 82, 194–5; alternative responses 205–8; alternative theorising 208–10; commercialisation 185, 188–9; governance 151, 153; interpreting processes 195–7; marketing of sports 202–4; media 197–201; politics 124, 126, 129, 137; resistances 204–8; socialisation 82–4; TV advertising 200–1
Goffman, E. 118
Golby, J.M. 7, 13, 15, 48
Goldblatt, D. 146
Goldlust, J. 88, 198
Goldstein, S. 22
golf 115, 146, 167, 173, 182, 206
governance 139–40, 154–5; cohesion and equality 151; Olympics 143–4; Paralympics 144–6; participation 153–4; reform 152–3; regulatory bodies 141–3; rule-breaking 149–50; rule-makers 146–7; rule-making 147–9; transparency and accountability 151–3
governing bodies 120, 125, 130–1, 141–2, 146, 152, 178–80
government *see* state involvement/intervention
governmentality 107
Grace, W.G. 26–8, 180
Gramsci, Antonio 46
Gratton, C. 185, 234
Greece 5, 51, 102, 123, 203, 208, 225
Greenberg, M. 184
Green, E. 59
Green, M. 135, 137–8, 140, 156
Griffin, E. 2
group identities 82
Gruneau, R. 6, 31, 88–9, 182, 185, 203–4
Grusky, D.B. 50
Guardian 132
Gunnell, Sally 22–3

269

272